STEPHEN
WILLIAMS

KARLA
A PACT WITH THE DEVIL

D1361809

First published in French in 2002 by Trait d'union.

National Library of Canada Cataloguing in Publication
Williams, Stephen, 1949-
    Karla : a pact with the devil / Stephen Williams.
    ISBN 2-89594-000-2
    1. Homolka, Karla. 2. Bernardo, Paul. 3. Trials (Murder) – Ontario.
4. Murderers – Ontario – Biography. I. Title.
HV6535.C32O65 2003   364.1'523'0922713   C2003-900546-1

Cover photo: Author archives
Author photo: Yvonne Berg
Typesetting: Édiscript enr.

Cantos International
459 King Street East
Toronto, Ontario M5A 1L6

Printed and bound in Canada

10 9 8 7 6 5 4 3 2 1

But corruption, or Evil, or Satan were objects of adoration to the sinner, man or woman, and dear to him or her. Pleasure plunged deep into Evil. It was essentially a transgression, transcending horror, and the greater the horror the deeper the joy. Imaginary or not, the stories of the Sabbaths mean something: they are dreams of monstrous joy.

> – from *Death and Sensuality* by George Bataille

Here is wisdom. For him that hath understanding count the number of the Beast: For it is the number of a man and his number is 666.

> – Chapter 13, The Book of the Apocalypse

Fairy tales can come true, it can happen to you...

> – from "Young at Heart" by Johnny Richards and Carolyn Leigh

> Give me crack and anal sex
> Take the only tree that is left
> and stuff it up the hole
> in your culture

> Give me back the Berlin Wall
> give me Stalin and St. Paul
> I've seen the future, brother:
> It is murder.

> – from "The Future" by Leonard Cohen

> Time present and time past
> Are perhaps present in time future.

> – from "Burnt Norton" by T.S. Eliot

There be none of the affections which have been noted to fascinate or to bewitch, but Love and Envy; they both have vehement wishes, they frame themselves readily into imaginations and suggestions, and they come easily into the eye... We see likewise the Scripture calleth Envy an Evil Eye.

> – from Essay IX, "Of Envy," Francis Bacon

Table of Contents

IN THE BEGINNING

There are abiding mysteries in life such as who cleft the Devil's foot or what song the Sirens sang? Two more contemporary mysteries have plagued me for the better part of the past decade: Who is Karla Homolka and how did she come to have a future?

Over the last ten years Karla has been examined by at least sixteen psychiatrists and psychologists. The majority of them diagnosed her as a battered woman suffering from post-traumatic stress disorder. A few contrarians concluded that she was a psychopath. One honest man described her as a "diagnostic mystery." Regardless, it seems the more she is studied the more mysterious and inexplicable her past behavior becomes.

Perhaps even more perplexing than what she is and what she has done is the fact that Karla has a future. How, in the name of all that is holy, does a woman like Karla, who did what Karla did, get the opportunity to pick herself up and just start over? Although there has been a great deal of speculation about what Karla is, and a great deal of anguished examination of what she did, no one has really addressed the fact of her future. After all, the facts of her past make the fact that she has a future inconceivable.

In the process of "giving" her younger sister to her boyfriend Paul Bernardo as a Christmas present in the basement of her parents' house in 1990, she killed her. Six months later, Karla lured a young girlfriend into the house she was by then sharing with Bernardo, drugged her in the exact same manner as she had her sister, and then proceeded to participate with her fiancé in a lascivious videotaped sexual assault on the comatose girl. This time, the girl, known only as Jane Doe, was a wedding present. Miraculously, Jane survived.

A week later, Karla's betrothed brought another schoolgirl home. He said it was merely reciprocity. He and Karla proceeded to repeatedly rape Leslie Mahaffy while again recording the action on videotape. Then they killed her, cut up her body, encased the parts in cement and dumped the blocks in a nearby reservoir. Two weeks later, Paul and Karla were married at historic Niagara-on-the-Lake. Their nuptials were a bizarre videotaped extravaganza marked by a horse-drawn carriage and a sit-down champagne dinner for their families and a hundred of their closest friends. They settled into seeming domestic bliss in a quiet St. Catharines' suburb, a ten-minute drive north of the Peace Bridge and Niagara Falls, New York.

After returning from their honeymoon in Hawaii, Karla called on her young girlfriend again. The impressionable Jane Doe became a fixture in the Bernardo household. In collaboration with her husband, Karla put Jane down for the second time in August, 1991. This time, the girl appeared to stop breathing. As she had done the night her sister died, Karla called 911. A few minutes later she called back. Everything was all right, she said. It was a false alarm. Her friend had come around.

There were a few other atrocities, such as the rape of a Port Dalhousie teenager who was jogging alone early one April morning. But other than the fact that Paul Bernardo quit his job with a large accounting firm and started smuggling cigarettes for a living, everything was perfectly normal.

A year into the marriage, Karla took the afternoon off work to help Paul kidnap another teenager. They grabbed Kristen French as she walked home from school in the middle of the afternoon. In their late-model Nissan, Paul and Karla pulled into a church parking lot. Holding up a map as though needing directions, Karla called the girl over. Over that Easter weekend, with the ubiquitous video camera ever present,

Paul and Karla repeatedly raped the fifteen-year-old. With vaporific demons almost visibly seething in the grainy frames, over the incessant, demonic gangsta rap that so preoccupied her husband pulsating in the background, Karla can be heard encouraging the teenager to smile and say just the right things while Paul is sodomizing her. Just before going to Karla's parents for the obligatory Easter Sunday dinner, they killed Kristen too. Later that night, Karla cut off the corpse's luxurious dark chestnut hair – as she later explained – to foil forensic analysis. Then she helped Paul dump the shorn, naked body in a ditch.

Among the more difficult facts in all these cases, Karla had numerous opportunities to save all of their victims. At one point during Leslie Mahaffy's captivity, Karla went out and walked the dog for half an hour while Bernardo stayed home and raped the girl yet again. There was nothing to stop her going into a nearby telephone booth and calling the police. On another occasion, Karla was left alone to "guard" Kristen French while her husband went out to get take-out and rent a movie.

In a controversial plea bargain, allegedly motivated by the authorities' need for her testimony against her husband, Karla pled guilty to two counts of manslaughter and received a twelve-year prison sentence. Almost as astonishing as the deal itself, the families of the murdered teenage girls sanctioned Karla's deals.

Subsequently, there has been a good deal of superficial commentary and public indignation about the fact that Karla has a future. Some say it was blind luck, while others say it was blind Justice. Wiser men than I have proclaimed it a combination of both. All of it has been characterized by the idea that Karla wove some kind of voodoo spell that confused and befuddled our purveyors of law and order.

Like her namesake Karla Faye Tucker from Texas, in many American states, Karla Homolka would have been given the needle. If there were any such thing as Justice she would at least be rotting in jail for the rest of her life. Instead, on July 6, 2005, at the age of thirty-five, "her debt to society" paid in full, she will be released, a free woman.

The questions about Karla and her future and what she might do with it are not as profound as the nagging arcana of life and death but for me they are especially vexatious because I cannot get away from them.

God knows I've tried. After I was arrested in 1998 and unsuccessfully prosecuted over the next two years for allegedly violating court orders while writing my first book about Paul and Karla's crimes, it became evident that I was not going to be allowed to end my quest where most quests end. I was not going to be able to settle comfortably somewhere between Heaven and Hell in the midst of a troubled acceptance that certain mysteries are unknowable. I had been unwillingly dragged back into the quagmire of sex, death and videotape that had defined Karla's short life. It was like a nightmare from which I could not awake. By the time I was acquitted on November 30, 2000, it was too late.

"If you are not a bird, beware of coming to rest over the Abyss…" the German philosopher Frederick Nietzsche wrote. I had come squarely to rest over the Abyss and could not help staring into it.

It was a shape-shifter.

Sometimes, it was quite attractive, with blue eyes, full breasts and cashmere-blond hair. Many times it was naked and I watched, both repelled and riveted, while it performed various sex acts on members of both sexes. Often, it looked exactly like Karla Homolka, as she appeared in those videos, bent over her sister or some other comatose teenager, naked, legs akimbo, rubbing her pubis, a demonic, feral grin on her face.

Other times, it looked exactly like Michael Code, the square-jawed, Buddha-worshiping, ex-rugger-playing prosecutor who ultimately sealed Karla's fate and delivered her a future.

Other times it was a huge blackness, like a starless country sky, under which it was impossible to get any bearing.

No matter how long I stared into it, or how much I read about it, or how closely I examined it, it stubbornly remained inaccessible and mysterious. Thus began my quest for the tarnished fleece of forbidden knowledge that might just stop the Abyss from staring into me.

With my first book, *Invisible Darkness*, I tried to write a straightforward, un-hyped, literate account of the crimes and the criminals and the police, and prosecutors who tried to bring them to justice. This time I am going to do a *Rashomon* and tell the story of Karla's life in prison and suggest what her possible futures may be in many voices and from many different points of view. Certain viewpoints are more illusive than others. For instance, the letters I wrote to Karla throughout the nineties went unanswered. My frequent requests for interviews with the architects of Karla's deals were ignored. Then something happened and things changed.

In myth and legend, mortals who embark on seemingly unattainable quests are aided by something – Fate, Coincidence, Divine Intervention. So was I.

CELLBLOCK A

Karla gave Paul everything he wanted, including her younger sister. When he wanted more, she gave and gave until finally, he gave her a beating that almost killed her.

Everyone saw the picture. It was on the front page of all the newspapers. Paul had hit her so hard on the back of her head with one of those big, black, steel flashlights that her eyeballs almost popped out and a mask of bruising welled up around her sockets. The doctor said it was the worst case of abuse he had ever seen.

When things had been better between them, before the atrocities began, Karla had sent Paul a love note that said "All men are not alike… You are so special, you mean so much to me… *amo nunquam obliviscar.*"

Amo nunquam obliviscar – Latin for "Oath of Love, never to be forgotten."

But he did forget.

Now, monitored by the same video technology with which he was so obsessed when they were together, day by day, month by month, year by year, Paul wastes away in a tiny cell in the Kingston Penitentiary's segregation unit with Karla's *amo nunquam obliviscar* eating his brain. It's a cinch he's never going to forget that broken oath now – at least not as long as he is *compos mentis.*

It only took Paul a few years to betray Karla. It took the prison authorities seven. Instead of packing up her belongings and getting ready to move to the Elizabeth Fry Society's halfway house on the outskirts of tony Westmount in Montreal, Karla found herself unpacking her posters and pictures in a tiny cell of her own, this one on Cellblock A in the Regional Reception Center at Sainte-Anne-des-Plaines in the province of Quebec.

Sainte-Anne-des-Plaines is a complex of correctional service facilities near the small rural town of the same name, about a fifty-minute drive directly north from downtown Montreal. A bunker-like compound made up of different pods that are distinguished only by the level and severity of the inhabitants' security classifications, it sits back off the road in the middle of a vast cornfield.

Karla was being "oriented" to the Center by the resident psychologist, a petite, bespectacled creature named Christine Perreault. Karla needed orientation. Even though she had been a model prisoner throughout the seven years she had been in prison, she had, by this point in early April, 2001, been in four different institutions in less than six months and moved by airplane back and forth across the country.

It did not take long to realize that this time she was in a very peculiar place indeed. It was not quite hell, but it was headed in that direction. The Regional Reception Center was the clearinghouse for all male prisoners in Quebec. Every man convicted of a crime which garnered a prison sentence of more than two years was first sent to Sainte-Anne to be assessed and evaluated for a period of four to six weeks. Each of them, Dr. Perreault explained – over a thousand a year – is watched, interviewed, given a few computerized psychological tests including the ubiquitous Minnesota Multiphasic Personality Inventory(MMPI-2) and assigned a security classification.

MMPI-2 is the nucleus of psychological testing because it is the test against which any other of the myriad tests a psychologist might chose to administer are measured. The test requires one of three responses to hundreds of statements about behavior, feelings, social attitudes and psychopathological symptoms. The subject answers each question with either a "T" for "true," a "F" for "false," or a "?" for "cannot say."

The answers are then scored on scales established by the tests' authors, a psychiatrist named J.C. McKinley and psychologist named Starke Hathaway.

In prison, one's security classification is everything. There are only three possibilities – minimum, medium or maximum. From the time Karla arrived in prison on July 6, 1993, she had been classified as a medium security prisoner. The security classification determines in which of a dozen different institutions a con will do his/her time and how hard that time will be.

Karla surmised during her orientation that the Regional Center at Sainte-Anne was going to be where she was kept, at least for the foreseeable future, maybe even until she had served her full sentence, four years hence. This was not good news. Karla had fully expected to be returned to Joliette, Quebec's only medium security prison for women from whence she had been so unjustly plucked that past Thanksgiving.

There were five other women on Cellblock A. As Karla wrote to a friend "This a very boring place to do time, outside of the regular self-injuries, headbanging, screaming, emergency interventions, etc. there is nothing much going on…The women here are in prison for a variety of things. Some of them are not max material, some are mental health [meaning women with identifiable mental defects or disease]. some are typical max women. They ended up in prison for various reasons, the typical abuse and drugs. Most women in prison have similar stories. They end up in max for various reasons, mostly violence in other prisons."

But none of them – regardless of whether they were "max material," "mental health," or Karla – were welcomed in Sainte-Anne and it did not take Karla very long to discover this fact of life. "This is not a place for women," she continued. "We are not wanted here by anyone. It is a fight to get anything. We are constantly insulted… It is not nice to be somewhere you are not wanted."

It was never intended that anyone, man or woman, be "housed" in the Reception Center for any length of time. Its sole *raison d'être* was the evaluation and processing of male prisoners. Women in prison have different needs than men. To be responsible for the long-term incarceration of six women in a facility specifically designed for the short-term evaluation of men made the administrators' lives hell.

As Camille Trudel, the Reception Center's Program Manager and a thirty-year veteran of the Correctional Service explained to me when I visited the prison in the summer of 2001, the entire complex was routinely locked down whenever one of the women had to be moved, whether to attend the medical unit or just buy cigarettes at the canteen across the pod. Things were a bit looser now, but not much.

There had been no real effort made to accommodate women either. For instance, there were no hairdressers. Karla's dark roots were already showing when she was flown back to Quebec in mid-January, after her fourteen-week stay in a psychiatric facility operated by Correctional Services in Saskatoon where she had been isolated and psychiatrically probed against her will.

Well, that was not entirely true. It was true that by law and by virtue of its own regulations, the prison system was supposedly prohibited from conducting psychiatric or psychological examinations without consent. However, Karla had recently come to clearly understand that they broke their own rules and regulations all the time, whenever it suited them.

Once she was ensconced in the Regional Psychiatric Center in Saskatoon and against her better judgement, she had decided to cooperate.

"I was basically threatened. Not outright, the threat was subtle. I was informed that if I did not cooperate then that could be used against me to increase my security level to maximum. And that was the last thing I wanted. Of course, back then, they were also promising me that when they were finished I would go back to Joliette."

Ever since Karla's plea bargains with the Ministry of the Attorney General in 1993 delivered her twelve years in exchange for guilty pleas to two counts of manslaughter and her testimony against her ex-husband, she had been led to believe in a fate very different than her recent experience and arrival at Sainte-Anne signaled.

Everybody had said that if she was a good girl, if she minded her P's & Q's, did her school work, applied herself to the prison's programs, bettered herself, did not do any of the bad things that women in prison do, such as fight, drink and take drugs, she would treated fairly. And in fairness, she would be released from jail – on parole – no later than July 6, 2001, after serving two-thirds of her sentence.

By law, all prisoners in the country are automatically released after they have served two-thirds of their sentence. It was very rare that the overcrowded prisons moved to detain a prisoner beyond that individual's Statutory Release Date, known throughout the system as an SRD.

Karla's lawyer, George Walker, had explained early on what a twelve-year sentence meant – four years, if she continued to behave as she had (this was when he used to visit her in Kingston before Paul Bernardo's trial, during the first two years of her incarceration) and eight years if she was the worst inmate in the world.

Although there was no impediment to Karla applying for full parole as early as July 6, 1997, after she had served only four years of her sentence, and indeed, the judge and the prosecutor at her trial had deferred parole recommendations, a sign that the authorities would not oppose any application she might bring, Karla herself demurred and decided to wait for her Statutory Release.

Karla had lived up to her end of the bargain. If her name weren't Karla, she would have been the poster girl for the country's new women's penology. She completed the necessary high school credits and then went on to get her Bachelor of Arts degree in Psychology through a Queen's University correspondence program. She had really wanted to read the law, but that was not possible by correspondence at Queen's. Sociology had been her next choice, but there were not enough correspondence courses to get a degree.

Waterloo University offered an abundance of courses, more than 300 Karla thought. She applied to change from Queen's but Waterloo rejected her. It was "not based on my marks, but based on my crimes," Karla said. They sent her an "unbelievable letter."

The majority of women in prison do not have the equivalent of a Grade Eight education and very few emerge with any further academic credentials. There are many ways to do time and the statistics show that most simply waste it or fight it.

After obtaining her degree in 1999, Karla applied to Simon Fraser University in British Columbia to begin a post-baccalaureate diploma in criminology. She got through one year, but then she ran out of money and decided to save whatever she had for when she gets out. Dropping out is one of her great regrets.

"Education did more for my self-esteem and growth than all of the prison programs I did put together," Karla wrote, with some pride.

The prison would pay for a community college-type correspondence Spanish course and Karla wanted to try that out. All she needed was proof of citizenship, but Correctional Services seemed to have lost her birth certificate. There was a whole "thinking world" out there that Karla longed to rejoin. As she observed, "It's amazing how quickly one can deteriorate inside these walls."

When Karla was not taking course, she read.

"Reading is like breathing to me," she explained. "I have to do it or I will die. Psychologically, at least."

When she was at the Kingston Prison for Women, the librarian was devoted to her work. After Karla finished reading everything in the prison library that interested her, the librarian took it upon herself to go to the public library, where she selected books she thought Karla would like.

At Joliette there was an extensive library of English and French-language books in the area devoted to inmate education. Karla could walk from the classroom where courses were offered in the use of computers, past a long wall painted with scenes of Egyptian life that had sprung from the creative wellspring of a prisoner, into the library where shelf upon shelf of books awaited her.

In Sainte-Anne, it was different. The library was much smaller. It was an airless, windowless room, and the selection was random and relative to the kindness of strangers who made donations. There were about 10,000 books in the library, one-third English and the rest French. The comic books were all in French, but Karla didn't care about them. One good thing was that every time Karla went to the library she got a smile out of the cartoon artwork on the walls, signed by Thibault, who she heard had been a heroin addict incarcerated in the early 1990s. His work was big and colorful. The piece nearest the library depicted some kind of jovial genie emerging from a bottle. No one seemed to know what became of Thibault.

Every Thursday morning, the women from Cellblock A were allowed to go to the library, but they were only allowed to take five books per week. No reason was given. That was just the way things were. Karla thought it was "ridiculous." But then, there were lots of rules at Sainte-Anne that didn't make sense to Karla. For instance, sometimes prisoners were allowed to receive pre-stamped envelopes and stickers that were sent to them from the outside. Then, suddenly, those things were not allowed. "They change their rules like most people change their underwear," Karla complained. "And they never advise us, either."

The prison did not tell Karla what to read, however, and she has sampled the library as much as possible. One week during the spring of 2001 she read *Caught Up in the Rapture* by Sheneska Jackson, a novel about a black preacher's daughter making it in the music industry ("really liked it"), *The Last Dive* by Bernie Chowdhury ("a gripping account of a fatal dive – very well written"), *The Secret of Shambhala* by James Redfield ("the third installment in the Celestine Prophesy – very good"), *A Painted House* by John Grisham ("not like his usual books. I *loved* it – hope he writes a sequel") and *From the Corner of His Eye* by Dean Koontz ("I really like Dean Koontz").

"How do I choose what I read? That's a good question. When I find an author I like, I try to read everything he or she writes." Also, family and a few friends had taken to donating books they think Karla will like to the library at Sainte-Anne with instructions to the librarian that Karla get first crack at them. That seemed to work.

Karla does not have access to English-language newspapers, only the *Journal de Montréal* ("the worst of the bunch), so she relies on recommendations from the book review pages of *Glamor* magazine, to which she subscribes.

"I liked it years ago when, in the backs of books, they used to advertise other books that you might like if you enjoyed the book you had just read. Why did they stop doing that?" she wondered. "I also love reading biographies – pretty strange for someone who values privacy so much."

As she did when she was a free woman, Karla continues to read true crime and crime fiction, and she has stopped worrying about what people think about that. "No matter what I do, I can't win," she acknowledges. "If every tenth book I read is true crime or crime fiction, I'm screwed. So I just don't care. I read what I like to read and that's it. People are always going to interpret what I do as bad. They'll pick out one bad thing from a sea of good and I'll be judged on that."

Television viewing is limited to the major networks – CBS, NBC, CBC and CTV, plus a couple of French channels and Super-Ecran, a French channel the women must pay for. Karla has her own TV and she watches a lot of televison, everything from *Family Law* and *Law and Order* to *Everybody Loves Raymond* and *Access Hollywood*. Occasionally, she will watch a news-magazine program like *Dateline* but current affairs are not a high priority. "I only watch news if I get a feeling that I should watch it (rare). When I do it's usually CTV at 11 p.m."

Karla also has her music to keep her company. When she has difficulty sleeping, which she estimates occurs every ten days or so, she stays up until 3 or 4 a.m. playing CDs on her Walkman. "I don't like country (except for the Dixie Chicks) or any of that 60s and 70s rock (CCR, Janis Joplin etc.)," she said of her tastes, which range from classical to modern. She loves 50s music and likes a lot of the music from the 1980s that pre-dates her relationship with Paul Bernardo.

While she was at Joliette, Karla had kept her nose clean and stayed out of trouble. She "graduated" from all of the programs the prison insisted she take such as "Anger Management" and "Survivors of Abuse."

With the prison's encouragement, she gladly took the "Peer Support" courses offered at Joliette and made a concerted effort to help other women who were having trouble on the inside. But the betrayal Karla felt at the Regional Reception Center in Sainte-Anne was more egregious still because not only did the system not live up to its end of the bargain, it was now patently obvious they were really trying to screw her in the process and make the remaining years of her sentence hell on earth.

What no one seemed to grasp was the fact that doing time in the Reception Center at Sainte-Anne-des-Plaines was a lot "easier" than doing time in Joliette. In Joliette, you were kept busy fourteen hours a day. It was a very structured, disciplined environment. If you were even a minute late for work, or one of your courses, you received demerit points on your record and demerit points directly affected your privileges and progress.

It was no picnic either, trying to live and keep up in a house with seven or eight other drug-addled, strung out women who came from all different walks of life, none of whom were very pleased with themselves or wanted to be where they were. Some women just couldn't cut it in that kind of environment and those women were sent to special segmented maximum security lockups in men's prisons like the Regional Reception Center or the big male pen out in Saskatoon.

In Sainte-Anne, they did not really care about the six women they housed. As long as they stayed out of the way and did not cause any trouble, everybody was happy. Not only were there no hairdressers, there were no programs, no therapy (Dr. Perreault was the only staff psychologist and responsible for overseeing and interpreting the administration of the psychological testing) and no work to speak of either.

"Oh well," as Karla wrote in one of her letters, "I still get paid the same $6.90 a day."

In Joliette, Karla was working thirty-three hours a week and getting regular therapy. She had responsibilities for which she was held accountable. And she had hope. No one had disavowed her of her obvious belief that she was going to be released on her Statutory Date, in fact quite the opposite. They encouraged her to work hard toward it.

At Sainte-Anne things were different.

"My average day is very boring," Karla explained, after she had been there for almost a year. "They unlock the doors at 7:30 a.m. There is really no reason to get up early, because there is nothing to do. So I usually stay in bed until around 8:30 or so. Contrast this with Joliette where I get up between 6 and 6:30 a.m.

"I take my shower, put on my makeup, dress, do my hair, etc. I usually draw this process out for as long as possible to fill the time. They open the yard at 9:30. When it's nice, especially in the summer, I usually go outside with one of the other girls. We talk and either walk around the big yard or sit on the bench near the hall windows and watch the guys walk by and talk. If I stay inside I usually talk to her in my room or in her room or read or write letters. The yard closes at 11 a.m. and that's when lunch comes…"

"I piss around until 1 p.m. when the yard opens again. We usually go outside again until 2 p.m. I watch my soap (*Passion*) from 2-3 p.m. Sometimes at 3 we go out again. If not, I usually read, write letters or clean up my cell. It all depends on the day. Supper comes at 4 p.m., If I eat, that takes about half an hour. I watch *Oprah* sometimes, or read again, and watch *Friends* at 5 p.m. At 5:30 I usually get ready to work-out. The yard opens at 6 and one of the other girls and I train, usually for about two hours. We do this pretty much every day. It's getting harder though, as it is getting pretty cold outside now. When we finish, I take another shower, take off my makeup and put on pyjamas. Then I spend the rest of the evening watching TV, reading or playing on my computer…I usually go to bed around 11:45 or 12 p.m."

"People want me in max so my life will be hard, but really it isn't. There are absolutely no responsibilities here. Everything is provided. We barely work. We can spend the day sleeping, suntanning, or doing whatever we want all day every day."

It was sure a hell of a lot easier than her first four years in Kingston's antiquated, gothic Prison for Women where she had been locked down in her tiny third-floor cell twenty-three of twenty-four hours a day, seven days a week.

Then again, now that she thought about it, maybe not. The first two years before she testified at her ex-husband's trial had really been the easiest time of all. She might have been isolated in the prison tower but they treated her like a princess. She was continually being coached by police and prosecutors in preparation for her appearance as their "star" witness, often for days, sometimes for months at a time. And the prison had provided a psychologist and a psychiatrist whom she could see as often as she wished. During the first two years, Karla often had three or four therapy sessions a week.

Things did change after she testified. Although Sergeants Bob Gillies and Gary Beaulieu came down to see her one last time as they had promised, she never saw another policeman or prosecutor. As far as the police and prosecutors were concerned, Karla had served her purpose. What happened to her from then on was no longer their concern. They got what they wanted – her testimony against her husband and his conviction, on all counts.

At least the prison did not abandon her. They seemed to redouble their therapeutic efforts on her behalf. She kept seeing the prison psychiatrist, Dr. Roy Brown, until he got sick in 1996 and left the prison. He was old and never came back. Then they sent a very prominent Kingston-based psychiatrist, Dr. Sharon Williams, to see her. Dr. Williams was very nice and helped Karla with some issues she had, particularly what she should tell someone whom she might meet after she was released about her crimes and time in prison. But that was a long time ago now.

Karla's thirty-second birthday was coming up on May 4. Her girlfriends from high school, with whom she used to celebrate around the pool in her parents' backyard, had long since stopped sending her cards. One by one, they had all betrayed her too. Her former very best girlfriend, Kathy Ford, nee Wilson, had even sold Karla's letters to a tabloid newspaper. Kathy said it was compensation for the fact that by simply being there, and being in so many of the shots, Karla and Paul had ruined her wedding videos. Karla had always been a bit jealous of Kathy and her seemingly perfect marriage – to a Marine named Alex Ford. Since coming to Sainte-Anne, Karla heard that they were now divorced. So much for happy endings. Karla took some solace knowing that other people "fucked up" too.

Karla would occasionally catch herself dwelling on some ridiculous artifact, like Kathy Ford and her letters, that meant absolutely nothing to her anymore. So much had changed over the seven years she had been in prison. After she had testified in the summer of 1995 and returned to Kingston, her mother started to suffer annual breakdowns between Thanksgiving and Christmas. The reality of what had happened finally sunk in and her mother's collapses were severe enough that she was hospitalized, sometimes for months at a time. And now her father, who, although quiet, had always been a bit of a rascal and robust, had multiple sclerosis. And her beloved Rottweiler dog, Buddy, was dying. On the plus side, her surviving sister, Lori, with whom she had remained close, had finally married and now had a baby that Karla absolutely *adored*. Her sister brought him to Joliette so Karla could see him when he was barely two months old. He was beautiful. Karla wanted children herself so badly that the visit had been strangely unsettling.

After years of haggling, the authorities had decided, once and for all, to close the dilapidated Kingston prison. Karla was transferred to general population in Joliette on June 1, 1997. In Joliette, Karla made many new girlfriends and she celebrated her last few birthdays with Tracy Gonzales and Christina Sherry, Linda Véronneau and Stivia Clermont.

Three and a half years later, in what was no more than a politically motivated publicity stunt, Karla's keepers unceremoniously transferred her to the Psych Center in Saskatoon where she was placed in maximum security isolation. They did not have hairdressers there either. Karla was almost able to look back on it now and laugh. For the first time in a half-dozen years, her mother had managed to stay out of the booby hatch and there Karla was, locked down in one four thousand miles away. She and her mother had actually chuckled about it on the phone. For the first little while out there, every time she phoned her mother the call would not go through and she had to redial two or three times, a sure sign that the prison was monitoring her phone calls. Calls were not supposed to be monitored unless the prisoner was advised, but they were anyway. She confronted the Warden. Naturally, he denied it but after that her calls went through on the first try.

After years in the open environment with eighty other women in Joliette, other than a couple of nurses, two shrinks, a psychologist named Cindy Presse and a couple of her grad students, the only other person she talked to over the four months she was there was her mother.

When they finally shipped Karla back to Quebec in January, they did not immediately place her in Sainte-Anne. There was no room. They had to wait for one of the six cells on Cellblock A to become available. Instead, they put her in Institut Philippe Pinel, a psychiatric hospital on the northern boundary of Montreal. They did not offer her any therapy in Pinel either. It made absolutely no sense.

Karla's favorite place of all the places she had been was Joliette. Not only was it a structured and a disciplined environment where all the inmates were required to work and attend programs, everyone was responsible for the upkeep of their property and for cooking and feeding themselves. The groceries were bought with pooled wages.

Each woman earned $6.90 a day, a minuscule sum given that a bag a potato chips at the prison store or canteen was $3.50. The store in Joliette was well stocked and run by the inmates. However, groceries were as expensive, perhaps in some cases even more expensive, than groceries in those twenty-four hour mini-marts on the outside. Meager wages and healthy prices meant there was no way to opt out of the cooperative thing. The only way to get sufficient food was for each woman to contribute her share to the house fund and buy enough groceries to feed everyone. Some of the women could not cook, others would not cook. Practicing a primitive form of democracy, the house members quickly had to select cooks and cleaners and divide functions in some semi-equitable way. This was not easy. It was actually very difficult. And just when you seemed to get things working the way they should, one of the women would be paroled, and another, new, disoriented or disgruntled con would take her place and everything would become tenuous again.

Celebrating someone's birthday in Joliette in 1998 – Karla did not think it was hers – she and Christina and Tracy got dressed up in their best dresses. Karla wore a little, black cocktail sheath. They all put on lots of makeup. It was no big deal but they made a birthday cake and had a lot of fun.

The prison recreation committee made a camera available so inmates could take pictures and send them to their family and friends. Two years later, Karla's picture showed up on the front page of the September 22, 2000, edition of the *Montreal Gazette*.

A firestorm of publicity ensued. Everything, from her styled blond hair, to the dark eye makeup, painted lips and sleeveless dress, incensed the public. What did they think? That they wore sackcloth and shuffled around in leg chains. All the women in prison wore their own clothes. As far as she knew, it had ever been thus. "It makes me laugh," Karla wrote in the aftermath, "how little the public knows about what really goes on in prison."

Newspapers across the country picked up the pictures and extrapolated the story with verbose editorials by indignant columnists. People wrote letters to the editors. They telephoned, faxed and e-mailed their Members of Parliament, the Solicitor General and the Commissioner of Corrections. Members from the right-wing Alliance Party howled.

Even though birthday parties and other gatherings are common in prison, prison officials expressed regret and a sense of helplessness. This was somewhat pawky too, given it was the prison that supplied the camera with which the pictures were taken in the first place.

Karla instantly scanned a mental lineup of possible betrayers. It was not Tracy Gonzales. She was still in Joliette. Linda Véronneau would not do it. At that time, Linda was in love with Karla and Karla would have been the last person Linda would betray. Neither would Stivia Clermont. It was not her style.

Christina Sherry had been paroled but it wasn't her either. Christina would not have wanted those pictures published anymore than Karla did. As it was, Christina was on the outside when the pictures appeared and she lost her hard-won waitressing job because of them.

The paper said that they bought the pictures from an ex-con for $500. It could have been Mary Smith, it was the kind of thing she would do. Like Karla, she was doing time for manslaughter but she was incredibly bossy and belligerent and everyone was really happy when she had been paroled.

But Karla was skeptical. One would think that even an idiot like Mary Smith would have known that she could have easily sold the pictures to one of the Toronto newspapers for thousands of dollars just as one of Karla's own uncles had done with her wedding photographs years earlier. And given the timing, and how bad it was for her, Karla would not put it past the prison to have been the source. For them, the timing was perfect. The pictures portrayed Karla as a vamping slut, living *la vida loca* in what the media dubbed "Club Fed" and the "Hen Pen."

Tracy Gonzales and Christina Sherry had been involved with a notorious Montreal pimp named James Medley and had been convicted on sexual assault charges to do with some kind of bizarre, violent tryst of his design. They were very different women than Karla – both much younger, drug-addled street kids who had run away from abusive homes. Their stories and their crimes were dramatically different. The one common element, perhaps, was the fact that all three women had somehow fallen under the spell of a sadistic sexual predator. But the press made it sound as though Joliette were a sandbox in which women who committed heinous sex crimes spent their time cavorting in townhouses with color televisions. In retrospect, Karla realized that the party pictures and the attendant furor raised the specter of Karla the Sex-Crazed Killer again and made it much easier for the prison to do what it had fully intended to do anyway.

Karla's family had long-standing plans to visit her in Joliette that Thanksgiving weekend. They had not seen each other since the previous year and the visit was much anticipated. Sixteen days after the pictures appeared in the *Gazette*, on the Friday night that began the long weekend, at 11 p.m., Karla found herself the only passenger on a seven-seat Pilatus 7, flying into the oblivion of the prairie night with her legs shackled to the seat, two, silent, armed guards on either side and a soggy egg-salad sandwich in her lap.

* * * * * * *

Situating her beloved Disney and Care Bear posters, collating the dozens of pictures she had collected of her nephew and thinking about all this in her new cell at Sainte-Anne, Karla decided to do a little "housekeeping." Looking around, she determined that her new cell was really about the same size as the sub-basement room she used to have when she lived at home with her parents. The metal cot with its roll-up mattress and the stainless steel toilet made it a little different but there was a desk and chair and a built-in ottoman. The heavy, steel door was typical of max units. She had a window though. It was about waist-high. Although there were bars embedded in the concrete structure, the window itself opened pretty wide, and on that particular day the sun was shining brightly and there was a very pleasant early spring breeze.

At the bottom of one of her boxes, she found Dr. Hans Arndt's business card. Running her fingers over the embossed lettering, good memories of him and his sleep therapies came rushing back. At various times between the day they first met on March 4, 1993, and the time Karla went on trial on July 2, 1993, Dr. Arndt would check her into Northwestern General Hospital in Toronto and mix up drug concoctions that knocked her out for three days at a time. It was bliss. Once he kept her in the hospital for eight weeks, prescribing copious amounts of drugs and giving her daily therapy. Dr. Arndt was the first psychiatrist Karla had ever met. He really helped her and she really liked him.

A kindly, German-born man, he would have made a far better Freud than Montgomery Cliff in John Huston's 1962 biopic. Tall, lean and prone to tweedy jackets, his wire-rim glasses had a tendency to slip down his nose and the balding pate of his head was endearingly shiny. Dr. Arndt had been on Karla's side. There was no one on her side now.

For a while, during her first few years of incarceration, she had written to Dr. Arndt. She told him all about what her life in prison was like, about the other women in the segregation unit where she was kept at P4W, the university courses she was taking by correspondence, the police and prosecutors who were then coming to see her regularly and her growing sense of self-assertiveness. She asked for his advice and counsel about her psyche and the medication she was being prescribed by the prison psychiatrist.

He replied with spirited, chatty, supportive letters. In one of her letters to Kathy Ford that had just been published in the paper, Karla said that she hated her psychiatrist. Dr. Arndt wrote saying that he hoped she was not referring to him. Karla laughed and immediately sent him another note. Of course it was not him. She had meant the psychiatrist the prison had assigned her, Dr. Roy Brown.

But now, here in Sainte-Anne, very far away from those halcyon days before her trial when she had been under Dr. Arndt's care and protection, Karla felt a strange emptiness when she looked at his card. They had not corresponded for a long time. And there was nothing Dr. Arndt, or anyone else for that matter, could do for her anymore. Psychiatrists and psychologists had become agents for her detention, rather than advocates for her rehabilitation. She threw the card out.

A few days later she was given her mail. Among the cards from the usual crackpots offering to pay her if she would send them pairs of her panties, and a chatty letter from her sister talking about the kid and how wonderful married life was, Karla found a letter from someone she truly despised and from whom she had never expected to hear again.

Although the envelope had been opened by the prison, Karla resolved not to read the letter and tossed it out. As she did, a photocopy of Dr. Arndt's obituary, clipped from the April 9, 2001, *Globe and Mail* newspaper, fell to the floor. In elegant script, there was a single hand-written line: "Thought you would want to know."

The obituary said that Dr. Arndt, who was just sixty-years old, had died at his cottage after a long illness and spent his last hours sur-rounded by his family. It noted that he was a devoted father and grand-father. "Perhaps on some level I knew? Things like that happen to me often," Karla wrote in a letter dated April 27, 2001.

Coincidences have always had special meaning for Karla. She had always interpreted them, from the time she was a teenager, as omens or signs with adumbrative significance. Like the tabby cat that had found its way out of the woods and through the chain-link fence at Joliette. Imagine a cat showing up, as it did, on *her* doorstep – not on any of the other nine houses' doorstep but *her* doorstep – just as she learned that her dog, Buddy, who still lived with her parents in St. Catharines, was in declining health.

After that, more cats made their way into Joliette and the prison bent to Karla's will, and permitted the inmates to keep the strays. It was such a good thing, coming out of her bad news.

Karla loved her dog so much that she used to send her unwashed socks to him when her family returned to St. Catharines after a visit. That way, the dog would retain the scent of his mistress and remember her when they were reunited. Thanks to the prison, now she knew she would never see him alive again and they would never be reunited and it made her very sad – and resentful.

Karla had been in the process of presenting the prison with a plan to bring dogs into Joliette as therapy for the inmates when they low-ered the boom and hustled her onto that silly airplane.

Perhaps they were small things, a sick dog coincident to a found cat and an obituary notice, a reminder of one kind voice lost to her forev-er and the pure serendipity of its arrival right after she had found his card and thrown it out. Even more significant, to Karla's way of think-ing, was the fact that she had been toying with Dr. Arndt's card and thinking about him just about the time he had taken his last breath.

Magnolia, a critical hit in 1999, was a movie about the dramatic effects of coincidence on the lives of six different characters. It opens with a series of vignettes recounted by an omniscient, soto-voiced narrator, played by the internationally renowned sleight-of-hand artist, Ricky Jay.

Mr. Jay repeatedly tells the audience, as one short story after another about disaster brought on by unbearable coincidence unfolds on the screen, that he is constantly "trying to think that it was all only a matter of chance."

The last vignette in the prologue is about a failed suicide attempt by a seventeen-year-old Los Angeles teenager named Sidney Barringer that nevertheless results in his death.

Sidney was an unhappy young man. His parents, Faye and Walter Barringer, were always fighting and at the height of their domestic arguments, Faye would grab an unloaded shotgun which was kept in the closet and threaten to shoot Walter with it.

Sidney and his parents lived on the sixth floor of a nine-story apartment building. Sidney decided to commit suicide by jumping off the roof. He wrote a suicide note and put it in his pocket. Just before he went up to jump off the roof, he took the shotgun out of the closet, loaded it and put it back.

A young friend of Sidney's told police that Sidney had said "they (his parents) wanted to kill each other, and that's all they wanted to do was kill each other and that he (Sidney) would help them do that if that was what they wanted to do…"

On March 23, 1958, Sidney jumped. As he did, his parents' arguing three stories below swelled to a crescendo. His mother grabbed the shotgun from the closet, pointed it at Sidney's father and threatened to shoot him. Just as Sidney passed the sixth-floor window, the shotgun discharged, missed Walter and hit Sidney.

A safety net installed for window washers three days earlier would have broken Sidney's fall and saved his life, except, as Ricky Jay notes, "for the hole in his stomach." Faye Barringer was charged with killing her son, and Sidney himself was named as an accomplice in his own murder.

"It is, in the humble opinion of this narrator," Mr. Jay continues, "not *just* something that happened; this cannot be *just* one of those things; this, please, cannot be that, and, for what I would like to say, it can't. This was not just a matter of chance. Whoa. These strange things happen all the time."

In Karla's cosmology, these strange things do happen all the time. And as far as she is concerned, these things, like Dr. Arndt's obituary appearing as it did, just after she had tossed his card, were not just chance occurrences. They had meaning, they were signs. And the significance of the timing of the receipt of Dr. Arndt's obituary was magnified by how it had come to her attention. She decided to read the bulky, type-written, single-spaced, eight-page letter after all and retrieved it from the garbage.

DOCTOR ARNDT

I met Dr. Hans Arndt by pure coincidence. It was in September, 1993, a few months after Karla's trial. I was having dinner with my accountant on a Sunday evening in early September. We were in a little cafe called Episode in a downtown Toronto neighborhood called Cabbagetown.

A somewhat effete, well-dressed stranger approached our table and sat down. I had never laid eyes on him before but it appeared he and my accountant knew each other. His name was Doug Elliott. He was a lawyer who focused on gay rights and civil litigation. At that particular time, he was engaged in a hundred-million-dollar class action suit to do with tainted blood and the Red Cross.

Mr. Elliott turned out to be a welcome diversion. He was garrulous and witty. Turning to me, he remarked that I looked familiar. There had been a recent front-page magazine article about me and my Paul Bernardo/Karla Homolka writing project. "Perhaps that's it," I offered.

"I know *her* psychiatrist very well," he said. "I sit on an advisory board with Hans. We review release applications for inmates from Penetanguishene. Hans is a great guy."

"You mean *Karla's* psychiatrist?" I asked incredulously.

"Just what I said. She was in Northwestern General Hospital, right?"

I knew this to be true, having attended her short, secretive trial two months earlier.

"Well, it was Hans who admitted her. And it was Hans who treated her for four months. He was hired by her lawyer."

By this time, I had put it together. He was talking about Dr. Hans Arndt, the psychiatrist to whom Karla's lawyer, George Walker, had referred when he addressed the Court during Karla's one-day trial. Walker had also tabled two other psychological reports by experts who had assessed Karla as a battered woman suffering from post-traumatic stress disorder. I remember thinking at the time that I would give my right arm for a look at those reports.

The judge at Karla's trial had levied a publication ban on the details of Karla's crimes and most everything else that was said in court that day. The experts' reports were not entered as exhibits but rather, as previously agreed between prosecutor Murray Segal and Karla's defense lawyer George Walker, tabled for the record and inclusion in the file that would follow Karla into prison. There were no witnesses called, nor any evidence entered except agreed upon statements. The media had access to exactly nothing. Barring the general public and the American media from the Courthouse, the judge said he could not trust either of those two groups to respect his order. He allowed the Canadian media to stay but imposed a pernicious gag order. Approximately ninety reporters sat through the recitation of Karla's offenses in stunned, disbelieving silence. The cursory details were so horrific that many cried. The publication ban and the expulsion of the American media immediately made Karla and her trial international news. Information about the details of the crimes became a commodity, while rumors ran rampant in coffee shops, at dinner parties and on the Internet.

I thought that perhaps Mr. Elliott had quaffed one too many glasses of claret. "You don't really know him, do you?"

"Would you like to meet him?" Elliott asked.

Within the week, we convened for dinner with Hans at Bistro 990, a film-star friendly eatery where lamb from my wife's farm was featured on the menu. And Doug Elliott was right. Dr. Arndt was a warm, intelligent man with a great tableside manner.

After talking of many things including Bora Bora and Ojibway Dreamcatchers, I broached the topic of Karla. In response, Dr. Arndt asked me if I knew how Karla had happened to get George Walker as her lawyer.

In retrospect, I realize this was some sort of acid test to make sure that I really knew the people I said I did – including George Walker, Karla's lawyer. Walker was not talking to anybody in the media and he certainly would not be talking to me if he did not trust me implicitly. I told Hans what no one outside of a very closed circle knew at that time. George and his second wife, Laurie, had three dogs – two Dalmatians and a mixed breed. With literally hundreds of options on the Niagara Peninsula, many years earlier, just about the time Karla began to work there, the Walkers just happened to take the dogs to the Martindale Animal Clinic. In fact, one of the Dalmatians, whose name I had forgotten, which I knew to be deaf, had been a gift to the Walkers from one of the vets at the clinic, Dr. Patti Weir. Karla had facilitated the adoption. But it was Karla's kind treatment of Walker's beloved Dalmatian, Kelly, who had died after a hard fought, expensive battle with cancer, that facilitated Walker's taking Karla on as a client. Karla had called Laurie Walker at home, first thing in the morning on February 10, 1993, asking to see George about a "domestic matter." George Walker did not practice family law. His specialty was murder and major crimes and he had practiced long enough and been successful enough to be exclusive. Because of their connection through the vet clinic, Laurie pencilled Karla in to see George at 3:00 p.m. the following day.

Dr. Arndt was delighted. "Right, right. The dogs. She's a dog lover. So am I. So is George. We are all bound together by the dogs!"

With his wire glasses tilting down the bridge of his nose, he looked up from his grilled chicken and said enigmatically in a lyrical German accent, "You know, it is just as I told George; I really don't know whether she is mad, or bad. Of course, that does not matter. I am not her God or her judge. I was her treating physician."

Although I did not know it yet, Dr. Arndt made a number of decisions that night. I thought he opened up a bit because he decided that

I could be taken at my word. Or perhaps, he recognized that everybody at the table was both equally fascinated and repulsed by this "little wisp of a girl," as George Walker had taken to calling his diminutive client. But there was more to it than that.

"You know, she sat around the hospital in these little baby-dolls, clutching her teddy bear and I do not know what it was – normally, I am the kind of person who hugs people. I would not hug Karla." Riveted, no one said a word.

"And her drug consumption, I still cannot believe. It was truly heroic. I believe in drug therapy, but she outstripped my scripting. She was on enough junk to stun a horse but everyday she was perfectly lucid."

The next morning, at his suggestion, I met Dr. Arndt at a Toronto courtroom where he was giving expert testimony about the state of mind of a defendant who was on trial for arbitrarily stabbing a taxi driver. I sat alone in the large courtroom's gallery and listened, totally perplexed. I could not see any connection between the defendant for whom he was testifying and Karla Homolka.

Afterward, he offered me a ride from the courthouse to the Sutton Place Hotel at Bay and Wellesley where I kept an apartment. As I was getting out of his car he told me not to forget my bags and flipped open the hatch-back. Bending over to look in the trunk, I saw two large, somewhat worn, brown attaché cases.

"These aren't mine," I said.

"Yes they are," he replied, with a wink. "Take them."

I did as I was told, but did not fully understand the import of what he was doing until I opened the cases on my dining room table and discovered they contained all of Karla's school, medical and psychological records, including her recent hospital charts with the nurses' daily observations and remarks; everything to do with her eight-week stay at Northwestern General in March and April 1993, including very detailed records and charts documenting her prescriptions and drug consumption. The three reports I had coveted were there as well, even the scraps of paper on which Dr. Arndt scribbled notes during Karla's therapy sessions, as well as Karla's handwritten private diaries of abuse.

Most disturbing and peculiar of all, was the letter she wrote to her parents apologizing for having killed her sister.

"Dear Mom, Dad, & Lori,

This is the hardest letter I've ever had to write and you'll probably all hate me once you've read it. I've kept this inside myself for so long and I just can't lie to you anymore. Both Paul and I are responsible for Tammy's death…"

It was two pages long, totally coherent and neatly composed, although its author was taking among other things at the time 150 mg. of Valium. It ended with "I don't expect you to ever forgive me and I will *never* forgive myself. I love you all,

Karla – xoxo."

Psychiatrists never share patient files, yet here he was, handing me the keys to the kingdom. Here was the foundation of the real story of Karla Homolka, which, except for this remarkable gesture might never have come out.

GENEALOGY

Dr. Arndt did not have much use for Karla's father. Given the bizarre, unusual circumstances, and the heinous nature of the crimes Karla had committed, curiosity got the better of him and he decided to involve and interview "mother, father and sister." Karel Homolka communicated, when he communicated at all, with shrugs and monosyllabic grunts. After forty years in Canada, he retained a thick Czechoslovakian accent, which made many of those grunts unintelligible. Born in the industrial city of Stokov, Czechoslovakia, on January 24, 1943, at the apex of World War II, Karel Homolka had come to Canada in 1950 at the age of seven with his mother, father and ten siblings.

He was immediately put to work on their patron's tobacco farm near Woodstock, Ontario. It was not uncommon in those days for farmers to sponsor entire families. Immigrants represented a kind of slave labor, at least for the indenture period stipulated by the Ministry of Immigration.

Many of the farms around Woodstock and along the north shore of Lake Erie west toward Windsor grow tobacco, tens of thousands of tons a year. The only way to get it off the fields, then as now, was to pick it. Picking tobacco is hot, dirty work. By comparison, the lush market gardens and orchards of the Niagara Peninsula were a veritable Eden. Fruit and flowers had become big business by the fifties. There was ample work for itinerant pickers. Vaclav Homolka decided to pull his family out of the tobacco fields. Fourteen-year-old Karel got his first exposure to St. Catharines picking fruit in nearby orchards in the mid-fifties. To this child of a peripatetic picker, the small, prosperous city built around the intersection of Dick and Twelve Mile Creeks, was like an oasis in Paradise.

Somehow, by the late fifties, the Homolka patriarch morphed into a self-employed salesman and began dragging his large family across the vast, empty expanse of the Canadian prairies, pedaling trinkets and trash. Suddenly, 1957, Vaclav Homolka dropped dead. Having been a nomad since he stepped off the boat, Karla's father had only managed to get a Grade Five education. Given his family's pecuniary situation when his father died, he never had an opportunity to complete Grade Six.

An immigrant himself, Dr. Arndt's glib assessment of Karla's father was more the consequence of his own prejudices than any kind of psychiatric assessment. Since immigrating to North America a decade after the Homolkas, Dr. Arndt had become a well-to-do, successful psychiatrist. His English was impeccable. It is easy to suppose that Dr. Arndt consciously maintained his slight accent because he knew it was a nod to mythology and irresistibly charming.

Dr. Arndt did not make anything of "Father," as he called Karel Homolka, psychiatrically speaking; he did not see any clues to solve the mystery of Karla's psyche in her father's background or in the nexus of the father-daughter relationship – he just did not particularly like the man.

On the other hand, he had warm regard for Karla's mother. Dr. Arndt saw Dorothy Homolka as an "earth mother" figure. To him, "Mother" was a rock solid, attractive, head-strong, determined peasant, exactly the kind of person for whom one might imagine benevolent psychiatrist could have empathy.

And it was true: the Homolkas were the penultimate urban peasants. They met in a trailer park in Mississauga in the early sixties. Mississauga was then a rural enclave on the western outskirts of the City of Toronto. In the aftermath of Vaclav Homolka's untimely death, the Homolkas returned to Ontario and settled in that park, which was all they could afford. Dorothy Seger was already living there with her family.

With a broad, open face, fine skin, and a full figure, Dorothy was very attractive. She had also completed Grade Twelve and secured a secretarial job at the nearby Lakeshore Psychiatric Hospital. A bit like Cinderella, Dorothy had been relegated, by forces beyond her control, to a way of life that was increasingly beneath her expectations. Although Dorothy's mother was neither evil nor her stepmother, she was sickly. Ever since Dorothy could remember, she had to be both daughter and mother, wife and housekeeper. Dorothy told Dr. Arndt that her life was no fairy tale, it was more like a television sitcom.

Her father was a dead ringer for Archie Bunker, the loud-mouthed, misogynist that actor Carroll O'Connor played in the hit TV sitcom *All in the Family* in the seventies. A construction worker, most often gone from sunrise to sunset, Donald Seger, like Archie Bunker, affectionately called his wife "The Dingbat." Although Dorothy described her childhood as "happy," Dr. Arndt did not think there was anything care-free about the role Dorothy was forced to play.

She had virtually raised her brother and younger sister. Before and after school, she did all the housework. Baby Calvin, her third sibling, Dorothy barely knew. He was a "mistake," born only a few months before Dorothy left home. Calvin's cradle was the one that broke the bough. The way Dorothy figured it, if she had to keep house and raise children she might as well do it for herself.

John Kennedy had been assassinated in Dallas on November 22, 1963. On Christmas Day, 1964, Myra Hinkley and Ian Brady, better known as the "Moors Murderers," abducted 10-year-old Lesley Ann Dowley from the fair grounds in the Ancoats district of Manchester, England.

In 1965, Malcolm X was assassinated, Winston Churchill died and the first American to walk in space, Ed White, drifted outside the spacecraft for twenty-one minutes. Oblivious to such other-worldly events and happy, on December 11, 1965, Dorothy Seger and Karel Homolka were married in Cooksville, Ontario, a quiet village about an hour's drive north of Toronto. Dorothy Christine Seger, born September 26, 1946, was nineteen when she became Mrs. Dorothy Homolka.

The newlyweds moved to an apartment in Port Credit, a small west end Toronto suburb on Lake Ontario, close to the hospital where Dorothy worked. Karel and his brothers did whatever they could to get by, which wasn't much. The newlyweds were thankful for Dorothy's job.

Karla Leanne Homolka was born by Caesarian section on May 4, 1970, at Mississauga General Hospital. The Homolkas had no idea they were on the cusp of a New Age.

The Rolling Stones concert at Altamont Speedway outside San Francisco on December 6, 1969, had been pegged by social critics as the official end of the Age of Aquarius. Apparently, the sentiments of Peace and Love evaporated once and for all the night Mick Jagger sang his dark anthem "Sympathy for the Devil" while the Hell's Angels stabbed a man to death in front of the stage. Flower children were suddenly replaced by acolytes of the Beast.

* * * * * * *

It was a bright Saturday morning in August. Mrs. Winifred Chapman, a domestic, ran screaming from the house in which she worked at the end of Cielo Drive up in Benedict Canyon, north of Beverley Hills in Los Angeles, California. She ran across the huge grounds and parking lot, through the iron gate and down the road screaming at the top of her lungs: "There's bodies and blood all over the place!"

Each victim was stabbed or shot to death. Steven Parent in his white Rambler. Wojiciech Frykowski in front of the house. Twenty yards down the rolling lawn, underneath a fir tree, Abigail Folger was curled up in her bloody nightgown. Inside the house Jay Sebring and Sharon Tate lay near the living-room couch, connected by a single nylon cord wrapped around their necks and thrown over a rafter. Sebring had a pillowcase over his head.

The District Attorney for Los Angeles county sifted through the deck of color Polaroids taken by staff photographers from the county coroner's office and the Los Angeles Police Department, trying to read them like Tarot cards.

Some are slightly out of focus which makes them even more horrific, reminiscent of Francis Bacon's popes, or the old sepia late nineteenth-century photographs of Jack the Ripper's last victims. All the relevant graphic details are there – the wounds, the nakedness, the blood; shots of the rooms, the bullet holes, the bizarre blood-writing on the walls – RISE, HELTER SKELTER and PIGGIES.

Try as he might the pictures were as impenetrable as the future. Although such random, senseless murders had spawned an industry of experts and explainers since World War II, when the deck is made up of all the same cards nothing can be divined. What in God's name would make a bevy of women brutally stab to death a dozen strangers, including the pregnant wife of a famous Hollywood film director? Charlie Mason was not even there. The killings were carried out at his "instigation."

"Spring is the cruelest month…" In May, 1970, Charlie is sitting in his Los Angeles county jail cell, humming a Beatles song: "Everywhere there's lots of piggies/Living piggy lives/You can see them out for dinner/With their piggy wives."

Meanwhile, thousands of letters are pouring in from all over the country. A middle-aged lady in Bel Air wants to be his "mother." Teenage girls from New Hampshire, Minnesota, Los Angeles, Toronto, and St. Catharines, deluge the jail with love letters that say things such as "We knew you hadn't done it anyway when we saw your face in the newspaper, Love…"

* * * * * * *

As far as twenty-two-year-old Dorothy was concerned the birth of her first child marked an end and a beginning as well.

From where she sat, Karla Leanne Homolka was a little princess who looked and behaved like an angel and the world was a very bright place indeed. By the summer of 1970, just as Charlie Manson and a dozen female members of his "family" went on trial in Los Angeles, things were going a whole lot better for Karel Homolka. Following in their father's footsteps, he and his brothers had established a thriving trade in trinkets and trash – framed Elvises and mulatto girls on black-velvet backgrounds and the like – which they sold in open-air country markets and shopping malls. With sprawling suburbs, came faux culture with spiraling taste and the attendant explosion in the market for such things. Things were going so well that Dorothy was able to become a full-time mother and housewife. She would not return to work for twelve years.

Karla's first sister, Lori Priscilla, named after Priscilla Presley, was born on June 22, 1971. A few months after a disgraced Richard Nixon resigned the American presidency, the Homolka's third and last child, Tammy Lyn, was born on New Year's Day, 1975. In March, the Homolkas moved into a rented trailer in the trailer park at 241 St. Paul Street West, St. Catharines.

Niagara Falls, ten minutes away by car, was the Mecca of the trinkets trade. St. Catharines had more than its share of open-air markets and shopping malls. To Karel Homolka, St. Catharines was the paradisal garden from which he had been banished as a child. If he had anything to do with it, he and his young family would never leave.

Suddenly Karel Homolka became his father. No sooner had he regained Paradise than was he expelled by some inexplicable twist in his neural wiring. He abandoned trinkets (which, for him and his brothers, had become a thriving retail operation) and became a self-employed lighting fixture salesman who was required to call on hundreds of small furniture stores all over the province. For the next twenty years, like Willy Loman, Karel Homolka would be on the road far more often than he was at home.

In September, 1975, little Karla was enrolled in kindergarten at Westdale Public School. She was described by her teacher, Mrs. Joanne Berry, as "a quiet little girl who enjoys all aspects of the kindergarten program. She is cooperative and well behaved and is encountering no difficulty in any area."

Karla began Grade One at the same school the following year. Her Student Achievement Form for the first term shows excellent, above-average grades.

In the section for the teacher's comments, Mrs. Maureen Nield spoke directly to Karla: "Congratulations Karla! You read very well. We will be very sorry to see you go Karla. We hope you will enjoy your new school."

Living in a trailer park was too much like Dorothy's life before she quit the Seger sitcom. The Homolkas moved into a small townhouse at 64 Foster Street.

Karla was transferred to Parnall Public School for her second and third term. The move did not effect her academic performance as Miss Betty Bates, her new teacher, acknowledged:

"Karla has made a very good adjustment to her new school situation. I am pleased with her very good work... Karla is an eager pupil. She has made very good progress. Karla reads with fluency and expression from her reader as well as from library books and magazine articles... Karla has made excellent progress in all areas of the Grade One programme. She is ready to begin Grade Two work."

Karla's Grade Two teacher, Miss Diane Lawless was equally enthusiastic:

"Karla is an eager student who seems to love learning. I am pleased with Karla's work this term. She is an enthusiastic student who tries to do her best at all times."

While her father moved happily from town to town, little Karla gasped for breath. Severely asthmatic, the child was hospitalized a dozen times between 1976 and 1978. The doctors tried to control it with drugs and inhalers but nevertheless, whenever Karla got scared or excited, particularly around holidays, birthdays, the start of school, her father's comings and goings, she would often have a severe attack.

A great deal of speculation in the medical community, particularly on its fringes, has been given over to the psychosomatic nature of asthma.

However, in 1964, the year before Dorothy and Karel were married, a Dutch scientist named Voorhorst implicated the dust mite (*dermatophagoides pteronyssinus*). As the name implies, millions upon millions of microscopic living organisms thrive in the universe of dust, skin flakes, hair and other detritus that blankets the average household. Sufferers, such as Karla, sensitive to this ever-present, microscopic insect, have the most difficulty at night or early in the morning.

As a consequence, Karla was raised on the use of emollients and taught aggressive housekeeping techniques. Like her mother, Karla would become obsessive about maintaining a hospital-like cleanliness in her home which, to one extent or another, would become her salvation.

In September, 1978, Karla entered Grade Three. Her teacher, Mrs. Sarah McLaughlin, observed that "Karla is a good independent worker. Her work is always neat."

Late that same year the Homolkas moved into the house where their children would be raised. In the heart of a new working-class subdivision known as Merriton, 61 Dundonald Street is directly behind the Victoria Lawn Cemetery, which is briefly noted in *Ripley's Believe It or Not* because it is the only cemetery in the world with a highway running through it. More than sixty thousand graves line the road in and out of Merriton. In those days, a double plot went for sixteen hundred dollars, about an eighth of the cost of Homolka's new house.

Based on a design by Fredrick L. Olmsted, the nineteenth-century architect who designed Central Park in New York, Victoria Lawn has a carillon that plays eight-track tapes. For some reason, in those days, it was playing the theme from *The Sound of Music* – "The hills are alive, with the sound of music..." over and over again.

Semi-detached, 61 Dundonald seemed much larger to the Homolkas than its tiny 800-square feet because it was split on four levels. To the family of five who had lived most of their lives in tiny apartments and trailer parks, it felt like the mansion on the hill, complete with deck and in-ground pool which took up most of the small backyard. The illusion was further compounded by the fact that the house backed on a Hydro right-of-way. Those huge towers that support the vast network of hydro wires that span continents, strode like Colossus over an endless horizon.

Once again, Karla changed schools.

Mrs. Mary Steele, Karla's new Grade Three teacher at the Consolidated School remarked that "Karla shows industry and interest in her work. Karla has very good work habits."

Before she had a chance to graduate Grade Three Karla transferred yet again, this time to Ferndale Public, closer still to her new home.

In these early years, Karla established what would become a lifelong academic pattern – poor performance in maths and sciences, against a proclivity for English, languages and the arts. "Karla found this term's math very challenging. She had to work hard to master her two-digit multiplying and long division. Karla has done an excellent job in her language-related subjects. Very good, Karla!"

She completed Grade Four with an 80.0 average against a class average of 69.2 and was placed in Grade Five with honors.

Karla finished Fifth Grade with an 84.3 average, again, way above the class average of 68.4.

In a groove, Karla completed Grade Six with an 86% average. Her teacher, Mr. Paul Kachan, pointed out that "Karla's excellent marks are a good indication of the thought and care that she puts into her work."

Karla's teachers' remarks by now had become a sustained litany of praise. Echoing his colleagues before him, her Grade Seven teacher added his voice: "Excellent standing and work habits. An excellent year. Karla has been a pleasure to have in the room." Karla had virtually outgrown asthma by this point. She finished the year with an 82.1 average and went into her final year of grade school with honors.

With all her daughters now in school during the day and the cost of living rising, Dorothy Homolka returned to work as a secretary at the

Shaver Clinic, St. Catharines' chronic care hospital. Karla's father continued to roam the countryside and Karla continued to excel in school. Upon graduation, once again she was toasted by her teacher: "Congratulations on fine work in all subject areas Karla." Her final Grade Eight average was 83.9%.

While in public school, Karla was not only an excellent student but she also participated in track and field, gymnastics, the choir and school plays. Outside of school, she was involved in figure skating and "Pioneer Girls," an Anglican Church group.

Her mother still keeps a picture of Karla in her little Pioneer Girls' outfit; blond, wide-eyed, smiling, she is a portrait of sweetness and light.

Karla had walked and talked and read from an early age. When tested in her later grade school years she scored a very high intelligence quotient – 131. As well as being pretty, Karla Leanne Homolka was a very smart little girl.

By the time she entered high school, Karla had come to view her parents benignly, but with a certain wry bemusement. She was smarter than they were and she knew it. In the Homolka household, her mother was a submissive yet strangely dominant force. There was a dynamic between mother and father that Karla instinctively understood. She also came to understand that part of her mother's strength lay in her ability to behave submissively.

Dorothy Homolka always talked about what she was feeling, and thinking, particularly when it came to matters of money, or the lack thereof, a subject about which she thought and talked about more and more as the years went by.

Karla's father never talked about anything and that was somewhat frustrating, especially to an intelligent, curious little girl like Karla. The fact that her father still struggled with English after twenty-five years in Canada was something about which Karla became ever so slightly ashamed.

However, Karla also recognized in her father a certain inner strength. Not only did she perceive it but she also understood it was derived from the fact that he was a poor immigrant whose sense of displacement and desperation had never quite dissipated. It was, ultimately, a strength rooted in fear.

It also occurred to Karla that it was entirely possible that her father did not say anything because he had absolutely nothing to say. About this time Karla started to lead the chorus of Homolka women in referring to Karel as the "dumb Czech."

Whenever one or the other for some reason came into contention with Karel, they would all start twittering about the "dumb Czech." This moniker became a kind of standing family joke in which even Karel himself taciturnly participated.

"I would never marry a man like him," Karla nodded in the direction of her father, who was busy with the barbecue in the corner of the yard. "He's always away and never has any money," she said right out of the blue, quite sternly. "And that just won't do."

Karla was so fixated on her perception of her father's shortcomings that she latched onto Arthur Miller's *Death of a Salesman* for a Grade Ten English project. With two of her best girlfriends, she made a rather innovative video that exaggerated certain aspects of Willy Loman's character.

Karla saw Willy as a caricature of her father. She played Willy as if he were Steve Martin's ridiculous, jiggling immigrant, the somewhat arrogant yet happily oblivious "wild and crazy guy."

Although the Homolkas were friendly with a few of their neighbors and often entertained around the pool, Karla's father did not really have any "guy" friends. To Karla and her sister Lori (Tammy Lyn was too young to participate in this perception) he always seemed sort of "out of it."

On the other hand, Karla was the center of attention, always surrounded by a flock of friends, only alone when she wanted to be. In those days, Karla was universally perceived to be smart, sweet, active, fun loving, outgoing, and a leader.

Of her own accord, Karla started to visit the new library in downtown St. Catharines, near the Market Square. Her visits became a weekly ritual that Karla would maintain until she went to prison. Her mother often told co-workers and friends, regardless of Karla's academic and social success, Karla always demanded her "quiet time" – time by herself to read and think.

"Karla got along with her sisters and was a well-behaved child," Dorothy told Dr. Arndt. "Karla was a normal little girl who liked to play with her friends. She liked to swim and play little girl games. Mind you, something did change when Karla got to high school."

Although the kids still came to the side door in droves, and hung out around the pool or in the basement recreation room where Karla had her bedroom, Karla and her friends were no longer "as open as they had once been."

* * * * * * *

There is an old Czechoslovakian saying: "The darkest spot is under the light." Karla seemed to have sought the spotlight almost instinctively from the moment she was born. In the beginning, she had been encouraged, perhaps subconsciously, by the extended Homolka family, to compete with her infant uncle, her mother's younger brother, Calvin Seger, but as she matured Karla began to insist that she stand in the light alone.

Karla had a very dark side, a strange compulsiveness that drew her to gruesome books about crimes, real and imagined, the occult, satanic ritual, horror stories with offbeat titles such as *Brainchild* and *Michelle Remembers*. This dark side was a side of Karla of which few were aware and even fewer had seen.

Karla knew all about her dark spot. She saw it, in the only place where such things can be seen – in her mirror image and in photographs. There is a snapshot of Karla and two girlfriends taken in the school gymnasium just prior to the Grade Eight graduation ceremonies. Karla is the little girl in the middle and has an arm around each of the other girl's shoulders. One girl looks decidedly unhappy, the other quite radiant. They are all wearing glossy, pastel polyester party dresses. Karla is the only one wearing a corsage.

On the back of the photograph Karla inscribed: "*Oh-me & my bestest buddies, Vicky and Lisa. Poor Lisa's been crying over Tom. What am I planning? (There's that devilish glint in my eye!) June 21st, 1984.*" Karla had just turned 14.

* * * * * * *

The culture of Karla's high school was a mirror image of St. Catharines': white, blue collar, homophobic, jock. With approximately 2,000 students, Sir Winston Churchill Secondary School was the largest in the city, and Karla was no longer the only pretty blonde in the corridors. There were a lot of pretty blondes in St. Catharines. The spotlight became diffuse, elusive and fickle. Karla's grades remained above average, but she started to lose focus.

There were few rules in the Homolka household. Europeans view "drinking" differently than North Americans. So did Dorothy Homolka. Although her mother and father allowed Karla to drink, they encouraged her to do so at home and she was not allowed to go out with boys in cars. Hardly Czechoslovakia under Alexander Dubček, but it was enough to set the increasingly independent-minded Karla off.

Karla's closest girlfriends, Lisa Stanton, Debbie Purdie, and Kathy Wilson, remember regular arguments, particularly with her father, whom they all perceived to be as strong-willed as Karla.

Others, who were closer to the family, such as next-door neighbors the Andersons and the Youngs, saw a different kind of tyranny, the more accurate one. This version portrays Karla's father as a man subjugated by the collective will of a household completely dominated by strong women. Not only did the four women regularly call Karel a "dumb Czech" – derisively, spitefully – Karla and Lori also frequently told him to "fuck off." When the beleaguered man could not stand the heat, he would flee the kitchen for the rec room in the basement.

After her involvement in the atrocities became public, after her arrest, Karla's friends and family were encouraged by the police and the media to dredge their memories for any morsel that might have revealed Karla's dark side.

Amanda Whatling, a portly tomboy whom Karla had befriended talked about a book called *Brainchild* which Karla had inscribed and given to her about the time they were going into Grade Seven. The police and prosecutors determined it was a B.F. Skinner-inspired horror story about behavioral psychologists who program human beings for their own miscreant purposes.

Around this period, Karla's interest in the occult intensified. She took to applying dark, heavy eye makeup, wearing black, dyeing her hair different colors every other day and changing its style as often.

She also started lighting candles, burning incense and conducting seances. In their background work-up, the prosecutors document Amanda's breathless description about how Karla *even* advertised in newspapers for Ouija boards. According to Amanda, in those days she talked about spirits and the "Screaming Tunnel" all the time.

The Screaming Tunnel was a train underpass made of rough-cut stone, almost five metres high and 38 metres long, about a 12-minute drive from Niagara Falls, on the outskirts of St. Catharines. It passes beneath a railway bed at an isolated spot off Warner Road, not far from the Queen Elizabeth Way. In 1983, David Cronenberg used the location in his film *The Dead Zone.*

According to legend, a young girl had burned to death in the tunnel. Her agonizing screams were said to be audible if one entered the tunnel and then lit a match. According to Amanda, Karla struck many matches in the Screaming Tunnel and claimed that she heard the horrifying screams after every strike. Amanda did not know where the Screaming Tunnel was and had never been there. She had only heard about it.

"When we were in high school she was a little rebel, you know," her close friend Debbie Purdie told the police. "Wore black nail polish, wore the longjohns and boxer shorts. Nobody ever told Karla what to do. She was her own person and her own boss."

Another classmate, Iona Brindle, described strange carved marks, like scarifications, on Karla's arm. She said they looked like circles carved into skin and then filled in with nail polish.

Karla also inscribed the book *Michelle Remembers* for Iona. She wrote "There is always something more left to say" inside the front cover.

First published in 1980, *Michelle Remembers* was the first and probably the most influential "true" story about satanic ritual abuse (SRA), co-authored by the "victim-patient" Michelle Smith and her therapist, Dr. Lawrence Pazder.

It allegedly documented the horrendous abuse suffered by Smith at the hands of a satanic cult. The book single-handedly kick-started the entire SRA movement in the early 1980s.

Much of the book's content was derived from Dr. Pazder's personal studies of African native rituals, rather than Michelle's memories. When its accuracy was questioned, Dr. Pazder said that he and his patient had never claimed events in the book actually happened but it certainly reads as though they did.

In the plethora of "recovered memory" cases that went to court throughout the 1980s thousands of lives were destroyed by this facetious concept. Ironically, at least in terms of Karla's life, Dr. Pazder has shifted gears, and now proselytizes about "sadistic" rather than "satanic" abuse.

Karla told Dr. Arndt that she had started smoking a little dope around that time and once popped a little pill called a "White Cross" in Grade Ten. She told Dr. Arndt the pill really made her feel good, but then she "crashed" and had to call in sick for work. She was working part-time since she started high school at the Number One Pet Center in the Pen Center Mall.

Dr. Arndt thought it was probably contraband Ritalin.

School records show that while in Grade Eleven Karla was accelerated to Grade Twelve English. Language skills came easily to her and she served as a French tutor to other students. Alas, pi, integers, and isosceles triangles remained impenetrable mysteries and she continued to struggle with all things mathematic. Even though she liked to dissect frogs and took a strong interest in biology, she only managed passing grades. Karla squeaked through History but scored high marks in Law.

One of Karla's girlfriends, Tracy Collins, described Karla to the police as "a thirty-year-old in a seventeen-year-old's body."

"You know what I'd like to do…?" Karla had whispered in Tracy's ear one afternoon in the cafeteria. "I'd like to put dots all over somebody's body and take a knife and then play connect the dots and then pour vinegar all over them." Tracy was enthralled by the remark and never forgot it.

Karla also started talking about suicide. Her high-school sweetheart, Doug Liddell, whom she met in typing class, liked Karla's moodiness and found the fact that she was constantly threatening to commit suicide attractive.

Doug was not the only one who noticed Karla was obsessed by death. "Remember: Suicide kicks and fasting is awesome. Bones rule! Death Rules. Death Kicks. I love death. Kill the fucking world" was how she inscribed another schoolmate's yearbook. At best a casual acquaintance, the lurid inscription shocked Lyn Cretney and she never forgot it and now she never would.

Karla and two of her closest girlfriends, Debbie Purdie and Kathy Wilson (later Kathy Ford) formed a little clique they called the Exclusive Diamond Club (EDC). Its charter was conservative and simple: recruit rich, slightly older, good-looking men, get a diamond, marry and live happily ever after. This tidbit was discovered by the police. Karla never mentioned it to Dr. Arndt.

The composition, behavior and attitude that members of the Exclusive Diamond Club adopted mirrored the fictional *Heathers* portrayed by Winona Ryder, Shannon Doherty and Lisanne Falk in the 1988 cult film classic of the same name. The woman who conceived and produced *Heathers* was a Canadian, Denise Di Novi, and the movie was developed and made contemporaneously with the advent of the Exclusive Diamond Club.

The Los Angeles district high-school girls played by Ryder, Doherty and Falk, call themselves the "Heathers" and all take the name Heather. The Heathers' obsessions with their looks and their status and their aspirations (all of which are, like the Diamond Club members, disarmingly normal and ultra-conservative) eventually lead, in dark, hilarious ways, to murder and mayhem.

The relationship between the head Heather (played by Winona Ryder) and her boyfriend (played by Christian Slater) becomes a destructive, lethal weapon. They are somehow transformed by their relationship into an instrument for revenge and retribution for which they, and they alone, determine targets and justification.

The otherwise demure Ryder becomes a conduit for some kind of a dark force within the cradle of Slater's misanthropic intellectualism. They infect each other with something psychiatry currently calls Shared Psychotic Disorder or *folie à deux*.

The concept of folie à deux has been around for a while. In the *Textbook of Psychiatry*, translated from the French by A. A. Brill and published in New York in 1930, *folie à deux* or "double insanity" was said to happen "when paranoid or paranoiac patients not only can make those with whom they live close together believe in their delusions, but so infect them that the latter under conditions continues to build on the delusion…"

It was invoked by psychiatrists for decades to describe the occasions when two people closely associated with one another suffer a psychosis simultaneously and particularly, when one member of the pair appears to have influenced the other.

The way the *Textbook of Psychiatry* describes it, if one psychotic incident turns into a spree, the influence one has over the other can shift from one to the other arbitrarily. Was it Macbeth or Lady Macbeth who first took leave of their senses and, between the two, who leed whom to destruction and insanity?

Like many psychiatric diagnoses, such as the modern antisocial personality disorder or psychopathy (which is no longer included in the

Diagnostic and Statistical Manual of Mental Disorders, DSM-IV-R, as a psychiatric disorder) *folie à deux* is wonderful fiction, evocative and descriptive, but ultimately, as a diagnosis, meaningless because it explains nothing and is impervious to treatment and cannot be cured or even ameliorated. It describes a condition which is only identifiable in retrospect. It is not preventable or manageable. Either a person leaves another person who is acting crazy and tries to get help or stays and joins in.

In the Diamond Club, Karla was *numero uno*; "the tough one in the bunch," as fellow member Kathy Wilson put it. Karla had a pair of real handcuffs, "with keys and everything."

In a move worthy of a Heather, Karla hung the cuffs over her negligee on the back of her bedroom door for all Diamond Club *cognoscenti* to see.

In high school, besides planning her suicide and running the Diamond Club, Karla joined the Dance Club and participated in school variety shows and musicals. For three years she studied music, taking voice and singing lessons.

Like her mother, Karla was preoccupied with money and worked part-time from when she was in Grade Seven; as a telephone solicitor for a local photographer, as a nanny for her neighbor's two small children, and at the Number One Pet Store, after school and on weekends.

On May 4, 1987, the Diamond Club assembled to celebrate Karla's 17th birthday. By July, Tracy Collins's parents were among the few who had seen Karla's dark spot and they forbade Tracy to see Karla anymore. Tracy's schoolwork was faltering and her parents attributed disturbing changes in their daughter's personality and behavior to the negative influence of that strange, domineering Homolka girl.

Lost in love that summer, Karla defied her parents and, in August, bought a plane ticket and flew to Kansas. Doug Liddell had moved there with his family a few months earlier and she and Doug had plotted her visit by mail. Although Karla called her parents once she got there, she stayed for two weeks.

She told Dr. Arndt that during her stay, she snorted cocaine and had sex for the first time. Doug Liddell told the police that there was nothing unusual about what happened, it was "just sex." He did not mention anything about cocaine.

Karla's girlfriends told a different story. When Karla returned, she regaled them with tales of profligate sex with whips, dog collars and cocaine. They were shocked. Everyone talked a good game back then but Karla walked the walk.

Only a few years hence, Dorothy Homolka would look back over Karla's life and her own, time and again, examining every incident, every stingy little memory, searching for answers about what went wrong, finally wondering herself into the psych ward, not as an employee as she had been when newlywed, but as a patient, severely depressed and the perfect candidate for one of Dr. Arndt's specialties, electro-convulsive therapy (ECT) or, as Hans liked to call it, "buzzing."

For Dr. Arndt there were no answers in Karla's biography. Wanting to be in control, or being a domineering bitch were not symptomatic of any pathology he knew of. Quite the opposite. Most teenagers were rebellious to one degree or another. Millions of people, otherwise perfectly levelheaded, were interested in the occult. There were hundreds of witch covens scattered throughout Europe and North America whose memberships were comprised of perfectly "normal" suburban housewives who never committed any crimes. Neither were reading habits or preferences predictors of behavior or indices of psycho-pathologies.

There was absolutely no evidence that Karla had ever been subject to any physical or psychological abuse. Tens of thousands of fathers frequently travel on business, as Hans did himself. Absent, distracted fathers, were a norm of twentieth-century life, hence the universal appeal of Willy Loman. There was nothing in Karla's background that helped explain why Karla did what she did. If anything, her happy childhood and uneventful teenage development made her subsequent deviant and murderous behavior even more mysterious.

THE LETTER

The letter was addressed to Karla Leanne Teale at Sainte-Anne-des-Plaines Institution. It was dated Tuesday, April 10, 2001. She sat down at her desk to read it. "You have a future, a rather bright one, if the tea leaves I'm reading are any indication" was the opening lines. No one had spoken to Karla about a "bright" future since grade school. She read on.

"Suffice it to say that historically, there have been a number of very high-profile women in exactly your position: that is, sentenced for heinous crimes but ultimately released. They have all, to a woman, thrived and prospered...

"You have never had more power than you have at this moment..."

What was this person talking about? Karla had never felt more helpless or less powerful than she did at this moment. Intrigued, she read on.

"You had it right early on, particularly as you expressed it in some of your letters to Dr. Arndt when you talked about standing up for yourself and your rights because no one else was going to do it. Your affidavit to the Federal Court in support of your application to have the Warden's decision reversed spoke to some of these same issues.

"I think you made a mistake backing down from your court challenge against the Warden's decision to refuse your request for day parole. Whatever, that is water under the bridge and I am not suggesting that the outcome would have been any different.

"I also think you made a mistake when you decided not to appear in front of the Parole Board to defend yourself and plead your case. You have a case but no one, not even a lawyer (particularly a lawyer who is being paid by Corrections Canada and Legal Aid to service prisoners), is going to plead your case for you. Your initial instincts were correct. You need to go back to first principles.

"To get a true perspective on all this, follow the money.

"When Drs. Arndt, Long, and Malcolm examined you and wrote their reports, they were in your employ. Rightly, they did their job.

"When Drs. Hatcher, Hucker and Jaffe reinforced Drs. Arndt, Long and Malcolm's opinions, they were being paid by the Ministry of the Attorney General and the Province of Ontario to do exactly that.

"Not to forget old Dr. Roy Brown at P4W. He was a wild card, one which you have under-utilized. He was, in retrospect, one of your staunchest allies and supporters. Few people know about Dr. Brown. And as far as his employer CSC is concerned, the fewer the better. Neither CSC, the National Parole Board, nor the Federal government want to be reminded about Dr. Brown or his opinions.

"Regardless, none of these doctors remain on your bond. Therefore, none of them are going to stand up on your behalf – unless you invoke them.

"Following the money: There were psychologists and psychiatrists during and after your ex-husband's trial who held very similar views to the ones held by Dr. Hubert Van Gijseghem – the guy who wrote the "expert report" upon which your Case Management Team relied to justify your involuntary transfer to RPC in Saskatoon. The psychopathy or antisocial personality disorder and narcissistic personality disorder, call it what you will, is old news. Nevertheless, it should not escape anyone's attention that the few experts who held and hold these opinions were and are being paid to do so. Nevertheless, back in the days, such opinions were superceded and negated by your phalanx of experts.

"Your point should be that the opinions of Drs. Arndt, Long, Malcolm, Hacker, Hucker, Jaffe and Brown are just as valid as the current crop of psychological henchmen that CSC has brought forward to justify the

Warden's and CSC's opinion that you be "gated." (I understand there is at least one dissenting opinion from Saskatoon; a useful happenstance.)

"There are, in fact, grounds for substantive arguments that your experts' opinions are more valid, particularly with respect to individual psychologists of Drs. Peter Jaffe's and Chris Hatcher's stature."

Karla grew more curious with each line she read. Not only because of the profound dichotomy between her perception of her circumstances and what the letter said but also because the writer knew about the Montreal psychologist Hubert Van Gijseghem's psychological report. Van Gijseghem did not work for CSC. He was an outside consultant, hired for the specific purpose outlined in the letter.

As far as Karla knew, no one knew about his report. Even though some media had obtained copies of her Federal Court file, Van Gijseghem's report was not in it.

The prison had indeed used Van Gijseghem's unsupportable and irresponsible psychological report to facilitate her transfer to the Psych Center in Saskatoon last Thanksgiving.

The letter continued: *"On a related topic, you seem to think that there is something you need to keep secret or hidden, particularly with regard to the CSC psychological and psychiatric reports.*

"This is exactly what authorities hoped you would think and want. The last thing CSC or the Parole Board or any of them want, is to be challenged. The last thing they want the public to see is your prison records and these new, commissioned assessments. Challenges to their authority and so-called wisdom are way too public.

"Consider this: Coming into prison you were a clinically depressed, abused spouse suffering from post-traumatic stress disorder. After eight years in custodial care, in a system that is now, according to its own public relations, all about healing and rehabilitation, you have become an unredeemable psychopath. How is that possible? What does that say about the system and its effectiveness? What a paradox. Heaven forfend that this unredeemable anomaly be made public and highlighted by debate.

"No, no, they just want to lock you down and keep you quiet and out of the public eye. Your compliance relieves enormous political pressure on

*CSC and the incessant public controversy that surrounds their manage-
ment of you.*

"*As far as I can determine, you have been a model prisoner – but this
is an anti-fact.*

"*If your name were not Karla Homolka you would be the poster girl
for the new penology evolved after Madame Justice Arbour's scathing
report in 1993 instigated the changes that saw P4W closed and regional
institutions such as Grand Valley and Joliette grandly opened. They do
not want anyone thinking about such dichotomies, such outrageous
anomalies and paradoxes.*

"*One other thing. Why be concerned about your privacy? What privacy? Nobody's secret, private life has ever been more public than yours.
Your privacy is unredeemable. Get over the notion of a private life. At
least, until you get out of prison and disappear. Until that day, you do not
have a private life.*"

Reading this almost made Karla dizzy. These were all excellent
points. Karla was astounded that someone else, someone other than
herself, had ever thought about them, let alone given them a moment's
consideration.

Her correspondent even had a point about her obsession with the
media and her privacy, and although it was antithetical to every
instinct upon which she had relied over the past eight years, she recognized in it a glimmer of truth.

"*What more can the CSC psychologists and psychiatrists contribute
that has not already been said? What could possibly be in any of these new
reports that has not all ready been articulated and written about by other
psychiatrists and psychologists, such as the ones retained by your ex-husband's lawyers… There was Dr. Graham Glancy, Dr. Nathan Pollack and
from Johns Hopkins, Dr. John Money and Dr. Fred Berliner. Or the psychiatrists and psychologists and criminologists quoted by Patricia Pearson
in her voluminous article on you in* Saturday Night Magazine, *or more
recently, Trish Wood in her article in* Elm Street Magazine *about the very
real possibility that you deliberately killed your sister. Man, you have been
called every name in the book and then some.*

"You once wrote in a book you gave to one of your high school friends that there is 'always something left to say'. In your case, there is a hell of a lot left say. But no one is going to say it for you. You have to have the courage and the strength to stand up and say it in a restrained and organized fashion yourself, no matter how difficult.

"Believe me when I tell you, the authorities do not want to hear it nor do they want the public to hear it. They do not want publicity. They do not want to be reminded about this sham of so-called psychological experts' one-up-manship they have perpetrated.

"They do not want to see the bundle of letters from your supporters – including those two jurors from Bernardo's trial. That two people who sat on that jury bought your story and the Crown's portrayal of you as a battered woman is powerful stuff. Your recent reticence has wholly discounted it.

"They do not want to be reminded about all those renowned experts' opinions that you were a battered spouse suffering from post-traumatic stress syndrome. They do not want your file made public. They do not want to hear about your academic achievements or your excellent performance in their programs. They took a big gamble that you would cave and capitulate. And you did.

"As for the helping professions, there is nothing left to say, nothing more to be revealed; it's all old news. Like the media, they are recycling old, tired concepts.

"We all know about the antisocial personality bit, the malignant narcissism, all the 'isms' have been laid bare. The real question is, what does it all mean? And what relevance does it have? How might it affect the inevitability of your release on July 6, 2005? Or your life after your release? It may but I suspect not in ways that you might think or ways that you would necessarily be able to predict. This would be very worthy of discussion – for you."

This was startling because these were all questions that Karla had recently been asking herself over and over again. What about her life after she got out? She had no idea what she was going to do.

She started re-reading the letter immediately after she read through it the first time. It was constructed around a series of observations or thoughts which the writer started to designate:

"_NUMBER THREE_: I think you are far too concerned about the media. Whatever, you have definitely spoken, through your current lawyer, to the wrong media.

"There are profound distinctions and differences between media and the effect of certain media are profoundly different than others. There is a huge difference between, say, a program such as A Current Affair which is now defunct, and 60 Minutes.

"When they were both on air, they were billed as "current affairs broadcast magazine programs" but their modus operandi, their effect, their journalistic rigor, integrity, and their audiences could not have been more different.

"There are media that might be useful to you but those media assuredly do not include the daily news media, the wire services, tabloid newspapers or programs such as A Current Affair.

"First and foremost, you should not be speaking (directly or indirectly – i.e. through your lawyer), to any daily news media, most especially the wire services.

"If that lawyer in Montreal still represents you and he was speaking at your behest or with your permission, you should immediately silence him. If he will not keep quiet you should fire him. No one in Canada cares what you think or want. Whether you want to stay in jail or not, is immaterial. Nobody – with the exception of your loved ones – cares whether you fear for your life?

"By the way, just as an aside, the so-called Internet Death Pools that your lawyer pointed to as evidence that your life is in danger on the outside – I strongly suspect that Web site was built by the Toronto paper that originally reported its existence – it's a tabloid technique called 'manufacturing news.' There were no 'death pools' or any other kind of threat, or implied threats against your life on the Internet prior to the appearance of their first story. We have been closely monitoring the Internet since 1993. And we know what we are doing. Lawyers, yours included, are Luddites when it comes to the new technologies. Most of them do not know a bit from a byte.

"If you ask the average man or woman on the street, the large majority would probably say that if something should befall you, a tragic acci-

dent perhaps, then Justice would have been served. So what? Justice is notoriously blind. Let people say and think what they want. You cannot change what people say or think. The Canadian public hates you – sort of. Broad sweeping generalizations seldom have any real meaning. Conversely, in the same vein, the American and British public do not know you exist. There is a great deal more to be said about the media and its relation to you and reality, the places where you are known and the places where you are unknown...

"NUMBER FOUR: The media does not have any where near the power that you think it does. Many years ago, if I recall, you were most concerned, even agitated when A Current Affair *and* The Sunday Daily Mirror *an English broadsheet, published banned details about you, your crimes and trial.*

"If memory serves you called Inspector Vince Bevan in a frenzy, concerned about the impact such accessible broadcast and publication might have on your status. You seemed to have actually believed that the sweeping publication ban that old Doc Kovacs levied at your trial, would keep the sordid details of your crime out of the public domain. The cops were so cheap they would not accept your collect call but Bevan did have Sergeant Bob Gillies get back to you eventually. By the way, did you know that Sergeant Bob's colleagues used to call him Bob 'Homolka' Gillies and there were rumors swirling around that you and he were sleeping together?

"If my research is correct, both the prison psychologist you were seeing, Jan Heney, and Sergeant Gillies told you to not to worry about the Current Affair *programs or the British newspapers, even though Canadians could easily watch and read them, it would have no appreciable impact. They were right. The media are sound and fury signifying nothing. And all they do now, those that pay you any mind, is recycle the obvious.*

"Another illustration: certain media, particularly one crusading newspaper in Toronto, have actively campaigned to have your deals rescinded. Hundreds of thousands of people from Southwestern Ontario have signed petitions. Tim Danson, the lawyer for the families, rants and raves. If the people and the media are so powerful how come your deals stand and you will be released once and for all no later than July 6, 2005?

"*NUMBER FIVE: Should you be cooperating with CSC and their idea that you, after eight years of actively treating you as a battered woman suffering from post-traumatic stress disorder and depression, now need to be treated as a sex offender?*

"*There are still serious hurdles to be overcome. And serious questions to be asked. First, there is no standardized treatment for female sex offenders. I don't know about you, but I would not want to be the guinea pig for its development.*

"*You were not convicted as a sexual offender although sexual assault charges were on the table at one time. Did you know sexual assault charges were on the table? Did you know that George Walker had a prominent Toronto lawyer named Robert Bigelow advising him about this very issue? (Bigelow has since been appointed to the bench and is now a sitting judge).*

"*The Ministry had all the opportunity in the world to charge you, along with manslaughter, with numerous sexual assaults. In their wisdom, they decided not to. Should the Parole Board and your many detractors not be reminded about this fact?*

"*If you comply with the authorities' wishes now, what is the effect? More importantly, what are the optics? What does it look like if you allegedly undergo treatment as a female sex offender? Appearances have an uncanny habit of becoming reality. Would it not, in a large part, negate the fact that you were not charged with or convicted of any sexual offences.*

"*Believe me, no one, not CSC, the Ministry of the Attorney General of Ontario, Chief Vince Bevan, the National Parole Board, or the legion of red-necked politicians and pontificators running around Ottawa, wants to be reminded that you could have been charged with sexual offenses but were not. No one is going to raise this issue unless you do. Why would you do that? Because otherwise, they may pull a Section 810.a on you when you are released. This is a whole other discussion.*

"*At any rate, it is a* carpe diem *situation…*"

Karla did not know what to think. What was a Section 810.a? But one thing she did know was the fact that there was a glaring problem with this astounding letter. The writer had some seminal facts wrong. The letter writer linked the devolution of Karla's relationship with Hans Arndt to the evolution of her bad judgement, and pointed out that anyone who had ever watched a movie about prison knew that challenging the authority of the Warden, as Karla had done at Joliette, was improvident. But what Karla had done, with regard to the Warden and her application for escorted temporary absences (ETAs) had nothing to do with bad judgement or some vague notion about prison life gleaned from watching too many B-movies about women in prison. The reality was at once both more mundane and bizarre.

Karla decided that this time, for the first time ever, she would respond. After all, look what keeping her mouth shut and her head down all these years had got her. She opened her drawer and took out her stationery – mini letter-sized paper bordered by cartoon-like teddy bears and fat flowers. She picked up her pen and began her reply.

* * * * * * *

The whole thing about passes and the prison and the Warden had not been Karla's idea at all. In the spring of 1999, she had been strongly encouraged, if not coerced, by representatives of the Elizabeth Fry Society to apply for escorted temporary absences (ETAs)in anticipation of her statutory release date on July 6, 2001.

With ETAs, Karla could leave the prison, at first escorted by a Primary Worker (the new politically correct terminology for prison guards or "screws," as cons still called them) and later by herself for a few days at a time, and begin a much-needed, gradual reintegration into society.

It was *de rigueur*, Karla was told, that an inmate coming up for statutory release apply for an ETA. After being locked up for as many years as Karla had been, the world outside prison was all that more forbidding and frightening. Karla knew that to be true.

"I am scared to death of getting out of jail," she wrote. "Everyone who has been in a long time is. Everyone thinks that they have "ex-con" tattooed on their foreheads. In my case, it's even worse because it seems the whole world knows me and is out to get me. Not physically…the idea that I am terrified for my life is incorrect. That is a lawyer and media creation, something that has got totally out of hand… but everyone wants to know where I am, what I'm doing…"

Karla did not want to apply for an ETA. She was positive that the prison would not grant it. She had long ago resolved not to apply for early parole or day passes or any of that stuff. After all, she had been eligible to apply for ETAs after she had been in jail only eighteen months and she never did.

She told the people from the Elizabeth Fry Society, a prisoners' advocacy and rights organization, with regional offices in major cities across the country, that she was content to wait until her actual release date in July, 2001. Then she would adhere to whatever stringent parole conditions the prison and the Parole Board would invariably impose until her sentence expired on July 6, 2005, at which point she would be completely free. She told the lawyer and other E. Fry volunteers including carceral lawyer Sylvie Bordelais, in no uncertain terms, that the prison would never grant her an ETA, so there was no point in applying.

They agreed. They did not think the prison would give Karla ETAs either. But an application for these passes was an unwritten prerequisite to Statutory release. If Karla did not apply, it would indicate to the prison that she was not interested in her own rehabilitation. It would give them an easy excuse to do what they were undoubtedly trying to figure out how to do anyway – to keep her in jail until she had served her full sentence. The way it worked, the prison would develop a dossier (any point of controversy would do) and six months prior to that person's statutory release date, apply to the National Parole Board for a detention order to keep them in prison until the last day of their sentence.

Ninety-nine percent of all prisoners in federal penitentiaries are released on their stat dates. The prison only "gated" prisoners who routinely broke rules and committed crimes on the inside. Those who committed violence against the staff and other inmates, who had a string of infractions that might include drunkenness or the importation of drugs into the prison for the purpose of trafficking; prisoners whom the prison could not seem to "reach." Historically, the prison hardly ever sought to detain women. The very small minority that they kept were men.

Karla was different. If she did not apply for ETAs, Karla would be putting her statutory release in more serious jeopardy than it already was, they said. Even though she was a model prisoner, because she was who she was, Karla was going to have to fight for those things, such as statutory release, that otherwise came automatically to even the most recalcitrant prisoners.

Karla and the E. Fry reps conceived a strategy in anticipation of the Warden's rejection. The Society would agree in advance to let Karla use one of their halfway houses in downtown Montreal as a "home base" when and if she was released. That would bolster her application and give it some credibility. When the application was refused, as everyone one agreed it would be, Karla would immediately appeal through the Federal Court. The Elizabeth Fry Society would supply her with a lawyer in Montreal, a man named Pascal Lescarbeau. Monsieur Lescarbeau was a specialist in such matters, they said. In effect, Karla would be "suing" Correctional Services and the Warden for that which she had earned and was her legal right.

The Warden at Joliette, Marie-Anne Cyrenne, did as was expected and turned Karla's application down flat. Pascal Lescarbeau filed Karla's appeal with the Federal Court on September 20, 1999.

In a hand-written, five-page affidavit that was a mandatory component of the appeal, Karla spoke about her personal growth and increased self-awareness. Monsieur Lescarbeau and her E. Fry reps vetted the document half-a-dozen times before it was deemed cogent and good enough for inclusion in the file.

Karla noted her accomplishments, particularly the Bachelor of Arts in Psychology which she had received from Queen's University. She noted her high grades. That aside, the thing Karla was most proud of, she said, was her smooth transition from segregated isolation in Kingston's old Prison for Women to the general population at Joliette in June, 1997.

"Before I transferred to Joliette, people predicted that I would have an extremely difficult time integrating into the population. When I first arrived, I did have some difficulties with some of the women, but I was accepted by the majority. I managed to integrate quickly with no major problems. Considering my history, I believe that this is a huge success for me. I think that my success in integrating is due in large part to all the work I did on myself while in Kingston."

Karla talked about her good behavior and all the prison programs from which she had "graduated," including "Improving Your Inner Self," "Anger Management," and "Survivors of Abuse and Trauma." She stated that she gained "increased assertiveness" and "self-esteem" and "met all the required objectives" of her "correctional plan."

In conclusion Karla wrote that "although some of the information contained in my file may be perceived as negative, it is clearly out-weighed by the number of positive assessments and recommendations."

The case never got before the Court.

Karla had been assured by Pascal Lescarbeau that this court challenge would·never become public. All he had to do was file an application to keep the proceedings *in camera* and it would be done. The Federal Court was not like the provincial criminal courts with which Karla had her only direct experience.

Alas, Monsieur Lescarbeau forgot, or neglected to file the necessary application. Not only did the media find out about Karla's case, they walked into the federal court office and freely copied hundreds upon hundreds of pages from her confidential prison files which the Correctional Service had filed in defense of Karla's motion. Ironically, it was some clerk in the Federal Court who had arbitrarily imposed a publication ban on the material and the proceedings, but by then it was too late, the damage was already done.

Three months after she launched her appeal of the Warden's decision, some of the best tidbits of information from her confidential files were splashed all over the front pages of the newspapers and broadcast across the country. Caught completely off-guard, Karla became unhinged. She quit Pascal Lescarbeau and retained new council. Even though there had been a publication ban levied by the court, Karla's new lawyer told her that the media would invariably challenge the legality of the ban and quite possibly win, that the only way she could really hope to protect her file and her privacy was to withdraw the court challenge. So that is what she did.

It had not happened the way the letter writer described it at all. It had nothing to do with Dr. Arndt or Karla's lack of resolve or willingness to stand up for herself. It was not her fault that she had been banished from Joliette. She had been betrayed. For her good behavior and good intentions she was rewarded with lockdown in a maximum-security male prison.

Frankly, it was a consequence of listening to other people's advice, people whom Karla thought knew better. And the media. When talking about Karla and anything that happened to her you could not forget the media. The timing was very bad too. There had been an election and the incumbent Liberal government perceived themselves to be under pressure from the conservative parties for their softness on crime and criminals. Karla and her situation became a subcutaneous election issue, a diversion; forces outside of her control turned her into a symbol and made her, if not a sacrificial lamb, then at least a sacrificial goat.

Although Karla made these notes, and reflected on these things, she did not send this explanation right away. She was very, very leery of engagement. Particularly with this person. Instead, she sent a short note. It was dated April 27, 2001:

"I received your letter this week. I want to thank you for letting me know of Dr. Arndt's death. I had no idea. The world has lost a truly wonderful and compassionate man. He was incredibly helpful to me at a very difficult time as I'm sure you know…

"Well, they say 'never say never' and they're right. Never in a million years did I think I would ever write a letter to someone (like you)…

"However, I was raised to be a good girl and good girls write thank you notes. It means a lot that you thought to let me know about Dr. Arndt. Of course, it could just be a ploy, a way to suck me in. Who knows? I've become very suspicious these last eight years and with good reason…

"I must say, however, that your letter intrigued me…

"You say you have a great deal more to say than what you said in your letter. I'm curious to hear what it is…

She signed the letter *Karla* and as Karla had been doing all her life, she sat back and waited to see what would happen next.

SEXOLOGY

Karla's life-long infatuation with Walt Disney, Disney World, and particularly that Disney institution, Mickey Mouse, troubled the Montreal psychologist Hubert Van Gijseghem. That Karla was still decorating her room in House 10 at Joliette with such juvenilia was, like Freud's cigar, symbolic of something. Dr. Van Gijseghem could not quite put a finger on it, but there was something – suggestive, nefarious, evil. As were her reading habits and her persistent use of the surname "Teale."

Dr. Van Gijseghem had never met or examined Karla. By the time he was commissioned by the prison to assess her in the early summer of 2000, Karla had realized that she was being set up and the psychologists and psychiatrists in the employ of the Correctional Service had an agenda other than her mental health and rehabilitation. As was her right by virtue of the prison's own rules and regulations, she refused to see Dr. Gijseghem. Undaunted, he wrote his report based on his review of Karla's file and interviews he conducted with her handlers. Since he had never met or spoken to Karla, he could not have known that the use of the surname "Teale" in prison was not Karla's idea, it was the prison's.

After she had married Paul Bernardo on June 29, 1991, they had resolved to change their name. For different reasons, neither of them liked his surname. Karla suggested the name "Teal" based on a character in a movie. The character's name in the movie was actually spelled "Thiel" but that bit of arcana was not readily acquired from watching it. To Karla, it was the name of a color she liked. When they were in Florida that year, she and Paul coincidentally came across a "Teale" family coat of arms in a gift shop. They made an application to the government to change their surname from "Bernardo" to "Teale." Ironically, the notification that it had been approved arrived as everything was unraveling, shortly before Paul Teale was arrested on February 17, 1993.

Legally, Karla's last name was Teale. Karla was tried as "Karla Bernardo, a.k.a. Karla Teale" in July, 1993. After she went to prison, Dr. Arndt found it queer that she signed her letters to him "Karla Teale" and he queried her.

"I have been reluctant from the beginning to use Homolka," Karla explained in a letter dated October 24th, 1994, "simply because I didn't want my family to be dragged into this whole media circus."

She conceded that this strategy had not worked; the press stubbornly persisted in using her maiden name. But, she said, the prison made the ultimate determination. Because she had been indicted as "Karla Bernardo, a.k.a. Karla Teale," she was given only two options when she arrived in prison – she could either be known as Karla Bernardo or Karla Teale. Not surprisingly, she chose the name of a fictitious monster.

The thing that got Dr. Van Gijseghem bent out of shape was the fact that Karla had chosen the name based on the fictional serial killer, Martin Thiel, as he was portrayed by Kevin Bacon in the 1987 B-crime thriller *Criminal Law*. It had been one of the couple's favorite movies.

What Dr. Van Gijseghem did not know was that it was Karla herself who had voluntarily explained this to the police during her induced and cautioned statements in May, 1993. Otherwise, no one would have been any the wiser.

Dr. Van Gijseghem also found sinister shadows in her reading habits. But exactly what his perception of those shadows meant in terms of Karla's psyche he did not say. Millions upon millions of people read Stephen King and Dean Koontz and other books about horror, crime and the occult. Besides, Karla's interest in these genres was well known to the police and the prosecutors with whom she had made her plea resolutions and they still saw fit to give her twelve years in exchange for guilty pleas to two counts of manslaughter and her testimony against her ex-husband.

Dr. Van Gijseghem's extrapolations were absurd. Karla's favorite books in the whole world were Sylvia Plath's *The Bell Jar* and John Knowles' *A Separate Peace*. Sure, she liked police procedurals like those written by Michael Connelly and Ed Bain and was trying to read everything either man had ever written, but so did hundreds of thousands of other people. And she liked Dean Koontz – not Stephen King, except for *Christine*, *Cujo*, *Thinner*, and *Gerald's Game*. What would the good doctor have made of her preference for Koontz over King, or her specific choices from King's oeuvre, particularly *Gerald's Game*.

Gerald's Game is about a woman who reluctantly indulges her husband penchant for sadomasochistic sex in an isolated cabin where they are vacationing. When the husband dies of a heart attack, she finds herself handcuffed to the bed unable to reach the keys, the telephone or food and water. The book documents her struggle, both psychological and physical, against demons both real and imaginary.

It was also true that Karla liked some true crime, if it was well written and provocative like *Perfect Victim*. But by no means to the exclusion of everything else.

Looking at her from afar, Dr. Van Gijseghem went for the superficial, sensational effect, just like everyone else did. Her choice of name and her reading habits did not mean anything, psychologically speaking. Nor were they indicative of any kind of psychopathology, any more than her enthusiasm for *The Bell Jar* and *A Separate Peace* said anything about her mental state or her level of dangerousness or her potential to reoffend.

Karla was between the proverbial rock and a hard place. When she read Dr. Van Gijseghem's report, shortly after it was tabled in August, 2000, it finally sank in that no matter what she did, she could not win. The fix was in. No matter what any individual parole officer, or primary worker, or warden said or did or thought, the promises made to Karla were not going to be fulfilled.

Dr. Van Gijseghem, an occasional consultant to Correctional Services in private practice in Montreal, had been retained by the Correctional Service's Director of Psychological Services for the Region of Quebec, Jacques Bigras, despite the fact that numerous psychological assessments already existed.

For some reason, Monsieur Bigras and his masters at Correctional Services in Ottawa were not satisfied with what they had, even the psychological reports from their own pre-eminent psychiatric consultant, Dr. Sharon Williams, who had seen and evaluated Karla at the Correctional Service's behest in 1996 and 1999.

Dr. Williams, an expert on incarcerated sex offenders and psychopaths, found that Karla was not a psychopath and did not think she was a danger to reoffend. Obviously, for the prison's purposes at this particular time, Dr. Williams' conclusions were not helpful so they carefully selected Dr. Van Gijseghem, from whom they knew they were likely going to get a more useful report.

In retrospect, from her second year in Joliette, Karla realized the CSC had been sending psychologists such as Joanne Racine-Rouleau in to see her for the distinct purpose of calling into question the diagnoses that followed her into prison and that they had previously accepted unquestioningly.

Dr. Racine-Rouleau was an associate professor at the University of Montreal. She had co-authored a few articles about the role of the expert witness in the courts, sexual disorders and sexual predators. Hardly prolific or well known, Dr. Racine-Rouleau was handy and she had a new instrument to which Karla had yet to be subjected. In mid-1998, the prison invited Dr. Racine-Rouleau to give Karla the Abel Screen Test.

The Abel Screen is a software-based, assessment "tool" developed and managed by Dr. Gene Abel, a psychiatrist from Atlanta, Georgia, with whom Dr. Racine-Rouleau had co-authored a paper entitled "Sexual Disorders in G.W."

The test is given on a computer. It takes a number of hours to complete. The software package necessary to administer the test is purchased from Dr. Abel for approximately $2500 US. No matter who administers the test or where it is done, the raw data is sent back to Dr. Abel's lab in Georgia to be scored, a service for which the data provider pays handsomely.

On the computer screen, the subject sees a series of pictures of fully clothed young people of both sexes as well as various objects known to be fetishes. The test measures visual reaction to stimuli by recording the amount of time that it takes the person to hit the enter key and move on to the next picture.

This reaction time provides the core data and is based on the premise that a homosexual pedophile, for instance, will unconsciously stare at a picture of a young boy longer than he would a young girl. The test was designed to screen for sexual preferences and fetishes in adult males.

The test results could be used in a variety of ways. For example, a group of psychiatrists and psychologists in Toronto were planning, in consultation with the Catholic archdiocese, to set up a novitiate-screening program around the Abel test to identify pedophiles *before* they were ordained.

Dr. Abel, a tall, gangly man with a shock of long, white hair, well known in professional circles for his work with sex offenders, had developed a large, standardized database – for men. As such, testing Karla was an exercise in pure symbolism. There were very few women in Dr. Abel's database. His test had not been standardized for women.

Any conclusions drawn about Karla's sexual preferences and fetishism by virtue of her Abel Screen Test results would be skewed and unreliable. Even if the test were infallible – and it is not – Karla's test results would have no credibility and could not withstand even a scintilla of professional scrutiny.

Karla does not remember what Dr. Racine-Rouleau looked like or how old she was. She remembers that she did not like her. "Her report was full of lies and mistakes," she later wrote. "I wasn't impressed. I tell the truth and it bothers me when others don't. If someone can't even get the bare facts right what does that say about the rest of what they have to say?"

Dr. Joanne Racine-Rouleau's report, dated October 2, 1998, appears to be, given its inherent flaws, deliberately negative. It is as irrelevant as it is innocuous. It hints that Karla may be bisexual but does not detect any identifiable deviance or fetishism. Of course, bisexuality has nothing to do with sex crimes or murder nor is it a predictor of dangerous behavior.

Prisoners were allowed to access and review their files. But Karla had become lackadaisical and was not paying much attention. She realized too late that there had been a sea change over the past two years in what psychiatrists and psychologists in the employ of Correctional Services were saying about her.

She had become blasé because she had been seeing and talking to Correctional Services' psychologists and psychiatrists since she arrived in prison. Her own lawyer, George Walker, had assured her that it was alright for her to be open and forthcoming with her prison therapists and, in the beginning, it was.

At the Prison for Women in Kingston, Ontario, where Karla was first incarcerated, there had been that kindly old soldier, Dr. Roy Brown, who aggressively treated her on the prison's behest as she had been diagnosed – as a heavily depressed, battered woman suffering from post-traumatic stress disorder.

During those first few years there was also the fledgling psychologist Jan Heney – an inmate favorite because she was an activist who, with the prison's taciturn permission, advocated on the prisoners' behalf. In those days, between Dr. Brown and Ms. Heney, Karla was getting three and four therapy sessions a week.

After she returned from testifying at her ex-husband's trial in the summer of 1995, Dr. Sharon Williams came to see Karla for the first time. Karla had just spent nineteen days on a witness stand in Toronto and the prison thought it would be wise to have her thoroughly checked over and evaluated. Karla found Dr. Williams to be "a warm and open person."

Dr. Williams was the Corporate Advisor to the Commissioner of Correctional Services on Sex Offenders Programs, as well as an Adjunct Assistant Professor at Queen's University in Psychology and Psychiatry.

Karla's first sessions with Dr. Williams were long and involved. Karla thought she had taken every test known to man. Both before she went to prison and after she arrived, Karla had been given the Halstead Reitan Neuropsychological Test, the Halstead Category Test, Tactile Finger Recognition Test, Fingertip Number Writing, Reitan Indiana Aphasia Screening Test, the Reitan Klove Sensory Perceptual Examination, Seashore Rhythm Test, Seashore Speech Sounds Perception Test, Tactual Performance Test, Trail Making Test Forms A and B, Hand Dynamometer, the Wechsler Adult Intelligence Scale – Revised (WAISR), the Wechsler Memory Scale – Revised (WAMSR), the Forer Sentence Completion Test, Adjective Checklist, Thematic Apperception Test (TAT) – Part A and B, the Cattell 16 P F Test, California Psychological Inventory and Jackson's Personality Research Form – E, the Rorschach Psychodiagnostic Instrument or ink blot test, the Rainwater Interpretive Report and (on three different occasions that she could remember) the Minnesota Multiphasic Personality Inventory or MMPI-2.

Dr. Williams did another MMPI-2, but she threw in a couple of new tests that Karla had never heard of, including the MMCI (Minnesota Multiphasic Clinical Instrument) SMAST and a DAST (Karla did not remember what those initials stood for) and some sex knowledge and denial/minimization inventories.

SMAST (Short Michigan Alcoholism Screening Test) and DAST (Drug Abuse Screening Test) are used to identify individuals with drinking or drug problems. Given that Karla was a drinker, not a druggie, and had not had a drink since she went to prison, they were somewhat irrelevant. They are basically long lists of questions, such as "Do you ever feel bad about your drug abuse" or "Do you abuse more than one drug at a time," to which the subject answers either "yes" or "no." The sex knowledge and denial/minimization inventories were innocuous and Karla's results were quite normal.

Of all these tests the MMPI-2 and MMCI were the most important because they established benchmarks against which all the other psychological tests were measured.

Dr. Williams' first "Psychological Assessment Report" was dated March 12th, 1996. Karla viewed it benignly. "I don't have a problem if someone says something negative, as long as it's fair," Karla wrote. At Joliette Dr. Williams also administered Dr. Robert Hare's famous Psychopathy Check List – Revised (PCL-R). Karla scored very low, a 5 or something, if she remembered correctly. To be diagnosed a psychopath, an exceedingly rare conclusion with women, Karla would have had to score a twenty or thirty.

Dr. Williams was a student and acolyte of the architect of the world-famous Kingston-based Sex Offenders Program which had been developed over the past thirty years by her mentor, Dr. William Marshall, in conjunction with Queen's University and Corrections Canada. She did not find that Karla was a dangerous psychopath or even recommend that the therapy Karla had been receiving as a battered woman suffering from post-traumatic stress be discontinued so that she could be immediately admitted into a sex offender program.

On the contrary, Dr. Williams remarked about how well Karla had responded to the prison's programs over the years she had been in jail.

In the first instance, Correctional Services relied on Dr. Williams' assessment, as well as two reports by Dr. Roy Brown and the fledgling psychologist Jan Heney's clinical notes, to support Karla's transfer into the general population at Joliette on June 1, 1997.

After she was transferred, Karla had regular sessions with the resident psychologist there, a woman named Frances Arbut. But talking to Ms. Arbut was like "talking to the wall" as Karla put it in one of her letters, and Karla eventually stopped consulting her.

At least Dr. Van Gijseghem begins his report honestly by admitting that he was unable to prepare a "primary source" assessment without an extensive interview and stipulated that Karla had refused to see him or submit to any of his tests, he would, therefore, only rely on certain "select items" in Karla's file and on the opinions of the various members of her case management team. Conveniently, Dr. Van Gijseghem says that he will not name any of these individuals or attribute any of the statements they allegedly made to him about their observations of Karla and he was doing this at their request. Their rationale for this, according to Dr. Van Gijseghem's report, was a fear that without anonymity any future relationship they may have with Karla would be jeopardized.

Dr. Van Gijseghem then states that it is his opinion Karla's tastes and her personality have not changed since Karla was first sent to jail.

Referring to himself in the royal "we," he begins with a tautology: "We agree with the thesis that a personality structure changes little if at all over the years, which leads us to continue to ask ourselves about the state of her mind when the crimes were committed."

The intrinsic problem with this rumination is the fact that questions about Karla's state of mind when she committed her crimes and what Karla really was like, were rampant from the first moment Karla Homolka became a public figure in early 1993.

During her trial that July, fed by insidious rumors accelerated by a pernicious publication ban on any details revealed during the trial, such questions became the stuff of national debate and legend.

During Paul Bernardo's trial in the summer of 1995, when all the lurid details seeped into the national consciousness, day by day, in small poisonous doses, the answers to those questions appeared to be obvious and provoked public outrage.

After Bernardo was convicted and sent to prison for life on September 1, 1995, 320,000 citizens signed petitions demanding that the Ministry revoke Karla's deals.

But the authorities had long since answered those questions about Karla's tastes, personality and state of mind to their own satisfaction. The police and the Ministry of the Attorney General had based their decisions to do their deals with Karla on the opinions of nine experts – many of them far better qualified and experienced than Dr. Van Gijseghem.

Regardless, in the face of such vociferous public disapproval the government stepped back and appointed two judges to conduct "independent" inquiries into the plea bargaining with Karla and the police investigations of the rapes and murders.

After lengthy and arduous reviews, the judges tabled their reports in 1996.

The Honorable Archie Campbell found that the police had completely bungled their investigations and the forensic scientists had dropped the ball.

For his part, Justice Patrick Galligan found that the deals with Karla were proper and correct, justified both by circumstance and in law, and would therefore stand. Thus, the matter was settled, once and for all.

But not as far as the politicians, the prison and Dr. Van Gijseghem were concerned.

In his report, Dr. Van Gijseghem concedes that Karla entered the prison system diagnosed by a number of experts as a clinically depressed, battered woman suffering from post-traumatic stress disorder.

Although Dr. Van Gijseghem does not elaborate, three of the doctors – Hans Arndt, Alan Long and Andrew Malcolm – had been retained by Karla's defense lawyer George Walker and made their diagnoses in 1993.

Four others – Drs. Chris Hatcher, Stephen Hucker, Peter Jaffe and Angus McDonald – had been retained by the Ministry of the Attorney General and the prosecutors to make independent diagnoses in 1994 and 1995 which would either confirm or deny Drs. Arndt, Long and Malcolm's original assessments.

The latter four unanimously agreed with the diagnoses of the first three. A few of these doctors – such as Dr. Peter Jaffe from London, Ontario, and Dr. Chris Hatcher from Los Angeles, California – were internationally recognized experts in Battered Spousal Syndrome and post-traumatic stress disorder.

This was not true of Dr. Van Gijseghem. Although Dr. Van Gijseghem was recognized as an "expert" by the courts in Quebec it was for his "particular interest in research into the study of and treatment of sexual abuse problems" which would seem to make him a very odd choice indeed to assess Karla's readiness to be paroled on her statutory release date.

Rational thinking would suggest that, as a specialist treating the survivors of sexual predators, Dr. Van Gijseghem would have a predisposed bias that might interfere with a fair and impartial assessment of someone with as high a profile as Karla, who had been involved in crimes characterized by aggravated sexual assaults and murder.

There are several distinguished psychologists in the greater Montreal area who are recognized experts in the determination of a prisoner's readiness for parole, which was the only real issue, technically speaking, of concern to the Correctional Service. The Correctional Service is the punitive and rehabilitative part of the law-and-order equation, never, or at least ideally, not judge and jury.

Dr. Van Gijseghem goes on to erroneously state that none of the doctors who diagnosed Karla had reviewed the infamous videotape tape evidence. On the contrary, Drs. Hucker, Hatcher, and Mcdonald had all reviewed the videotapes, as had the prison's own Dr. Roy Brown.

Although the only so-called "expert" in Karla's lengthy psychotherapeutic history who had not conducted numerous "primary interviews" with her, Dr. Van Gijseghem simply dismisses the consistent diagnoses of all his learned predecessors out-of-hand.

"It seems to us," he wrote, "that this [referring to the diagnosis of a depressed battered woman, suffering from post-traumatic stress disorder] is wrong-headed."

He goes on to say that in all the reports "it is taken for granted that the disorder is due to the ill-treatment she experienced at Bernardo's hands and the horrors he ordered her to perpetrate."

Singling out Dr. Arndt, the psychiatrist who spent the most time with Karla, Dr. Van Gijseghem observes, "Nowhere is it said [in Dr. Arndt's report] on what trauma the PTSD is based."

When I met Dr. Arndt at Bistro 990 with Doug Elliott in September of 1993, he was dying of leukemia. He had been diagnosed about six months before George Walker asked him to see Karla and was undergoing aggressive treatment, including chemotherapy, to slow the deadly disease.

I do not remember where exactly we were when he told me – not long after he had entrusted his files to me at any rate. He had labeled them the "Lorenzo" files in an early attempt to protect the privacy of his notorious patient. Both Dr. Arndt and the hospital staff at Northwestern General anticipated a media blitz when it became known that Karla had been admitted. Although the hospital chose to admit Karla under her mother's maiden name – Karla Seger – Dr. Arndt continued to mark all his Karla files "Lorenzo." He was quirky that way.

Between the time he gave me the files and Paul Bernardo's trial in 1995, we spoke on the telephone and saw each other often. Sometimes it was in his office on Keele Street, just south of the 401 highway where it rages across the top of the city of Toronto, or in the basement of his elegant home in Hogg's Hollow off Yonge Street. Early on, shortly after he gave me those attaché cases, he began talking about his illness.

He realized he had been feeling flu-ish and fatigued for about a year, so he went for a checkup. His condition was not something that was generally known and he did not look the slightest bit ill – quite the contrary. Dr. Arndt was robust and athletic. He suggested that it had slowed him down but I never saw any evidence of that. He was still seeing all his patients and had not changed his rounds at the hospital. He continued to respond to any and all requests for expert testimony. Accredited as an expert in the Northwest Territories, he often flew up to Yellowknife to testify. He and his wife, who was a social worker, continued to provide marriage counseling twice a week in their basement in the evenings.

He was dying, though. And as with many of the more dangerous cancers, it was impossible to predict whether death would come sooner, or later.

Dr. Arndt kept his copy of the *DSM-III-R* (*DSM-IV* was not published until 1995) on the shelf beside his Ojibway Dreamcatcher and a piece of the Berlin Wall behind his office desk.

Having thoroughly reviewed all of Karla's files, I had suggested to him that his diagnosis of Karla as a depressed, battered woman, a victim of post-traumatic stress disorder too boot, seemed bogus. "Tammy was the hook," he said to me definitively one evening.

Citing the trial of Lorena Bobbit, the woman who had been exonerated for cutting off her sleeping husband's penis because the experts said she was abused and was suffering from post-traumatic stress disorder, I suggested that PTSD had become a diagnostic fad. Virtually every woman accused of a violent crime who had come before the courts throughout the late eighties and early nineties had been diagnosed with post-traumatic stress disorder. He dismissed my observation saying that there were always controversies between psychiatrists, and psychiatrists and the public-at-large over diagnoses.

Originally derived from the condition called shell shock, first observed in veterans of World War I, post-traumatic stress disorder and its symptoms were fully extrapolated in a book by Arthur Kardiner, first published in 1941, called *The Neuroses of War*. The disorder had since been hypothecated and broadly diagnosed in veterans of the Vietnam War.

Not satisfied, I sarcastically asked how Karla could have contracted a condition that evolved out of the unimaginable atrocities of war?

What catastrophic events in her daily life could have caused such an exacerbated, difficult condition? Although there was no question Paul Bernardo had beaten Karla, there was no evidence that Karla was suffering from battered spousal syndrome, at least not in the classic sense, as it had been set out in Lenore Walker's 1979 book, *The Battered Woman*.

The Battered Woman proposed a diagnostic model for assessing abused women. All subsequent clinical experience had reinforced its validity and Walker's three-phase cycle of abuse had been universally accepted in the therapeutic community.

Ms. Walker postulated that battered spousal syndrome was only possible if a spouse went through this three-phase cycle of abuse numerous times.

The first cycle was a "tension-building phase," characterized by verbal abuse, minor physical abuse and attempts by the woman to actively try and prevent more severe abuse by placating the abuser.

This was immediately followed by an "acute-battering phase" distinguished by physical assault. This phase, in turn, was followed by the "loving-contrition phase," in which the batterer expresses remorse and makes amends.

In abusive relationships, this cycle had to be repeated over and over again for the actual syndrome to develop. Eventually, the woman would develop a sense of helplessness about her situation – hence the term "learned helplessness."

"Learned helplessness" meant that the repeated cycles of abuse "taught" or brainwashed the woman into becoming a passive, anxious, depressed, confused, self-effacing shell who felt trapped in what she comes to perceive as a hopeless situation. There are many women who are battered and abused. There are very few who actually have battered spouse syndrome.

I suggested that the statements of her friends and family showed that Karla, being the avid reader and student that she was, picked up on Lenore Walker's two most famous phrases: "cycle of abuse" and "learned helplessness," early on.

After Paul beat her with that flashlight and Karla was hospitalized, everyone with whom she came into contact – the police, doctors, nurses, social workers, friends, family – told her that she was an abused woman and began to provide the fodder to bolster their own, untutored perceptions.

Her divorce lawyer, Virginia Workman, encouraged her to create the "diary of abuse" that was included in Dr. Arndt's "Lorenzo" files, listing all the things, conceived like fiction in calm retrospect, significant or not, physical or psychological, that Paul Bernardo had ever done to her. The meticulously handwritten document became thirty pages long.

I suggested that this exercise in composition was a touchstone and focused Karla's thinking about abuse and her status as an abused woman. She shared it with Dr. Arndt and the other doctors and also told them elaborate, detailed stories about her recollections of the abuse she had suffered, exfoliating, at least within the context of these stories, the concepts of "learned helplessness" and "cycles of abuse."

Had she not told Dr. Arndt that Paul had hit her all the time, unpredictably; that he made her eat feces and drink urine and that he made her go out on the front lawn and strip at 3:00 a.m. in the morning while he watched her from the darkened living room and masturbated?

How could anyone be certain that any of these stories and details were true? Also, as far as I could tell with what I had been able to gather, Bernardo had beaten her up badly only once, then she left. Someone suffering from battered spouse syndrome stays. Surely Karla was not only Paul Bernardo's accomplice in crime but also Dr. Arndt's diagnostic accomplice?

With a patient smile, Dr. Arndt listened to what I had to say. To my surprise, he agreed with me. There were discrepancies; things that did not fit.

In the early years of their relationship, Karla lived at home, in the bosom of her family and friends. During their courtship, Paul worked full-time in a city two hours away. They only saw each on weekends.

Even after they were married, Karla saw friends, family and co-workers virtually every day.

He allowed that it was rare for a woman to suffer the conditions that he had diagnosed, and that the patient who does is most often isolated by her abuser from the outside world.

Although it was not an area in which Dr. Arndt claimed any special expertise, it was certainly an area with which he had passing, professional familiarity.

Another discrepancy was the fact that once Karla had abandoned the matrimonial home, she set out to systematically undermine Bernardo. She instigated divorce proceedings. She called Customs and reported him for the cigarette smuggling. She called him in to the Humane Society for abusing the dog. She engaged his friends in telephone conversations and pumped them for information. Dr. Arndt allowed how none of this was typical.

Also, there was the appliance salesman she met in a bar. Less than a month after she left the marriage, she hopped in bed with another stranger, just as she had done with Bernardo when he was a perfect stranger that fateful night they first met in October, 1987.

She had told Dr. Arndt that this time the sex "was for her." The way she explained it, it was therapeutic. Everyone is different, but heavily depressed, post-traumatically stressed women do not tend to behave in this way. And it was a harbinger of a disturbing pattern – between the way she behaved with the appliance salesman and the way she had behaved when she met Paul Bernardo. In both cases, the sex had been almost instantaneous.

The fact that Karla continued to correspond with her new lover and send him nude Polaroids of herself, even though she had been instructed by her lawyer to cut off contact – all of this was inconsistent with a diagnosis of post-traumatic stress disorder.

While she was in the hospital under Dr. Arndt's care, Karla would make sure the nurses recorded the fact that she was awake at 4:00 a.m. This vigilance was not typical of heavily depressed persons with PTSD either.

Dr. Arndt said he had never satisfactorily reconciled these dichotomies, or resolved any of his other doubts. As he explained it, when the prosecutors made it clear to Karla's lawyer, George Walker, that Dr. Arndt and his colleague Dr. Long were not sufficiently credible – a communication that precipitated the recruitment of Dr. Andrew Malcolm to the team – Dr. Arndt's original position as Karla's assessor was compromised and he had to reinvent himself.

Within the reinvention or redefinition of his role was the resolution of his conflicts and doubts. With the arrival of Dr. Malcolm on the scene, his mission became a healing one. "You see," Dr. Arndt explained, "I became her treating physician. As her treating physician and therapist, the reconciliation of contradictions and inconsistencies was irrelevant. That was up to the others."

The way he saw it, his only responsibility became Karla's well-being. If they subsequently took his opinions – and that was all they were, opinions – as gospel, that was hardly his responsibility.

And what I had said was also true, the part about how, to a large degree, he and his colleagues, took Karla's stories at face value. But they were not stupid men. What else could they do but listen to their charge carefully and weigh the details with what facts were on offer? They all had hundreds of other patients and busy practices. Medicine, and particularly psychiatry, was every bit as much an art as it was a science. There were no unlimited budgets for far-reaching psychiatric inquests. After all, the police had burned through millions of dollars during their six-year investigations and were obviously none the wiser about Karla's relative guilt or innocence.

According to Dr. Arndt – and the key here was that his colleagues had ultimately all agreed – Karla's sister Tammy was the unimaginable trauma, "the hook," as Dr. Arndt so cryptically called her, that induced post-traumatic stress disorder.

This did not explain or exonerate Karla's behavior by any means. But Dr. Arndt did not think that Karla intended to kill her sister, either. If my opinion differed, so be it. After all, everyone is entitled to their opinion. Of course, proving it, one way or the other, in a court of law would be another matter. And, if he was not mistaken, the sister's death had been ruled an accident in January, 1991. Without Karla voluntarily offering the correct information about her sister's death, no one would have ever known the truth about what happened. And the offer of that information was certainly as damning to her, perhaps even more damning, than to him. "So what's up with that?" he asked. It was a reasonable question within the limits of Dr. Arndt's knowledge of the circumstances.

"It was important, also, to remember that different people react differently," he said. The scholarship suggested that only ten percent of any population is even susceptible to post-traumatic stress disorder. In his opinion, Karla was one of those people.

As Dr. Arndt described it, in a case as extreme as Karla's, PTSD was akin to entering a state of psychological shock characterized by psychic "brown outs." The patient very often continues to participate, to combat both their demons and daily life, without having any specific knowledge or awareness of exactly what they are doing. To others, the person appears to be functioning perfectly normally. He suggested to me that "each subsequent event," referring to the crimes against Leslie Mahaffy and Kristen French and whomever else, was more trauma piled upon trauma. Contrary to Dr. Van Gijseghem's statements in his report, this was clearly stated in Dr. Arndt's report.

According to Dr. Arndt, Karla was like a tourist at a massacre.

There was at the time an unbelievable news report about English tourists deliberately going to strife-torn Rwanda to tour mass graves sites that contained thousands of corpses rotting in the African sun. The way Dr. Arndt portrayed Karla, she was just like one of those people, only she got caught up in one of the massacres. The modern marriage could easily be compared to guerrilla warfare and was often characterized by psychological and physical torture. If you were already in a war zone, getting caught up in a massacre was not so difficult, Dr. Arndt taciturnly suggested. It was certainly within his, and his colleagues' abilities to imagine, and they all had far more experience of the matrimonial battlefield than I did. As Dr. Arndt explained it, for Karla, as for many soldiers, it simply became a matter of self-preservation and survival.

Dr. Arndt said, "Once she was an accomplice, it didn't make any difference what happened afterwards... she had to go on."

He talked about Karla's fantasies about the perfect marriage and her capacity for naive, magical thinking and how it had transformed her life into a kind of unreal, malevolent fairy tale.

"You see, it is only in our Western culture where the young have been raised watching the *Wonderful World of Disney* and taught to believe in happy endings that such fantasies can become pathological," Dr. Arndt explained. "The real fairy tales, which are very often Germanic in origin, have very dark antecedents and there are no such thing as happy endings."

I too had read the English folklorists, Iona and Peter Opie, as well as Bruno Bettelheim. Dr. Bettelheim saw big trouble in the incessant revisionism of the modern idea that children should only be exposed to politically correct stories that were all sweetness and light. The Opies relentlessly documented the real thing.

The story of Cinderella was a good example. Well over a thousand years old, the story bore absolutely no resemblance to the Disney version with which almost every child born in North America in the last fifty years had been raised.

In its original form, the princess Cinderella is forced to leave her royal home and take up menial employment elsewhere. That is where any similarity between the original and the modern version ends.

Cinderella's banishment has nothing to do with being sent into domestic servitude by a wicked stepmother, foot size or weird glass slippers.

In the authentic version, Cinderella's mother, on her deathbed, commands her father not to marry again until he finds a woman who is as lovely as she herself once was. After much searching, the king realizes there is only one person as beautiful – his own daughter. When he discovers that his deceased wife's ring perfectly fits Cinderella's finger as per his wife's dying fiat, he determines to marry his own daughter. Shunning incest, Cinderella takes flight.

Dr. Arndt mentioned the story *Three Heads in a Well*, from the fourteenth century in which a princess willingly picks up one talking, severed head after another, washes it, combs its hair and places it gently aside, actions which required a good deal of courage as well as the placid acceptance of a totally bizarre, unbelievable situation.

"If you look at it a certain way, Karla was like this princess. She had courage, or was at least stoic, and she placidly accepted difficult, bizarre circumstances; these are traits that many women possess, don't you think?"

Possibly. Karla's crimes certainly seemed to be rooted in mundane yet pervasive schoolgirl fantasies of the Heathers and Exclusive Diamond Club variety, and her gruesome story's many twists and turns sort of qualified it as the modern equivalent of a classic fairy tale.

In those old fairy tales, as in real life, many events are remarkable for their unpleasantness. Unbelievability, nary a fairy to be found and resolution through some form of enchantment or supernatural element are predominant characteristics of the genre. But the supernatural or magic in these tales is really a magic of coincidence through which people and creatures are shown to be what they really are.

Karla's knight in shining armor was certainly shown to be a Svengali and what Karla had done was truly unbelievable. If a preponderance of coincidence is seen to be supernatural and serendipity a sign of Divine Providence or malevolent intervention, as it is by most religions and legions of the gnostically superstitious, then everything about her story fit the paradigm perfectly – like a glass slipper.

Meanwhile, Karla was unusually adept at compartmentalizing the various aspects of her life and soldiering on. This was not unusual with people who were really suffering from post-traumatic stress disorder, Dr. Arndt said.

Preoccupied as she was with her parents' perception of Paul as the "son" they never had, Dr. Arndt referred to her almost pathological devotion to the happily-ever-after prototype.

"I think it was Tammy that just sealed it for her, because at that point… she was a participant in the killing of a daughter." He offered me a cold beer and got up to get it from the refrigerator.

"She did not want to have the 'son' killed or the other daughter and so it goes."

Dr. Arndt explained that it had been a hard sell. Dr. Andrew Malcolm, the wellknown and highly respected psychiatrist who was, at the prosecutor's insistence, a late addition to Karla's "team," had been particularly skeptical.

The magnitude of the crimes and Karla's involvement in them seriously troubled Dr. Malcolm.

Dr. Arndt had, as he described it, become her "treating physician," rather than simply an evaluator or assessor as was originally contracted. He had treated Karla intensively and given her numerous therapy sessions over a four-month period. He had the most hands-on, clinical experience of her and as such he was the one who had suggested the diagnoses.

"I wasn't suggesting that Dr. Malcolm was susceptible to suggestion was I?" Dr. Arndt asked. Or that Karla had somehow put him under a spell? Or that perhaps Dr. Arndt had hypnotized Dr. Malcolm?

If such were the case, Dr. Malcolm did not behave as though he was in a trance. He strenuously questioned who and what Karla was and what her state of mind was at the time she committed the crimes and, therefore, was very reticent about Dr. Arndt's diagnostic propositions. It was Dr. Arndt's conception of Tammy, as the originating traumatic event of inconceivable magnitude, that finally won over a skeptical Dr. Malcolm.

Dr. Arndt argued that had Karla "squealed" then she herself would have been susceptible and her well-being severely threatened – on many fronts. The way Dr. Arndt conceived it, in Karla's mind it would have been the equivalent of committing suicide.

"It would be shown to them [her parents, in particular, and the authorities in general] that she was involved with Tammy," Dr. Arndt said. "And then she was also constantly under the threat that he (Paul) would harm the others."

"Whether this was truly the only thing that happened I don't know, but this is what she explained and it certainly makes some sense."

DREAMS OF MONSTROUS JOY

"Like I said," Karla wrote to her new correspondent in January, 2002, after spending her first Christmas on Cellblock A, "I have really not been here in my head too much these days."

Her problem was really exactly the opposite: Karla was increasingly way too much "in her head," way more than she had ever been previously. In Sainte-Anne-des-Plaines, there was nothing else for her to do, no place else for her to go.

Her first years in P4W had been the easiest because she had a really good "job" – talking about herself, her ex-husband, their crimes, her role in them, her feelings and fears. She had a steady stream of interlocutors – policemen and women, prosecutors, psychiatrists and psychologists. All were dedicated to wringing, with impunity, as much detail out of her as was humanly possible while preparing and coaching her to be a witness at her ex-husband's forthcoming trial.

While doing this, they also made sure she was comfortable and protected. Under those conditions, talking about what had happened and what she did was both cathartic and liberating. In her visitors' quenchless curiosity there was sinecure from the reality of what had happened. Her role as blameless documentarian allowed her to distance herself. And with the additional balm of a plethora of psychiatric pharmaceuticals prescribed both before and after she went to prison by Drs. Anrdt and Brown, she had an added buffer that turned her immediate, horrific past into something like a spiritually confused, horrific fable by Dean Koontz or a bizarre series of episodes on her favorite afternoon TV soap opera, *Passions*.

When she returned to Kingston's Prison for Women after testifying in late July, 1995, she was talked-out and exhausted. The police and prosecutors had praised her performance on the witness stand. Elated and relieved, she found herself happier than she had been since before she killed her sister.

She remembered it as though it were yesterday. One of the guards from her unit was waiting for her at the back door. It had been a blistering hot summer and on that particular day the temperature was well over 90. The prison was an inferno – it was probably 120 inside – and the guard's face was beet-red but Karla didn't care, she was just so happy to be back she felt like crying. The guard led her up the four flights of stairs to her tiny 8' x 10' cell. As far as Karla was concerned, it was a sanctuary, a haven in a heartless world, a suite at the Hilton and with her posters, pictures and books, the most welcomed sight in the world.

Normally, P4W was a noisy, raucous place, much as prisons are portrayed in Hollywood movies but because it had finally been condemned and was slated for closure the following summer, half the women had already been transferred to other prisons, and it was especially quiet up in the segregation unit.

Sergeants Bob Gillies and Gary Beaulieu came down to see her one last time as they had promised. And "Gary" – Karla called everyone by their first name – wrote her a very nice letter, thanking her for all of her help and telling her not to listen to all the critics. She never did see the prosecutors again. From time to time she would call and talk to Sergeant Bob Gillies and he often had a kind word from prosecutor Ray Houlahan.

The only woman left in segregation was Karla's friend, Kim. Kim had been sentenced to four years for killing her two-year-old son. She and Karla had hit it off from the beginning. Karla had written Dr. Arndt about Kim, asking if he would take her on as a patient after she was paroled.

Technically, they were supposed to be locked in their cells all day and only allowed out for a few hours in the evening but the guards, unburdened as they were by the ever-diminishing population, became "super nice" and left the two of them unlocked most of the time for the remainder of the summer.

Kim and Karla hung around in the common area, talking about this and that, drinking cappuccino and doing crafts. Every night Karla would call her mother for a report about what had happened at Paul Bernardo's trial that day.

When his jury began to deliberate on August 31, Karla was in the Private Family Visiting Unit by herself and she heard Paul Bernardo's so-called "suicide tapes" and a bunch of other things they were playing on the news. It was totally surreal. She came back to her cell in segregation a few hours before the jury came in with its "guilty-on-all-counts" verdict.

"When they announced the verdict and it was crazy – I heard people yelling from the other units, everyone was cheering," Karla wrote. "It was unbelievable. I was crying because I really thought that I would magically feel better once he was convicted, but I felt no relief at all. Strange."

In late 1996, Dr. Brown became ill and left the prison for good. She really did not need him anymore and had only been seeing him occasionally anyway. But Karla missed him. She had really come to appreciate the old soldier. It was her understanding that he had been in the British Army. He was very good with her – hard sometimes, but good.

By the beginning of 1997, things had changed dramatically. There had been almost a hundred inmates in P4W. With the exception of seventeen maximum-security and mental health prisoners, now all the women had been transferred out, most to the recently opened Grand Valley Institution outside Kitchener, Ontario.

P4W was virtually empty and Karla was totally alone in her unit. She was the last medium-security prisoner in the house. From her standpoint, it was a grand time.

"I was alone in my unit and it was a welcomed change. P4W was so loud and noisy and it was great to finally have some peace and quiet. I was waiting to transfer to Joliette and was the last medium-security offender to leave the prison. Because of that, I had tons of different jobs. I worked outside, in the library, in the unit and there was even talk of going to work at the canteen. (I didn't though.) It was a nice time where I began to mentally prepare for my upcoming transfer."

Before she knew it, it was summer again. On Friday, May 30, they told her to get her family down for a last visit over the weekend, they were going to transfer her first thing Tuesday morning. She could stay in the "little house," as she called the Private Family Visit (PFV) unit, until they came for her.

Her sister and her mother came rushing down. They had their best visit ever. On the Monday night, Karla did not think she would be able to sleep but she did. Very early in the morning, they drove her out to the Kingston airport and put her on an RCMP Pilatus prop plane and flew her to Joliette, Quebec. It only took forty-five minutes and was totally uneventful. The first time Karla actually realized that things were going to be really different was when she saw the townhouses behind a barely visible chain-link fence and how nice the grounds were as they drove toward Establishment Joliette on Marsolais Street. Suddenly she became very nervous and afraid. For four years, she had been mostly locked up for twenty-three of every twenty-four hours and otherwise escorted everywhere, and now suddenly she was completely on her own.

She was put in the Mental Health Unit for evaluation, but this time for less than twenty-four hours and then released into the yard to fend for herself. The first two cons she met only spoke French. Then she got lucky. She met Ines Barbosa, the strongest and "most respected" con among the eighty some odd women who were detained in Joliette. Barbosa took Karla under her wing and introduced her to everyone. She took it upon herself to make sure that she had an easy integration. She knew Karla's story and that she had been in segregation for a long time and that it would be hard for her to adapt. Just going for walks with her was a way to let everyone know to back off, that she had friends. There was another woman too, Angel, a friend of Ines' who did the same thing. And there were also a couple of people who had come from Kingston who did it too.

"There is nothing sexual or 'Hollywood' about it. I even do that with some of the new girls that come in. Everyone does it. It is just a way to help people out." As a consequence, Karla was quickly accepted.

The way it worked in Joliette, you had to find your own way. The first thing the newcomer had to do was find a house that not only had a vacant room but also occupants who were willing to let "new fish" move in. In less than a day, Karla found herself accepted by four different houses. She chose one, and immediately settled in. On her third day, she started working in food services. Over the next few months, with the exception of a few rocky patches, she was able to adjust and get along.

"I should also say that for the first little while I hated Joliette. I found it really hard to be free, but not free at the same time," Karla wrote. "It was a real adjustment. That is why it is so important that we be allowed to live in prisons like this. Imagine if I had been released from P4W after twelve years!"

Every con in the joint was expected to not only fit in and hold up their end as part of a commune of eight women living in one of ten well-appointed townhouses, they were also supposed to work. For all these various prerequisite activities – communal living, compulsory programs such as "Survivor of Abuse" and "Anger Management" and work – they were graded – on performance and punctuality, just as they would be on the outside.

How well or badly the individual performed affected their privileges as well as the quality of their daily lives and ultimately their parole eligibility.

Karla continued the correspondence courses she had begun in P4W and ultimately got her Bachelor of Arts degree in Psychology from Queen's University in 1999. She had taken one correspondence course in criminology from Simon Fraser University and was contemplating a degree in that discipline as well. Karla also "graduated" from all of the courses she was required to take by the prison.

She was a model prisoner. Karla incurred no disciplinary infractions, mostly got along with everyone and required no special monitoring whatsoever. She continued to work thirty-three hours a week in food services – the equivalent of a grocery store clerk on the outside – until she was transferred to Saskatoon in October, 2000. Between her house duties, her correspondence courses, her job and her prison programs, over the three years, four months she was in Joliette, Karla rarely had a minute to herself.

In Sainte-Anne, she had nothing but time. Karla begged for work, she made suggestions at every chance she got, she gave anyone who would listen a resumé of her capabilities. She was computer-literate, she had done inventory and invoicing for food services at Joliette, she could type, sixty or seventy words a minute, she could do this, she could do that.

To shut her up as much as anything else, they gave her a job preparing the files for the constant stream of new male arrivals at the Center. The women housed in the Regional Reception Center were not allowed to work off their secure unit. Her boss would bring the list and a stack of files to her cell late Friday afternoon. But that was desperately simple and, if she fussed over it, it took her at most an hour on Friday night, and another hour or two on Saturday.

"It's boring," she admitted "but better than mopping stairs."

Christmas, 2001, was by far her worst holiday since she had been in prison. "You know, I'm not getting stronger, I'm getting weaker. I am really starting not to care about whether or not I go back to Joliette… I am very discouraged. I see things here that make me lose all faith in human beings."

Every morning they unlocked her door at 7:30 a.m. But Karla never bothered to get up until 8:30. What for? There was nothing to do. In Joliette, she had to get up at 6 a.m. and help prepare breakfast for her seven roommates, make sure the house was in order and then get ready to go to work. In Sainte-Anne, once she got up, all she did was spend two hours showering, doing her face and fussing with her hair. "I usually draw this process out for as long as possible to fill the time."

With nothing else to do, particularly in the mornings, she started going inside her head and it was not a place where anyone would willingly want to spend much time.

Looking at her reflection in her makeup mirror, Karla remembered the way she had looked through her reflection in the plate-glass window in Bluffer's Atrium, the bar restaurant in the Howard Johnson's Hotel on Pharmacy Avenue in Scarborough, Ontario. She could almost see the car pulling up to a stop in the parking lot.

Looking at her reflection in the plate-glass window, she remembered thinking that she looked pretty good. She certainly had that "devilish look" in her eye. And she knew exactly what she was planning. It was about 11 p.m. on October 17, 1987, and she and her friend "Dirty" Debbie Purdie were on a mission to fulfil one of the key Exclusive Diamond Club mandates – meet older, good-looking men from whom they might acquire a diamond and a future. And sure enough, there they were, getting out of a car in the parking lot.

Karla was determined to meet someone that night. That it was Paul Bernardo was pure coincidence. Karla was just seventeen and her parents had not even formally allowed her to "car date" yet. This was her first trip to Toronto. She was there with her boss, Kristy Mann, the manager of the Number One Pet Center in the Penn Center Mall where she and her friend Debbie worked as clerks. The occasion was a pet store suppliers' convention and Kristy had invited Debbie and Karla to go along – just for fun. They had already picked up a couple of boys in the disco downstairs early in the evening, but those two looked a lot better in a dark bar than in the austere light of their hotel room. Kristy and her supervisor had to come to Debbie and Karla's rescue and have the two drunks thrown out by hotel security.

If at first you don't succeed…

As though he truly were Karla's destiny, the tall, sandy-blond, well-groomed, good-looking one strode up to the window and seemed to look right through her and into her soul. He obviously saw something he liked because he immediately walked into the restaurant, ignored the "Please Wait to Be Seated" sign, brushed the maitre d' aside, and sat down at their table. Or at least that was how it seemed. Karla could not remember what was said, if anything. The next thing she knew, they were up in her room doing it and doing it, over and over again.

Karla was not in her head then either except then it was different. Karla had only had sex once before. Her defiant trip to Kansas to see her high school sweetheart, was only a few months old but it seemed a lifetime ago.

With Doug, it had been nothing special. But this, this stuff that she was doing with this guy was rapture. He was experienced. He whispered things to her, dirty things. He wanted her to say things to him. She had never been more excited. He touched her in places where she had never been touched. She was somehow irrevocably transformed by that night.

It was one of those small HoJo rooms with one double bed and a couch. Even though they were only a few feet away, Karla had no idea what Debbie and Paul's friend, who had been relegated to the couch, were doing and she didn't care. Nothing else, except Paul, and what he was doing to her, mattered. As far as Karla was concerned, he was it. Showering with him the next morning, they exchanged phone numbers and thus it began, the satanic fulfillment of the Exclusive Diamond Club charter.

The next weekend Karla invited Paul to come to her house in St. Catharines. He quickly agreed. Soon he was mounting her from behind, quickly, quietly, in her tiny room in the basement of her parents' house, while their friends amused themselves on the other side of her locked door in the adjacent recreation room or just outside her open window, around the pool. Although there was nothing really unusual about what was going on – looking back, Karla could see that Paul Bernardo was really quite a clumsy lover – there was something deliciously forbidden about what they were doing and Karla very quickly became totally obsessed, not exactly with him but with the idea of him.

The handcuffs sealed it. When she revealed her strange keepsake that day, she immediately saw surprise – and recognition – in his eyes. And then he said he had a pair exactly like them. It was at that moment that they seemed to know that they were made for each other, or rather he seemed to know – Karla already knew, or, at least, thought she knew. She may have seen their destiny differently than he did, but she could no longer remember.

All she is remembering now, in this godforsaken place, is what happened next. Glossing over the detritus of all the silly love songs, the glittering Niagara Falls nights, sappy letters and love notes, their engagement and her ring, the intense, debilitated longings, the frenzied, violent lovemaking, the dirty pictures and the videotaping and all the other jiving around, the next thing Karla remembered was Christmas Eve, 1990. While her parents and her other sister were asleep upstairs, she was fingering her younger, comatose sister in front of the Christmas tree in the recreation room, while he watched, playing with himself and his video camera, getting ready to replace her finger with his penis.

THE WEDDING PLANNER

Paul Bernardo fit all the criteria. He was older – twenty-six when they met. (Karla was seventeen.) He had a nice car and appeared to be well-off. He had a good job with a big company and a university education. He had credit cards and money and he bought Karla things – jewelry, stuffed toys, dinner. Between the time Karla entered high school and the time she met Paul Bernardo, she had somehow developed a pathological aspiration for a conventional life defined by diamonds and white picket fences, while having acquired no worldly experience and no wisdom.

At first, all the teenage girls in the Exclusive Diamond Club agreed that Karla had really lucked out. He was handsome (if you like that sort of bottle-blond, boy-toy look, and the majority of the girls Karla grew up with did). He appeared to be the epitome of what they were all looking for. She was cock-proud. He had a collegial air about him, something girls in blue-collar St. Catharines didn't see very often. A few of her girlfriends were visibly jealous and Karla reveled in it.

He talked a good game too. He had been all over the place. When he and Karla collided in the Howard Johnson's that night he had just come back from a friend's wedding in Texas. He frequently vacationed in Florida. One day, he took her to Florida. She lied to her parents; she could not even remember what she had said; probably something about going up to his grandparents' cottage for a week, then off they went to Disney World.

He had big plans; he was going to get really rich. They went to see the movie *Wall Street* and he glomed onto the Gordon Gekko character. He culled a bunch of things the character said in the movie, neatly printed them out in large, black letters on pieces of paper and plastered them all over his bedroom wall. "Words to live by," he said.

He told her that one of his old girlfriends had told him that he reminded her of Jay Gatsby. Gatsby was a character in some big, important book. "You read a lot," he said, "you must know it." She demurred. He told her to read it and tell him if it was true. Karla took to calling him her "big, bad businessman."

Between October, 1987, when they met, and December, 1990, when they killed Karla's sister, another world opened up for Karla and a great deal of it was captured on film.

In the summer of 1988, she posed for a series of pornographic still photographs. Paul still lived at home with his parents in Scarborough – which, had she let herself think about it, might have seemed a bit odd except now she wondered, in retrospect, whether she really would have known enough at that point in her life, to have come to any meaningful, ameliorating conclusion. She was smitten. She was under some kind of spell enhanced by hormonal fury. What other explanation could there possibly be? While in prison she had seen a television program about how Italian men frequently live with their mothers until they are in their fifties. That might have explained it – Paul Bernardo was of Italian descent – but in the television program all the men really loved their mothers and Paul hated his and he wasn't just saying it either and Karla could understand why. She was a pig. She seemed to live in the basement of the Bernardo's large, spacious home in the Guildwood Village area of Scarborough, on the periphery of the Scarborough Bluffs. The house was three times the size of Karla's parents' and it had a really nice, big swimming pool in the backyard, but Paul's mother was like a large troll, always hunkered down in the dark basement. Even on the nicest day, you could hear her rummaging around or see her looming in the shadows at the bottom of the stairs. She was loud, and shouted a lot. Paul said she had something wrong with her thyroid or something and that was why she was so fat and stayed the basement. Come to think of it, the whole family was strange. Paul's older brother David had some kind of disease that made all his hair fall out. He wore an ill-fitting wig that made him look like a child molester. Without his hairpiece, he looked like an alien.

By the time Paul and Karla had met, his older sister Debbie had left and moved up north. She was married and had a kid. And Paul's father, tall and gangly, his limbs akimbo when he walked, peering out through coke-bottle glasses that made his eyes appear to be the size of saucers, made her uncomfortable. According to Paul, he was an accountant who made a lot of money. Sometimes, in the middle of the night, Paul said he would hear his father creaking down the cellar stairs to have sex with his mother, which was really disgusting and an image Karla could have lived without. Her relationship with Paul was destined to deliver a lifetime of images she could have lived without.

Paul also said that his father was not really his father, that his mother had told him on his sixteenth birthday that he was a bastard and showed him a picture of his real father, some wealthy businessman from Kitchener where his mother and father came from. Paul's mother called Karla "a slut," but knowing what she had done with her life, Karla just laughed, thinking about the proverbial pot calling the kettle black.

Later, Karla found out that Paul's father (or stepfather) had molested Paul's sister. Eventually, when he started molesting his seven-year-old granddaughter bouncing her on his lap and fingering her while they were watching cartoons on the television early in the mornings during family visits, Paul's sister called the cops and had him charged. By the time Karla found this out, she also knew that Paul, like his stepfather, was an unrepentant peeping Tom. But Paul had gone his father one better. Since she and Paul met, he had become a serial rapist. Although he talked about being a rapist during their lovemaking, it would be a few years before Karla realized that there was no distinction in Paul's world between fantasy and reality. Karla became the fulcrum for that transaction.

On that blissful, ignorant summer day, the day he took all the pictures, one of Paul's grandparents had died and his parents had gone to Italy on some kind of pilgrimage. Paul set up his camera on a tripod, handcuffed and gagged her, set the timer on the camera, and holding a knife to her throat, mounted her from behind. The sex went on for hours. He had her pose masturbating with a wine bottle. For one picture, he put whipped cream on her nipples and vagina. The picture looked stupid – as though someone had dabbed white-out on those strategic spots.

In another, with a black gag tied around her mouth and her handcuffed hands stretched above her head, she was captured spread-eagle, dripping with semen. Using the timer again, she was immortalized fellating him while he posed holding a knife in his raised, left hand. He talked dirty to her. She talked dirty to him.

Karla regaled the membership of the Exclusive Diamond Club with certain details, not about the knife but about dog collars, and handcuffs and being tied up and doing it doggy-style, and they were shocked. Karla liked the fact that they were shocked. Forbidden knowledge was a power trip.

The years went by and Karla's obsession grew with experience. She liked the fact that their outward appearance belied their growing deviance. He worked five or six days a week, sometimes fourteen hours a day during tax season, for Price Waterhouse, a big accounting firm in Toronto. He worked in their Scarborough offices. Karla attended one of their Christmas parties. Coincidentally, it was held in the same Howard Johnson's where they had met. A senior partner wondered out loud, in reference to them, who had brought their children? They had their picture taken together at the table and they did look very young. During dessert they slipped away and had sex in a stairwell.

For the first six months of their courtship, Paul would often surprise her and show up on a Wednesday night and tap on her window. They would hang out and have sex in his car on the deserted roads out by Lake Gibson and then he would drop her home and drive back. But it was too much – two hours there, two hours back – and he couldn't keep it up, so he started just coming down on the weekends.

At first, he drove back and forth but then her mother, who really liked him and starting calling him "her weekend son," said it was silly, going back and forth like that. He was invited to stay on the couch in the rec room which happened to be right outside Karla's bedroom door.

Looking back, Karla could no longer rationally explain everything that happened, but remembered that the first few years were rhapsodic. As she told Dr. Arndt, "He treated me like a princess; he swept me off my feet... You have to understand, I liked him back then. He was the one guy who was very nice to me; he never bored me like the others. With the other guys I could always do what I wanted and that was boring. In all my previous relationships, I was in total control. I never cared what others thought."

* * * * * * *

In the summertime at Sainte-Anne, they opened the women's yard at 9:30 a.m., and if it were not pouring rain Karla and the one woman on the unit with whom she felt remotely comfortable would go out. It was a big yard – maybe half an acre – and they would walk around and talk or sit on the bench near the hall windows and watch the guys walk by and sunbathe. But now, rising from her toiletries to gaze out over the vast, forlorn, snow-swept landscape that surrounded the prison, Karla could not even imagine trees.

Over the summer, the vast acreage around the prison had been planted in corn, but otherwise it was as flat as the prairie, and there was nothing for it when the wind was up but to shut her barred window and hunker down in the quickly oppressive, dry prison heat. Quebec winters were unforgiving, let alone when one was on the lee side of the Laurentians, as the prison was. In the winter, it was too often far too cold to spend more than five minutes in the yard.

Someone had donated James Ellroy's L.A. *Confidential* to the library (in English, thank God; Karla could not lose herself in French the way she could in English). Madeleine the librarian knew Karla liked police procedurals. Thursday mornings were reserved for women and the librarian brought Ellroy's book and Mordecai Richler's *Solomon Gursky Was Here* to her attention. They were allowed five books a week. (Karla wondered why in the world prisons restricted the number of books inmates could read – in Saskatoon it had been two! What did they think? That too much reading was bad for people in prison? It was totally bizarre.)

Anyway, she was trying to read *L.A. Confidential* over the Christmas holiday. But that probably was not a good idea because it was dense and dark, not anything like Ed Bain's and Michael Connelly's books and Karla's mood over every holiday season since she killed her sister was always dense and dark. Left entirely to herself in the dead of winter as she was in Sainte-Anne, eventually she would start remembering Tammy Lyn's blue, lifeless body lying naked on the harsh, violent-colored rug in her parents' recreation room.

Somehow, between their storybook engagement in the miniature Christmas village in Niagara Falls over the holidays in 1989, when he proposed and gave her the ring and a little glass unicorn and Christmas, 1990, Paul persuaded Karla that his sexual obsession with her youngest sister was something that Karla ought to help satisfy – if she really loved him. It was absolutely sick. In retrospect, Karla could not believe that it was her, that it was the same person that had gone along with it. What she did was insane.

He was putting enormous pressure on her. She had come to realize over the two years they had known each that he was by no means the perfect realization of the Exclusive Diamond Club prototype as it had been originally conceived. He was definitely seeing other women and did little to conceal it, and that both enraged and inspired her. After she had so publicly laid out her perfect future like a long, red carpet in front of all her family and friends she was not about to let it unravel under the stiletto heels of some vapid office slut. She knew more about Paul Bernardo than anyone else. She knew about his dark, perverted side. And she knew that there were lots of other women who would willing do what he liked to do – up to a point. But Karla figured she had an edge. Karla thought she was smarter than most women. She also knew about his weaknesses. There was a craven aspect to his character. She not only believed she had to control him, she believed she could. At any rate, she was determined not to lose him. She had too much invested. Sure, she was jealous of her youngest sister. Shortly after they were engaged, the kid began to flirt more willfully with Paul. And he did nothing to discourage it. But she was not jealous enough to kill her. Even the thought of such a thing was ridiculous. Both her sisters and her mother made a big fuss about him. He had a real way with women, at least the Homolka women, and in their minds, it must therefore have been so with all women.

Her parents had an impromptu block party around the pool in the summer of 1990, and somehow Paul ended up going off in mid-afternoon with Tammy Lyn across the border to replenish the quickly diminishing liquor supply and did not return for six or seven hours. No question, Karla was hysterical. The party had long since disbanded by the time they finally returned and everyone witnessed Karla's humiliation. That moment must have been the fulcrum. It must have been the straw that broke the camel's back because, after that, there was no denying that she did start trying to help him fulfil what he said was an increasingly urgent need for her younger sister. He kept saying that if she really loved him she would help him do it but still, even though she did, how to explain exactly why and what she did? One thing for certain: no other woman would ever be prepared to go as far as Karla did.

Although neither Paul nor Karla were drug users, far preferring the classic middle-class stimulant of mixed drinks, Karla immediately turned to drugs to facilitate her sister's rape. She was familiar with stupefying drugs because she was in charge of the drug cabinet at the veterinary clinic where she worked, and often assisted in the surgery where she would be responsible for the administration of anesthetic. Her mother occasionally used sleeping pills and there was Valium in the house. Excepting the absolute insanity of trying to help your fiancé have sex with your sister, one might have thought that after crushed

Valium sprinkled on your sister's food and in her summer drinks did not have the desired effect, such a depraved goal would be abandoned. But Karla was never one to give up easily and this was not so much a matter of love as it was control. Left unattended, he would probably figure out a way to have sex with her sister anyway, and then where would they be?

Looking back it was difficult, but not impossible, to rationalize how she could have spent her time between September and December not only trying to rigorously figure out how to fulfil his perverted wishes but also, with equal vigor, plan for their absurdly overweening nuptials which they had targeted for the end of next June. Beside her wedding planner and her phone book, she kept a copy of the *Compendium of Pharmaceuticals and Specialities* (a slightly out-of-date version which she had "borrowed" from the vet clinic) by her bedside. She used it to research drugs, trying to find a suitable agent to render her sister unconscious long enough for him to have his way.

By the time she was jolted awake by an incessant tapping on her ground-level bedroom window on Wednesday evening, November 20, she had figured it out.

At the clinic they often sedated larger dogs to make them more manageable before giving them anesthetic. Occasionally, they used Halcion, a common sleeping pill for which even Karla's mother had a prescription. Karla frequently called the pharmacy across the road from the animal clinic to obtain prescriptions on behalf of the veterinarians, and this was the false pretense she would use to obtain a sufficient number of Halcion pills to crush into Tammy Lyn's drinks. But pills alone had not worked before, so she decided to do to her sister what they did to dogs in surgery and administer the anesthetic Halothane, just to make sure once she was out, she stayed out.

Karla marked the passages that described Halcion and Halothane with highliter. This indicated to the police, who later found the book, that the stupefaction of her sister was premeditated and that Karla was fully aware of the contraindications which described, in no uncertain terms, how dangerous the non-professional use of Halothane could be.

Halothane was not like chloroform, it was not to be used unadulterated, poured on a rag and held over someone's face, the way they did in movies. Regardless, that is exactly what Karla decided to do. Paul was very happy when Karla told him she had figured it out.

She stole a bottle of the anesthetic from the clinic and stored it in her room. (Unlike most prescription medicines, including all the narcotics, Halothane was not a restricted substance and therefore not something that had to be reported to a registry, rather just another inventory item in an inventory for which Karla was responsible.)

However, Karla was so vigilant of her wrongdoing that she preempted any possible notice that the supply of Halothane was suspiciously depleted. She told the vets that the atomizer which mixed the oxygen with the Halothane during surgery, had been malfunctioning and using too much anesthetic. They accepted her word and replaced the atomizer with a new unit.

* * * * * * *

What a surprise! It was Paul at the window. He never came down anymore during the week. Opening the window, her demeanor changed from pleasant surprise to concern. "What's the matter?" she asked.

"I need to talk to you. Don't tell your mother. Just say you're going out for a walk."

He was hysterical. He had just come from the police station in Toronto where he had been interviewed as a suspect in the massive Scarborough rape investigation. A month after he and Karla had met, Paul Bernardo had started raping strangers in earnest. His *modus operandi* marked his work. Most of the rapes occurred relatively close to his parents' house on Sir Raymond Drive. However, in recent months, he had stopped off a couple of times in Mississauga on his way to see Karla.

He cruised bus stops and when he saw a woman get off a bus alone, he would follow her. Sometimes he stalked his subjects, sometimes not.

Invariably, they would head into a densely populated suburb. There he would attack them from behind, pull them between the houses, most often only a few doors away from their own homes, and violently, repeatedly rape them, vaginally and anally, for as long as an hour and a half. He used a knife and threatened to kill them if they screamed. He invariably insisted on oral sex. Often, he would put a length of coaxial cable around their throats. In the summer of 1990, the police had finally published a composite drawing in the Toronto newspapers and a number of people had called to say that Paul Bernardo was a dead ringer. The police came calling and he was compelled to go in for an interview. They wanted samples – hair and spit – and he voluntarily supplied them. What else was he going to do? What if they made a mistake? What if they just nailed him so they could say the case was solved? After all, the cops were under pressure. There were fifteen or more unsolved rapes since 1987 and it had a high profile in the media.

The police told him they would have the test results in a couple of weeks. Karla had never seen him that upset. She tried to reassure him. She told him that wasn't the way the police worked. That weekend she took him to the library and they looked up all the rapes from microfiche newspaper files, and made a written chart that included the date and time and the intersections where they occurred. At least half a dozen, maybe more, had occurred on days or nights Karla seemed to remember they had been together. She would be his alibi. She distracted him by telling him all about how she had figured out her sister. By the following week, he had calmed down and refocused on Tammy Lyn.

They had to abort Karla's plan two or three times that December; either Tammy Lyn had one of her friends over, or she went out herself or everyone stayed up late. Karla had vivid memories of certain events during the day leading up to the night they did it.

She remembered the sound of Paul crushing the Halcion pills with a hammer in the basement and her mother's censorious query. His vociferous disappointment when they found out that one of Tammy Lyn's girlfriends was coming over to spend the night that night, too. Once again, they reluctantly abandoned the project and went cross-border shopping. In the late afternoon, a sudden blizzard shut down the Peninsula and Tammy's friend's mother called and cancelled her daughter's visit. Karla could still see the glowing Meatland neon sign like a beacon in the blowing snow as they sat in the deserted parking lot of the nondescript, box-shaped butcher shop and crushed the rest of the pills into powder in his car. They arrived home around six o'clock.

These scenes played in her mind like a series of movie trailers but instead of a concourse of phantasmagoric shadows they seemed, in her idleness and isolation, to be becoming more real than they ever had before.

She has told the police about the details of what happened next – how they had mixed Tammy's drinks for her and watched her as she got progressively more stoned; how her sister Lori spoke out about it and, most disturbingly, in her stupor, Tammy Lyn announced that she was sure that Paul and Karla were trying to poison her. Karla was at first shocked and then totally surprised and then somehow emboldened when the girl's imprecations went right over her parents' heads.

It was like a dream sequence. Although Tammy was clearly drunk, instead of passing out while everyone was still awake and being quietly put to bed by her father, she belligerently insisted that she wanted to stay up with Paul and Karla and watch the movie they had rented.

Karla no longer remembered which movie it was because they had no intention of watching it. Just after they got it into the VCR and pushed the play button, probably before the titles came up, Karla poked Tammy, who had laid down on one of the two couches in the small rec room and discovered the pills had finally taken hold. She was out cold.

Later Karla told the police that she had only wanted to crush a couple of the 10 mg. Halcion pills into Tammy's drinks but Paul crushed all thirty and probably used the equivalent of twelve or fourteen. But what difference did that make? The pills alone would never have killed her. She might have slept for the next sixteen hours but she would have eventually awakened.

Karla knew that a person or an animal being given anesthetic was not supposed to eat for at least twelve hours prior to its administration. Tammy had been eating and drinking all night. Regardless, Karla got out her bottle of Halothane, soaked a rag and held it over her sister's mouth and nose while Paul pulled off her track pants and pushed her shirt and bra high above her breasts. While her other sister and parents slept upstairs, Karla steadfastly replenished the Halothane on the rag and held the soaked rag on her sister's face and watched while Paul lubricated the comatose girl's labia and fumbled with his penis, trying to insert it in her vagina at the same time as he tried to videotape himself doing it.

To Karla's surprise, her sister was menstruating. In urgent whispers, she urged Paul to "hurry up" and get it over with. She implored him to use a condom. He ignored her and made her perform cunnilingus on her menstruating sister. He made her stick her fingers inside and then lick them. Karla was enormously displeased. She looked directly into the camera and said, in a harsh, loud whisper "Fucking disgusting." And then they changed positions again and he stuck his penis in her sister's anus and asked Karla if she would "suck him off" afterward. To her amazement, she said, "yes" and again encouraged him to hurry. For some reason, he just stopped. And Tammy Lyn vomited. Then they realized she wasn't breathing.

At least that was how they had configured it. Was that the way it had really happened? Of course it was.

While watching the video with the police much later, in late February, 1995, in the final months of her extensive preparation for her role as a witness in Paul Bernardo's prosecution, she would have seen the way Tammy's right hand, resting comfortably over her naked stomach above her pubis during most of the remarkably short video record, suddenly fell lifelessly to her side just as the screen went to black.

PASSIONS

They lock up the women's yard at 11 a.m. and serve lunch. Karla was only eating three or four meals a week. A lot of women gained weight on prison fare and Karla had no intention of sharing their fate. The food prepared and served by prisons tended to be starchy and the vegetables were always overcooked.

There were certain things that Karla really missed. She was a candy addict, something she had been working on and had to keep working on although it had become a lot easier in Sainte-Anne because there was no good candy there.

Prison food is terrible. "There are things I really miss," she confesses in a letter. "I love red wine – Beaujolais and Chianti and would really appreciate a glass now and then. As for food, my whole sentence I have dreamed of having a Harvest Barn salad, cheese bread, and a slice of their bumbleberry pie. Havest Barn is a little fruit vegetable market/bakery on the same street as Martindale Animal Clinic. I used to go there for lunch often. I adore salad."

In Joliette, she had not missed much because of the way food services and the cooperative housing was set up and because Stivia Clermont did the cooking for their unit. Up until then, she had missed restaurant food but Stivia was as good as any restaurant chef.

There were limited cooking facilities on Cellblock A, an oven with a few pots and pans. The women were allowed to order food every two weeks from the local grocery in Sainte-Anne-des-Plaines. The list was very limited (compared to Joliette)– bacon $4.00 for 250 grams; broccoli, $3.99 a head; Saputo mozzarella cheese $3.79 for 300 grams. It went on: pork chops, ham, chicken breasts and a small assortment of vegetables. The only fish on offer was filet of sole. "It's expensive, but at least we can order it if we have the money."

What Karla had started doing, with the con she had befriended, was take her food – a special, basically vegetarian diet, with chicken provided by the prison, (something that Karla was fighting to get for herself but figured it might take the rest of her sentence before they acquiesced) and whatever Karla could scrape together and they would make three or four meals a week. They often had salad and cheese toast.

Since arriving at the Regional Reception Center, Karla pretty much existed on what she could buy at the canteen and those three or four dinners.

Regardless, even if she ate lunch it took no more than half an hour. If she did not eat lunch, in the summertime she would "piss around" until 1 p.m. when they reopened the yard and go out again for an hour and sunbathe. In the winter there was nothing at all to fill those midday hours until *Passions* came on at 2 p.m.

Karla liked *Passions* because it was different from other television soaps. It was way beyond your basic incest, betrayal, Jim and John trading Jill and Jane, *Days of Our Lives*, *Young and Restless* fare. It had bizarre, Koontz-like plot lines surfeit with the supernatural. On January 2, 2002 for instance, there was a totally surreal scene set in a psychiatric hospital with an axe-wielding, gender-bended patient dressed up like a doctor chasing a middle-aged, bottle-blond woman named Tabitha who happened to be a witch, and had turned her doll into a real little boy named Timmy, played by an adult, dwarf actor who bore a striking resemblance to malefic Howdy Dowdy.

Tabitha was upset because, after she granted Timmy's Christmas wish to become a real boy, she lost her powers and could not make another doll. She had originally created the life-size doll to keep her company. Now she was convinced that Timmy would grow up and leave her.

Norma (the axe-wielding axe-murderer in the psychiatric hospital) wanted to kill Tabitha and Timmy because they had somehow unknowingly insulted Norma's dead father whose skull she carried around in a pouch.

The psychiatric scenes in *Passions* reminded Karla of the three months she had spent in Institut Philippe Pinel, the psychiatric hospital in Montreal's north end where they had parked her until a cell opened up at Sainte-Anne. Talk about truth stranger than fiction. Although there were no axe-murderers running around trying to kill middle-aged witches clutching Chucky dolls, there was just about everything else.

Karla did not think such places still existed. Placed on an open, co-ed ward, Karla watched in stunned silence while men and women were paraded through the hallways in their underwear. Given that she had just returned from four months in maximum-security isolation at the Regional Psychiatric Center in Saskatoon and had not been in the company of the opposite sex for at least the past seven years, and further, that the Parole Board had just ruled her too dangerous to be released on parole, her placement in an unsecured, co-op ward without police or prison guard supervision was nothing short of institutional insanity. But no one seemed to notice, and Karla had certainly learned enough over the past seven years to know that discretion was the better part of valor. She said nothing and that was a good thing because, as it turned out, in Pinel, if you spoke your mind, they got big men to drag you to the isolation room where you were tied to the bed and pumped full of drugs.

In Joliette, Karla had heard stories about Pinel from people who had been there but she was always skeptical because they were all mental health cases. Then she saw it first-hand. "A friend of mine from Joliette came in while I was there. She has been severely abused in her life and was really agitated when she arrived. Joliette told Pinel that they were scared of her, so the first thing Pinel did when she arrived was to get the "miradors" [orderlies *en anglais*] to grab her and drag her to isolation. This woman had been abused all her life. So how do you think she reacted to big men grabbing her? She tried to fight them off, was tied to the bed (how do you think a rape victim would react to being tied to a bed by several men)? And then was drugged up and left there for days. Nice treatment."

Breakfast was served at 8 a.m. Then the men had their showers. Then you sat and did nothing. At noon hour, everyone was locked in their rooms for "nap time." Then the doors were unlocked and everyone did nothing again.

It seemed to Karla that everyone in Pinel, staff and patients alike, smoked. Unlike virtually every other institution in Canada, there was only one small TV room where smoking was not allowed. To avoid the smoke, Karla either hung around in there or in her room. For this, she was harassed by the staff for not associating with the other patients.

Contrary to what the staff perceived, Karla did associate with a number of people. There was a guy named Guy who she thought was "really nice but very spinny." He could not stand to be locked up and freaked out whenever they put him in his room.

"Another was a guy named Yannick who was kind of creepy. He was very cute but very strange. He used to cry about being locked up in Pinel for a couple of months. Finally, one day I couldn't take it any more and told him that I have been locked up for eight years so stop whining about a couple of months. He liked me and kept saying that he would wait for me to get out of jail. He didn't even know anything about me "

Then there was a guy named Raymond who she really liked. Karla thought he had been diagnosed a schizophrenic and that was why he was there. Raymond had been in the infamous maximum-security Archambault (one of the satellite facilities joined by a long tunnel to the Regional Reception Center pod). Karla would tell him stories about P4W and he would in turn tell her stories about life in "the Shoe," as Archambault was disaffectionately known among the cons.

She also met an eighteen-year-old girl named Audrey with whom she got along. She was there for some kind of evaluation and was supposed to go back to a group home or something like that.

There was absolutely nothing to do but associate and Karla associated a lot, she just didn't make a big deal about it. After dinner, everyone was locked up in their rooms for another nap. After that, it was shower time for the women and phone calls (fifteen minutes only). At 7:30 p.m. they were finally offered an activity. The choices were swimming (once a week), skating and tobogganing, and sometimes they showed a movie. "BORING " was how Karla characterized it.

In the summer there were some other things but since Karla was transferred in April she never found out what they were. The activities lasted until 9:30 p.m. They were locked in their rooms for the night at 10:30 p.m. Even though they were only allowed two books a week, Karla's mother was able to send her books and Alain, her caseworker, managed to borrow books from other units, so Karla spent her time reading and writing letters. She was, by that time, corresponding regularly with a few of her fellow inmates from Joliette, who were just as upset and outraged as she was by her unjustifiable transfer.

Although Pinel was a psychiatric hospital, Karla was not offered any therapy or counseling. She was seen by a Dr. Brault Da Silva (once) and someone else for a short time. (She couldn't remember the person's name.)

"I told them I was never going to tell my story again because it has been told enough and I don't see the need to repeat everything over and over again when it is all in my file."

She kept asking them when her program would start and they kept asking her what she wanted to do. She told them that she was supposed to be doing a sex offender program but they never did anything. They just kept asking her what kind of therapy she wanted and with whom she wanted to do it and where? Then her caseworker told her that she was just there for another evaluation. It was crazy. She felt like she had fallen down the rabbit hole. Nothing made any sense.

Passions made sense to Karla, so she watched it every day. It was set in Maine, in an imaginary town called Harmony, and focused around the Crane family and its matriarch, Ivy, who was confined to a wheelchair. Everyone in Harmony seemed to be Catholic, although Karla did not know why. Further, she did not necessarily approve of the Catholic Church, although she admitted in a letter that she found it "very interesting" that the Pope had declared Hell a state of mind.

"My how the Catholic Church is changing," she wrote. "That is what I don't like about it – religion is not supposed to change with the times."

There was a *Passions* character named Kay Bennett who sold her soul in order to have her way with Miguel, her cousin Charity's boyfriend. Kay's misdeed resulted in Hell coming to Harmony – specifically located in Charity's bedroom closet. Kay then watched nonchalantly as Charity opened her closet and got sucked into hell. Kay's sister's name was Jessica.

There had been big deal in the newspapers a couple of years back about how Karla was having an affair with another inmate at Joliette named Linda Véronneau. In the article, it was reported that Linda had told her family that she was in love with a woman in Joliette named Jessica and was going to live with her when they both got out of jail. The article also reported that Karla's mother had told the reporter that Karla's favorite television soap opera character was named Jessica. From that, the article inferred that Karla must be Jessica.

"As for Jessica she is Kay's sister and a very minor player in all of this. So much for what you read in the newspaper – she is not at all my favorite character. My favorite is Theresa. The whole storyline about her and Ethan is my favorite. So don't believe what you read "

To Karla's chagrin, toward the end of January, just as winter was setting in with a vengeance, *Passions* took a turn for the worse. "They started to revert to a very typical storyline," Karla wrote, " – about 5 different people were out to kill Julian Crane. He got shot yesterday and now it will be a typical 'whodunit' with the requisite trial. Oh well."

THE DEVIL'S ADVOCATE

Love blooms in dark corners. During the Bernardo trial, in the summer of 1995, Inspector Vince Bevan and a dozen of his hand-picked Green Ribbon Task Force officers considered essential to Bernardo's prosecution were holed up in the Colony Hotel on Chesnut Street, kiddy-corner to the University Avenue Courthouse in downtown Toronto. Bevan ordered Green Ribbon Task Force letterhead with the hotel address and telephone number on it, as well as Green Ribbon Task Force Visa cards for all his men. They were in for the long haul. After hours, the large bar off the hotel lobby was an oasis for the purveyors of law and order.

One evening, in August, a few weeks after Karla was cross-examined by Paul Bernardo's defense lawyer John Rosen, I happened to sit down for a drink with a couple of prosecutors, including Assistant Prosecutor Leslie Baldwin.(Ms. Baldwin has since been appointed to the bench and now sits in St. Catharines.) An intense, attractive blonde with a bird-like aspect, she shared with her two male colleagues, Tom Atkinson and Shawn Porter, a prodigious thirst. The men were tossing back shots with beer chasers. For her part, during the two and a half hours I spent at the table, Ms. Baldwin downed at least six or seven glasses of white wine.

The more Leslie Baldwin drank, the larger the heart she was wearing on her sleeve became. Me, she regarded with suspicion, but with my researcher she laughed and cried and spoke of many things, including details about images on the restricted videotapes that were daily being played as evidence in the courtroom. The judge had ruled that certain portions of the tapes would be restricted to audio only, and during those segments that depicted the rapes of Tammy Lyn Homolka, Jane Doe, Leslie Mahaffy and Kristen French, the public television monitors were turned off and the sound turned up.

For instance, Ms. Baldwin spoke about how unattractive Karla looked during a sequence in which Karla and Kristen French were, at Paul Bernardo's direction, playing schoolgirl friends. When instructed to bend over and pull up their tartan skirts, something about the way Karla's loose-fitting underwear which had bunched between her buttocks, seemed to both disgust and fascinate Ms. Baldwin. Kristen French was not wearing underwear.

This image had become some kind of emotional black hole into which all the other atrocities and cruelties depicted on the tapes imploded. Its contemplation caused Ms. Baldwin to burst into tears. After all, she had been the person designated to explain the contents of the vidoetapes to the victims' families and was traumatized by the idea that her voice would be the voice "those families" heard for the rest of their lives whenever they thought about what their dead daughters had gone through. Toward the end, I was amazed that she was able to get up and walk, albeit a little unsteadily, to the ladies' room.

At one point, during these happy hours, the lead prosecutor Ray Houlahan joined the group but left almost immediately, perhaps disquieted by my presence and the obviously fragile psychological state of Ms. Baldwin.

Shortly thereafter, Inspector Bevan also sidled up to the table. Pool cue in hand, he quaffed a beer and, citing the need for intense preparation for the forthcoming day's proceedings, excused himself. This was somewhat anomalous given that the only thing he had to do was supervise the officer who was manning the video cassette recording device, pausing and playing and replaying segments of the lurid evidence when requested.

During the ten minutes he was there, he gave no indication that he and I were already well-acquainted. Stiff and aloof with everyone except Ms. Baldwin, I thought I detected something more between the policeman and the prosecutor than professional collaboration.

After the Inspector left, I expressed my contention that he was single-handedly responsible for the fact that Karla Homolka was a witness at her husband's trial rather than his co-defendant. The protestations from the three prosecutors were loud, but loudest among them were those of Leslie Baldwin who profusely sang the Inspector's praises. Slurring slightly, she exclaimed "HE'S A GREAT MAN!"

Much later in the evening, around midnight, I cruised the bar looking for a straggler from the press corp with whom I might share a nightcap. I found the large room deserted except for Ms. Baldwin and Inspector Bevan, huddled together in a dimly lit corner. They did not acknowledge my passing.

* * * * * * *

I had first met the Inspector a year and a half earlier, on February 11, 1994, at 12 noon in Grant Waddell's office. At the time, Grant Waddell was the Chief of the Niagara Region Police Service. I had spent a great deal of time and effort over the previous year, between the time Paul Bernardo was arrested on February, 17, 1993, and that auspicious day in Chief Waddell's office, trying to get an interview with Vince Bevan.

During that year I learned that many of Inspector Bevan's peers perceived him to be a bit of a mountebank. I heard anecdotes illustrating his inexperience, ineptitude and bad judgement. The fiery, Italian-Canadian civilian employee with whom he was allegedly having an affair was pointed out to me. Although virtue and competence have never been hallmarks of promotion or success, there were obviously those in the senior ranks of the Niagara Regional Police Service who disagreed with this portrayal or else Inspector Bevan would not have been in the position he was. I do not think Chief Waddell was one of them.

A rather good-natured Scot, with a thick, endearing brogue, Chief Waddell was a recent appointee, imported from the ranks of the Toronto police on the shaky premise that a politic, experienced immigrant to the Niagara region might just be able to quell decades-old corruption and partisan back-biting that made the eight-hundred-some-odd person Niagara force not only an object of ridicule and derision within policing circles, but formal judicial inquiries as well.

At the time, I did not fully appreciate the dynamics of the situation. It had taken some doing to get the Chief to act as a go-between and set up this meeting. As I now realize, the Chief and Inspector Bevan disagreed about virtually everything, including issues of openness and media management and that fact worked in my favor. Still, there were no guarantees. The Chief could not compel Inspector Bevan to do anything. He had to coerce and cajole him.

Shortly after Kristen French's nude body was found in a ditch on April 30, 1992, and before Chief Waddell's appointment, the government had agreed to finance the organization of a task force around Inspector Bevan. From that day forward, Bevan was his own master with a vague responsibility to a few senior bureaucrats at the Ministry of the Attorney General in Toronto. He certainly did not answer to Chief Waddell. If anything, at the time of our meeting, the two senior police officers' relative power was the reverse of their rank.

Bevan had been born in St. Catharines and came from a local, Irish Catholic family with a long tradition in policing. His father had been a Deputy Chief of the regional force and his mother the daughter of another senior officer. His brother was a priest and a minister to the police. Even Bevan's father-in-law was linked to the police and had made his fortune supplying the force with mechanical services.

The Niagara Police Service was a government-enforced amalgam of eighteen little police forces that dotted the region between Hamilton and Niagara Falls in the 1950s. One day seventeen police chiefs found themselves back walking a beat. From that day forward, deep-seated resentments and chronic nepotism precluded any possibility for stability and unanimity.

Police work, in the real world, is essentially a test of an individual's ability to endure boredom. The vast majority of police officers never have occasion to draw their guns. Postings to Inspector Bevan's well-financed Green Ribbon Task Force were coveted by the rank and file and Bevan had the singular responsibility for staffing. As a consequence, he had more parturient power than any one chief in any of the ten forces from which he cherry-picked his personnel.

Having failed to get any response to dozens of phone calls and half a dozen notes sent directly to Inspector Bevan, I started lobbying the Chief shortly after he was appointed to the job in May, 1993. It took him eight months to make the meeting happen.

From a distance, and in press photographs, Inspector Bevan bore a resemblance to the American actor, Tom Selleck. In person, he was not as tall, fit, or good-looking and his eyebrows seemed to form a thick, single, black furrow that extended temple-to-temple across his forehead. This fact of physiognomy gave him a somewhat Snidely Whiplash, cartoon-like demeanor which made his resemblance to Selleck more caricature than striking. He was also wearing a brown suit and cowboy boots.

The Chief had barely introduced us when the Inspector proclaimed that I had "spelled her name wrong."

"I beg your pardon?"

"In your letter to the Frenches. You spelled Kristen's name wrong." He held out a copy of the letter.

I had written letters of condolence and sympathy to both the families of the dead girls when I began research for my book about the case, *Invisible Darkness*. In the letters, I told them that it was probably not necessary that we talk – unless, for some reason, they wanted to talk to me.

I told them that by pure happenstance I had rather close ties to parents who had lost children in similar diabolical circumstances; Sharon Morningstar Keenan, a little, nine-year-old girl who was abducted from a park, raped, murdered and stuffed in an unused freezer, was our next door neighbor and played with my daughter when we lived in the Beaches area of Toronto in the 1980s.

I had worked for a multinational advertising agency with Alison Parrot's mother, Lesley. Twelve-year-old Alison had been lured to her death by a man posing as a photographer in broad daylight in downtown Toronto one summer afternoon in 1983. As a consequence, I said in the letter, I had become more than a little preoccupied with these kinds of horrible cases and the people who are capable of such evil, catastrophic acts.

I meant the notes to be considerate and respectful. In retrospect, the letters were far too long and self-absorbed; nothing anyone can say or do means anything to people who have gone to the place where the Mahaffy and the French families had gone. Even though I had asked Lesley Parrot to read them in draft so that I did not unwittingly say anything inherently stupid or insensitive, the very fact that someone in my position would send such verbose missives was stupid and insensitive. The fact that I proclaimed that I did not see any need to talk to them was also a misstep. One of the only things both families could do, or wanted to do, was talk.

"See," the Inspector said, pointing to a highlighted line. "You spelled it K-I-R-S-T-E-N. Her name is Kristen, not Kirsten."

The misspelling of Kristen's name was one of those typos that somehow stubbornly elude even the most studied eye. I had reversed the "r" and the "i" and in spite of dozens of proof readings by various individuals, there it was: "Kirsten."

As Inspector Bevan intended I should be, I was immediately put off-balance and embarrassed. As I was to discover, Bevan was the kind of man who saw huge significance in small mistakes and became easily fixated and mislead by irrelevant details.

Satisfied that I had been firmly put in my place, and that my ignorance and insensitivity were duly exposed, the Inspector proceeded to listen politely to my five-minute pitch about why he should talk to me. When I was finished, I asked for a private interview. Both the Chief and

I were stunned when Inspector Bevan agreed. The Chief offered the boardroom adjacent to his office to which the Inspector and I adjourned. Would the Inspector mind if I taped our conversation?

"No problem," he replied.

I put the tape recorder on the table and asked him if what I had heard was true; that the Niagara Regional Police first learned that the Toronto Police had a man under twenty-four hour surveillance in St. Catharines by accident. I had heard that two uniformed officers from Niagara just happened to stumble on a couple of Toronto undercover cops in the Robin's Donut Shop on the outskirts of the St. Catharines' suburb, Port Dalhousie, where Karla and Paul Bernardo lived.

It was well known that Inspector Bevan had control over every aspect of the task force's business, including media relations. Because of the way Inspector Bevan had managed, or rather mismanaged, the media during the course of his protracted investigation, he had alienated many reporters, particularly those from the national press in Toronto. I thought that this cops-and-donuts story was probably apocryphal, meant to embarrass Bevan and even further denigrate what was already perceived as a kind of Keystone Cops' tragi-comedy. I was surprised by his answer.

"May be true; in fact, I think it is true. I don't know who the guys were but I believe that's true… But, of course, that is not how we learned about it." Inspector Bevan was another one who often referred to himself with the royal "we."

"A call came from Metro (Toronto Police) and I was invited to a meeting in Toronto. This was shortly after they had positive DNA results in some of the rapes – in January," he explained.

Part of Inspector Bevan's problem with the press seemed to be the quirky anomalies in almost everything he said. For me he was making no exception. Shortly after our meeting I discovered that according to his own voluminous, sworn statement which documented – for the use of both prosecuting and defense attorneys – the chronological details of his two-and-a-half year investigation into the rape and murder of Leslie Mahaffy and Kristen French, the meeting to which Inspector

Bevan alluded had actually taken place at 10 a.m., Monday, February 8, 1993. That was a full week after the Toronto police initiated round-the-clock surveillance of Paul Bernardo. The Staff Superintendent in Toronto, David Boothby, called Bevan to invite him to that meeting late Friday afternoon, February 5, 1993. Prior to that call, according to his own report, Inspector Bevan was clueless.

Even though he admitted to me during our interview and documented in his report that he knew eyewitness accounts were universally regarded by knowledgeable police investigators as unreliable, right after Kristen French's abduction, Inspector Bevan became convinced, based on eyewitness accounts, that the young schoolgirl had been abducted by two scruffy men driving an old, cream-colored Camaro.

Not only did his obsession infect the entire task force with an ultimately indomitable myopia, it morphed into a public witch hunt riveted on that one make and model of car.

Putting on his copywriter's hat, Inspector Bevan developed an elaborate advertising campaign to try and convince anyone who owned a Camaro to turn themselves in. Putting on his database manager's hat, he then developed a system whereby Camaros that had been checked out by task force personnel were designated with a specially designed Green Ribbon sticker. Reporting fathers, sons, and uncles became a pastime among all the dysfunctional family units in the Niagara region. Tracking them down and clearing them consumed almost all of Inspector Bevan's massive task force's time, energy and money.

In the meantime, putting on his television producer/director's hat, Inspector Bevan spent months producing and directing a special, ninety minute, television program called *The Abduction of Kristen French*, in collaboration with a Hamilton television station and featuring an old cream-colored Camaro, FBI profilers, and virtually all the misinformation the Inspector had accumulated.

The Inspector could never have anticipated that I would come into possession of his report, called a "will-state" in legal circles. Will-states are part of what is known as Crown disclosure and generally never available to anyone outside the policing and legal communities.

During large criminal investigations such as the Bernardo and Homolka cases, the prosecutors and police develop massive amounts of information and evidence, including interviews with family, friends, victims, victims' families and friends, forensic evidence of one kind or another, experts' opinions and the like. Crown disclosure is like an iceberg. Only a very small portion of it is ever seen as evidence in the courtroom. The vast majority remains unseen, hidden below the surface. This massive information pool can be damaging to all and sundry because down there, in the deep, dark intricacies of intersecting interviews and cross-references and chronologies, in veritable oceans of accumulated, often un-collated information, lies the truth and it seldom sets anyone free.

For instance, in Bernardo's case, there were approximately two hundred and fifty police will-states – everything from three-paragraph, one page statements from policemen who drove Bernardo at various times from "A" to "B," to Inspector Bevan's novel-length record.

The will-state is supposed to contain everything a police officer has direct knowledge of, anything to which he or she could testify, under oath, in a court of law. And to illustrate the integrity of my iceberg metaphor, in the end, only three or four policemen were called as witnesses at Bernardo's trial, and Inspector Bevan was not one of them.

It is called Crown disclosure because the prosecutors are required by law to disclose all of the information and evidence they collect to the accused's defense attorneys. Very few people outside the legal profession know that such a thing exists, let alone understand what it is. It was certainly news to the majority of press covering the Bernardo trial who were not aware of its existence until long after my book, *Invisible Darkness*, was published and I was charged with breeching court orders restricting access to certain videotape portions of the material in 1998.

Although Crown disclosure is technically "owned" by the public, by taciturn agreement taken by committees comprised of judges, prosecutors and defense attorneys within the Law Society itself, no one in the media is normally allowed access to it. Historically, the Crown disclosure in a major criminal case has never been shared with anyone outside of the legal profession, at least not in a timely fashion.

For me, someone made an exception.

As documented in Inspector Bevan's will-state, Paul Bernardo had been interviewed by two detectives at Bevan's behest in mid-May, 1992, shortly after Kristen French's body was found. Up to that point, both Inspector Bevan and one of his sergeants had had numerous conversations with various Toronto police officers including Steve Irwin, the Toronto detective responsible for the Scarborough rape investigation.

Bevan had his first conversations with Detective Irwin shortly after he was assigned responsibility for the investigation of Leslie Mahaffy's death and dismemberment in

July, 1991. Either he or one of his detectives was meeting with, or talking to Detective Irwin as late as March, 1992, a few weeks before Kristen French was kidnaped.

Even though there were stalking reports made by two women in St. Catharines that identified Paul Bernardo as their stalker, and Bevan knew, or should have known, that Bernardo remained a major suspect in the Toronto rape investigation, he never made any connection between Bernardo and the bizarre sex crimes and murders that had begun to occur shortly after Bernardo moved in with the Homolkas in late 1990. At least, not until an anonymous May, 1992 tip provoked the Inspector to finally have Bernardo interviewed. In preparation for this interview, not only did they miss the stalking reports, they also missed the fact that Paul Bernardo and Karla Homolka were alone with Tammy Lyn Homolka when she mysteriously died in the Homolka's basement on Christmas Eve, 1990. Never mind the failure to communicate that characterized the relationship between Bevan and his task force and the Toronto police, there was no effective communication between Inspector Bevan's Green Ribbon Task Force and his own employer, the Niagara Regional Police Service either. In spite of the fact that Bevan worked for Niagara as did two dozen of the forty-odd handpicked senior investigators who stuck symbolic Green Ribbon pins on their labels, his task force was not "in touch" with his own, local police service. It was as though the head was severed from the body or there was a complete synaptic breakdown. No electronic sparks jumped cell-to-cell. No one connected any of the dots.

Even though the Toronto rapes had mysteriously stopped after 1990, and Inspector Bevan's detectives discovered during their interview with Paul Bernardo that he was unemployed and did not have an alibi (except for his wife), for the weekend Kristen French disappeared, and that his name had mysteriously been run through CPIC seventeen times between 1990 and 1992, Bernardo did not drive a Camaro. Therefore, Inspector Bevan cleared Bernardo as a suspect and deleted his name from his suspect database.

In a newspaper article published in the *St. Catharines Standard*, on Saturday, February 6, 1993, two days before Bevan attended that precipitous meeting in Toronto, he even stated that "there is no clear evidence to suggest the two cases (the Mahaffy rape and murder and the French rape and murder)are linked."

In his will-state, Inspector Bevan confirms that the first inkling he had that the murders were linked and that Paul Bernardo was probably the man who had kidnaped, raped and murdered the young girls, came after Toronto Staff Superintendent Boothby told Inspector Bevan in that meeting that he should seriously consider Paul Bernardo as a suspect for "his murders."

Among the investigative techniques detectives are taught are "tricks and lies." In pursuit of a suspect, in the course of a criminal investigation, the police are allowed to play fast and loose with the truth, to practice tricks and tell lies for the sake of law and order. At its extreme, and it is done all the time, the police set up elaborate "undercover" sting operations as they pursue their quarry. Everyday, the police cross the line and become what they behold in order to solve a crime. Some policemen, once they have crossed that line, just never seem to be able to find their way back.

* * * * * * *

In that anteroom next to Chief Waddell's office, almost a year to the day after Inspector Bevan's meeting in Toronto, he went on to confide in me about events that never took place.

"When we were consulted about Bernardo and the DNA results we almost immediately became suspicious…" Arching his eyebrow, he went on to explain to me that it was not just the exhortations of Staff Superintendent Boothby that caused him to look very hard at Paul Bernardo but also "for a number of reasons, including evidence found at the scene of the abduction." Kristen French was abducted in broad daylight around 3 p.m., Thursday, April 16, 1992, from a church parking lot on Linwell Road while she was walking home from school.

Leaning forward conspiratorially, the Inspector lowered his voice, as though he were telling tales out of school, "A piece of a map of a very significant place…" He brushed aside my attempt to interrupt him. "A piece of a map was found at the scene of the abduction, with the hair and the shoe. As things unfolded in the parking lot, the hair was probably cut off accidently during the struggle."

These things – the piece of map, the hair and the shoe – were discovered the day after Kristen disappeared, on Saturday, April 15, 1992, a month before Inspector Bevan sent his detectives to interview Paul Bernardo in his Port Dalhousie home and two weeks before her body was discovered. The torn piece was from a map of Scarborough, Ontario (Paul Bernardo's home town); "the hair" referred to a lock of Kristen's hair which had been accidently cut off by the knife Paul Bernardo was wielding during her abduction), and "the shoe" was one of Kristen's maroon Bass loafers which had come off in the brief struggle to force her into the car; these clues had remained pieces of a jigsaw puzzle that Inspector Bevan, by his own sworn statement, never managed to put together.

More curious still, Inspector Bevan was relaying all these nonsequiturs and rhetorical subterfuges eight months after the grim details of Karla's participation in the crimes had been read into evidence during her perfunctory, plea-bargained trial on July 6, 1993.

He was, in a veiled, secretive way, talking to me about selective details, as though they were a holy grail, to do with that period of time between the discovery of Kristen French's body on April 30, 1992 and 11:30 p.m. on February 11, 1993, when he sent two of his detectives to lawyer George Walker's home to tell Walker that he would do whatever deal was necessary with his new client, Karla Homolka, in return for her testimony against her husband, Paul Bernardo.

The Toronto police had three DNA matches that strongly suggested that Paul Bernardo was the Scarborough rapist and they could have arrested him on the strength of those preliminary forensic results any time they wished. At that Monday morning meeting, they had assured Inspector Bevan they would hold off and give him a couple of days to get his ducks in a row. What ducks? As it stood, Inspector Bevan could not write his own search warrant because he did not have one shred of evidence upon which to base its composition. And, if he could not write a search warrant, he certainly would not be in a position to arrest Paul Bernardo for murder, or anything else. Further, it was perfectly clear to the Inspector that some time, in the very near future, he would have to stand there, impotent and apologetic, while the Toronto police popped Bernardo for the Scarborough rapes and merrily took him out of the jurisdiction to be arraigned in Toronto. A complicated prosecution such as the Scarborough rapes prosecution promised to be, could take years. And what of Inspector Bevan and his murders? Given all the givens, that the Inspector might have seen in such a scenario the end of his stellar career, or at least its severe retardation, is perfectly understandable. In hindsight's twenty-twenty, little wonder then that he sent his detectives to George Walker's doorstep in the middle of the night on February 11, 1993, singing Karla's redemption song.

In response to a comment I made about the apparent animosity between his task force, the Niagara Region and Metropolitan Toronto police forces he said, "You have only gotten six or seven feet below the surface of the iceberg… The nature of the relationship between the Toronto police and Niagara region and the dynamics of the circumstances surrounding his [Bernardo's] arrest bear a great deal of explanation… Metro and Niagara were both preparing very detailed search warrants so that we could arrest him jointly – that was the plan but I grant you the deal [with Karla] is a good topic for discussion."

HELL HATH NO FURY

Toronto police Detective Mary Lee Metcalfe returned to work on Monday, February 8, 1993, after a week's holiday, to discover all hell had broken loose. On February 1, a scientist at the Forensic Center had linked Paul Bernardo through partial DNA matches to three of the Scarborough rape victims. The Scarborough rapes were a particularly egregious string of violent attacks that began shortly after Paul met Karla in 1987 and continued unabated until late 1990 when he moved in with her family in St. Catharines. Although Detective Metcalfe worked for the Metropolitan Toronto Police sex assault squad with her long-time partner Ron Whitefield, they had not previously been involved. The case had been in the hands of another detective on the squad, Steve Irwin. The assaults had abruptly stopped in 1990 and the case went cold.

Serial rapists were relatively rare beasts in the criminal landscape. Anyone with any experience in the field knew that there were only three possibilities why a serial rapist suddenly stopped. Either they were dead, in jail for other crimes, or had moved out of the jurisdiction. Obviously, in this case, it was the latter.

Sitting in the conference room on the third floor of the Toronto police headquarters on College Street first thing that morning, Detective Metcalfe familiarized herself with the investigative reports. Her colleagues had put Bernardo under twenty-four-hour surveillance on February 3. The files showed that Bernardo had been charged with assaulting his wife – with a weapon – on January 5, 1993. Her name was Karla Bernardo, nee Homolka and she had been hospitalized as a result of the beating. There were pictures of her taken at the St. Catharines General Hospital on January 6. He had hit her so hard on the back of the head with a steel flashlight that severe bruising welled up around her eyes. The emergency room doctor's report said, "On examination today, Karla is in distress, quite anxious and understandably so. Her eyes reveal racoon's eyes, bruising all around the orbits, large contusion to her head and what feels almost like a depressed fracture, although x-rays have ruled this out. She has a subconjunctival hemorrhage in the left eye, which was seen by Dr. Marriott, and she was reassured. She has several bruises down the left side of her neck, along her arms, with a very large bruise on the upper right arm which is about three centimeters by three. About 75% of her legs from mid-thigh down are bruised, quite dramatically and swollen to touch. She cannot move them due to pain. On the right thigh, about 3 cm. above the right knee, there is a puncture wound which she says was caused by Paul Bernardo when he punctured her leg with a screwdriver. On the left leg, there is a large isolated contusion about 6 inches by 3 inches, quite warm and tender."

There was a picture of Karla with the "racoon eyes" in the file. It was startling. Racoon eyes were caused by a "*contra coup*," which refers to a blow of substantial force delivered to the rear of the head causing the brain to collide with the front of the skull, which in turn precipitates bleeding into the tissue around the eyes.

When released from hospital on January 7, Karla had moved in with her aunt and uncle in Brampton, Ontario. Detective Whitefield had interviewed the Homolka family on February 3, but for some reason Karla put him off. Detective Metcalfe discovered that she and Ron would be interviewing Karla the following evening, with their immediate supervisor, Detective Sergeant Bruce Smollett, at the apartment in Brampton.

At 9:35 a.m., Detective Metcalfe was interrupted and called into a meeting by Detective Sergeant Smollet. Among others, that meeting included Detective Steve Irwin and the Crown prosecutor from

Scarborough, Mary Hall. At its conclusion, she and Detective Whitefield were introduced to Inspector Vince Bevan and instructed to fully cooperate with him.

For the past two years, Inspector Bevan had been in charge of a fruitless investigation into the kidnaping, rape and murder of two teenage schoolgirls in the Niagara region. Detective Metcalfe learned that he had been invited to a meeting with the Toronto brass which had taken place upstairs coincident to the meeting Mary Lee Metcalfe had attended downstairs. As she noted in her will-state, Inspector Bevan was already aware that they were going to interview Karla Bernardo the following evening.

* * * * * * *

Karla did not want any part of any police action against her now-estranged husband. He was crazy. If he thought she was helping the police, he would implicate her. Besides, she was busy getting on with her life and starting to have a really good time.

Detective Whitefield had first tried to find Karla on February 2. Even though she was at her mother's house in St. Catharines when he called, Karla's mother and sister told him that they did not know exactly where she was and that they would get a message to her. When Karla finally responded to the messages on Thursday, February 4th, she said that it would be impossible for her to talk to him any earlier than the next Tuesday evening, February 9th. She had commitments Friday afternoon and evening which could not be broken.

Her aunt and uncle were having company over the weekend and she wanted them to be present during the interview, so the weekend was out. She had appointments with her divorce lawyer and her doctor in St. Catharines on the Monday. That's why Tuesday evening was the earliest possible time. Detective Whitefield agreed that they would come to Brampton on Tuesday, February 9, at 7:30 p.m.

That Karla had put off meeting with the Toronto detectives until Inspector Bevan was called to Toronto would be one of those "strange things" that happened to Karla "all the time." It not only changed her life – immensely for the better – it also changed Inspector Bevan's.

* * * * * * *

While Detective Metcalfe was being brought up to speed in her meeting downstairs, Inspector Bevan had been upstairs with Deputy Chief Chuck Maywood, Staff Superintendent David Boothby, Staff Inspector Steve Marrier, and Inspector Bob Strathdee.

Although he does not exactly say so in his will-atate, its tone and descriptions allow one to easily imagine that Inspector Bevan emerged from that meeting feeling somewhat ambivalent and conflicted.

In spite of numerous previous discussions with Steve Irwin and others aware of the nature of the Scarborough rapes and that Paul Bernardo was a prime suspect, he finally learned about Bernardo's *modus operandi* and the fact that all of his rape victims reported that he used a knife to threaten them.

He did not share with this august body of senior police officers that he had already interviewed, and cleared, Paul Bernardo in May, 1992. Neither did he mention the unsolved Henley Island rape case which had exactly the same *modus operandi* as the many Scarborough rapes. He would share that information soon, but not just yet.

Bevan must have felt like a deer caught in the headlights. He was swirling in what appeared to be, on the surface at least, a hopeless maelstrom of his own incompetence. As it was, his obsession with the Camaro, an obsession which had blinded him to the obvious, and his failure to assimilate the few clues he had – the piece of map, the shoe and the shorn hair and correlate them with the stalking reports that had clearly identified Bernardo as some kind of roving pervert – was destined to become a matter of public disgrace.

It was all well and good for Staff Superintendent Boothby to tell Inspector Bevan to have a hard look at Paul Bernardo. The fact was, he had absolutely no evidence, circumstantial or otherwise, to link Paul Bernardo with the sex slayings of Leslie Mahaffy or Kristen French. The tiny fragment of a map, the lock of Kristen's hair and her Bass loafer were not evidence that would support anything. In fact, they were not evidence at all. They were *clues* that he had not been able to decode.

To Bevan, Boothby's advice was worthless. His opinion had no probative value. Without some reasonable and probable grounds, without some hard evidence, Inspector Bevan could not write a search warrant for Bernardo's house, let alone arrest the guy for murder. And it did not go unnoticed by Inspector Bevan that Staff Superintendent Boothby, and the powers-that-be at the Toronto police headquarters, did not feel sufficiently motivated to have called him and shared the positive DNA matches before they put Bernardo under twenty-four-hour surveillance. Inspector Bevan was no Sherlock Holmes, but he was relatively intelligent and politically savvy. He could tell when he was being disrespected.

To make matters worse, it was also made abundantly clear that the Toronto police were preparing to arrest Bernardo on a moment's notice, as soon as their search warrant was ready. After all, they had been watching him for ten days and seen enough to realize that he represented a clear and present danger. They had real evidence; the best kind – DNA. They were in a position to arrest him, whether or not it suited Inspector Bevan. During the meeting, they agreed to give Inspector Bevan a few days in which to get his ducks in a row. But what good would a few days do? How was he going to make something out of nothing?

And then he was told about the Toronto detectives and their forthcoming interview with Paul Bernardo's estranged wife, Karla Homolka. Inspector Bevan was not invited to participate in the interview but they were instructed to cooperate with him and he was allowed to confer with them. It was at this moment the worm turned.

Detective Whitefield had reassured Karla and her mother that it was not Karla but her estranged husband they were after. As he had told Karla's family, the police always interview the women close to a rape suspect. It was always from the women – the mothers, daughters, wive, lovers – that the police got the most definitive chronologies and sense of a suspect's perverse behavior and sexual preferences.

* * * * * * *

If Inspector Bevan was off-balance he did not let on to Metcalfe, Whitefield and Smollett. He treated them just as he would his own rank and file. He told them what he wanted and what they were to do – in no uncertain terms. Detective Metcalfe's will-state documents Inspector Bevan's instructions:

"At this time, Inspector Bevan made specific requests of this (forth-coming)interview (with Karla):

- to obtain elimination fingerprints from Karla Homolka. Ms. Homolka's fingerprints to be compared to any findings on a piece of map located at the abduction scene (Kristen French).
- the nature of any physical beatings received by Karla Homolka.
- the nature of sexual relations and any propensities during the marriage of Karla and Paul Bernardo.
- the nature of any changes of physical appearance of Paul Bernardo.
- activities of couple during time periods of June 15-29,1991; and the time period of April 16-30,1992.
- the description of any jewelery worn by either Paul or Karla Homolka. Specifically, Karla Homolka was photographed by Niagara Regional Police, following Paul Bernardo's arrest for domestic assault, wearing a Mickey Mouse wristwatch. We were advised that Kristen French was wearing a similar watch at the time of her abduction and the watch was never recovered."

It continues: "At approximately 11:20 a.m., I attended the afore-mentioned conference room for an additional meeting. Present at this time were:

– Detective Sergeant Smollet
– Detective Ron Whitefield
– Inspector Vince Bevan, Green Ribbon Task Force
– Detective Sergeant Robert Waller, Green Ribbon Task Force
– Staff Sergeant Murray Macleod, Green Ribbon Task Force
– *There were discussions regarding the proposed interview of Karla Homolka and reiteration of Inspector Bevan's requests for informa-tion (jewelery worn by Paul Bernardo; elimination fingerprints of Karla Homolka; the Mickey Mouse wristwatch)"*

* * * * * * *

Karla was so sure of herself that she did not even seek advice from her recently retained divorce lawyer, Virginia Workman, or anyone else for that matter, about her imminent police interview.

She felt no threat. Their interest was in Paul and the Scarborough rapes. These police were from Toronto, not St. Catharines or the Niagara Peninsula. It only made sense.

And Karla had no intention of blowing any whistle. What was done was done. After all, she could not bring back the dead. As she noted in her "diary," all she really wanted to do then was "get on with her life," have some fun and get her stuff back. She wanted her "hope chest, champagne glasses" and everything else that was rightfully hers!

Even on the day of the interview, Karla considered delaying the interview again but her curiosity was peaked. Karla knew they had some good stuff on Bernardo. Her mother and her sister Lori had been interviewed the previous week and discussed with her what they had been asked.

The interview started at 7:30 p.m. with a discussion about her wifely status.

"Former wife," Karla quickly pointed out.

If only Karla had submitted to the interview when they had first asked, then they would never have asked the question, the one question that changed everything, and then everything that happened next would never have happened and she would have been left alone and could have just gotten on with a new life. At least, that was her fantasy.

Det. Metcalfe:	Okay, what about watches, did he ever buy...
Karla	Oh yeah, he bought me a watch; that's right, an Alfred Sung watch with a leather strap. That was for my birthday, or no, that was for Christmas. I think that was Christmas 1990, maybe. I can't remember (sniffs)
Det. Metcalfe:	Okay. We got some photographs?
Karla	Yes.
Det. Metcalfe:	Of when you were injured.
Karla	*Oh, you did get those?*
Det. Metcalfe:	Yeah.
Karla	Okay.
Det. Metcalfe:	You're wearing a watch in those photographs...
Karla	*The ones that the police took?*
Det. Metcalfe:	Yeah.
Karla	*Oh. Okay okay, that's, that's a Mickey Mouse watch?*
Det. Metcalfe:	Yeah.
Karla	That's my sister's.
Det. Metcalfe:	Your sister's watch?
Karla	Yeah, I switched watches with her because I didn't want any of his jewellery on so I gave her the Alfred Sung watch and she gave me her Mickey Mouse watch.

Det. Metcalfe:	Okay, when did you do the switch?
Karla	In the hospital. So, so it was after January 4th.
Det. Metcalfe:	Who would have given your sister the…
Karla	The Mickey Mouse watch? I couldn't tell you, huh, um, my parents or she bought it or off her boyfriend, I really don't know.
Det. Metcalfe:	When did you first see…
Karla	The Mickey Mouse watch? I don't know. We just, never really noticed her getting it…
Det. Metcalfe:	Okay.
Karla	I don't know.
Det. Metcalfe:	Have you got it with you now?
Karla	Yeah, do you want to see it?

The fact that Detective Metcalfe, a Toronto policewoman, had the pictures of Karla taken in the St. Catharines hospital the night after Paul had beaten her up, and was now asking questions about the Mickey Mouse watch Karla had been wearing that night told Karla that a connection had been made between the Scarborough rapes and the murders in which she had direct involvement. Kristen French had been wearing a Mickey Mouse watch the day Paul and Karla had abducted her and Karla had kept it after they killed her.

The question about the watch came up more than two hours into the interview and it took Karla's breath away. She had not had an asthma attack since she was a little girl but suddenly she could not get her breath and started to get that terrible panicky feeling.

To Karla the Mickey Mouse watch question meant that these cops from Toronto had somehow connected the dots and were, contrary to what they said, after her as well. All this business about Paul this and Paul that and what he was like then and how were his hands, opened or closed, when he hit her, did he like anal intercourse, suddenly, at the moment the words "Mickey Mouse watch" came out of Detective Metcalfe's mouth, Karla just *knew* it was all a ruse to put her at ease and pull her guard down.

The fact that these detectives had somehow noticed the barely discernable Mickey Mouse watch in those Polaroids, taken specifically to document how badly Karla had been beaten by Paul, said it all. Suddenly, just when the interview was winding up, the sky fell in. It was at this moment, a moment unbeknownst to Karla constructed by Inspector Bevan, that Karla knew that she, too, was in very, very deep trouble.

Detective Metcalfe noticed the sudden change in Karla's demeanor. *"This request seemed to initially upset Ms. Homolka; her explanation for the upset was that it was her only watch and was a borrowed item from her sister, Lori Homolka. Detective Whitefield took possession of this watch and departed the premises to obtain an official property receipt."*

The color drained from Karla's face and, for the first time since the interview began, Karla started to stammer and moisture beaded on her upper lip.

It is also recorded in Detective Metcalfe's will-state that Karla then asked a curious question. She wanted to know how much time someone might get for crimes like the ones the detectives were investigating.

The detective also noticed that the request for Karla's fingerprints discombobulated her. *"Karla Homolka was inquisitive regarding where and why her fingerprints would be compared. I advised her that I could not discuss the piece of evidence. She appeared satisfied with this explanation."*

Far from being satisfied, Karla was almost hysterical which speaks eloquently about her thespian talents. She was somehow able to regain her composure so quickly that in her will-state Detective Metcalfe put the sudden change in Karla's deportment – her shortness of breath, the sweat beads on her upper lip and her agitated responses – down to nerves and the strain of being interviewed and fingerprinted for the first time.

Although terrified, she had not taken leave of her senses. Karla had a strange, uncanny capacity to distance herself from the immediate moment – to step outside herself, as it were, and objectively regard any predicament in which she found herself from a distance. Realizing that the detective had noticed the sudden change in her comportment and that the interview may well be far from over, she did her little mental trick.

* * * * * * *

In fact, Detectives Metcalfe, Whitefield and Smollett were focused on Paul Bernardo and the Scarborough rapes. The murders in St. Catharines were out of their jurisdiction and not really their concern. It was Paul Bernardo's DNA that had been matched to three rape victims, not Karla's. What were the odds that this diminutive, little girl was a rapist and a killer too? The thought never occurred to them.

The dramatic change in Karla should have triggered alarm bells but it didn't. Right after the exchange about the watch, Detective Metcalfe moved from the profound to the banal. Referring to the Niagara Police report made the night she was taken to the hospital, Detective Metcalfe suggested to Karla that Paul Bernardo had, on occasion, made her bark like a dog. Karla expressed surprise that such a thing was in the police report from that night in January when she had been hospitalized and he had been charged.

"That must have been something my sister said because I was asleep on Christmas Eve and I don't remember this. My sister told me that I was sleeping and he woke me up and said, 'Karla, bark.' And I guess I did but I don't really remember that."

Detective Metcalfe asked if she had taken it as a kind of joke and Karla chuckled and said, "Yeah, I took it as a joke."

Toward the end of the interview Detective Sergeant Smollett, who had left most of the questioning to Detectives Metcalfe and Whitefield, asked Karla if she had any response to the fact that the police were investigating Paul Bernardo for a violent sexual assault. Karla said, "Nothing shocks me, I knew you were coming." All three detectives noted that remark in their will-states.

The detectives had arrived at 7:30 p.m. They left almost five hours later around midnight. Karla's aunt and uncle knew as soon as the apartment door closed behind them that something was drastically wrong. Karla was white and shaken. She sat across from them and it just poured out. She told them that she had been there and watched while Paul repeatedly sexually assaulted and murdered Leslie Mahaffy and Kristen French. She told them that he had made her participate and help him. Her aunt told Karla that she had to call a lawyer.

* * * * * * *

First thing in the morning, Karla called Laurie Walker in Niagara Falls. Laurie was an attractive blonde and like Karla, petite and fun-loving. Laurie liked Karla. She also happened to be married to the most prominent criminal lawyer in the Niagara Region, George Walker. Karla knew George and Laurie through the Martindale vet clinic where Karla worked and the Walkers brought their dogs. The Walkers also perceived Karla to have treated George's dead Dalmatian Kelly kindly. Walker was so enamoured of Kelly that he had the dog cremated and kept her ashes on his mantle piece.

Karla told Laurie that she had to see George about a "domestic matter." She said it was very important. Although Walker had restricted his practice to the defense of murderers and drug dealers, for Karla, he made an exception. Laurie arranged for her to see George at 3 p.m. the following day, Thursday, February 11, 1993.

Strangely, or perhaps in an attempt to try and stay close to Karla, before they left the previous night, Detective Metcalfe had offered to drive Karla any place that she might need to go. On Thursday morning, Karla took her up on the offer.

COMPLIANT VICTIM

At 9 a.m. on February 11, 1993, an otherwise unassuming tall, gray-haired man arrived at Toronto International Airport. One of the very few Canadians trained as a "profiler" by the FBI Behavioral Sciences Unit at Quantico, Ottawa-based RCMP Inspector Ron MacKay was a frequent consultant to the Metropolitan Toronto Police. As he records in his will-state, he flew into Toronto that morning to "attend a joint meeting of the sexual assault squad and Green Ribbon Task Force members." MacKay made a note to himself to involve Dr. Peter Collins, a forensic psychiatrist from the Clarke Institute in Toronto with whom he frequently worked. Inspector MacKay called Dr. Collins and asked him to bring his copy of "Compliant Victims of the Sexual Sadist" to the meeting.

The sexual sadist was a relatively new figure in the ever-expanding lexicon of criminology. The lower the crime rate plunged, the more dramatic the creative explanation for deviant criminal behavior seemed to become.

As he is known in law enforcement circles, the sexual sadist was a concoction of FBI Supervisory Special Agent Roy Hazelwood, legendary California psychiatrist Park Dietz, and a psychiatric nurse named Janet Warren. In 1990, the trio introduced this very scary character in an article entitled "The Sexually Sadistic Criminal and His Offences" published in the *Bulletin of the American Academy of Psychiatric Law*.

Between 1990 and 1993, the same team published numerous articles and abstracts extrapolating his characteristics and features, culminating with "Compliant Victims of the Sexual Sadist" which was scheduled to be published that spring in *The Australian Family Physician*.

Between the airport and the police station, Inspector MaKkay tracked down Roy Hazelwood to check on the article's status and make sure they had permission to use it.

Explaining criminal behavior and trying to profile unknown killers had become a multi-billion dollar industry. Roy Hazelwood's immediate predecessor, John Douglas, the figure upon whom Jonathan Demme based Clarice Starling's boss, FBI profiler Jack Crawford, in *The Silence of the Lambs*, was making millions of dollars promulgating and pontificating about profiling and characters like the sexual sadist on the law enforcement lecture circuit.

As Hazelwood put it to me, in reference to his imminent retirement from the FBI, "now I can get on with it and make some real money."

According to "Compliant Victims of the Sexual Sadist" Supervisory Special Agent Hazelwood had identified and interviewed seven women who were "compliant victims," although neither they nor the crimes in which they were involved were identified or described.

After recapping the definition of a sexual sadist, the article goes on to document a panoply of abuse levied by sadists on their female partners: "All the women were sexually abused by the men. Three victims were forcibly penetrated by large foreign objects. One subject used a 12-cell flashlight and also a long cylindrical piece of wood. Almost invariably these items were inserted anally, so as to cause maximum suffering.

"Six of the women reported anal intercourse to be their sadistic partner's preferred mode of sexual release. Forced fellatio was also reported by all seven women, and these same women reported that the sadists enjoyed ejaculating on their bodies, primarily on their face or mouth...

"Three of the women were forced to have sex with others; two were raped by friends of the sadists, and one was forced to engage in sexual acts with another woman who had been kidnapped by her husband."

The article concludes: "This intermeshing of attachment of perversion raises interesting questions about criminal responsibility. As indicated, several of the women eventfully became co-conspirators with the sadists in serious criminal activities. The past decade has seen the 'battered woman syndrome' being recognized as evidence supporting the claim of self-defense when the abused woman kills her abuser. From a somewhat different perspective, kidnapped American heiress Patty Hearst argued that she had been brainwashed by her captors and was thus not fully responsible for her behavior in support of their crimes. While the former addresses the issue of guilt or innocence and the latter the issue of diminished capacity, neither suggests that the impairment the abused or 'brainwashed' woman experiences is significant enough to warrant a finding of legal insanity under either the McNaughten or Model Penal Code Standard…

"In the current sample, the wife of a sexual sadist who became involved in the kidnapping and murder of victims acquired for her husband, was convicted on a guilty plea and is now serving a substantial prison sentence. Although her criminal behavior began and was perpetrated exclusively within the context of her relationship with her husband, she entered a guilty plea in exchange for a shorter sentence than she might otherwise have incurred." This unlikely and highly speculative, unscientific article was to become the blueprint for delivering Karla's future.

* * * * * * *

Although February 11, 1993, was a very busy and important day for Inspector Bevan, perhaps the most important day in his twenty-year career, there are no entries for that day in his will-state. To read Inspector Bevan's will-state with its lengthy entries for February 9, 10, and 12, one could be forgiven for thinking that he had called in sick or taken the February 11th off.

According to Inspector Bevan's will-state, absolutely nothing worthy of note to do with his involvement in the Bernardo case happened on that day.

To fully understand what happened, and how helpful it was to both Karla and Inspector Bevan, one has to turn to other officers' will-states, including those of RCMP Inspector MacKay, Toronto sexual assault squad Detectives Metcalfe, Whitefield, Smollett and Marrier as well as those by Sergeants Mike Riddle, Bob Waller, Bob Gillies and Constable Michael Matthews from Bevan's own task force.

Documented in the will-states of Metcalfe, Whitefield, Smollet and Marrier is the fact that Inspector Bevan had been fully debriefed about the four-and-a-half-hour interview conducted with Karla on Tuesday evening, February 9, 1993.

From what he heard and saw in their notes, Bevan was of the opinion that Karla was lying to police and knew a hell of a lot more than she let on. The Mickey Mouse watch thing was just too coincidental. There is no record about whether or not he shared his sentiments, which means it is likely he did not.

The fact that Karla was lying to the police from Toronto was confirmed for Inspector Bevan when he learned from Staff Sergeant Bruce Smollett early in that afternoon that Karla was being driven by Detectives Metcalfe and Whitefield to the Niagara Falls law offices of a man very well known to Inspector Bevan, renowned criminal defense attorney George Walker. After all, it could not just be a matter of chance that Karla suddenly decided to scurry off and consult the most prominent criminal lawyer in the Niagara Region a day after she was interviewed by police. To an experienced police officer like Inspector Bevan, Karla's action spoke eloquently about "consciousness of guilt."

* * * * * * *

"On Thursday, February 11, 1993, I attended the sexual assault squad of the Metropolitan Toronto Police force, along with Inspector Bevan…" Sergeant Mike Riddle recorded in his will-state. "We arrived at the sexual assault squad about 11:00 a.m. We met with Staff Sergeant Bruce Smollett, Detective Steve Irwin and other members… Inspector Ron MacKay of the Royal Canadian Mounted Police was also there, and provided information regarding the profiles of the offenders."

For Inspector Bevan, "Compliant Victims of the Sexual Sadist" was a godsend. It explained Karla's criminal behavior as that of a woman under a spell, beaten into submission by a sexual sadist, not entirely responsible for her own actions, and therefore as much a victim as an accomplice. This article not only provided an elaborate explanation but also a rationale for Karla Homolka and her criminal behavior. There had been others, Karla was not unique, and she was powerless to resist the Rasputin-like will of her sexual sadist. He immediately hit on it the way he had that old, cream-colored Camaro.

This was hardly surprising. With his question about the Mickey Mouse watch he had flushed his bird of paradise out of the bush. If Karla was the key to reconstituting his botched investigation and salvaging his career, the article was the key to her behavior – "Compliant Victims of the Sexual Sadist" was Karla's ornithology and the rationale for what would arguably become the most important relationship with a member of the opposite sex in Inspector Bevan's life. It was also the catalyst which would allow him to wrestle control of the ongoing investigation away from the Metropolitan Toronto Police. All one had to do was look at the photographs taken of Karla in the hospital on January 6 to see that she had been battered. Her husband was clearly a violent, serial rapist and a sexual sadist. No one could argue with that.

That this concept of Karla as "compliant victim" was then allowed to spread throughout his task force, with the same virulence as the earlier, erroneous concept of a cream-colored Camaro, was implicit in remarks that one Sergeant Riddle made a few days later while preparing to interview Norma Tellier.[1]

Norma was another local St. Catharines' teenager whom Karla had entrapped as a sex toy for her sadistic husband in late 1992. Sergeant Riddle opened the interview by telling Ms. Tellier that "... nothing will surprise us; we have studied greatly compliant victims as far as people who are abused and Karla is an abused wife; that man, I don't know what your feelings of him are at this time, has magical powers of some sort over individuals. We know that Karla has lived a living hell for quite some time and would not be surprised at anything she did under the powers of Paul Bernardo..."

* * * * * * *

Inspector Bevan states for the record that he first became aware that "counsel for Karla Bernardo, Paul Bernardo's estranged wife, wished to speak to a Crown attorney about his client" on Friday, February 12, 1993.

According to Staff Sergeant Smollett, Inspector Bevan was made aware of this fact much earlier. In his will-state, Smollett documents a telephone call he had with Karla's Toronto police chauffeurs at 5:50 p.m. on February 11, 1993.

Detective Whitefield informed Smollett that he and his partner, Mary Lee Metcalfe, had driven Karla to George Walker's law offices, that Karla's meeting with Walker had taken about an hour and a quarter, and that when Karla came out she no longer wanted to talk to them and did not talk all the way back to Brampton.

Whitefield told Smollett that Walker said he was going to speak with a Crown attorney. Detective Smollett notes that, at his invitation, Inspector Vince Bevan "sat in" on this call.

1. Norma Tellier is a pseudonym. Ms. Tellier's identity is protected by court order.

Staff Sergeant Smollett goes on to say that he also advised the senior prosecutor from Scarborough, Mary Hall, about Karla Homolka and George Walker and told her what Walker had said about going to a Crown attorney. During that evening, Ms. Hall placed numerous calls to both Walker's office and his residence, none of which were returned.

* * * * * * *

There was also something else that Inspector Bevan learned during the meetings with Metropolitan Toronto Police on February 11 that strongly affected his thinking and his subsequent actions. Again, from Sergeant Riddle: "There was discussion about the evidence that the sexual assault squad had against Bernardo, regarding DNA evidence and the fact that they (the Toronto police) were going to be executing a search warrant in the near future."

From Inspector Bevan's point of view, this was omnious. The Toronto police had the strongest possible evidence upon which to base their warrant. For all Inspector Bevan knew, they could be hours away from having it sworn and executed. In the meantime, he had absolutely nothing. If they arrested Bernardo and executed their search warrant, control of the investigation would be ceded to Toronto. In that scenario, Paul Bernardo would be taken into custody and moved to Scarborough to stand trial for the Scarborough rapes and Inspector Bevan would simply have to stand down and, like most of his colleagues, quietly wait for retirement.

* * * * * * *

Sergeant Bob Gillies and Constable Michael Matthews both say in their will-states that they attended a Green Ribbon Task Force "team meeting" led by Inspector Bevan on February 11 around 10 p.m.

Acting on instructions from Inspector Bevan, Sergeant Gillies noted that he called George Walker at 11 p.m. and arrived on his doorstep at 11:25 p.m.

"I explained to Mr. Walker that the police had an interest in his client's husband and if his client had any knowledge or could be of assistance, the Crown attorney in all likelihood would be willing to negotiate for her cooperation. At 11:45 p.m., Constable Matthews and I left the Walker residence and met with Inspector Bevan…"

Constable Matthews' record confirms Sergeant Gillies' record of these events. While both officers' entries reflect that Walker told them that he would speak with a Crown attorney the following morning, what they do not say is that Walker also told them that he had been dodging calls all evening from Toronto prosecutor Mary Hall and that he had no intention of returning them. It was his intention, he said, to speak with the local prosecutor, Ray Houlahan, first thing in the morning. Walker believed that people from the region should stick together. The crimes with which his client was involved were committed in St. Catharines and they should be resolved in St. Catharines. George Walker was an old stick-in-the-mud that way. And Inspector Bevan was very pleased to have what he suspected about George Walker's attitude confirmed.

Inspector Bevan worked out of an office in the Green Ribbon Task Force headquarters in Beamsville, a small town north of St. Catharines, about a thirty-minute drive from downtown Niagara Falls. However, on this particularly evening, he had arranged to meet his detectives at the Niagara Regional Police Niagara Falls' headquarters a few blocks up the street from George Walker's house. He wanted to hear Walker's reaction right away, first hand.

* * * * * * *

That late night visit from Inspector Bevan's emissaries told George Walker everything he needed to know and guaranteed Karla a future.

Walker had been shocked by what he heard from Karla that afternoon. Within a short hour and a quarter, he heard things about Karla's
involvement in the rape and murder of her younger sister, Leslie
Mahaffy and Kristen French, things that would cause Gilles de Rais to
spin in his grave. But he was not so shocked that he failed to take stock
of the situation.

Karla had been driven to his office by two Toronto detectives who
were investigating her estranged husband as a serial rapist. As Karla
said to him, since Paul Bernardo was the Scarborough rapist, she had
always wondered why it had taken them so long.

To Walker's amazement, after they had interviewed her on Tuesday
evening, they offered to chauffeur Karla where ever she might want to
go and she had actually taken them up on it! Either she was very, very
smart, or incredibly stupid. He soon came to believe it was the former.

The moment Walker heard Karla's story the "Battered Woman"
defense popped into his head – and out just as quickly. He knew that if
he had to defend her in an open court against the many charges that
could be laid against her, including kidnaping, aggravated sexual
assault, the administration of a stupefying substance, at least two
counts of first-degree murder, he would lose and she would go to
prison for the rest of her natural life.

Although it was true Paul Bernardo had battered her and she had
been abused, it would not work as a defense with crimes as deliberate
and heinous as the ones she and her husband committed. The
"Battered Woman" defense seldom worked in cases where the woman
lashed out and killed her abusive partner. It would never work with a
woman who, after participating in the kidnaping, confinement and
rape of teenage strangers, also participated in murdering them.

But it would work perfectly for Inspector Bevan's purposes, and
that is what Inspector Bevan told George Walker by sending his detectives to his doorstep. After thirty years practicing criminal law, Walker
knew how the police worked. He, more than most, understood the ter-
ritorial imperatives that characterized the relationships between police
forces.

Cops do not routinely pay midnight visits, hat-in-hand, to criminal defense lawyers. It confirmed what Walker had surmised; that the Toronto police were very close to arresting Paul Bernardo and they did not need his client to do it. If they were after her, or had anything on her, they would have arrested her already.

The visit told Walker that Inspector Bevan needed Karla badly and needed to become her new best friend quickly. The Ministry of the Attorney General had funneled countless millions of dollars into Inspector Bevan's high-profile task force and as late as the past weekend's local paper, the Inspector publicly said he had no concrete leads and did not believe the murders of Mahaffy and French were linked. As soon as Inspector Bevan sent the two detectives to tell Walker they would do whatever deal necessary to get his client's cooperation, the Inspector may as well have sent Walker a handwritten note saying, "I'm desperate, please help me, neighbor."

Where Inspector Bevan went, his masters at the Ministry were sure to follow. This case was like one of those brown paper bags full of excrement kids used to plant on people's doorsteps at Halloween. Lighting the bag on fire, the little bastards would knock on the door and then run away. The unsuspecting dupe opened the door and instinctively started to try and stamp out the fire, covering their shoes and pants cuffs with shit in the process.

Talking to Karla that afternoon, Walker felt something like he had that day when he sat in a Toronto courtroom in 1985 and watched helplessly as his adopted son, Robin Sloan Walker, then seventeen, was convicted of second-degree murder and sent to prison for life; a kind of numbing, total, stunned incredulity. From that day forward he stopped trying to reconcile what he saw with what he heard.

It had been a hot July day in 1983 in Niagara Falls. Robin Sloan Walker and Janet Zeiter had just met that morning and spent the day drinking beer, smoking a little hash – nothing heavy – just having a good time. Janet was eighteen, blond and beautiful. Robin was sixteen. Even though Janet had thwarted his advances, Robin insisted on walking her home. They cut through Greendale Public School on their way to her house on Dorchester. Robin knocked Janet down. Then he strangled and raped her.

Although troubled, there had been no previous indication that Robin was capable of such a heinous crime. He was a relatively normal teenager. The Walkers – George's first wife, Pamela, and George – were having problems, but otherwise they thought everything was fine.

Robin left Janet's nude body in the ornamental bushes at the front of the school and went back to his friend Chris Boyd's house where he spent the night. The Boyds' house buttressed the schoolyard. The next morning Robin and Chris watched from Chris's bedroom window while an old caretaker showed Janet's body to the police.

At Robin's trial there had been considerable argument about whether or not Janet was raped before or after Robin killed her.

The most difficult part of the trial for George had been watching the police-made videotape re-enactment of the crime in which Robin had played himself.

Since he was allowed time served before and during the trial, Robin was just about to be paroled when Karla walked in and told George a story far more diabolical than his son's; a tale of such nightmarish, unimaginable degradation, sex, murder, lies and videotape as to defy even the most febrile, deviant imagination. What Karla readily admitted she had done and witnessed made young Robin's crime look like youthful transgression.

There was a terrible cruelty in coincidence: because the Walkers took their dogs to a particular vet (and there were literally hundreds of options in the Niagara region where vets were as ubiquitous as doughnut shops) Walker became Karla's father confessor and her defender.

Paul Bernardo could not be allowed to leave the Niagara region without being arrested for the murders of Leslie Mahaffy and Kristen French, and now George Walker knew that the only way that was going to happen would be when a deal was struck with his newest client. This was going to be one of the easier plea bargains Walker ever did but he still went to bed that night thinking, "Won't they be surprised."

Sure, they knew Paul and Karla had killed Leslie and Kristen. But they had no idea about the sister and that was really ugly and could be a deal breaker – if they found out some other way than through George. He resolved to get the sister out on the table tomorrow, at the first opportunity.

* * * * * * *

In his will-state, Inspector Bevan states that he was an "experienced investigator." As such, did he know what he was doing when he gave Detectives Metcalfe, Whitefield and Smollet his list of questions? Did he know what he was doing when he insisted that they ask Karla about the Mickey Mouse watch? Did he know that Karla was malingering up there at her aunt and uncle's apartment in Brampton, with no intention of coming clean? Did he know she would bolt the moment she was asked about the watch? Did he imagine his reinvention in the nexus of all of the what-happened-nexts? Did he see his salvation immediately when he saw that copy of "Compliant Victims of the Sexual Sadist"? Or was it all just a matter of chance and blind luck?

One thing is certain: When he learned on February 11 that Karla indeed was on her way to George Walker's office, Inspector Bevan did not know anything about Karla Homolka or the exact nature of her role in the crimes or even the extent of the crimes themselves – he just knew that he had to have her.

DIVINE INTERVENTION

If one were to look at it from Inspector Bevan's perspective, Karla's fate could be described as an unfortunate by-product of Divine Intervention.

It was not unfortunate for her. It was not unfortunate for him but it was certainly unfortunate on the higher planes of Justice, Law and Order.

The deal made with Karla really had nothing to do with her and everything to do with him, which was the kind of syllogism that had so far defined Karla's short life. If Karla had not become the "compliant victim" Inspector Bevan needed her to be, then she really would have been crazy. Her future was handed to her on a platter. Is anyone really surprised that she took it?

After all, Karla not only looked and felt battered, she was battered. The doctor in the emergency ward at St. Catharines' General Hospital said that she had received the worst beating he had ever seen in a decade practicing medicine.

The only question was whether she was sufficiently battered to have been unable to discriminate between right and wrong and exercise free will, and that question, thanks to Inspector Bevan, was never going to be asked.

People started telling Karla she was an abused woman – the police who attended that night in the hospital, the hospital social worker, her mother and sister. Girlfriends and co-workers sent her literature about battered woman's syndrome (strictly speaking, it is called battered spousal syndrome (BSS). Her general practitioner confided in Karla about a period of her life during which she had been abused. Her divorce lawyer encouraged her to start a "diary of abuse" and write down everything she could remember that Paul had done to her. Karla's "diary of abuse" became a long, variegated list of slights, real and imagined. It expanded exponentially over the next three years with Karla's growing exposure to the lexicon of the Battered Woman.

Regardless, it was a fiction and George Walker quickly brought Karla back to reality. Were she to face the panoply of charges that could be brought against her – if for some unknown reason she were to look the gift horse in the mouth – the so-called "battered woman defense" simply would not work. Neither George Walker nor Karla nor anybody else was ever under any illusions about what would happen if those seminal questions about Karla's responsibility and free will were ever asked in front of a judge and jury.

Before he ever laid eyes on her, or knew anything about her crimes, Inspector Bevan, via Dr. Peter Collins and RCMP Inspector Ron MacKay, had defined Karla as the "compliant victim of a sexual sadist." That definition would stick because it was destined, primarily as a consequence of the Inspector's actions, never to be challenged in an courtroom.

At that moment in time neither Karla nor George Walker had any idea how Inspector Bevan defined her or just how far that definition would go toward limiting the administration of Justice. They did know that the Inspector was very eager and instinctively Walker knew that time was of the essence.

First thing in the morning on February 12, 1993, Mr. Walker went to prosecutor Ray Houlahan's office in the St. Catharines courthouse. Houlahan had already been apprised of the situation by Inspector Bevan and told Walker that negotiations of this magnitude were beyond his authority. He had already referred the matter to Murray Segal, the Director of the Criminal Division at the Ministry of the Attorney General's law office in Toronto.

George Walker and Murray Segal were already acquainted. They had met decades earlier when they both worked in the appellate courts in Toronto. Murray had become a well-respected jurist and George a successful criminal lawyer. They renewed their acquaintance on the telephone early that afternoon. Walker told Segal about his client's participation in the kidnaping, rapes and murders of Leslie Mahaffy and Kristen French. He also told him about the sister.

Tammy Lyn Homolka's death had been ruled accidental and forgotten. If Karla had not come clean, in all likelihood the authorities would never have known exactly what happened. Or they might have found out from a vengeful Paul Bernardo. It was very smart of Walker to share this sinister information. In exacerbated circumstances such as these, surprises were anathemas. Leading with this would prevent any future prosecution of Karla with regard to her sister's death while establishing an immediate good-faith basis for the negotiations. It showed that he and his client were coming to the table with nothing to hide.

Mr. Walker and Mr. Segal had a meeting of the minds right then and there. Karla would be charged with two counts of manslaughter for which she would receive an appropriate penalty. But, as far as Murray Segal was concerned, he was being forced to buy "a pig in a poke" and he wanted George Walker to know that.

Under the circumstances, what else could he do? It was the police who gathered evidence. If the police did not have any evidence, prosecutors cannot prosecute. This was a very high-profile case and the Ministry had spent millions of the taxpayers' dollars propping up Inspector Bevan's Green Ribbon Task Force. And what did Inspector Bevan bring him as evidence – a twenty-something, waifish blonde from St. Catharines. Karla was it, they had nothing else. The murder investigations, for a host of reasons, not the least of which were financial and political, took precedence over the lesser offences in Scarborough. Even though the offenses in Scarborough were serial, and they had some preliminary DNA matches with Paul Bernardo, no one had been murdered. All that was left to agree upon between Walker and Segal after that telephone conversation on February 12 was how much time Karla would do and where she would do it.

For years, I puzzled over Murray Segal's "pig in a poke" remark. When men in Murray Segal's and George Walker's position negotiate over something as potentially explosive and controversial as any deal with Karla Homolka promised to be, they do not keep detailed notes. They occasionally scribble things on scraps of paper and restaurant napkins. George Walker was so amused by Murray Segal's "pig in a poke" remark that he scribbled it down. He knew what it meant. It meant that Segal was dealing in the dark and didn't like it. He had no idea who or what Karla Homolka was. He had no idea, other than what his old courtroom confrere told him, about the scope of what she had done. It was not that he thought George was lying or withholding information, it was just that Walker was biased by definition, only privy to his client's side of the story. Segal had no idea why Karla did what she did nor did he have any real sense of her true culpability. Nor did he have any time to find out.

Inspector Bevan had committed the authorities to a deal when he sent his men to George Walker's doorstep in the middle of the previous night. All that was left for Segal to do was work out the details – how much time was she going to do and where? Even with respect to those issues, he was not in a strong position. Karla was absolutely necessary for Inspector Bevan to be able to write a search warrant that was executable and would withstand legal challenge. She was also absolutely necessary for Inspector Bevan to be able to participate in Paul Bernardo's imminent arrest. Were Bernardo arrested by the Toronto police and returned to Scarborough to stand trial for the rapes he could, potentially, be lost to Inspector Bevan and the murder prosecutions for years.

Prosecutors usually insist on knowing with whom they are doing deals and the full extent of the individual's culpability. But in this case Inspector Bevan had already committed their side and he was in a big hurry. Because the Toronto police were poised to arrest, there was little time for sober second thought.

George said no jail time, but, if his client had to be incarcerated, it should be in a psychiatric hospital.

Murray said twenty years in jail.

Experienced lawyers such as Segal and Walker knew that meant they would invariably meet in the middle. Ten years for guilty pleas to two counts of manslaughter. They hung up, agreeing to take their first face-to-face that coming Sunday. Segal would drive down to George's office with assistant prosecutor Michal Fairburn. They would continue their negotiations then. After their meeting, he would meet for the first time with Inspector Bevan in Beamsville. Afterward, maybe Mr. Segal, Ms. Fairburn and Mr. Walker could go across the border for dinner? There were a couple of fine Italian restaurants on the American side of Niagara Falls. After all, it would be Valentine's Day.

* * * * * * *

At 1:45 p.m. on February 13, 1993, Toronto Detective Sergeant Bruce Smollett was advised by his superior, Staff Inspector Marrier, that the Staff Inspector had received a call from Vince Bevan. Marrier told Smollett that Bevan had told him that "George Walker had contacted the Crown Attorney in Niagara Region and further that she (Karla) had admitted that she had assisted Bernardo in the murders of both Mahaffy and French."

* * * * * * *

Now that the Ministry was involved, the two police organizations were supposed to play nicely together. And they did, sort of. They were to help each other prepare their respective warrants, but it was of necessity more one-sided, given that Toronto's warrant was almost ready to be sworn and Inspector Bevan had just started to prepare his. The Toronto warrant made a good template. It had been developed with an

expert from the Ministry of the Attorney General who was now seconded to Inspector Bevan and the Green Ribbon Task Force. Like
everything else about police work at this level, it would take some time
and concentrated effort. Search warrants are tricky.

In his will-state, Detective Smollett records that he and a number of
other members of the Toronto Sex Assault Squad including Staff
Inspector Marrier made the trip to Beamsville on the afternoon of
February 13, to meet with Inspector Bevan and a few members of his
task force. "There was further discussion as to the status of the search
warrants for 57 Bayview as it was felt that the best situation would be
to have the search warrants prepared and ready to execute at the time
of arrest.

"During the course of the evening Inspector Bevan and myself spoke
to Special Agent Greg McCrary of the Behavioral Sciences Unit of the
Federal Bureau of Investigation in Quantico, Virginia. The topic of conversation was the criminal behavioral profiling of Bernardo. After
lengthy discussion with McCrary both Inspector Bevan and myself were
of the opinion that Bernardo met the profile descriptors of a sexual
sadist." That Bernardo met the "profile descriptors of a sexual sadist"
was absolutely meaningless claptrap as far as his culpability and the
courts were concerned, but it was very convenient for Inspector Bevan.

* * * * * * *

On Sunday, Murray Segal and George Walker reached an agreement.
Karla would do two concurrent ten-year terms in prison. In return, she
would waive her right to a preliminary trial, give her full and complete
cooperation to the police, enter guilty pleas to the two manslaughter
charges during a short, expedited trial, and then testify against her husband at his murder trial. As Walker well understood, how and where
Karla would be incarcerated was not within Segal's sphere of influence.
It would be up to the federal Correctional Service. However, Segal

undertook that neither he nor the police would interfere with any petition Walker and his client might bring to arrange for Karla to serve her sentence in a secure psychiatric facility.

This was a great deal for Karla. Under the terms and conditions of the laws that govern incarceration, Karla would be eligible to apply for full parole within two and a half years of her first day in prison.

Segal also agreed that the authorities would not oppose any parole applications Karla might bring in the future. If she was well behaved and a good prisoner, Karla could be out of jail on parole by the summer of 1996. Even if things did not go smoothly, at the very latest, she would be out on statutory release after she had served two-thirds of her sentence, sometime in 2001. That was the law.

Were she to have to go to trial as a full accomplice, Karla would have been convicted of at least second-degree murder, and gone to jail for life. This would have meant that she would not be eligible to even apply for parole until she had served seven years and depending on how well she was represented, could easily do as many as ten or twelve years before she actually got paroled. Of course, there was always the possibility that great lawyering would get her manslaughter convictions anyway and, from where Murray Segal sat, that would be a needlessly expensive, highly public, protracted zero-sum game.

* * * * * * *

Talk about money and expense – convoys of senior police officers were now going back and forth between Toronto and Niagara on an almost hourly basis. Detective Smollett records in his will-state that he and a number of detectives from the Toronto's Sex Assault Squad once again went to Beamsville on Sunday, February 14, this time for a meeting with Inspector Bevan and Murray Segal.

At approximately 12:10 p.m. he had a conversation with his immediate superior, Staff Inspector Marrier. Marrier told Detective Smollett "that if an arrest was to be made on our charges only [referring to the Toronto rape charges] then Bernardo was to be taken to the nearest Metropolitan Toronto Police facility and processed as per our regulations." He told Smollett that he would personally explain this fact of life to Inspector Bevan.

There was friction between Staff Superintendent Marrier and Inspector Bevan. They did not see eye-to-eye on a number of issues. Marrier probably thought Bevan was a loose cannon and inexperienced whereas Bevan had other, more salty opinions about Marrier. At any rate, Bevan had proposed that when they arrested Bernardo jointly he be taken to Halton Regional Police headquarters which was right off the Queen Elizabeth Highway, equidistant between St. Catharines and Toronto. Marrier was obviously not convinced that Toronto should wait for Bevan and was fully prepared to take full charge of the arrest himself and told Bevan so.

* * * * * * *

As George Walker explained to Karla the following day, there was nothing not to like about the deal to which he had committed her. Although very frightened about going to prison, Karla knew that she was damned lucky. She implored George to try and figure out how to make sure she served her time in a psychiatric hospital.

It would be a long while before Karla would come to realize that it was not transposed depravity and relative innocence or mysterious, benevolent, occult forces that deserved thanks for her good fortune, but rather the very corporeal Inspector Bevan and three will-o'-the-wisps – Dr. Dietz, FBI Special Supervisory Agent Hazelwood, and Nurse Warren – of whom Karla had never heard.

* * * * * * *

Inspector Bevan and Murray Segal met for the first time on Sunday afternoon, February 14, 1993. During that meeting the Inspector learned that Segal and Walker had pretty much figured out a deal for Karla's testimony and that was good enough for him.

On the premise that the media was going to expose the allegedly clandestine Bernardo stakeout on the six o'clock news, Inspector Bevan precipitated Paul Bernardo's arrest three days later, on Wednesday, February 17, at 3 o'clock in the afternoon. As it was handled, Inspector Bevan's impetuosity came perilously close to immunizing Bernardo against prosecution for the murders of Leslie Mahaffy and Kristen French.

Two days later, the Ministry of the Attorney General quietly withdrew the Inspector's murder charges. The Toronto police had solid evidence to back up their arrest on sexual assault and rape charges. Because Bernardo was a multiple offender and the rape charges were sufficiently serious, they would be able to hold him without bail indefinitely on those charges alone. The forensics lab was optimistic that at least another six or eight samples would pan out and the Toronto police would simply be able to continue to lay charges each time they got a new match. Thanks to Inspector Bevan's impetuousness, if that had not been the case, Paul Bernardo (and his wife with him) could have conceivably gone free.

When Inspector Bevan arrested Paul Bernardo on that Wednesday afternoon, he had never laid eyes on Karla Homolka, let alone taken a statement from her. His arrest was done in a complete evidentiary vacuum. The arrest on the murder charges was an incredibly stupid move. Inspector Bevan's bosses in the Ministry of the Attorney General shook their heads and thanked their various gods that Paul Bernardo really was a monster with inexperienced legal representation and a documented past of singular evil doing.

Regardless, at 6:00 p.m., on February 19, shortly before the murder charges were withdrawn, Inspector Bevan executed his sworn search warrant, and took full control of the crime scene investigation. After the execution of his search warrant, there was no turning back. Actions speak louder than words. Karla's future was sealed and delivered.

CANADIAN PSYCHO

At George Walker's insistence, Karla had reluctantly moved out of her aunt and uncle's apartment in Brampton and back to her parents'. When she showed up at his office for her appointment at 2:30 p.m., on February 19, she was unhappy. The media were onto her – the fact that she wanted immunity – everything had been published. Her parents were beside themselves. The boyfriend she had just met in Brampton did not want to talk to her. She demanded to know who told them? Walker shrugged. "It's only going to get worse."

Later in the day, Murray Segal called and advised him that the search warrants had been executed. He said that he might not have the authority to stay in communication but Walker understood when he was being four-flushed. Now that Bernardo had been arrested for the murders and the police were in the house the deal was done, and done again, as the American writer Richard Brautigan might have put it, in "watermelon sugar."

* * * * * * *

The search warrant itself was an interesting document. According to Inspector Bevan's will-state, he virtually wrote it himself because there was no one else competent enough or sufficiently motivated to do it.

However, on the nineteenth, it was sworn by an Ontario Provincial Police officer who had been seconded to the Green Ribbon Task Force. In the section where the reasons for the search warrant are given, and the basis upon which it has been written are itemized, the officer repeatedly states that the warrant was based on what he had been told by Inspector Bevan and other senior staff sergeants on the Green Ribbon Task Force. It also included a copy of "Compliant Victims of the Sexual Sadist."

* * * * * * *

With the exception of two crime scene investigators who were placed under his command, Inspector Bevan banished all Toronto police from the Niagara Region; no more consultations with Marrier and Smollett, no more division of the spoils.

In accordance with the principles of Crime Scene Investigation 101, the house at 57 Bayview was divided into a grid, and the grid sections assigned numbers. Identification officers, hermetically sealed in white spacesuit-type garb, pulled out all their toys: laser lights, metal detectors, high-powered industrial vacuums, jackhammers, magnifying glasses. They assiduously collected all manners of visible and invisible artifacts including wall spots, fingerprints, flakes of skin, hairs, fibers and various unidentified dried secretions. Everything that came out of the house was assigned a number and a grid designation. Even though the number of exhibits would eventually exceed a thousand, virtually none of them had any probative value.

On Inspector Bevan's first tour he was shown numerous suspected blood spots, a collection of newspaper clippings about the crimes, and various test tubes containing a curious blue liquid. There was also a chronological list of all the Scarborough rapes, with Detective Steve Irwin's business card attached. Dated November, 1990, it was hand-written on legal-size paper. There were detailed descriptions of the attacks and various descriptions of suspects and eight dates in reverse order from May 4, 1987, through May 26, 1990. Beside each date the main intersection nearest the location of each assault was noted. Half of the documentation was in Karla's handwriting.

There were hundreds of books in the house including Karla's well-marked copy of *The Compendium of Pharmaceuticals and Specialities, 22nd Edition*, with Halcion and Halothane highlighted, and a copy of Bret Easton Ellis's *American Psycho* under Karla's side of the bed.

Because various members of the Green Ribbon Task Force had been prepped by the FBI about the reading habits of sexual deviates, they took particular notice of certain kinds of books.

In conjunction with Dr. Dietz, the forensic psychiatrist and consultant from California, the FBI had, over the past two or three decades, determined that 83 percent of men accused of violent sex crimes maintained collections of items related to sexual and/or violent themes.

They do not say anything about the percentage of women accused of violent sex crimes who maintain such collections or anything about the percentage maintained among the general population.

They found dozens of appropriate titles in the house and seized them. An officer was assigned to read *American Psycho* and prepare a book report, itemizing the similarities between its protagonist, a wealthy, thirty-something, New York investment banker named Bateman and Paul Bernardo. The fact that they had discovered a copy of *American Psycho* was leaked to the press which henceforth referred to the satirical novel as "Bernardo's Bible." The police never bothered to correct the mistake when they discovered that all of these books, including *American Psycho*, belonged to Karla.

There were also hundreds of videotapes in the house. Most of them were taped television shows or purchased movies. It would take half a dozen police officers a number of months to fully review all the video material, but they had great expectations.

At five o'clock in the afternoon on Sunday, February 21st, they found a one-minute-and fifty-eight-second homemade pornographic video in a briefcase tucked away in a closet. The tape confirmed what they had been told by Karla through George Walker – that Paul and Karla had made homemade sex tapes. This one, however, was not what they were expecting. Divided into three "scenes," it showed Karla willingly, lasciviously participating in explicit lesbian sex acts with two unidentified females, one of whom was quite obviously comatose.

The identification officers first viewed the tape on the videotape equipment in the Bernardo's living room. They thought they had something important. It was marked and taken to the mobile command post, a big trailer parked outside the house.

Inspector Bevan notes in his will-state that he heard about the tape on the twenty-first but did not view it until 10 a.m. on Monday, February 22.

Because the young woman in the second and third segments was obviously comatose and had dark pubic hair, and because the scene had been shot in the Bernardo's master bedroom, Inspector Bevan assumed it was Kristen French. Leslie Mahaffy had been a natural blonde and this victim was not.

Bevan's note in his will-state is short and circumspect. "I viewed a copy of those tapes." He does not bother to mention the first segment in which Karla is shown with a naked, blonde woman, who was clearly a consenting adult. The two are ensconced on a king-sized bed in a hotel room, apparently putting on a show for Paul Bernardo who can be partially seen in frame. The two women are obviously enjoying themselves. The blonde fondles a spread-eagled Karla's genitalia. They giggle about lipstick on Karla's right nipple. Hardly hard-core stuff or evidence of a crime.

It was the other two scenes, both of which showed Karla gleefully sexually assaulting the same comatose teenager that should have concerned Bevan. The blasé tone of his will-state record would seem to suggest otherwise.

"The video revealed Karla and an unidentified young woman involved in sex acts in the master bedroom of the house. I made arrangements to have the tape transferred to the OPP laboratory for expert examination."

That afternoon, Inspector Bevan met with Murray Segal, and other senior prosecutors, including Jim Trelevan, the Regional Director for the Niagara region, and Casey Hill, the search warrant consultant and Ray Houlahan in Houlahan's St. Catharines' courthouse office. He showed them the videotape. Whoever the two women with Karla were – the first one was an adult, wide-awake and appeared to be a willing participant. But the other woman, who Inspector Bevan believed to be Kristen French, was obviously drugged or dead.

This tape added to the problems created by the Inspector's premature arrest of Paul Bernardo. There was a distinct difference between the way Karla behaved and acted on this videotape and the way her lawyer described her involvement in the crimes, and the way the prosecutors and police imagined a "compliant victim" might behave. She looked like she was really enjoying herself and she did not appear to be battered or coerced at all. In fact, she appeared to be in what might be described as a frenzy of monstrous joy.

Again, Murray Segal found himself in an impossible position. If they reneged now, called Walker and said "Forget it, deal's off," then the search warrant would follow Bernardo's premature arrest on the murder charges into the toilet. Any evidence, including this inculpatory videotape, collected over the past two days, would be inadmissible, and they would not likely be able to write another search warrant and re-enter the house for a matter of months, if at all.

It was classic Catch-22. Since the search warrant was based on what Bevan surmised about what George Walker told Murray Segal Karla knew, he would be back at ground zero. The 1:58 videotape would be inadmissible as evidence against her. It had only been found as a result of a search warrant based on information she had provided on a good-faith basis during privileged negotiations between her defense lawyer and a senior Crown law office official.

If the Toronto police had executed their search warrant based on their three DNA matches and taken control of the crime scene investigation then, hypothetically, things would have been different. The tape would have been extremely damning evidence of Karla's complicity and her state of mind and likely sufficient, in and of itself, to put her away for the rest of her life.

There has also been a great deal made out of Inspector Bevan's failure to find the rest of Paul and Karla's treasure trove of videotaped trophies which were hidden in a pot light in an upstairs bathroom. Although Inspector Bevan has been lionized in the policing community and promoted (he is now the Chief of the Ottawa-Carlton Police Service in the nation's capital), that failure to find all the videotape evidence is cited as the singular reason why Karla got off so lightly.

Nothing could be further from the truth. Karla's deal had everything to do with getting Inspector Bevan in the house to see if there was any evidence of any kind, and nothing to do with specific types of evidence such as videotape. If it had, the 1:58 videotape was more than sufficient evidence to arrest her and charge her with an array of serious offences, all of which would have been a stepping stone to full accomplice status, making Karla subject to every charge eventually levied against Paul Bernardo, including two counts of first-degree murder, both of which Karla and George Walker knew she was guilty.

In spite of the fact that the Inspector renewed his search warrant three times and remained in the house for almost three months, the 1:58 videotape starring Karla Bernardo was the only real evidence he found. All the police found was evidentiary innuendo – the kind that make novels about serial killers interesting – such as newspaper clippings, bags of soiled panties hidden in closets, and books with titles such as *Perfect Victim* and *A Killing in the Family* but absolutely nothing probative. (It was only after Bernardo's lease ran out and the police rented the house for $1200 a month and returned with Karla on a sunny day in mid-June, just before her trial, that she pointed out a spot where Kristen French had vomited. Thanks to Karla, and in spite of Inspector Bevan's horribly botched crime scene investigation, the forensic lab was finally able to come up with Kristen French's DNA mixed with samples of Paul Bernardo's semen.)

There is an unexamined reason for Inspector Bevan's failure to find all of the videotape evidence. As a strong advocate of community policing, Inspector Bevan developed an unusual and arguably inappropriate relationship with the owners of the house that Paul and Karla rented. He met with the Delaneys, local entrepreneurs – Rachael Delaney, a life insurance saleswoman who liked to speculate in real estate, and Brian who owned an extermination business and had a part-time career as a catalogue model – listened intently to their concerns and agreed to pay them rent out of the Green Ribbon Task Force coffers. In the end, like a good landlord, he withheld the internal devastation that another police force, such as Toronto, would have invariably unleashed on the interior of the house.

Rather than tear off the drywall and expose all the possible hidden surfaces and potential hiding places in the house, Inspector Bevan's investigators selectively punched holes. Although they dropped many pot lights and felt around, they did not remove ceiling panels.

This dutiful reticence on the part of Inspector was ironic in the extreme, given that the province, in a histrionic bow to voodoo logic, eventually bought the house (not the land) and demolished it. The land remained with the Delaneys who sold it years later in a soaring market.

* * * * * * *

It was Murray Segal's idea to have Karla evaluated by a psychologist and a psychiatrist. He and George Walker met again between 4:00 and 6:30 p.m. on February 25th in Walker's offices. Murray had a draft of the deal: two counts, manslaughter – one for Mahaffy and one for French. Karla's sentence would be ten years for each victim, but the two terms would be served concurrently. Written in was the proviso that the province would not ask for increased parole eligibility – if she behaved herself in prison, she would be eligible to apply for full parole in three years and four months from the date she went to prison.

Further, Segal agreed the Crown would write a letter to the parole board supporting parole for Karla, on behalf of both the Attorney General and the police. The parole board would be officially advised that Karla had been helpful and that her testimony had been essential for the conviction of her ex-husband.

Both sides would go before a judge in chambers to establish judicial approval prior to her formal trial. Theoretically, judges were independent and if they did not like a plea agreement, they could scuttle it. Seeing the judge privately in chambers before a trial to get him on side with a plea bargain was very rarely done, but Walker was not taking any chances. They agreed that there would be a court reporter present at this closed-door meeting, just to make doubly sure.

The draft was exactly as they had agreed during their many conversations and meetings over the past ten days. The police would formally arrest and charge Karla. Karla would then be released to her parents on their surety. Karla would waive her right to a preliminary hearing.

They went on to discuss some of the things that the police had found including the 1:58 videotape. Inspector Bevan had been waving around one of those FBI, law enforcement articles called "Compliant Victims of the Sexual Sadist."

Walker was amused. It made interesting reading but it was not relevant. The article mixed two, almost impossible defenses, the Stockholm syndrome, used in the Patti Hearst case, and the battered woman defense, as it was used in a California case called "People v. Hooker."

"People v. Hooker" was called the "sex slave" or "girl-in-the-box" case, because the victim was often kept in a box under the perpetrator's bed and was somehow psychologically enslaved by the sadistic beatings and sexual torture to which she had been subjected. Or so the theory went.

There was a book about it called *Perfect Victim*. It documented how a twenty-year-old woman from Oregon named Colleen Stan was reduced to sexual slavery – for seven years – by a seemingly, mild-mannered fellow named Cameron Hooker.

The bespectacled Hooker had short, sandy-brown hair and was married. Always well-groomed, he appeared harmless. His young wife was, like Karla, a full accomplice in his crimes.

Mrs. Hooker got off the hook, based on her willingness to testify against her husband. The prosecution used the battered spouse syndrome as a justification for their deal with her. But Colleen Stan had not been murdered. And details of the case were certainly bizarre. The Hookers would actually let the victim go into town by herself and shop. Once, they even let her visit her family for two or three days. She always returned.

This idea that Karla was the "compliant victim" of a "sexual sadist," abused and forced to commit one heinous crime after another against her will was all well and good. But the way Murray Segal saw it they were going to need a lot more than a cockamamie theory to justify this deal.

Walker readily concurred. He and Segal agreed that the psychological and psychiatric assessments that Walker would solicit would then be treated as pre-sentencing reports, but not entered into evidence. That way they could be kept out of the hands of the press and strictly confidential.

In this way, the actual trial would take no more than a day, providing there was no encumbrance from any third parties, such as the media.

Segal agreed that between Karla's arrest and trial, she would remain at liberty and make herself available for police interviews as well as psychological and psychiatric counseling. Segal would make every effort to get the Attorney General to agree to transfer Karla to a provincial psychiatric institution where she would serve her sentence, but Walker would also look into that and have the assessors explore what criteria would be necessary to ensure that it happened.

The deal would be contingent on Karla's absolute truthfulness. She would disclose the full extent of all her participation and impart all her knowledge, regardless of whether or not she deemed it relevant. Any perjury – any lie – either by commission or omission – would scuttle the deal.

* * * * * * *

Karla came to George Walker's office at 7:00 p.m. that night. During the hour and a half she was there, Walker told her about his discussion with Segal and showed her the draft deal. He told her about how much material was coming out of the house – not that any meaningful forensic analysis had yet been done – but the police had found a videotape which Walker described to her and said was potentially damaging to her position.

Walker told Karla that it would be complicated, at that point, for the police and the prosecutor to renege, but any deal of this magnitude was fragile. Whether or not Karla's position would withstand the legal challenge were they to renege was moot. It was clear that, for some reason, there was no real will to prosecute Karla to the full extent of the law, but it was unwise to look gift horses in the mouth. This was definitely a *carpe diem* situation.

As defense lawyers are wont to do, Walker assumed an exaggerated amount of credit where perhaps less was due. All he had really done was get out of his La-Z-Boy at 11:30 p.m. on February 11th and answer his front door. This immutable fact did not stop him from telling Karla that this deal for two ten-year manslaughter terms to be served concurrently was nothing short of miraculous. Given the crimes and the fact that she could have saved the dead girls' lives, and that Kristen French would probably never have been kidnaped but for Karla's participation – a jury would ignore the abuse, of which there had been only one provable incident, and send her to the gallows – figuratively speaking.

As Karla and George well knew, there was also the distinct possibility of witnesses offering testimony that Karla was into kinky sex, that she herself was sadistic. The issue of her sister was messy. After all, she had admitted to Walker that she had been jealous of Tammy Lyn.

* * * * * * *

Late that same afternoon, Inspector Vince Bevan spoke to Murray Segal and told him that the video-lab technician had pointed out many similarities between the comatose girl in the video and Kristen French.

Segal told the Inspector that the terms of the deal had been finalized and that he and George Walker were arranging to bring Karla to the Green Ribbon offices to give an "induced" statement.

"Induced" statements are statements made by a witness, of their own free will, to the police and the prosecutors. By virtue of the relevant information (which by law is evidence if it reflects that individual's direct knowledge) contained in said statements the authorities may be sufficiently motivated or "induced" to make a deal with that witness.

Nothing said during an induced statement can subsequently be used against the individual in any criminal or civil action, therefore there is little or no risk. Giving an induced statement is largely a formality. Obviously both sides have already fully discussed what the witness has to offer and agreed that what they have to say is sufficiently probative to justify a deal.

Upon hearing that Karla was going to come in and give her induced statement, the Inspector went directly to the families of the dead girls to get their permission. In this day and age, without the victims families' blessings, Karla's deal could not have been made. It would appear that the Inspector had failed to apprise the families of exactly who was saying what to whom when it came to any potential relationship with Karla. Once again, Bevan's career was hanging by a thread.

As he recorded in his will-state: "During my discussions with them [the French and Mahaffy families] I told them about a proposal arranged between the Crown and Karla Bernardo's counsel and sought their input. I was candid with them about the evidence gathered to date and about what we had learned about the nature of the relationship between Paul and Karla Bernardo..."

According to him, he "was candid" – but one surmises only up to a point. Apparently, he did not tell them about the 1:58 videotape which, at the time, he firmly believed depicted Karla sexually abusing an unconscious Kristen French. Nor did he tell them that he had already done the deal two weeks earlier. If he had not done the deal, he would have not been able to arrest Paul Bernardo for their daughters' murders or get into the house to search for the evidence he did not have. At least, these nuances are not recorded in his will-state.

What he did tell the families was that without Karla the chances were that Bernardo would go back to Toronto and be tried for the Scarborough rapes first. In that case, it could be years before Bernardo stood trial for the murders of their daughters.

He also told them that from friends of Paul and Karla's whom his officers were furiously interviewing – as well as from George Walker and Karla herself – they had learned all about the bizarre nature of the relationship between the couple. He explained to the families all about the compliant victims of sexual sadists. And that's what Paul and Karla were. Paul was a "sexual sadist" and Karla was a "compliant victim." He explained the predicament from his perspective, spinning it in order to make the families' compliance almost impossible to withhold.

In the final analysis, Inspector Bevan said, it was really up to them. They could wait and let the Toronto police take Bernardo back to Scarborough or endorse Karla's deal and see that Bernardo was tried and convicted for their daughters' murders.

The parents were confused by all the jabberwocky about "compliant victims" and "sexual sadists." Unable to conceive that a woman would be anything but a "compliant victim," unsteady on their best days, fearful that were Bernardo to go back to Scarborough and justice for their daughters' brutal murders might never be done, the families told Inspector Bevan that they would accept the deal.

* * * * * * *

Karla was completely drunk and stoned on tranquilizers when she showed up at George Walker's office that night. She had been drinking all afternoon with the receptionist from the animal clinic where she used to work. After Karla signed a "Plea Resolution Authorization" and left the office, Walker phoned Murray Segal and called off Karla's imminent meeting with the police. Walker might have even suggested to Segal that his client was suicidal. Just for the record, he and Segal euphemistically agreed to cancel "further negotiations." Segal would confirm it in writing.

* * * * * * *

"However, all these discussions were premature," Inspector Bevan concluded in his will-state entry for February 25, "because I was advised later that night that an impasse had developed and Karla Bernardo would not be meeting with us as anticipated."

* * * * * * *

In the midst of a media blackout which Vince Bevan had announced on Saturday, February 26, the Ontario Provincial Police issued a press release that declared Paul Bernardo a suspect in the unsolved sex killing of Cindy Halliday. The student's nude and partially burned body had been found along a highway a hundred miles north of St. Catharines on April 20, 1992, within days of the disappearance of Kristen French.

Halliday's case was only one of over a hundred unsolved sex slayings of young women in southwestern Ontario since the early eighties.

George Walker was not surprised by the news reports. Typically, the police were going to try and pin all unsolved sex killings from the last hundred years on the latest monster to have reared his ugly head. It

could not have been a better development for his client if he had
scripted it himself.

* * * * * * *

Robert Bigelow congratulated Walker on the fact that Walker had managed to avoid any sexual-assault charges against Karla. Sexual assault
convictions would have made her life immeasurably more difficult
after she got out of prison.

Walker had retained Bigelow, a well-known Toronto lawyer, to
advise him about the red tape and subtleties involved in getting an
individual convicted of a capital offense moved from a federal penitentiary to a provincial psychiatric hospital.

He told Walker that they would need to establish that Karla required
significant psychiatric treatment that was unavailable in the penitentiary. An appropriate program of treatment would have to be identified
in one of the provincial psychiatric facilities, and both the penitentiary
and the hospital would have to consent to a transfer. Under those conditions, it might be possible. However, the Ministry of Health was facing significant government cutbacks, therefore the case would have to
be very convincing before a hospital would be likely to agree.

He was also providing advice about parole issues and, at Walker's
request, some names of consultants to examine Karla.

He pointed out that anyone sentenced to a determinate federal
prison term, other than life, would be eligible for full parole at one-
third of their sentence. Six months before full eligibility, the person
would be eligible for day parole. In Karla's case, she would be eligible
for full parole at approximately 3 years and 4 months, day parole at 2
years and 10 months, and unescorted temporary absences at 1 year, 8
months.

He recommended the forensic psychiatrist Dr. Graham Glancy, but
Glancy turned Walker down. Walker then called an old, defense stal-

wart, psychologist Allan Long. Dr. Long, in turn, suggested his colleague, Dr. Hans Arndt, for the psychiatric assessment. If Karla needed to be hospitalized, Dr. Arndt could easily arrange it, given that he was the head of psychiatry at Northwestern General Hospital in Toronto. Walker had not even thought about hospitalization but seeing Karla as she had been the other night, it occurred to him that a few weeks on the psych ward might not be a bad idea.

George Walker filed a plea resolution "Authorization" with the court in St. Catharines first thing Monday, February 28, 1993. It read:

I, Karla Leanne Homolka, of 61 Dundonald St., St. Catharines, Ontario, do hereby authorize and instruct my counsel, George F. Walker, Q.C., to continue towards finalizing my plea bargain arrangement with Murray Segal, Esq., of the Ministry of the Attorney General for Ontario.

I understand that I must co-operate fully with the investigating officers, be truthful and frank in providing answers to all questions asked, and to provide full details of my knowledge and/or participation in the Mahaffy and French investigations and any others. That I will provide induced statements to the investigators at a time and place convenient to the officers.

I understand that I will be called upon to testify against my husband at his trials and I hereby agree to do so. That this agreement is null and void if I commit perjury. I understand that I will enter a plea of guilty to 1 count manslaughter, vis-a-vis, Mahaffy and 1 count manslaughter, vis-a-vis, French and at least one other charge in relation to each victim.

That I am to receive sentences totaling 10 years in custody.

That the Crown will not seek an increase in the period before parole eligibility.

That the Crown will write to the Parole Board, will include a record of my trial proceedings, will indicate my co-operation, remorse, etc. and will indicate on behalf of the police and the Crown that they will leave the matter of when releases and/or parole should commence, up to the Parole Board without further comment.

That my counsel and the Crown will go before the Justice before hand to ensure the terms of the agreement are acceptable.

That when charged I will go before a Provincial Court Judge, waive my preliminary hearings, be brought before a Justice, enter my pleas of "guilty" and be released pending sentencing.

That the Attorney General's office will indicate to the Federal Correctional Authorities and Provincial Authorities that they are not opposed to the offender being transferred from a Federal to a Provincial Institution to serve my sentence.

That I have had all my rights explained to me by my counsel and have been advised that I am free to contact another lawyer for another opinion but have advised my counsel that I fully understand and wish to proceed with the agreement forthwith.

DATED at the City of Niagara Falls this 26th day of February, 1993

Witnessed by Karel and Dorothy Homolka.
Notarized by Geoffrey Hadfield
Signed, *Karla Leanne Bernardo*

This document which officially recognized the details of a deal between Karla Homolka, the police and the Ministry of the Attorney General, was filed with the court only 8 days after the police entered Karla's house looking for evidence and almost two months before the search warrants expired forcing them to abandon the site.

In spite of the discovery of the damning 1:58 sex video on February 20, Karla's books, reading habits and demeanor, and in spite of the fact that both Inspector Bevan and Murray Segal knew that she was nobody's "compliant victim" (or any other kind of victim for that matter), the deal offered to Karla on George Walker doorstep at 11:30 p.m., February 11, 1993, by Inspector Bevan's minions was now officially a matter of public record.

VICTIMOLOGY

On March 4th, 1993, George Walker arranged with Dr. Hans Arndt to have Karla admitted to the psychiatric ward of Northwestern General Hospital. That way, he could relax knowing Karla was secure and not likely to get into any trouble while he was away.

Returning from his annual month-long Christmas sojourn at their oceanfront villa called "Journey's End" in Montserrat in January, George had booked the last seasonal return "excursion fare" before he left the airport. There had been no foreseeable reason why he could not return to the island for the second week in March and spend seven days by himself.

If Walker had not got that "authorization" filed with the court, "suspended negotiations" with Segal, and put Karla in the hospital, he would have had to forfeit that extra week in paradise. And excursion fares were non-refundable.

He bought a paperback copy of *Perfect Victim* and climbed on the last excursion fare plane bound for Montserrat on March 7th.

* * * * * * *

Shortly after he returned, it was made clear that Drs. Long and Arndt were viewed with a degree of skepticism by the prosecutor's office.

Dr. Long was getting a bit long in the tooth. Both he and Dr. Arndt most often testified as expert witnesses for the defense. They were considered "liberal." Dr. Arndt was not considered an expert with battered or abused women and so on and so forth.

Even though the experts would not be called as witnesses, nor their reports entered as evidence at Karla's trial, with this high profile case, and under the circumstances, it would be prudent if they could deliver expert opinion that had as much credibility as possible – for posterity, as it were.

Dr. Andrew Malcolm, a dour psychiatrist whose abrupt manner and deep cynicism meant he was highly regarded by prosecutors, would be ideal. Dr. Malcolm had frequently been called to testify on behalf of the prosecution over his thirty years in practice. Even though he was not an expert in the field of abuse, he would nonetheless make an ideal addition to the team. Dr. Arndt was instructed to call Dr. Malcolm.

* * * * * * *

From Karla's diary, entry dated 12 April 1993

PAUL
  1. made me eat food I didn't like (i.e. snails)
  2. forced me to drink alcohol
  3. made me stay up late even when I had to work the next day
  4. didn't allow me to seek medical care even when a) he hurt me or b) I had bruises from him
  5. strangled me with his hands
  6. threw knives at me
  7. held a knife to my throat
  8. hit me with a piece of firewood
  9. hit me with his shoes
  10. hit me with a flashlight

11. hit me with a screwdriver
12. stabbed me with a screwdriver
13. stabbed me in the back of the head with keys, causing my scalp to bleed
14. did the same with a screwdriver
15. ripped handfuls of hair from my head
16. punched me
17. kicked me
18. slapped me
19. anally raped me
20. pushed me into a board with a rusty nail in it and punctured my foot
21. pushed me down the stairs
22. called me names i.e. stupid, worthless, etc.
23. made me feel like I had no self-worth
24. told me I would have to have sex with anyone he said
25. told me when we had children he would have sex with the girls
26. he would force me to find young girls to have relationships with
27. he whipped me with a leather belt
28. he put me down repeatedly
29. he physically and emotionally abused my dog to get to me
30. he didn't allow me to see my friends
31. I was allowed very limited contact with my family – If I was bruised I couldn't see them
32. he isolated me from everyone
33. I wasn't allowed to drive
34. he always accused me of things I didn't do
35. he hit me for washing dishes with dish soap – I was only allowed to use water
36. I got hit for using cleaning products and smelling up the house with them
37. he was always suspicious of me
38. he threatened to kill me – he said if I ever left he'd hunt me down and kill me

39. he told me to always watch my back – that he'd find and get me
40. he spit at me
41. he spit in my food
42. he dumped my dinner on the diningroom table
43. he kicked me in the back and caused me to have blood in my urine
44. he punched my ear and pushed my earring right through my ear
45. if Paul and I were driving and I was wearing a jacket that would make a rustling noise, he would hit me every time the sound could be heard, so I took to wearing heavy sweaters to work instead of a winter coat so there would be no noise, therefore I would get sick a lot
46. he hit me for holding my hand on a patch of James Dean on my jeans
47. he hit me for scratching one foot with the other
48. he hit me for making any metal against metal noise in the kitchen (for example a spoon against a pot)
49. he hit me for cooking with the crock pot all day while he was on a diet
50. he hit me whenever he picked me up after work for smelling of disinfectant, even though there was no way I could help it
51. he hit me for "flicking" my toes
52. he hit me for scratching too much
53. he hit me for disciplining the dog
54. one time he was so outraged at the dog he picked him up and put him right through the wall
55. on another occasion he repeatedly smashed the dog's head on the concrete basement floor until I told him to stop and that he would kill the dog if he continued
56. he chopped my iguana's head off, made me skin him and then cooked him on the barbecue and made me try a piece
57. he would hit me if he caught me using dish soap. He didn't think it was necessary except for very dirty pots and pans

58. I was never allowed to wear perfume unless he was wearing cologne of his own

* * * * * * *

During her hospital stay, Karla told Dr. Arndt that the video "with the hand," as she called the 1:58 videotape the police found in her house on February 21 – she knew that the girl was still alive, so it was not Kristen French.

Karla was discharged from Northwestern General Hospital on April 24, 1993. In his will-state, Inspector Bevan notes that he arranged further funding to facilitate twenty-four-hour surveillance.

* * * * * * *

On April 29, 1993, Karla's general practitioner, Dr. Christina Plaskos, perceived her to be "rather flat…" In the file, Dr. Plaskos noted that Karla had "gained 15 lb… she is on a number of meds… I'm not really sure why she was put on these meds… I found her not to be depressed but basically lacking emotion…"

Karla was sufficiently sentimental to make a specific note in her date book on April 30. She recorded that the search warrants for 57 Bayview had expired. The police had been in the house for 69 days. She also noted that this occurred on the anniversary of the discovery of Kristen French's body.

* * * * * * *

On April 30, Murray Segal and George Walker had a telephone conversation. They agreed it was time to formally conclude their deal. They met in Segal's office in the Ministry building at 720 Bay Street in Toronto. Murray said that there was a small impediment. There was some internal dissonance within the Ministry and among the police. Segal said he thought that there would need to be additional charges for Karla's role in her sister's death. Walker could not have disagreed more.

If Karla had not come forward, the authorities would still think that Tammy Lyn's death was an accident – that is, if they thought about it at all.

* * * * * * *

Karla Homolka and Paul Bernardo had come to the attention of police in the Niagara region many times before Inspector Bevan sent his men to Walker's doorstep on February 11, 1993.

There was significant Niagara Regional Police involvement in the suspicious death of Tammy Lyn Homolka. There were interviews with both Karla and Paul on record as well as reports by forensic pathologists and the coroner.

In his haste to make a deal, it would appear that Inspector Bevan never bothered to do a search through the Niagara Regional Police files for any earlier occurrences that involved either Karla Homolka or Paul Bernardo.

For instance, by July 15, 1991, when Bevan was appointed head of the Mahaffy investigation, the file on Tammy Lyn Homolka's death had only recently been closed. One would have thought that any "experienced investigator," confronted with such a violent and unusual discovery – a young teenage girl's dismembered body parts encased in cement blocks and dumped in a lake – would have opened every file that involved suspicious death or sex crimes or strange stalking behavior going back at least a decade.

For instance, there was a exchange of letters in February, 1991, between two pathologists a few months before the discovery of Leslie

Mahaffy's body parts that should have raised red flags and given even an inexperienced investigator pause.

Dr. John Groves, a pathologist from Hamilton General Hospital, wrote to Dr. John Hillsdon-Smith, a forensic pathologist at the Center of Forensic Science on Grenville Street in downtown Toronto.

Dear Dr. Hillsdon-Smith,

Re: Tammy Homolka, Deceased, Aged 16

Our Reference – Hamilton ML 3435/90

"I would greatly appreciate your help with the following problem related to the sudden death of this 16-year-old girl.

He describes Tammy Lyn's condition when she was admitted D.O.A. to hospital. The tone and wording in his letter clearly communicates the doctor's skepticism about the veracity of Paul and Karla's stories about Tammy Lyn's demise.

There was a questionable delay in calling the ambulance. The coroner considered that there may have been a delay in calling the ambulance and that perhaps evidence at the scene had been interfered with. On discussion with the investigating officer, P.C. George Onich, St. Catharines Police, his opinion was that there had been no unreasonable delay in calling the ambulance and that there were no suspicious circumstances. The coroner, Dr. J.M. Rosloski, thought that CPR had been attempted for fifteen to twenty minutes prior to calling for help.

On inspection of the body the striking thing was the presence of sharply circumscribed, erythematous patches over the left cheek, right upper lip and around the mouth and lips but no lesions were present on the tongue, mouth or esophagus. The stomach contained a large amount of semi-solid food material. She had had a meal of macaroni and cheese at 5:00 p.m. There was bloodstained fluid dripping freely from the right side of the nose but none from the left. The pharynx and trachea contained blood stained fluid and food material but no corrosive lesions...

A section of skin adjacent to the margin of the lesion adjacent to the left ear show coagulation necrosis of the epidermis and dilated vessels without inflammation but the changes I think are those of a burn, possibly chemical and antemortem. The fine facial hair over the left side of the cheek and in the hairline was not singed which I think excludes a flame burn.

I must admit to being unable to explain these lesions on this girl's face. My colleagues in forensic pathology are also at a loss for an explanation…

"I enclose two color prints and kodachromes which need not be returned. Also a section of the skin from the left cheek."

The letter, signed Dr. John Groves, was copied to the regional coroner, Dr. J. M. Rosloski, the man who would ultimately, and inexplicably, and in spite of such dramatic, unanswered questions, rule Tammy Lyn Homolka's death accidental.

Thirteen days later, on February 23, 1991, Dr. Groves got a reply from Dr. Hillsdon-Smith.

"This is, indeed, an interesting case. Firstly, I agree with you that the appearance and distribution of the facial lesions represent a chemical burn. The absence of any corrosive lesions in the mouth and pharynx and larynx would indicate to me that the skin burns are of a topical nature and not the result of splashing. [*Meaning, in Hillsdon-Smith's opinion, the burns were not caused by the acidity of the vomit.*] The color of the burns is consistent with being caused by a strong caustic alkali.

"I note from your letter that the deceased started to vomit in the presence of her two young friends. One possible scenario is that the friends attempted to wipe vomit from her face using a rag inadvertently soaked in some domestically available caustic alkali."

[There was no evidence, certainly not in the statements given police by "her two young friends" – Paul Bernardo was hardly Tammy Lyn's friend and Karla was her sister – about "attempting to wipe vomit from her face using a rag inadvertently soaked in some domestically available caustic alkali." This complete non-sequitur from Dr. Hillsdon-Smith should have at least raised somebody's eyebrows.

Neither does Dr. Hillsdon-Smith offer which brand name house-cleaning products contain "strong caustic alkali" nor does anyone ever try and bother to confirm there were such products in the house.]

Dr. Hillsdon-Smith continues:

"This in part would explain the local nature of the burns.

The cause of death would appear asphyxia due to inhalation of vomit after having consumed alcohol.

Thank you for letting me review this case. I may seek an opinion from a dermatopathologist at some later date."

Even though the pathology report categorically stated there were only trace amounts of alcohol in Tammy Lyn Homolka's blood, neither pathologist seemed particularly troubled by the inconsistency in the coroner's conclusion, rendered in March, 1991, that Tammy Lyn had died by "asphyxia due to inhalation of vomit after having consumed alcohol." And no one ever addressed the most important observation made by Dr. Groves, that the "lesions" or "burns" on the girl's face appeared to him to be post-mortem. It was a profound clue to what really happened. In all likelihood, Tammy Lyn had died a good hour before "the ambulance was called." In fact, Dr. Grove's tentative observation suggests that Karla was still applying the Halothane-soaked rag to her sister's face after she was dead.

Having met Identification Officer Sergeant George Onich, I would find it difficult to accept his assessment of any peculiar situation. He seemed to me naive in the extreme, inexperienced and more interested in taking pictures than investigating clues. He is the police officer who took a picture of the videotape Paul and Karla made of their attack on Tammy Lyn. It was sitting in plain sight on Karla's night table. Sergeant Onich took a picture of it but never bothered to look at the videotape. That said, even a cursory review of the police reports would have revealed that he and rookie Constable Tom Weeks strongly disagreed about the circumstances of Tammy Lyn's death. Constable Weeks thought everything about Tammy Lyn's death was suspicious. He was silenced by the senior officer. This conflict of opinion was ignored by Sergeant Onich's superior.

The explanation given by Paul Bernardo and Karla Homolka that the otherwise healthy, active, young girl had simply "stopped breathing" because she had to much to drink and the ugly, red lesions on her face were "rug burns," was so absurd as to be beyond comprehension. The Chief Coroner for the Province has since declared that "asphyxia due to inhalation of vomit after having consumed alcohol" is descriptive, not causal, and will no longer be allowed as a conclusion in any coroner's jurisdiction.

Dr. Groves' letter, generated out of his deep skepticism, and the opinions it contains, the questions it raises and the inconsistencies it highlights, were never made public. Dr. Hillsdon-Smith, the Forensic Science Center pathologist, never bothered to follow up with a forensic dermatopathologist.

A file search of the Niagara Regional Police records, using the name "Homolka" or "Bernardo" would have turned up Tammy Lyn Homolka's file. At the very least, the strange circumstances surrounding Tammy Lyn's death and the unexplained red blossom burn on her left cheek would have set off alarm bells with the type of criminal investigator Vince Bevan considered himself to be. The coincidence alone would have been overwhelmingly suspicious.

Between the time Bevan was assigned the Mahaffy case and the night of February 11th, 1993, when he proposed a deal with Karla to George Walker, there was a great deal more than Tammy Lyn Homolka's suspicious death that Bevan should have uncovered. Had he done so, the deal with Karla would have been unnecessary.

From the time Paul Bernardo had taken up residence at the Homolka house in late 1990, there were a series of strange, disturbing, violent sex crimes that were most unusual for the area. In the Niagara region, crime was the purview of biker gangs and organized crime and had more to do with money laundering, drugs and vendettas than sex.

Over the 1990 Christmas holiday a young, divorced woman named Krystal Connors was raped and murdered. Krystal was petite and pretty and looked ten years younger than her twenty-eight years. She met her killer in a Port Dalhousie bar Paul Bernardo frequented. After raping and killing her, the murderer set Krystal and her apartment on fire. The apartment was in Port Dalhousie. Neighbors noticed the smoke early that morning and called the fire department. Forensic investigators found more than one set of semen stains on Krystal's sheets, drew their obdurate conclusions about promiscuity, and Krystal's violent and ignominious end faded into obscurity. A few days later, Paul and Karla killed Tammy Lyn.

In April, 1991, a young jogger was raped on Henley Island, just blocks from the Bernardo's new house on Bayview Avenue in Port Dalhousie. The attacker's *modus operandi* was exactly the same as the Scarborough Rapist's. Still, no red flags.

In June, 1991, a young A-student and cheerleader named Terri Anderson disappeared one night without a trace. Her bloated body floated up at the Port Dalhousie boat launch six months later. Although hers was labelled "death by misadventure" because it was discovered she popped a cap of acid and drank two beers the night she disappeared, the fact that her corpse was minus pants and shoes but still had underwear and a t-shirt which was strangely inside-out, was ignored by Inspector Bevan.

It was as though, in taking up residence with Karla Homolka, their union somehow released an unholy, sex-crazed demonic force imprisoned since the Dark Ages in the bedrock of the Niagara Escarpment.

In July, 1991, Rachel Ferron reported being stalked by a man in a gold Nissan. She got the licence plate number and called police. One of Inspector Bevan's colleagues went to see her and made a report. He determined that the car belonged to one Paul Kenneth Bernardo who lived at 57 Bayview Drive in Port Dalhousie. Rachel reported being followed twice again by the same car before the end of the month. Inspector Bevan never read these reports. The official explanation was that they had been "regrettably" lost.

* * * * * * *

On the topic of more charges for Karla with respect to her sister's death: through his own sources and resources, George Walker knew that the police had found scant hard evidence in the house. Walker reminded Segal that they already had a deal, without which Bevan and his task force would not have been able to enter the house, let alone find anything.

Bernardo would simply have gone back to Scarborough, from whence he came. Murray Segal knew the Ministry and the police were in no position to bargain. Would they have ever known about Tammy Lyn if George had not shared the information with Murray in the first place? The question was moot since George had already put the sister on the table in February.

Lately, the Inspector had been prattling on about charges against Karla Bernardo. If it wasn't so sad it might have been funny. An additional charge for Tammy was really about placating Inspector Bevan's posturing even though prosecutor Segal's hamstrung position was a consequence of Inspector Bevan's actions. That being understood, Walker had to agree that when the details about the extent of Karla's involvement became public, the optics would be worse if there were no reference to the sister in her criminal indictment.

They compromised. Segal backed off the extra manslaughter charge and Walker agreed that they would accept two additional years tacked onto Karla's sentence.

By the time Walker and Segal met again on May 5, Karla's sentence had become two concurrent twelve-year, rather than ten-year terms. That would add an extra year to the mandatory time she would have to spend in jail. Instead of three and a third years before she was eligible to apply for full parole, it would be four years. Her statutory release date would now be the summer of 2001 instead of 1999.

Even though Walker took professional pride in the fact that he had been able to avoid any sexual assault charges, three manslaughter charges would have made Karla a serial offender and that would have been equally egregious.

Manslaughter is by far the most common crime for which women are incarcerated. In terms of their resonance, or "carry-forward" effect on a woman's record, a manslaughter charge carries negligible impact, on a par with the after-effect of drunk driving convictions.

Serial offender status on Karla's record would change everything with respect to that record's deleterious effect on Karla's life after she got out of prison. Depending on how the political winds blew, it even might have opened the door for a "dangerous offender" application.

In terms of the internal dissonance Murray Segal had to confront, this compromise could be rationalized. The charges against Karla would become a matter of public record. While the public might buy into the concept of Karla as a battered woman and "compliant victim," no one would buy into it if the exact details of Tammy Lyn's death were revealed, as they inevitably would be, were Karla charged specifically in relation to her sister's murder. Karla's mock trial promised to become high profile enough when the abbreviated, cursory facts were read into the record.

* * * * * * *

In his will-state, Inspector Bevan noted that for a second time he was forced to confront the families about the deal with Karla Homolka.

"As a result of all discussions with Crown counsel, and Mr. Segal's discussions with Karla Bernardo's counsel, I was asked to invite the families for a meeting. On Wednesday, May 5, I met with Debbie Mahaffy at her residence. I then traveled to the French residence and met with several family members. Finally, commencing at 3:20 p.m. that date, Mr. Segal and I met with Donna and Doug French and Debbie Mahaffy at the Task Force office. During these meetings it was *carefully explained* [italics mine] to the families about the proposal to resolve the potential charges against Karla Bernardo.

"Later that night, after the meetings with the families had conclud-ed, I was advised by Mr. Segal that Karla Bernardo's counsel had accepted the proposal and a schedule had been arranged for investiga-tors to interview Karla Bernardo..."

"On Tuesday, May 11, through negotiations between Crown counsel and Karla Bernardo's counsel, Mr. Walker, arrangements were made to interview Karla Bernardo. For security reasons facilities were rented at a hotel in Whitby, Ontario."

* * * * * * *

On May 13, Karla and her mother checked into the Journey's End. Not George Walker's "villa" in Montserrat which he had years earlier named "Journey's End." Frankly, the two women and George would much rather have been there, than at the motel of the same name at 1700 Champlain Avenue in Whitby, Ontario.

Karla felt very special. Ministry officials and the police had rented two entire floors. Assigned Room 204, Karla and her mother made themselves at home. Karla's induced and cautioned statements were to be given upstairs and down the hall in Room 338. They began the following morning.

Murray Segal had the final, official copy of the resolution agreement which he ceremoniously handed over to George Walker. Although Walker had repeatedly explained this scenario to Karla, as part of the ritual, Walker again deciphered the difference between an "induced" and "cautioned" statement.

An "induced" statement was just what it said – an "inducement" for the prosecution to make the deal. Since they were already sufficiently "induced," this day devoted to inducement was a formality.

The "cautioned" statements were given under oath and would be considered evidence. Karla would agree to be audio- and videotaped. No problem. Walker then went on to point out the significant clauses in the resolution agreement, clauses which, were they trespassed, could negate the deal:

"*If the authorities learn through any means that your client had caused the death of any person, in the sense of her stopping life, any pro-*

posed resolution will be terminated at the suit of the Crown, regardless of the state the process is at."

Technically, Karla had "*caused the death*" of her sister, "*in the sense of her stopping life*," but that pesky reality had been dealt with. Karla got "two for Tammy," as George had noted in his file, and that was it.

With regard to Leslie Mahaffy and Kristen French, it would invariably become a "he-said-she-said" scenario. Karla said that Paul did it. Paul would likely say that Karla did it. There was actually puzzling evidence that made it possible that he just might be right.

There were subcutaneous symmetrical bruises on Leslie Mahaffy's back, consistent with someone Karla's size kneeling heavily on her. For example, to hold her down and smother her while she slept.

There was also aspirated blood in Kristen French's lungs and evidence that she had been severely beaten around the mouth and face.

Karla never mentioned, in any of the many statements that she was destined to make to police prior to Bernardo's trial that Paul had hit Kristen in the face – on the shoulders and back and side of the head, yes. But never in the face and the mouth.

This evidence was contained in the forensic pathologist's reports. It would appear that either the pathologist's evidence was not closely scrutinized or it was simply ignored because it was not going to change anything.

Without Karla, there would be no timely murder prosecution. It did not matter what they found in the house – whether it was two minutes or twenty hours of videotape evidence, Inspector Bevan would not have been in the house without Karla. Therefore, it did not matter which of them had actually "stopped the breath" of any of their victims. Inherent in the deal with Karla was the State's acceptance of her word that he did it. Unless some form of evidence existed that conclusively proved otherwise, the situation would remain as it was then and forever shall be. After everything she had seen and been through Karla was certainly not going to incriminate herself.

When confronted on the witness stand under cross-examination during Paul Bernardo's trial in 1995, Karla had no explanation for these anomalies in the various pathologists' reports. To this day, the subcutaneous symmetrical bruises on Leslie Mahaffy's back and the aspirated blood in Kristen French's lungs remain stubborn mysteries.

The fact that Karla could have freed either Leslie Mahaffy or Kristen French, or at least, on numerous occasions, could have alerted the police, had been countenanced by the prosecutors and, given the position in which they found themselves, discounted.

There was also another salient fact that was ignored because it was antithetical to the position which the prosecutors were forced to adopt.

Paul Bernardo had never killed any of his rape victims. Nineteen documented attacks, no fatalities. No one died until Karla came on the scene. And even then, only when she was directly involved were people killed.

* * * * * * *

George Walker continued pointing out salient passages in the plea resolution to Karla. "*The statement [meaning the induced and cautioned statements that she was about to give] and any subsequent statements will be a full, complete, and truthful account regarding her knowledge and/or involvement or anyone else's involvement in the investigations into the deaths of Leslie Mahaffy; Kristen French; alleged rapes in Scarborough; alleged rape on Henley Island; the death of Tammy Homolka; and any other criminal activity she has participated in or has knowledge of. An 'induced' statement cannot be used against her in any criminal proceedings.*

"Any other criminal activity she has participated in or has knowledge of…" The point being, this was the time to get it all off her chest, "to spill" as Dr. Arndt liked to describe the process whereby the patient confesses and testifies, in no small measure because nothing Karla revealed or said during the induced part of this process could be used against her in a court of law.

"*They (the authorities) will provide no protection for a prosecution if it is discovered that she lied, including a prosecution for obstructing justice, public mischief, fabricating evidence, perjury, inconsistent statements and/or false affidavits*" was the next important clause.

In other words, lying by commission was as damnatory as lying by omission.

These conditions were nothing new. The bit about Karla not having "*caused the death of any person, in the sense of her stopping life,*" and that "*no protection for a prosecution*" would be provided "*if it is discovered that she lied,*" had been integral conditions of the deal since mid-February, 1993. They were in the Authorization that George Walker filed with the court on February 28 just before he left for his Journey's End in Montserrat the first week in March.

Walker finished advising Karla by pointing out the part about giving the prosecution "an opportunity to inspect a copy of any psychiatric, psychological or other medical reports" and reminding her that this was a good thing.

Walker then turned his attention to the police who would be facilitating Karla's statements. He spent a couple of hours discussing the forthcoming "interviews" with various officers, especially Inspector Bevan.

The powers-that-be in the Ministry of the Attorney General had conveniently decided to let the Toronto prosecutor and the Toronto police deal with all rape charges, whether they had been committed in Scarborough, Mississauga, or St. Catharines, including the rape on Henley Island.

The Green Ribbon Task Force and Inspector Bevan were only responsible for the first-degree murder and any other charges that may be levied against Paul Bernardo with respect to Leslie Mahaffy and Kristen French. They would share Karla's induced and cautioned statements with Toronto for the purposes of Bernardo's prosecution on the rape charges after he was tried for the murders.

This divisive move ensured that the opposing forces from the Niagara region and Toronto would continue to be their own best adversaries. The authorities had, for all intent and purposes, at least as far as Karla was concerned, divided and conquered themselves and that would become more and more apparent as time went by.

In the immediate instance it meant that Karla would have two interviewers, one from Toronto and one from St. Catharines, who would act as her facilitators and interlocutors for these formal statements. The empathetic, peach-complexioned Mary Lee Metcalfe and the sharp-nosed, thin-lipped Sergeant Robert Gillies were cut out from the herd of cops stampeding through the halls of the Journey's End.

Although they could ask questions, Walker cautioned, their tone could not be challenging or abrasive. After all, they were all on the same side now.

In the middle of the afternoon, a posture-perfect Karla Bernardo recited the prodigious list of drugs she was on.

"Do you feel that this medication that you described would affect, in any way, your participation in this interview?" Detective Metcalfe asked politely.

"Absolutely not."

"Okay. Thank you, Karla."

"You're welcome."

"What is the current status of your marriage?"

"Zero. Zilch. It's over."

"Do you see any prospect of any reconciliation with Paul Bernardo?"

"No. I have already spoken to a divorce lawyer and divorce proceedings will be put underway very shortly... *The* fact *that he assaulted me made it* absolutely *certain that I would not reconcile with him. There is no hope.* Absolutely *none. I hate him, I don't want anything* to do with *him.* I wish – like, I want him to be totally out of my life."

"You are aware that your husband is a suspect in several crimes, including the Leslie Mahaffy and Kristen French matters. What effect has his alleged involvement in these crimes had upon your marriage?"

"We really didn't talk very much because our marriage was falling apart..."

Primly dressed and well-groomed, Karla barely moved except to occasionally brush her hair aside. She began her sordid tale with a lie. "He liked tall brunette girls because they were opposite to me. He liked them to be virgins – I know that's what you're looking for."

He actually preferred blondes which is why early in their relationship he "forced" Karla to forego perms and dye her hair bleached blonde. The only victim that had dark hair was the one Karla had picked out – Kristen French. It was true that Paul liked virgins.

* * * * * * *

On her sister, Tammy Lyn:

"One night we were having like a kind of get together at my parents' house and Paul was there and Tammy was there and a bunch of other people were there, who exactly I don't remember. And we ran out of beer or wine or something and Paul said that he'd run across the border and get some. So, Tammy went with him. She wanted to go with him and she was calling, 'Oh, I got a date with Paul. I got a date with Paul.' And they left and they were gone for hours and hours and no one knew where they were.

"I was furious because I didn't know where they were. I was very upset. I was afraid. I didn't know if they'd been in an accident because they were gone forever.

"And they finally came back all laughing and happy. And I was just so mad because they had frightened me so much. I don't know if that means anything or what.

On the teenage rower Paul raped on Henley Island on April 6, 1991:

"And then that girl rower, it was April 6. I just remembered it was April 6 because that's my cat's birthday.

About Jane Doe and Norma Tellier:

"He always wanted me to find him young girlfriends and so I did. I found him two young girlfriends, which were friends of mine. And what they did was between Paul and them. What's the word I'm looking for? 'Voluntarily'– like they had relationships with him and that's about it.

"So I called Jane Doe up, she came over. And, you know, it was great to see her again because I really liked her, and Paul started to try to make her his girlfriend and it worked."

[Although Karla becomes otherwise very detailed, she neglects to mention that Paul was out when she first invited Jane over on June 6, 1991, and that she did to Jane exactly what she had done to her sister six months earlier entirely on her own. She does not tell them that she then called Bernardo on his cell phone and invited him to come home and see the wedding present Karla had procured. She also neglected to mention that Paul had been talking to her about postponing their imminent wedding because he thought he might be in love with an anal-sex-loving nurse named Alison Worthington who he met in Florida when he went down to spend spring break with his buddies in March of that year.]

"She [Jane] and him got together really well and they ended up being very, very close and then, I don't know, things kind of fizzled out because her mother didn't want Jane hanging around us because she thought we were too old, even though I knew her mother from way back when. [The police already had Jane Doe's statements and knew that this description of the relationship and the role of Jane Doe's mother in its dissolution were false.]

"So Paul got really mad at me and blamed me for that, of course. Everything was always my fault. Then I found him Norma, Norma Tellier, who was one of Tammy's friends. Again they got along really, really well and things went very well between the two of them. They became boyfriend and girlfriend, so to speak. The way it was, I always turned my head and looked the other way."

[The police also had Norma's statements and knew that Karla had facilitated her rape and that, although it was peculiar, to say the least, there was nothing "really, really well…" about the "relationship," as Karla called it, between Norma Tellier and Paul Bernardo.]

"At the very end of it all in December, which is when, like, Paul was getting desperate, he needed to have a young girl, he went out and, like, he thought that he was losing both of them. Jane and Paul had gotten back together again too."

[This was incorrect and the police knew it from their extensive interviews with both Jane Doe and Norma Tellier.) Perhaps the copious amount of various drugs Karla was on affected her memory or her apperception of the reality of recalled events. Jane left the Bernardo domicile at Christmas in 1991, never to return. Norma Tellier was the Christmas special in 1992. It was very convenient for Karla to blur the chronology.]

"So he spent hundreds and hundreds of dollars on them for Christmas. He bought them hundred-dollar stuffed animals, gold chains. He bought Norma an ankle bracelet. He bought Jane a watch. You know, he bought them all kinds of stuff. [Just as he had bought Karla "all kinds of (exactly) the same stuff."]

"Paul always thought that he could buy love. That is what he did with me. He tried to buy me and I guess in a way it worked. I don't know.

"But both of the girls in the end told him that they weren't interested which he blamed totally on me because I was supposed to let them know that we didn't have a husband-and-wife relationship anymore, which we didn't.

"I slept on the floor beside the bed. We barely talked. The only thing we did together was smuggle cigarettes."

When asked directly if there were any other crimes similar to those committed against Karla's sister, Leslie Mahaffy and Kristen French, Karla replied, "None that I can think of."

Karla's general comments about Paul:

"He was very caring at times towards these girls, like Kristen and Leslie, then at other times he was very vicious to them. Like, it's funny, I wouldn't diagnose him as a split personality but he really does go to extremes. He can be the nicest guy in the world and he can be the worst person you would ever want to meet. So I remember him, like with Kristen, you know, saying 'That's too bad. I didn't mean to cut you' kind of thing. And I'm thinking, 'What?' Like, why are you acting this way? Because it was just – it just seemed so out of – not right.

"She (Kristen French) took off her sweater because she was hot and her white turtleneck had blood on it, on her shoulder. And I remember Paul saying 'Oh no,' you know, 'you got cut' in a really nice way. I think he might have even cleaned it out with peroxide and then he put a band-aid on it.

What Karla thought she might have been doing the night Paul went out and came home with Leslie Mahaffy:

"I probably cleaned the house. I always cleaned when he left, because he didn't like me to use cleaning products because he didn't like the odor of them.

"So I always tried to clean when he was gone. I would have cleaned and played with the dog, talked to somebody on the phone, possibly Jane Doe, maybe Kathy Ford, possibly my sister but probably not. Then I would have probably read. I like to read true-life horror stories, or true-life crime books. V.C. Andrews, Dean Koontz and Robin Cook. Robin Cook writes medical mysteries. I like the mystery stories mainly. I don't like Harlequins or anything like that."

Champagne glasses:

"I was upstairs reading I'm sure. I don't know what else I'd be doing up there because I stayed in the bedroom to be as quiet as possible so I'm sure I was reading.

"Oh, and I was really mad too, because when I took Buddy out there were two expensive champagne glasses on the dining-room table and – we had these expensive Champagne glasses from France which we never used. He had those out. The two of them had been drinking Champagne from those glasses and I was really mad. It was a stupid thing, but I was very mad about that."

Karla on killing Leslie Mahaffy:

"So he (Paul) went downstairs and got a piece of black electrical cord which I am sure you found. It was in the basement, just sitting on the floor…It's round … the length of which I am not sure because I've only seen it like wrapped up and tied around people. It was cut at both ends, I believe, like, with scissors. So it looks like just a nice cord, nice round and black. If you showed it to me, I could identify it.

"And he strangled her with it…We were both freaking out because, like, we had never done this before… it kind of looked like his first time killing someone…

"The cord was off her neck and she was blue… that was the first dead person I'd ever seen and I was just sickened. And I turned away again and I got really crazy. I was saying to Paul, like, I was so hyper and just hysterical almost and I was jumping around saying, 'What are we going to do, like, what are we going to do with her?' And he said, 'Calm down.' And I said, 'Well, what are we going to do?' and he said, 'I don't know.'

"And then she took a breath and that freaked me out even more. He should have slapped me in the face because I was really hysterical then. So he went over to her and did the same thing. He strangled her more and I think I watched that time because, like, what the hell, she's dead anyway."

Karla on dismembering Leslie Mahaffy:

"Well, he kind of joked. Like, I guess he had to joke because he was, I don't know if he was sickened by it or not. But he was kind of joking about it and saying that, you know, when he – I don't even like saying it – you know, when he cut her head off, he just held it up to him and looked at it and just plopped it in the cement. And he told me that – he told me what each one contained. Like there was her head, her torso, her lower arm, her upper arms, and then the lower legs and her upper legs. So that was one, two three, four, five, six, seven, eight, nine, ten.

Karla on kidnaping Kristen French:

"It was definitely planned. Like he had it in mind. I didn't come home right after I got off work. I got off work at one o'clock and I think I went to the library or something. I went for a little walk past the old library in Port Dalhousie and he was mad at me because I didn't come right home because he had wanted to go out earlier. So, he had it planned.

Q: 'Okay, what day was that?'

A: 'Thursday'

Q: 'Do you normally take a Thursday afternoon off?'

A: 'Well, we used to do it... everyone used to work every Saturday, or sorry, every Thursday. And then we decided that we were going to take every other Thursday off, because the veterinarian has that day off every week. Then they decided that they wanted everyone working on Thursday. So, for a period of the time it was every other Thursday I had off. And I think that was the first Thursday that I had off.'

Q. 'So that was something that was scheduled rather than a specific request from you.'

A. 'Right...'"

[Another lie. The vet Karla worked for, Dr. Patty Weir, had, months earlier, during four police interviews conducted in February, 1993, described how Karla had planned and manipulated her co-worker to get that particular Thursday off.

Karla's statements were never cross-referenced with other witnesses' statements, or, if they were, and the many discrepancies discovered, like the 1:58 videotape found in the house and the forensic pathologists' evidence, they were simply ignored.]

Karla continued. "He told me, like, when we were leaving, he asked me to go through it. I had a problem with memory then, too. He kept saying, 'Go through what we're going to do.' So I said, 'Well, if we see a girl, we're going to stop. I'm going to ask her for directions. I'm going to try and get her over to the car. I'm going to get the map out... I'm going to say we're from a different city and that I need to find a certain place, probably the Penn Center.

"And I don't know if we discussed it or if it was just implied, or if I just knew to get in the back seat. I can't remember if we discussed it or not. But it made sense. I mean, I wouldn't want her (Kristen French) behind us either. So I could have just automatically jumped in the back."

On what Karla and Kristen did in the bathroom:
"She asked me if she could use my perfume and I said 'yes, of course,' because I had a whole bunch of little perfume samples and she wanted to try some of the Opium and I said 'sure.'" After all, they were samples and they were free."

Karla on raping and killing Kristen French:
"I remember Saturday night, Kristen had a Jacuzzi bath and she had seemed a lot happier and she had her bath and I had a shower and we both got dressed up. I had a kilt which was kind of similar to hers only it was a different color. It was my sister Tammy's kilt and I had a green sweater which was also my sister Tammy's which was a lot like Kristen's Holy Cross sweater and a turtleneck. So we dressed in almost identical uniforms and we put on make-up and we were giggling and laughing and it seemed like we're just friends getting ready to go out, kind of thing, we were doing what Paul had told us to do. I had all little perfume samples and she wanted to try some. I remember Paul saying that he was going to have a contest, that the girl who had the best perfume on didn't have to have anal sex with him. And it turns out that I had the perfume he didn't like, but he said he would give me preferential treatment because I was his wife and he would have anal sex with Kristen. So he did. He lined us both up together, kneeling on our hands and knees together and he had sex with us, her first, then me, or me first, then her, whatever.

"She was handcuffed, hands behind her back. Paul put her in as comfortable a position as possible. Her feet were bound…she wasn't gagged. I didn't want her to be gagged, because I didn't think that was right…

"We talked about her dog, and about her boyfriend, and she asked me – Paul had hit me in front of her – and she asked me if Paul hits me all the time and I said 'yeah.' She said 'I know you don't want to be part of this.' We talked about school and stuff like that. I should never have talked to her. Because I got too emotionally involved. Like, it's hard to explain because you've never been through this. But, you know, she became a friend. And when she said to me, you know, 'I know that you don't want to be involved in this,' I felt really close to her then, because I felt like, you know, two girlfriends talking…

"Okay. I remembered a couple of things… nothing of real significance, but I think I should tell you anyhow. It was before Kristen was killed. She had started to resist the things that Paul wanted to do with her. Like, she was starting to fight him. And she said things like, you know, 'some things are worth dying for.' She was very proud, she was very strong. And then he showed her the videotape of Leslie, the part where she says her name – in order to scare her. And Kristen was very strong and she didn't even act scared. And I just wanted you to know that, because I think that is something her parents would like to know, that she was very, very strong and didn't show a lot of emotion throughout the whole thing."

Detective Metcalfe: We appreciate you telling us that.

Karla: Like, I just want to help.

Karla on the discovery of Kristen French's body:

"I didn't call Paul to tell him, because I didn't want to, you know, say anything over the phone. I don't know why. And I figured I had better not call him, I had better tell him in person, but I think he had already – No, okay, I'm wrong here. He called me. He had heard the news during the day, and he had called me and said they found her. And I said, 'I know, I saw it on the news.' And he said, 'You saw it?' I am pretty sure he heard it on the radio. And I said, 'Yeah, I saw it.' And he said, 'Well, is it her?' And I said, 'Yeah, it's her,' because I could describe it by the news footage on TV, I could tell where it was. And obviously it had to be her.

"So we both went through our little panicky kind of stage. I was upset, well, we were both naturally upset. We had expected her to be found a long time before then, and I think it really threw us that it took so long for them to find her.

"And then when they started saying that she had been kept alive for the whole time. Like, Paul was kind of happy, he was saying, 'Well, this is great because we have got all these alibis, you know, we went to your parents' house for Easter dinner, Mike was over.' Mike Donald was over several times that week. You know, he (Paul) had gone out, we had both gone out together. There is no way we could have left this girl, there is no way the two of us could have kept her for that length of time. So he was happy about that. I can't think what else."

* * * * * * *

When Kristen French's body had been found, in the ditch on Sideroad One across from the Meadowlands Cemetery where Leslie Mahaffy's remains had been interred, they could not be sure it was her. But Inspector Bevan was sure it was her because the corpse was missing the tip of the baby finger on the left hand. Without waiting for confirmation from the pathologist, the Inspector rushed off to tell the French family.

"I said that there were a number of factors which prevented scientists from establishing an accurate time of death," he noted in his will-state. "If the body had been frozen or refrigerated or was left in a cool place those factors would inhibit decomposition and make an assessment of the time of death almost impossible. However, at that time there was no evidence to indicate that any of that had occurred. Under the worst case scenario, circumstances seemed to indicate that Kristen had been killed 12 to 24 hours prior to the discovery of her body…"

This was devastating news to the French family. Not only had their daughter's naked body been discovered in a ditch but it would appear, according to Inspector Bevan, that she had been held captive for the better part of two weeks. To what unimaginable torture and degradation had their beautiful daughter been subjected?

Inspector Bevan got lucky. One out of two of his guesses were correct. The body was that of their daughter's. His other guess was dead wrong. Kristen had indeed been killed two and a half days after she was taken, prior to Paul and Karla going to Karla's parents' for Easter Sunday dinner. It had taken two weeks for the body to be discovered.

He was also wrong about the identity of the comatose teenager on the 1:58 videotape. An expert at the Ontario Provincial Police laboratories in Toronto even backed up his supposition and, officially, Inspector Bevan stood by his guess that the comatose girl on the videotape was Kristen French. However, by the time he and Karla got to the Journey's End Hotel in Whitby to take Karla's induced and cautioned statements, the police had decided to explore the possibility that it was somebody else – a fourth, unacknowledged victim.

"Karla, can I stop you for a minute?" Detective Metcalfe interjected during the third day. "Were there any other occasions where you had oral sex with another female, other than Tammy, Kristen or Leslie? Perhaps while you were on vacation…" The short videotape segment on the 1:58 tape they had recovered from the house involving Karla and the older, blond woman was obviously filmed in a hotel room. The prosecutors and police decided to try and provide some mnemonics.

"On vacation? No, no, definitely not. There is no other incident that I recall." [Karla had apparently forgotten all about the prostitute who she had talked into having sex with her and Paul during a stopover in Atlantic City in August, 1992, on their way home from a Florida vacation.]

Detective Metcalfe tried another approach. "Was there ever any other time that you were videotaped…"

"Well…I was videotaped with my friends, I was videotaped with my dog."

[On June 6th, 1991, the first of two nights that Karla administered alcohol, Halcion and Halothane to Jane Doe, Karla videotaped Jane playing with Karla's dog, Buddy. Here, Karla does not mention Jane

Doe by name, even though she had previously when she discussed procuring teenage girlfriends for Paul.]

"Do you mean like videotaped in a sexual way?" That was what Detective Metcalfe meant.

"Yes, there was another time. There was a video that Paul and I made. It was – I think, it was after Tammy's death. Yeah, it was, it was while my parents were away at a furniture show, so it would have been in January. January or February, after Tammy's death. We made a tape of us having sex together, basically of us having sex together in front of the fireplace."

[Karla neglected to say that in this video she played the role of her dead sister and talked about procuring virgins.]

Getting ready for a break Detective Metcalfe told Karla that she was doing really well.

Karla: Okay. Good. I hope so. I just want to help.
Detective Metcalfe: I know. We just want the truth.
Karla: I can't live with this any longer.

* * * * * * *

Sergeant Gillies handed Karla another still picture taken from the 1:58 video. Karla looked at it closely. "That's me, I'm sure. And I don't know whose hand that is. I don't know who that is." The lifeless hand and the index finger which Karla can be seen inserting in her vagina had become an indelible image in the minds of approximately one hundred detectives and prosecutors.

"Whose hand might that be?" Gillies asked.

Studying the photograph intently, Karla digressed. "That's in our house, because I can recognize it from that thing there – that's the pull-out handle on the drawer of Paul's dresser. It's definitely not my parents' house, so it's our house... on Bayview. So that would have either been Kristen or Leslie," Karla said, even though she had told Dr. Arndt two months earlier that it was neither because who ever it was, they were still alive.

"Were there other incidents of digital intercourse?"

The interviewers showed a real preference for polite euphemisms.

"Oh, probably," Karla replied. "With both girls, I'm sure. I can't remember specifically, but with both, I'm sure."

"In this picture, what does it show the other girl wearing?"

"It is a sweatshirt. It looks like a sweatshirt, and I don't know if that's underwear or – I don't know if it is underwear or just the bottom of the sweatshirt... It looks like a sweatshirt to me, anyway."

"The fact that the girl would appear to be wearing a sweatshirt, does that help you identify who that party is?" Sergeant Gillies' voice had a hint of frustration.

"Well, I don't think..." Karla started backpedalling syntactically. "Like I said, I am pretty sure that I didn't lend anything to Kristen or Leslie, but I guess I was – I am sure I am incorrect, because it obviously appears that this person is wearing a sweatshirt. But I can't tell from the body."

"The picture I showed you earlier today is from the same video."

Karla absorbed Gillies' statement but did not acknowledge it. "It looks like my sister Tammy," she said, and quite naturally so, since Jane closely resembled Tammy.

"It just gives me an impression," Karla continued. "But that's definitely not Tammy." Obviously it was not Tammy because Tammy had been dead for a month when Paul and Karla moved into their house.

"Do you have any other pictures?" Again, Karla responded to a question with a question, which always seemed to bring Sergeant Gillies to a standstill.

"Not with me right now, but I will get some others."

"Like, are these clips right after one another or something?" Karla asked.

"Yes."

"Okay, then based on that, this is the bed." That was a revelation. "It's not a pillow, it's probably the bed, because if that's the door, then the bed was right here." Karla pointed at a small spot on the photograph. "I don't know. I am going to have to think about them."

Gillies, starting to give up: "The top picture depicts a hand which appears to have an article of clothing or a rag or something in it." That was a vague image of Karla's Halothane-soaked rag.

"Okay," Karla obfuscated. "Possibly – I don't know, I really don't know." Then Karla pulled her interrogative stunt again. "How come this one is so good, and this one is so blurry?"

"I don't know the answer to that question," Gillies replied.

"Oh, okay. But you can get a clearer one of this, you think?"

"I hope to, yes."

Toward the end of that day – it was a Sunday, at 8:30 p.m. – Karla said to the detectives: "I don't know if you are doing it because you feel I need it, but I don't need as many breaks as we are taking…so you guys break for whatever you want to break for, don't worry about me."

Karla consumed other people's emotional distress the way she consumed drugs. She was a sponge for attention; the closer and more intently she was scrutinized, the more she opened up. She fed on her facilitators' astonishment and abhorrence. The more difficult and trying her circumstances, the stronger she seemed to become. The stronger she became, the more intense the light on the dark spot. And, as had been the case all her life, the less those around her could see it.

Finally such intense light on so dark a spot got to be too much for Detective Metcalfe; on the morning of the fourth day, she became ill and had to leave the interview. Karla solicitously said that she hoped the detective would feel better soon. Detective Metcalfe was replaced by her partner, Ron Whitefield.

The interviews ended on May 18th, 1993. The police thanked Karla. "You're welcome," Karla said. "That's it?"

"That's it," the detective replied and thanked her again.

"You're welcome. I hope I have helped you," Karla rejoined. "Can I have this pen?"

"Yes."

"Thank you."

* * * * * * *

"On Thursday, May 27th, I attended at St. Catharines Court," reads one of the last entries in Inspector Bevan's will-state. "Shortly after 9:00 a.m. Paul Bernardo appeared in Court and was remanded on charges in our jurisdiction.

* * * * * * *

"I know that I am lucky," Karla wrote years later from her cell in Sainte-Anne-des-Plaines. "I was literally half an inch away from a life sentence. I know that I could have been dead. But sometimes I wonder if either of those options would have been better. If I had received a life sentence would there have been so much public and political reaction? I am doing more time on a twelve-year sentence than many women. I know who are doing life sentences (with parole eligibility at 10 years and you are eligible to apply for day parole at 7 years.) And if I were dead, I wouldn't have to live through all this. Well, enough of that."

DREAMS ARE NOT REALITY

Two days after Independence Day, 1993, Karla lost hers and was sent directly to jail. Almost immediately, Dr. Roy Brown – at the prison's behest – started providing the intensive therapy that Dr. Arndt said Karla urgently needed.

During her first session, shortly after she had been moved from the prison's medical unit to a cell in segregation, Karla told Dr. Brown that she was having "bad dreams." These bad dreams were haunted by a victim she thought she might have forgotten.

Presciently, Dr. Brown told Karla not to worry. "Dreams are not reality," he said.

Not convinced that her dreams did not reflect reality, Karla wrote a letter to George Walker. It was dated October 6, 1993. In the letter she tells Walker that she is "having a major problem" because she "forgot" to the tell police that "Paul raped Jane Doe, a friend of mine."

Karla goes on to say that she does not remember much of it, just that Jane was drunk and had passed out and she has a mental image of it happening in their living room. But she also has an image of Jane Doe falling off their bed.

"I've been racking my brains for days now, trying to piece the whole thing together but I just can't."

In the letter, Karla complains that she feels constrained. If she tells the doctors, they will report it to the prison. She cannot talk to Walker or anyone else on the phone because she believes all of her telephone calls are monitored and recorded.

She talks about the still photographs she was shown by Sergeant Gillies. She refers to the sergeant by his first name. At the time, when Bob showed her the pictures, during her induced and cautioned statements last May, she could not identify the girl. Bob kept showing them to her again, last June, during the gravel run she did with the cops, retracing her steps the night she and Paul dumped Kristen French's body, looking for the Mickey Mouse watch, going through her ransacked house. She could not identify the girl then, either.

"What if it was with Jane?" she wonders. Why didn't she remember it when Bob first questioned her? "What I'm really afraid of is that I was more involved than I can remember" and that they will "nail me for it, too."

Indeed, Karla was very "involved." In fact the stupefaction and rape of Jane Doe had been one of Karla's singular contributions to the depraved *guignol* that had been their married life.

She says she chose to write "George" about it because the prison authorities cannot review prisoners' mail to their lawyers and implores him to write back to her with advice. "Remember that I *want* to tell them! I feel guilty and have to get it off my conscience. Thanks, George. I feel like I'm going crazy."

"Going crazy?" George thought ruefully to himself as he read the letter. Regardless, he was not particularly concerned about this recovered memory. The girl in the 1:58 video probably was Jane Doe, but this fact would not change anything. Jane Doe was alive. The police had interviewed her. If the videotape itself had not scuttled the deal when Inspector Bevan reviewed it on February 22, only three days after he executed his search warrant, Karla's forgetfulness was hardly going to precipitate a sudden reversal of her good fortune now.

Without fanfare, and quite blasé, George passed the letter on to Murray Segal in early November.

* * * * * * *

On December 6, 1993, the police showed Karla the videotape itself. The past six months had been months of intense preparation. Paul Bernardo's preliminary trial was imminent and they had to ready Karla. The preliminary could, potentially, be more grueling than the actual trial because Bernardo's defense team would be allowed more latitude. Preliminary trials were automatically subject to publication bans. Like American grand juries the proceedings were held *in camera* and whatever was said kept secret. This gave the defense an almost unfettered license to probe and explore the prosecutor's case which, in turn, created an even greater prosecutorial vigilance over those aspects that were perceived to be weak or vulnerable.

This particular meeting with Karla was one of the rare police interviews with Karla that was not videotaped and transcribed. The only record of this meeting are barely legible, handwritten notes made by Sergeant Gary Beaulieu. Nor is there any mention of this meeting in Sergeant Gillies or Sergeant Beaulieu's will-states.

Sergeant Gillies started the meeting by telling Karla that he was going to show her the videotape from which they had taken the still photographs he had shown her on numerous previous occasions. He explained the circumstances surrounding the discovery of the tape and what she could expect to see and then played it. When the first, short segment ended he pressed the stop button and attempted to rewind the tape. The machine malfunctioned. After a little fiddling they got it running again and Sergeant Gillies replayed the section.

Karla had already acknowledged the videotaped sex with the hooker in Atlantic City when Sergeant Gillies had shown her new stills taken from the 1:58 videotape just prior to their tour of her house on June 17, 1993. Now, she elaborated. It was a hooker Paul hired when they were in Atlantic City in the late summer of 1992. They were returning home from a vacation to Disney World. This short segment was part of a longer tape. Paul had concealed a video camera in their hotel room and recorded the entire event. It was probably 90 minutes long in its entirety. Now she remembered the prostitute's name. It was Michelle Banks. She even recalled that Michelle had told Karla that she was pregnant. Karla portrayed the hooker as Paul's idea and his doing.

During the playing of the second segment, in which Karla molests an unconscious young woman who cannot readily be identified because her face cannot be seen, Sergeant Beaulieu noted that Karla turned in her chair to closely watch the monitor.

First, Karla thought it depicted something that occurred at 57 Bayview but she did not recall the tape being made. It must have been Paul doing the videotaping because he was the only one she had ever done things like that with.

After a moment of reflection, she reversed herself and said it must have been Tammy at her parents' house because the torso looked so much like Tammy's but she said it was hard to tell. So they rewound the tape and played it again frame by frame, freezing specific frames to try and pinpoint items in the background.

Karla then said that there could be no doubt that it was shot in their house on Bayview in the upstairs bedroom and probably not long after they had moved there. She qualified that by saying that she was not one hundred percent sure and did not recall the circumstances. "Nothing stands out," was how she put it.

The detectives replayed the tape from the first still – to no avail. Then they played the third segment.

Karla concurred that it was the same girl and probably another clip from a longer videotape because she was wearing the same shirt. Karla could not recall the circumstances.

"Perhaps, if I had some time alone to think," she said which echoed exactly what she had said when Sergeant Gillies first showed Karla the stills during her cautioned statements six months earlier.

It was certainly the same person, at least based on the sweatshirt the girl was wearing. It must be either Kristen French or Leslie Mahaffy. She had performed with them in that location. The two sergeants encouraged her to focus on the sweatshirt but Karla still wasn't sure. They replayed the segment, freezing it frame-by-frame again, and asked Karla this time to focus on the victim's underwear, maybe that

Oh - me + my bestest buddies,
Vicky and Lisa. Poor Lisa's
been crying over Tom. What
am I planning? (There's that
devilish glint in my eye?)
June 21st, 1984.

Caption on the back of photograph in Karla's handwriting: "Oh, me & my bestest buddies Vicky and Lisa. Poor Lisa's been crying over Tom. What am I planning? There's the devilish glint in my eye.) June 21st, 1984."

The Executive of the Exclusive Diamond Club circa 1988. From left to right: Karla Teale a.k.a. Bernardo (nee Homolka), "Dirty" Debbie Dalgliesh (nee Purdie), and Kathy Ford (nee Wilson)

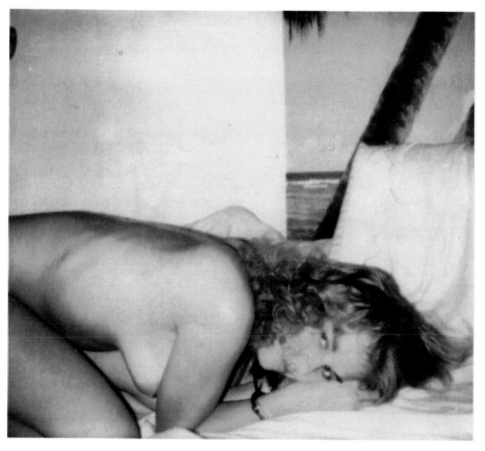

Karla, handcuffed, strikes a pose; circa May, 1988. Photo by Paul Bernardo

Karla, handcuffed, strikes another pose; circa May, 1988. Photo by Paul Bernardo

Paul and Karla celebrating on Karla's high school Prom Night; circa April, 1989. Left to Right: Karla Homolka, unidentified, Mike Donald, unidentified, unidentified, Paul Bernardo.

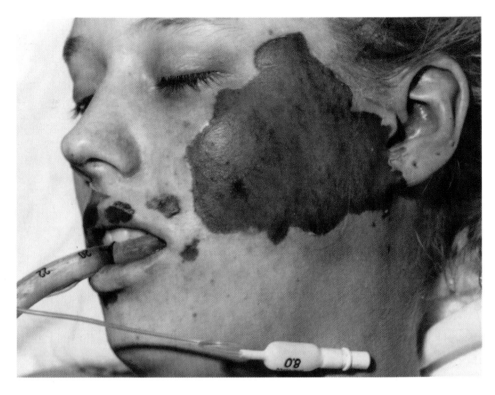

Post-mortem police photograph of Tammy Lyn Homolka taken at St. Catharines General Hospital, early in the morning of December 25, 1990. The violent, red chemical burns around her mouth, nose and on her cheek did not seem to give any of the medical or police personnel pause. The coroner found that her death was accidental and closed the file three months later.

Police photo: Karla's night table, December 25, 1990, shortly after Karla's sister Tammy Lyn was declared DOA. The videotape documenting Paul and Karla Homolka's attack on Tammy Lyn sits with a wad of American money. This picture was taken by one of the senior officers on the scene, Sergeant George Onich. For some inexplicable reason, the Sergeant took a picture of the videotape but did not bother to review the tape itself.

Photograph of Paul and Karla placed in Tammy Lyn Homolka's casket by Paul and Karla. This photograph was taken from Tammy Lyn's coffin by police during her exhumation in the summer of 1993. Karla's parents instructed the police not to return the photograph to the coffin.

Death letter addressed to Tammy Lyn Homolka with sections handwritten by both Karla Homolka and Paul Bernardo and placed in her casket with other bric-a-brac. It is written on Paul and Karla's wedding stationery. This item was also removed from the coffin during the exhumation. Along with the picture of Paul and Karla and a number of other items placed in the casket by Paul and Karla, Dorothy and Karel Homolka instructed the police not to return the death letter to the coffin.

Karla poses with a few of her shower gifts, June 7, 1991. Picture by Jane Doe

Karla with Jane Doe, circa June 7, 1991. Photograph by Karla using the automatic timer device

Police photo: Cement blocks containing Leslie Mahaffy's body parts at the edge of Lake Gibson, June 29, 1991.

Karla calls in Victoria Secret order, circa Christmas, 1992. Photo by Paul Bernardo

Paul and Karla celebrate Christmas in their living room at 57 Bayview Drive,
Port Dalhousie, 1992.

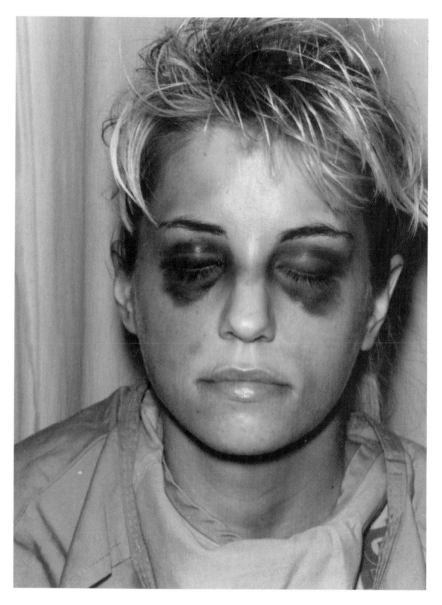

Happy New Year. The aftermath of Paul and Karla's holiday celebrations; Karla in police photo, St. Catharines' General Hospital, January 6, 1993. Notice the lip-gloss.

Karla's lawyer, George Walker, on the lawn of his villa, Journey's End, in Montserrat, circa January, 1994. He is holding a dead iguana and the machete with which it was dispatched, rough justice for the hibiscus-eating lizard.

would help. It didn't. They rewound the short tape and took it out of the machine.

In what must be in retrospect the perfect non sequitur, Karla then told the policemen that she thought they had come to interview her about Jane Doe. She told them she remembered giving Jane "booze and 1 pill," that Paul thought Jane had stopped breathing while he was assaulting her and Karla had called 911, only to cancel it a few minutes later. According to Sergeant Beaulieu's cryptic notes, the two topics, that is, Jane Doe and 1:58 tape, appear to have coagulated in Karla's memory at this point but without yielding any meaningful revelation or deeper insight into her "bad dreams," the "bad dreams" that the 1:58 videotape so graphically illustrated were grotesque reality.

The connection between the comatose girl on the short videotape and Jane Doe had definitely been established because Sergeant Beaulieu notes that Karla said, seemingly out of the blue, that the tape definitely had to have been made between February 1, 1991 (when she and Paul first moved into the house on Bayview) and their wedding day on June 29, 1991.

It was definitely before their wedding, Karla said, because Jane was at the wedding, information which would eliminate Kristen French as the comatose teenager on the tape because they did not kidnap and kill Kristen until a year after they were married.

Instead of seizing the moment and reading Karla her rights, Sergeant Gillies patiently explained to Karla that he and Sergeant Beaulieu were not prepared to conduct an interview about Jane Doe. That interview would be done sometime in the future, probably by the Toronto police because, if it was Jane Doe, Jane was still alive and therefore a rape victim. Even though Jane was from St. Catharines, it had been decided by the "higher ups" that all rapes would fall under the jurisdiction of the Toronto police.

He went on to say that any interview about Jane Doe would have to wait until the New Year and possibly until February. He advised Karla to forget about Jane Doe and enjoy the Christmas holiday. With that, wishing Karla a Merry Christmas, the two detectives took their leave.

* * * * * * *

In his psychiatric report dated March 23, 1994, Dr. Brown stated that Karla was doing very well. "At the present time she sleeps well considering her situations." He documented that she was having increased difficulty pushing "down her thoughts and feelings" and that to him was a sign that Karla was "healing."

Elaborating, he said that Karla was showing good insight and had assumed responsibility for her part in the crimes and was well motivated with regard to dealing with her sentence. "There is no further evidence of depression," he wrote.

In other words, the intense, comprehensive therapy provided by Dr. Brown was working and Karla was making real progress and getting better. That was good news to the police and prosecutors. They knew very well that Karla had been feeling intense pressure over the past months and they certainly did not want their star witness getting any worse.

* * * * * * *

Karla was informed at the beginning of April, 1994, that the Attorney General, Marion Boyd, guided by a bevy of senior Crown law office officials, had decided to "prefer" the indictment against Karla's erstwhile husband, thereby sending Paul Bernardo directly to trial.

There would be no preliminary hearing.

The Minister's rationale was succinct: The evidence against Paul Bernardo was strong and a preferred indictment would facilitate a speedier trial, but there were other unstated reasons such as concern that leaks during a preliminary trial might compromise his prosecution.

Their only real evidence against Paul Bernardo was Karla Homolka and they perceived Karla to be, if not a weak link, an assailable one. They also thought Karla was lying. The conundrum that was Jane Doe, and Karla's obvious complicity in these crimes, made the preliminary hearing a dangerous venue for the prosecution. The Minister was well . within her authority to make such a decision. Karla would not be going home for Easter after all.

* * * * * * *

Karla was torn. She had been really looking forward to getting out of her little cell and going "home" for a couple of weeks. Also, she had gone through all those months of intense preparation. For a brief moment, she was angry. Then she was happy, but frustrated, a cauldron of mixed emotions. On the fourth of May, Karla turned twenty-four. Then she was really upset. None of her friends sent birthday cards.

At the end of May, Sergeant Gillies came down for yet another visit and brought another new person for Karla to meet, Sergeant Scott Kenney. Karla liked meeting new people.

* * * * * * *

If it was not one thing, it was another. The prosecutors and police came back like a swarm of locusts to do last-minute prepping before Paul Bernardo's lawyers exercised their right to examine Karla.

When the Attorney General preferred an indictment, Karla's caretakers explained, the defense attorneys were given the option to examine the Crown's witnesses *in camera*. This was much preferable to a preliminary hearing. It was done behind closed doors without any press or outside observers, in secret just as the government wanted it.

Prosecutor Houlahan explained the rules and procedures in some detail, assuring Karla that she did not need George Walker. R.J. Houlahan would be there, looking out for her best interests. The State takes special care with their star witnesses. Karla had nothing to worry about.

* * * * * * *

After a good deal of preamble during which Paul Bernardo's two defense lawyers were introduced, the junior of the two, Carolyn MacDonald, started off by asking Karla about her aborted efforts to be transferred to a psychiatric facility shortly after she arrived in prison. Her efforts were thwarted by Dr. Brown – which might have partly explained why Karla expressed such disdain for the kindly, old psychiatrist in her early correspondence with friends.

MacDonald asked her why she had gone directly into the prison hospital rather than into segregation when she arrived at the prison.

"They didn't know what to do with me and I was on massive doses of medication – so they wanted me to be in the hospital," Karla replied.

Finally she admitted that Dr. Brown had told her on the second or third day that he did not feel Karla met the criteria for committal to a psychiatric facility such as St. Thomas.

"How did you feel about that?"

"I was a little bit upset," Karla said. "I didn't feel that this prison could offer me the degree of therapy that was necessary."

MacDonald told Karla that Dr. Brown's memo said Karla had spent most of their early time together talking about her fears of prison life, her drugs and the future; life after prison. MacDonald told Karla that Dr. Brown indicated in his notes that Karla was only interested in pursuing regular therapy sessions with a female – "he underlined that. Is that a request that you made to Dr. Brown?" MacDonald asked.

Karla emphatically denied that she had ever told Dr. Brown any such thing.

Dr. Brown had produced a formal psychiatric report on Karla on March 23, 1994. It was intended for the psychiatrist who was going to be with Karla at the cancelled preliminary trial – a Dr. Peter Collins, the psychiatrist who had originally supplied a copy of "Compliant Victims of the Sexual Sadist" to Vince Bevan in early February, 1993.

MacDonald made these observations and then asked if it was true, as Dr. Brown had indicated in his March 23 report, that Karla was sleeping well?

"Yes."

"Okay. Dr. Brown indicates you showed good insight and you are well motivated with regards to dealing with your sentence. Do you think that is a fair comment?"

"Yes, it is."

"He also shows no evidence of depression. Do you agree with that?"

"He must mean clinical depression, because I am depressed – not all the time, but I don't know what the definition of clinical depression is either."

MacDonald asked Karla whether or not she had anal sex or had penetrated her anus or her vagina with objects between October, 1987 and August, 1988.

MacDonald was making an undeclared reference to the series of pornographic Polaroids for which Karla had posed in the summer of 1988, one or two of which graphically shows Karla inserting a wine bottle into her vagina and anus.

Karla said she believed the anal sex had started in the summer of 1988, but not the sticking of objects into herself.

MacDonald asked Karla about oral sex and called it "oral sex on him," which somehow confused Karla.

"Why don't you say fellatio or cunnilingus? Use the words," Prosecutor Houlahan said curtly.

"The problem is I can't say them," Ms. MacDonald admitted. "I can't pronounce them. Yes. Okay. Fellation, we'll start with that… and I can't say it – *Cuneylunggus*. Is that how you say it?"

"Cunnilingus," said Mr. Houlahan.

"Yes, I enjoyed that," Karla replied.

* * * * * * *

During the cross-examination by Bernardo's lawyers it became abundantly clear to the authorities that Karla had been lying to them. And not just about Jane, but other things as well. Or, at least, that is what the police said they had come to believe when they were asked by Justice Archie Campbell. (Justice Campbell was charged by the government with reviewing the conduct of the police after Paul Bernardo was convicted and sent to jail for life in the fall of 1995.)

One thing was true at the point when Carolyn MacDonald and Ken Murray were conducting their examination of Karla. It was not from Karla's dreams or the depths of her subconscious from which her memory of an incident with Jane Doe had been "recovered," but rather by dogged police work, supplemented by pictures and videotapes.

The police had removed hundreds of videos from the house. On one of them, an innocuous homemade video, there was a young girl whom they had early on identified as Jane Doe, frolicking with Karla's dog. In that instance, it was Karla who was wielding the video camera and she could be heard giving Jane instructions. At one point, Karla clearly states, "I love videotaping."

In the background there was a wedding cake made out of bath towels. By the time Karla was to be cross-examined by Paul Bernardo's defense team in the summer of 1994, the authorities had come to the definitive conclusion that this girl, Jane Doe, was also the comatose girl in the two clips on the 1:58 sex video.

In another innocuous videotape also found in the house around the same, Karla is seen wrestling with her dog. Jane Does is also featured playing with the dog, wearing Karla's Oxford Hall sweatshirt, the same sweatshirt the comatose girl in the 1:58 videotape is wearing. A video-cassette copy of the movie *Ghost* can be seen on the coffee table. During their search of the house, the police had found a video store rental receipt dated June 6, 1991, for the movie *Ghost*. Further, they determined that the towel cake had been made by one of Karla's parents' neighbors for one of Karla's pre-wedding showers. They also considered the size and age of the dog. Using these tangential data, and things Karla had said, they were able to date an attack on Jane Doe late in the evening on June 6th or early in the morning on June 7th, 1991.

They had not yet "disclosed" this information to Paul Bernardo's defense team. Their excuse, were they ever called upon to make one, would be their confusion about a 911 call, which Karla herself had already tenuously linked to Jane Doe. It had been made two months later, on August 11, 1991.

This information would strongly suggest that Karla had put Jane Doe down with a combination of anesthetic and sleeping pills at least twice. That did not look at all good, given that Karla had, by her own admission, enticed Jane Doe entirely on her own.

On the other hand, and unbeknownst to the police and prosecutors, Paul Bernardo's lead defense counsel, Ken Murray, was not confused.

The search warrants for Paul and Karla's house had expired on April 30th, 1993, and the police were forced to abandon their search. A team of approximately twelve crime scene experts had occupied the house for 69 days. By law, search warrants are limited and can only be renewed three times. The police vacated the house with nothing probative except the 1:58 video.

Halfway through the police search, while Inspector Bevan was still in negotiations with the owners of the house, Ken Murray's co-counsel, Carolyn MacDonald, paid Paul Bernardo's rental arrears. When the warrants expired, the house and its contents reverted to Bernardo's possession.

On the morning of May 6th, following a rough, hand-drawn map given him by Bernardo, Ken Murray entered the house with Carolyn MacDonald and their law clerk, Kim Doyle. The three went to the upstairs bathroom where Murray climbed up onto the vanity and retrieved six 8mm videotapes from their hiding place behind a pot light in the ceiling. Miraculously, the police had missed them entirely. It was a literal case of the law's long arm coming up woefully short.

Later that month, Murray watched the entire set of videotape trophies, including the thirteen-minute tape of Paul and Karla's June 7, 1991, attack on Jane, from which Bernardo had spliced and copied the two segments on the 1:58 tape. Murray also learned that his client, Paul Bernardo, did not know Jane Doe prior to the first incident. Jane had been entirely Karla's idea. In fact, Paul Bernardo had been out of the house when Karla put Jane down with the same mixture of Halcion and Halothane that had killed her sister only six months earlier. Karla had called Paul on his cell phone that night and told him to come home because she had a surprise wedding present for him.

Murray also knew, as Karla admitted during her induced and cautioned statements, that Karla regularly pimped for Paul and had helped him establish a relationship with Jane Doe over that summer, a relationship that frequently included Jane consenting to fellate his client. His law clerk, Kim Doyle, and co-counsel, Carolyn MacDonald knew that Murray had culled videotapes from the house – he even showed them a snippet or two. He swore them to secrecy. He certainly did not share any of his esoteric knowledge with the prosecution or the police. Quickly, he became not only conflicted by his questionable possession of the videotape evidence but also confused about how he might use them. They were certainly damning to Karla, and put the lie to many of her specious interpretations of events. But the videotapes also showed his client to be a sadistic monster.

On the other hand, with good reason, Murray felt slighted by the prosecutors and police who, although compelled by law to release to the defense everything they had, were very slow in doing so. Murray believed that he and his staff were being treated with disdain by the police, who were smug and dismissive, even, at times, downright hostile to him and his staff. After all, the police had the wife as a witness against the husband. It was a slam dunk.

Ken Murray developed a strong, even virulent resentment toward both the authorities and Karla. For a while, the truculent lawyer comforted himself with the delusion that his secret and forbidden knowledge offset their obvious advantage. What Ken Murray was in a position to do was not only impugn Karla, but also expose the real reasons why the unconscionable deal had been made with her. His forbidden knowledge could, correctly applied, reveal the innate ineptitude and stupidity of Inspector Vince Bevan and his over-funded task force.

The arrest of his client, Paul Bernardo, was a sham built on the back of a flimsy deal with a woman every bit as evil as Bernardo was. The tapes showed that conclusively. If Bevan and his band of brothers were anywhere near as good as Bevan thought they were, the videotapes would never have ended up in Murray's possession in the first place.

For a time, these thoughts gave Ken Murray solace and perpetuated his delusion. But another more onerous issue would soon come to a head and then burst, overwhelming the besotted and vastly inexperienced defense attorney. If one lived in a glass house, as Ken Murray clearly did, it was always a bad idea to throw stones.

Although these videotapes impeached the police and their relationship with Karla, they were every bit, if not more, damning to his client. True, they clearly showed husband and wife as a team. But there was no question that Bernardo came out worse, if such a thing were possible. Not only did he repeatedly sodomize Kristen French and at one point, urinate on her while poised over her trying to defecate on her, he could be seen repeatedly punching her on her back whenever he was displeased by something she said or did. It was horrific.

In July, Mr. Murray was still wrestling with the question of how he might use the videotapes to incriminate Karla, destroy the deal, and expose the police and the prosecutors for the Machiavellian, amoral manipulators they were, without completely damning his client and himself in the process.

His obsession with Karla appears to have become almost pathological. For a long time it clouded his better judgement. As Inspector Bevan had done with the old Camaro and the idea that Karla was a "compliant victim," Murray instilled his distorted vision of Karla in his staff. When Ken Murray found those videotapes, watched them and decided to withhold their discovery, he opened a Pandora's box. From then on, he was running a hopeless defense based on an obsessed delusion.

At some point, either just before their *in camera* examination of Karla in the summer of 1994 or very shortly thereafter, Ken Murray came to realize that his undeclared possession of the tapes might put his entire career in jeopardy, and his confused ambivalence gave way to fear.

Rather than question Karla himself, Murray decided to have his co-counsel Carolyn MacDonald do it. The optics were better. As the police and the prosecutors had done with Karla, he tried to coach Ms. MacDonald. He gave her lists and lists of questions. Given that it is almost impossible to effectively ask questions when one has no idea of the context that determined their formulation, and considering her opponent, Ms. MacDonald actually acquitted herself admirably.

Over the three days she cross-examined Karla, Karla repeatedly lied under oath, contrary to one of the principal caveats in her deal.

For instance, she categorically denied, time and again, that she had ever administered Halothane to anyone other than her sister.

Carolyn MacDonald brought up the fact that Karla had called the Niagara Regional Police at 9:30 a.m. on February 22nd, 1993. She had made this call from her aunt and uncle's apartment in Brampton. This was significant because that was the day Inspector Bevan viewed the 1:58 videotape. Ms. Macdonald noted that Karla had been sternly warned by George Walker not to talk to the police and yet here she was calling the lead investigator.

This call marked the only time Karla disobeyed Walker's explicit instructions. MacDonald asserted that somehow both she and Walker knew that the police had found and screened the "sex" video, as they had, at 5:21 p.m., Sunday, February 21, 1993.

She suggested that Karla was so vexed that she decided to try and take matters into her own hands and determine exactly what was on that tape. The defense had not been able to get any information out of the police or the prosecution about this call.

Karla admitted she made the call, but she said she did not remember why. Shortly after the call, Karla went to Walker's offices with her parents but she had no recollection about the details of those discussions either. In fact, she testified that she did not even remember meeting with Walker on that date.

MacDonald moved on to questions about Karla's contact with Jane Doe. Yes, Karla had contacted her, once, after Paul's arrest, but she did not remember anything about the circumstances, the reason for the call or the conversation.

MacDonald pursued the short videotape and Karla's selective memory. "The police officers seized a videotape that I understand you have since viewed," she began. "I believe the videotape is a little bit less than two minutes in length and it has three episodes where you are involved in sexual acts with someone?"

"Yes."

"Were you aware on February 22 that the police had located this video?" MacDonald inquired.

Ray Houlahan interjected: "If this is something that you became aware of as a result of speaking to your lawyer, it may be privileged."

Karla turned to MacDonald. "I can't answer that."

MacDonald pressed, asking Karla whether she had seen the tape before the police screened it for her that past December and whether or not her lawyer had a copy of it. Karla started to flounder. Houlahan stepped in again to save her.

"If you're asserting privilege," he advised, "say you are, so it shows on the record. If you don't, you are just refusing for no reason that way."

"Okay, I'm asserting privilege," Karla said.

That line of questioning clamped, MacDonald turned to Dr. Arndt's notes from a session in early March, 1993, during which Karla discussed a videotape which showed Karla inserting the comatose Jane Doe's index finger in her vagina. MacDonald reminded Karla that she had told Dr. Arndt that the comatose girl, the one "with the hand," was still alive.

"Do you remember discussing that with Dr. Arndt?" MacDonald demanded.

"I don't remember that," Karla said, gently explaining, as though to a slightly retarded child, that her lack of specific memory was not really surprising since she had been under so much stress and she was still in shock.

Stymied, Ms. Macdonald asked Karla about her state of mind prior to her being hospitalized at Northwestern General – throughout the month of February, while she was staying at her aunt and uncle's. Everyone was surprised when Karla said: "I felt like killing myself all the time, I was severely depressed." It was a blatant and totally unnecessary lie.

"What do you mean by depressed?" MacDonald asked.

"I couldn't eat. I couldn't sleep." Karla's aunt and uncle had told the police that Karla ate like a horse and slept like a log. "I felt like my world was coming to an end. I felt hopeless."

"So before you get admitted to the hospital, describe for me your behavior," MacDonald requested.

"I was just hanging around the house all day, just moping around. I was tired all the time."

"Did you associate with friends?"

"Yes. I was seeing my friends. I was trying to reestablish friendships with my friends. I didn't see them very often."

"Were you drinking alcohol?"

"Not a lot, no."

Whether this was a lie or not would depend on one's assessment of what constituted a lot of alcohol. This also applied to whether or not clubbing, picking up men and having sex with them as often as possible, as Karla had been doing at least for the last few weeks she was in Brampton, fit the diagnosis of a clinically depressed, suicidal woman.

* * * * * * *

Although Ray Houlahan spoke slowly and deliberately he was by no means slow. After the first day of Karla's examination, he was aware that something funny was going on. The defense appeared to have some source of information to which his office and the police were not privy.

By the time Carolyn MacDonald began to question Karla, Ken Murray knew that Karla had used sleeping pills and Halothane on Jane Doe. It wasn't brain surgery. It was clearly visible on the thirteen-minute video of the June 7 attack on Jane.

Ms. MacDonald went on to establish that Karla had learned a good deal about drugs and their administration during her employment as a veterinarian's assistant. Karla knew how to give injections and had been exposed to narcotics. They had Demerol at the vet clinic and Karla was primarily responsible for the drug register.

MacDonald asked questions about Somnotol. Karla had run afoul of the vets at Martindale when she allegedly poured a bottle of Somnotol – another anesthetic that, unlike Halothane, was a controlled substance – down the drain. Karla explained, "I was dusting shelves and noticed a lot of drugs out of date, so I decided to throw away the out-of-date drugs…"

Karla's boss, Dr. Patti Weir, had already told the police during a series of interviews they conducted with her, and that were part of the Crown disclosure to which Murray and MacDonald had access, that Karla had been well-trained and knew better. According to Dr. Weir, Karla should have known that Somnotol was not date-sensitive, nor were veterinary personnel allowed to dispose of controlled substances in that manner. MacDonald brought this up. Karla had been trained, had she not? According to her boss, Dr. Patti Weir, Karla had been well-trained. Was Dr. Weir lying?

The defense was attempting to establish a pattern to show that Karla was preoccupied with anesthetic long before she alleged Paul Bernardo forced her to steal the Halothane.

Like most people, Paul Bernardo had never heard of Halothane, or any other kind of anesthetic. How could he have possibly counseled his wife to steal it?

The Somnotol incident at the Martindale Animal Clinic followed on the heels of the Ketamine incident which had precipitated Karla's departure from her previous place of employment. Was the defense supposed to believe that these strange things all happened purely by coincidence or were the Ketamine and Somnotol incidents failed experiments before Karla settled on Halothane as her anesthetic of choice?

After considerable obfuscation, Karla admitted she had stolen another bottle of Halothane after she and Paul moved to Bayview. She was quick to add the pervasive caveat that Paul had made her do it.

MacDonald wanted to know if Karla knew what the side effects of Somnotol were, whether or not she had ever looked that anesthetic up in her pharmaceutical compendium. For instance, had she highlighted it, the way she did the entry for Halothane? The answer to these questions was "yes."

MacDonald asked if Karla brought implements such as scalpels home from the clinic and Karla said "no."

MacDonald knew that the police had found a #10 scalpel, which had been taken from the animal clinic, among Karla's effects at 57 Bayview.

MacDonald wanted to know how much Karla knew about the process of administering anesthetic and if the animals were given some other sort of sedative before the anesthetic was administered. It turned out that Karla knew a great deal.

"Well, not always," she replied with the assurance of a professor at a veterinary college. "An animal can be what is called 'masked down', where they are given a high dose of Halothane through a face mask and they inhale it and go out that way, or they can be given… there's lots of different ways. There are different medications that can be given."

This would at least establish that Karla was very familiar with Ketamine, Somnotol and Halothane and their use as anesthetics, which contradicted other things she had said about her limited knowledge in her induced and cautioned statements.

"Is a sedative sometimes given in combination with Halothane?" MacDonald asked.

"Yes. Because, first of all, when an animal is being 'masked down' they resist, they become almost violent, and when you have a one-hundred-pound dog, you can't mask it down." Sedating the animal first made the surgical undertaking "less traumatic and easier."

* * * * * * *

Karla told friends in the Exclusive Diamond Club about how her new job at the Thorold Veterinary Clinic was "groovy." She cleaned kennels, answered phones and held the animals while they were prepared for surgery. But there was a problem. Karla's boss, the vet, Dr. Ker, had "practically" accused her of stealing Ketamine.

Ketamine hydrochloride was in wide use at the time as both a veterinary and a human anesthetic. In human use, a benzodiazepine such as Versed was used with Ketamine to induce unconsciousness and amnesia.

Why would Karla have stolen Ketamine? Because it was also a very popular recreational drug. Ketamine's action was "dissociative," meaning the user experienced a distinct mind/body separation. This separation caused hallucinations. Ketamine users often have the distinct feeling that they have left their body and entered a separate reality.

In the 60s and 70s, Ketamine was known as "Special K." It had occult associations which held great appeal for Karla. Karla had read *Journey's to the Bright Side* by Jane Roberts, the same author who wrote the Seth books such as *Seth Speaks: The Eternal Validity of the Soul.*

Journey to the Bright Side was about Ms. Robert's experience with "Special K." Apparently her husband, an anaesthesiologist, regularly dosed Ms. Roberts with Ketamine. The book documents how, in a Ketamine-induced state, she started going to the same familiar place or dimension and meeting certain beings. These sorts of places are called K-holes among K-cognoscenti.

Jane Roberts started a therapy group called Samadhi in Seattle, devoted to Special-K and enlightenment in the same vein Timothy Leary actively proselytized the therapeutic use of LSD.

Alas, Ms. Roberts came to a disquieting, violent end. Although the police found her body they never found her head. Her husband maintained that she was murdered because she was writing an exposé on a local Ssatanic cult. No one was ever charged with her murder.

* * * * * * *

Karla remembered that Tammy Lyn had called Norma Tellier after she drank a Rusty Nail the night she died. Ms. MacDonald wanted to know how in the world Karla could remember something as incidental as that but could not remember what happened to Jane Doe?

Because she had been talking to her mother a couple of weeks earlier and they had been discussing it, Karla replied. Besides, Karla had been in Tammy's room and had overheard her talking to Norma. She also remembered that Paul was wearing his UCLA sweatshirt that night.

Toward the end Ms. MacDonald asked Karla if there was, in her mind, a difference between the concept of the occult and Satanism.

"Yes. I believe that the occult is more involved in the spiritual world and doesn't necessarily have to do with the devil," Karla said matter-of-factly. "Although some people would say that being involved in the occult is being involved in Satan's world. Some people also believe that astrology is the devil's work." Karla concluded. MacDonald and Murray were stumped. There was nowhere else to go.

They adjourned, three years to the day that Karla had given Jane Doe to Paul as a wedding present.

* * * * * * *

A month later, on July 8th, 1994, George Walker received a letter from Greg Barnett. Barnett was the assistant prosecutor from St. Catharines who had been, with Ray Houlahan, working day in and day out for the past three months readying Karla for her ordeals. The letter informed Walker that the prosecution had agreed to make Karla available to Paul Bernardo's defense team for two additional days of questioning. Barnett acknowledged that this had not made Karla very happy and apologized to Walker for not discussing the matter with him first. He goes on to justify it a number of ways.

Firstly, the defense was demanding of a week or more but Mr. Houlahan, who at the time of writing was on holiday, thought two days a fair compromise. Barnett alludes to the fact that he was sure that Walker's client would not want to see an appellate court overturn the recent preferment of Bernardo's preliminary trial.

"This was offered to attempt to avoid an attack on the preferment of the indictment as an abuse of process. We do not, and, I think, your client does not want to see an appellate court overturning the preferment and order a preliminary hearing at which your client would face the prospect of further cross-examination."

Were Karla to refuse, Barnett cautions, it would likely be used against her during Paul Bernardo's trial and weaken her position.

Mr. Barnett then goes on to confirm that the prosecution has retained "two potential expert witnesses in the areas of Sexual Sadism and the Compliant Victim."

He states that the prosecutors see these experts' "potential evidence as, among other things, supporting the evidence of Karla Homolka by explaining, to the jury, the mechanism by which she was transformed by all the physical, emotional and sexual abuse into Paul Bernardo's compliant accomplice in these murders."

He goes on to say that the prosecutors also see this evidence (even though Mr. Barnett has yet to hear what evidence these experts might proffer) as potential rebuttal on "any attempts by the defense to shovel the blame onto Karla as a vengeful, homicidal lesbian, while attempting to exculpate Paul Bernardo.

"One of these experts is Dr. Stephen Hucker, a psychiatrist, currently at Queen's University, Kingston. You know Dr. Hucker, who was previously head of the Clarke Institute and director of METFORS. Dr. Hucker would like to interview your client, probably in early September, as part of the basis for any opinions he may express on these very important areas.

"The other expert is Dr. Chris Hatcher, a psychologist at the University of California. San Francisco. Dr. Hatcher is an expert on these areas who has testified numerous times in California and elsewhere in the United States. Perhaps his most well-known case was People v. Hooker, the case that involved the kidnapping of a woman in California and her sadistic abuse over 7 years, during which she was confined to a box for long periods of time."

Barnett also confirms that the prosecution had finalized arrangements to have a Dr. Peter Jaffe from London, Ontario, "provide an expert opinion regarding the battered spouse syndrome." This was something that Barnett had discussed with George Walker in early May of 1994.

As far as Walker and "his client" were concerned all of this was fine.

Walker dutifully passed a copy of this letter, as he did all correspondence and reports, to Karla.

Both Walker, and Karla, thanks to Murray Segal, were familiar with Dr. Hatcher and his role in the case "People v. Hooker." The book about the case, *Perfect Victim*, had been co-written by the woman who prosecuted the case and retained Dr. Hucker as an expert witness, Christine McGuire. One of Karla's favorites, it had been among the hundreds of books removed from her house in 1993 by the police. Walker had left his copy in Montserrat.

It was a strange story that, on the surface, had many parallels to Karla's predicament.

On May 19th, 1977, 20-year-old Colleen Stan was hitchhiking in California. She was picked up by a young couple with a baby. This couple, Janice and Cameron Hooker, had come to an agreement some months earlier. If Janice could have a baby, then Cameron could find himself a woman to whip and torture, as long as he promised never to have intercourse with her.

Janice and Cameron had met when they were fifteen and sixteen respectively. Over the ensuing four years Janice had been agreeing to and experiencing her husband's sadistic proclivities. She knew exactly what was going to happen to the hitchhiker the moment Cameron stopped to offer Colleen a ride.

In anticipation of finding the perfect victim, Cameron had constructed a heavy wooden box to isolate said victim's head. Stopping the car, he held Colleen at knifepoint, while Janice handcuffed her. They bound, gagged and blindfolded her and locked Cameron's homemade box on her head.

Back at the Hooker's home, the box was taken off. Cameron stripped Colleen, and hung her from a beam in the basement by her wrists and proceeded to whip her. Then Janice came down and she and Cameron had sex in front of the dangling Colleen.

When they finished, Janice went back upstairs and Cameron cut Colleen down. He put her in a small, three-foot square, cubed box. He chained her hands above her, removed the gag and locked her head back into the head box which he had lined with indoor/outdoor carpet. He then secured the head box to the ceiling of the larger box.

Because Colleen was kicking the side of the box, Cameron returned and bound her legs, wrapped a constricting band tightly about her ribs and inserted a small hairdrying device into her vagina. The idea was to turn it on and give her an electrical shock if she misbehaved.

The Hookers and their slave lived in a single-width house trailer in a park in Tehama County, Red Bluff, California. At some point over the next seven years, Hooker moved the box upstairs and placed it under the bed.

Later, after Hooker had Colleen sign a slave contract, she was allowed to roam about, go into town and shop, and even once visit her family in another state. Colleen was, true to the contract, convinced that she had to be with the Hookers and would return regardless where she was allowed to go. Upon her return, Cameron would promptly lock her into her box for the night and place it under the bed.

After seven years in captivity, and months after Colleen Stan had returned to her family, Janice Hooker got religion blew the whistle and both she and her husband were arrested on November 18th, 1984.

The parallel was being drawn by the prosecutor's office – both at 720 Bay by Murray Segal and his peers, and hence by regional prosecutors Barnett and Houlahan – between Karla Homolka and Janice Hooker.

Janice Hooker became the prosecution's key witness in the case against her husband. Unlike Karla, Janice Hooker was never prosecuted for her role in Colleen Stan's seven-year enslavement, although she was clearly a significant accomplice.

In People v. Hooker, the prosecutor, Christine McGuire, brought in Dr. Hatcher. According to his testimony, the husband, Cameron Hooker, was a sexual sadist and the wife, Janice Hooker, was his compliant victim. After Cameron was convicted, Janice divorced him and moved to another state.

The prosecutors were clearly expecting Dr. Hatcher to do the same thing with regard to the husband-and-wife team of Paul and Karla Bernardo. The fact that there were far more differences than similarities between the two cases – the most glaring perhaps being the fact that Janice Hooker did not stupefy, rape, or murder anyone, let alone her own sister – did not give anyone pause.

After all, Karla had already done the thing that took Janice Hooker decade to accomplish – she had already divorced her monster. Just like Janice Hooker, Karla had also resolved to move away – as soon as she got out of jail.

* * * * * * *

In a letter dated July 9, 1994, Karla told Dr. Arndt that he would be happy to hear that she had stopped taking the sleep-inducing tranquilizer Nozinan.

It had been Dr. Brown's suggestion that she try and wean herself off of it slowly, but that did not work – she was tired all the time – so she just quit, cold turkey. She goes on to tell him that she is functioning pretty well, although only getting five or six hours of sleep a night."

"I guess those years of sleep-deprivation imposed by Paul got my body used to less amount of sleep.

"I still have nightmares, but far less of them. They've shifted away from the actual offences and are mainly about Paul. I still do dream about the girls, but far less often than I used to.

"I'm starting to become less numb as well. I find I'm not nearly as able to push down my thoughts and feelings. At times they are so overwhelming I don't think I can survive it. But I will as I always have. Dr. Brown said this is a sign that I am healing. For so long I wished that I could feel raw emotion and now I hate it. It just hurts too much. I wish I could remain numb throughout the court process. Well, maybe my 'protection instinct' will kick in. I guess we'll see."

She tells him that he would be proud of her. "I am really starting to stand up for myself and my rights. A guard was treating me badly and doing something she shouldn't be doing, so I filed a formal complaint against her. A few months ago I never would have had the nerve to do that! And I am also standing up and requesting certain things for seg inmates that we should, but do not, have. I have come a long way in this past year."

She finishes up by telling him about how Bernardo's lawyers were trying to delay the court process, which she supposed was meant to upset her and make things harder for her.

"Well, all they are doing is giving me more time to get stronger and stronger. Paul is going to be really surprised. I'm sure he's expecting to see the weak "yes, sir, no sir" doormat that I used to be. I only hope that seeing him again doesn't bring back all of those old feelings or terror and cause me to become my scared, submissive old self."

Signing off, she says that her family is doing well and that her mother is taking anti-depressants "which she really needs."

On July 29, 1994, Dr. Arndt replied, reinforcing and encouraging Karla about the concept that Karla she was healing and making substantial, therapeutic progress.

"I am glad to see that you have started to stand up for yourself and not just always accept what people dish out to you. Of course, by not being just a 'yes sir, no sir' person, you will find that some people will not be pleased with this change in you, particularly those like Paul, who simply expected you to be a 'yes person,' something that unfortunately for the most part you actually had been with him."

He concurs that these traits and changes would seem to indicate that she was indeed "healing" and congratulates her on her mature attitude toward Paul Bernardo's defense lawyers' tactics.

He was also pleased that she was able to reduce or completely discontinue the many medications that he had put her on. This, too, was a very positive sign that she was making progress and getting better.

"I was feeling for you when you made reference to the nightmares that you are still having but I hope that they are much less than they were when you were at Northwestern. At times they must have been one of your most difficult ones, on the other hand it also probably was a time when you finally were able to start turning your life around."

He was glad to hear that her family was well and that her mother was on medication herself because he felt that she had long been in need of some help.

He observed that Karla's mother did not seem to be aware "of the enormity of the problems that were headed her way."

If Karla's mother wished it, he said, he would be able to see her, or anyone else in Karla's family professionally and that it might be a good idea because, "I am fairly familiar with the events and circumstances that now make it necessary for psychological intervention."

Telling Karla that he and his family had spent a couple of very pleasant weeks at the cottage during the summer, Dr. Arndt mentions that he had cases and obligations that were going to take him to Yellowknife and California in the near future. He closes by telling Karla that although he sent in the application forms he had not heard from the prison whether or not he had been approved as a visitor.

Karla finally replied to Dr. Arndt's July 29 letter on October 5th, 1994, By then, according to Dr. Brown and Karla, Karla was almost completely healed.

She apologizes for taking so long but says that she has been very busy taking courses, reading, receiving visitors and with "court matters."

She tells him that she no longer takes any psychiatric medication and that things are "going o.k. for me."

Dr. Brown felt, as Karla did, that she should try and stop taking any of that kind of medication prior to the trial, and so she did.

"I know you are in agreement. I am finally able to sleep rather well. My nightmares have decreased considerably, and I am now able to sleep through the night the majority of the time. I feel that I have been able to make significant progress with respect to my mental state. I now have great insight with regards to why I respond to things the way I do, and why I have such a hard time showing emotion sometimes. By the way, I am feeling and showing my emotions much more freely now, although still not as much as I should and would like. I know, in time though, that I will be able to."

Karla documents meeting with the psychologist Dr. Peter Jaffe who is considered one of the foremost experts in battered spousal syndrome as well as Dr. Stephen Hucker, a local psychiatrist with an extensive background in forensic psychiatry, sex offenders and their treatment.

She asserts that the meetings with these two specialists hired by the Ministry of the Attorney General had gone really well and that they had "definitely helped" her.

Over the summer, she had taken an English course as well as a sociology course called "Introduction to Women's Studies." She received excellent marks in both and enjoyed the courses. In the fall, she started two new courses: Principles of Psychology (first year) and Sociology of Deviance (second year) and was "enjoying them immensely."

"I find that the more courses I complete, the better my self-confidence gets." The Women's Studies in particular "opened my eyes to different ways of thinking. It was quite empowering – something I definitely needed. I am also doing a lot of reading for interest. I've started reading many of the classics. I'm also knitting, sewing, and doing various other craftwork. It's great fun, and passes the time really quickly."

She tells him that her family remains well. Her mother and sister went to Mexico for a week – "they really needed to get away" – while her father stayed home with the dog because "he doesn't like to fly."

Her mother was still on the anti-depressant and sleeping through the night. Karla called the trailer on the prison grounds used for conjugal and family visits – the prison term was PFVs, (private family visits) – the "little house." She reported that she had just had a weekend visit with her family and that they would be back for another one in November.

She looked into the status of Dr. Arndt's Visitor's Application and discovered that it was being held, pending Paul Bernardo's trial.

"Apparently, the Crown and/or police would prefer me not to visit with you until the other matter is taken care of" and she tells him that she will notify him when it is approved.

"In closing, I wanted to let you know that one of the girls who I have befriended here is getting ready for release (in the new year) and is looking for a psychiatrist in Toronto. Her name is Kim Wildeman, and she may be dropping you a line to see if you are accepting new patients. She is a very nice girl, in a situation somewhat similar to mine."

Kim Wildeman was serving seven years for manslaughter. She had murdered her four-year-old son. Like the prosecutors, Karla tended to draw analogies and see similarities liberally.

Karla wished Dr. Arndt good luck with his cases in Yellowknife and California and, in signing off, asked after a woman who had been in the hospital with her when she was under Dr. Arndt's care. Karla believed the woman had "killed her husband or something" and wondered what had become of her.

* * * * * * *

"Thank you very much for your letter of October 5, 1994," Dr. Arndt quickly replied.

"It was good to read that you are doing so well, in particular that you are doing so well without medication. You certainly have come a long way there."

Indeed, Dr. Jaffe had called and talked to him. Dr. Arndt also understood that Dr. Jaffe had seen her family for an assessment. "I am glad that you found the meetings with him and Dr. Hucker useful for you."

"It is good to read that you are doing so well with your course work at Queen's. The courses that you have picked seem to probably at least to some degree, give you some insights into what happened to you over the years and clearly your own experiences will make it so much easier for you to understand the course material and probably give you a chance to do quite well in these courses. As you wrote, you did receive good marks in the courses and that you enjoy them.

"As far as visiting is concerned, at least now I know that things were not forgotten and that for a reason, I have not been put on the visiting list yet. I believe I will be in the Kingston area sometime before Christmas and I could have seen you.

"You mentioned Kim Wildeman. I would be glad to see her and if for whatever reason I won't be able to take her on myself I certainly will endeavor to find somebody that she can get along with. It is so important to have some contact person you can relate with in order to get things organized so I am very glad to help her out.

"My case in Yellowknife was just postponed, probably until February because the judge who was to sit got sick and if they don't find a new judge for the beginning of the sentencing hearing that was to start on the 24th of October, then I guess I'll be up there in February.

"The case in California has been put on ice so I don't know what is happening with it. You mentioned that there was a girl from the Northwest Territories at the hospital who had killed her husband and you asked me how she's doing. Quite frankly, I don't remember who of the many people I have had from the Northwest Territories was with you at the time. Perhaps you can describe her a little bit to me such as whether she was Native or White and if you have any other recollections then perhaps I can remember who it was and let you know what's going on with her.

"I should let you know that some of your letters were printed in the Toronto Sun recently and in one of those letters you indicated that you 'hated' your psychiatrist. Several people approached my secretary and wondered whether I was the psychiatrist that you hated and Cynthia, of course, very quickly made clear that most likely you didn't mean me, you had somebody within the penitentiary system in mind. I hope she was right.

Keep up the good work and your spirits."

THE MEASURE OF A MAN

Once I discovered where he was, I sent an e-mail inquiry asking the recently appointed Chief of the Ottawa-Carlton Police Service, Vince Bevan, if he would be willing to clear up a couple of questions I had. And also explain why there was no entry in his will-state for February 11, 1993, a day that was certainly crucial to the fact that he was still in policing. I received a pointed reply: "I have no interest in speaking to you on any issue whatsoever."

Then I realized there was another source for what Chief Bevan had to say.

"Today is February 23rd, 1998. It's Monday. We're at the offices of the Niagara Regional Police, 4343 Morrison Street, Niagara Falls, Ontario, in the office of Superintendent Vince Bevan."[1]

Detective Constable Robert Kollee of the Ontario Provincial Police has turned on his tape recorder and was speaking for the record: "I'm with the Ontario Provincial Police. It's 2:28 p.m. If we could start off, Superintendent Bevan, by indicating to you that we are investigating an alleged breach of a publication ban. This is dealing with an admission that Stephen Williams, the author of a book called *Invisible Darkness* made to a newspaper columnist that he had, in fact, at one point, seen the videotape evidence restricted by a judge's order. Maybe we could just start off with any information that you could provide us

1. Vince Bevan had been promoted to the rank of Superintendent shortly after the conclusion of the Bernardo trial in September, 1995.

from your dealings with this Stephen Williams, any experience that you may have had with him either before or prior to the trial and during the trial."

"I think I first met Stephen Williams in the summer of 1993 during the Karla Homolka trial in St. Catharines. I know that I was present in court when Stephen Williams was represented by counsel trying to get standing so that he would not be excluded should the judge order that there be the exclusion of the public from the Homolka hearing.

"On one day he came to court and argued that he was not a member of the media but rather he was an author and was going to do a Truman Capote-like work that chronicled Bernardo and his unfortunate events.

"The judge, Justice Kovacs, ultimately ruled that Williams, in particular, would be excluded, along with members of the public and the American media.

"I recall getting some measure of the man when the next day he showed up, despite the things that his counsel had said about the media being the great unwashed, with a press pass. I think, if memory serves me right, he was then representing the *Wingham News*, which was a monthly publication.[2]

"It was some time following that I actually met Stephen Williams. He had made a number of telephone calls to us even shortly after the Bernardo arrest....

"Our first contacts were from Little Brown, trying to make arrangements for us to speak to somebody.[3] We wouldn't speak to anyone and

2. In fact, I was given media accreditation by CKNX FM 102 an "easy listening" radio station located in Wingham, Ontario. Any writer or journalist worth their salt would have done exactly as I did when confronting a judge who had the temerity to rule, as Justice Francis "Doc" Kovacs did with respect to me, that a contracted writer who had publishers in Canada, the United States and England, was not a member of the "media" and therefore would, along with the Canadian public and the American media, be excluded from the courtroom during Karla Homolka's "trial." At no time did I or my counsel refer to the media as "unwashed."

3. No one from Little Brown & Co., Toronto, or Bantam Books, New York, or Little Brown PLC in London, England ever contacted anyone in policing or the judiciary with respect to my project.

then ultimately it came to my attention that it was Mr. Williams who was under contract with them.

"One day I was called to a meeting in Chief Grant Waddell's office where the Chief introduced me to Stephen Williams and that had been arranged because I had refused to have any contact with Mr. Williams.

"I wasn't speaking to him on the telephone and I had declined an opportunity to meet with him. I listened that day to Mr. Williams present himself and what his intention was and when we left that meeting, there was certainly no commitment that I would speak to him to give him insight into the case at all.

"But I did agree to speak with him from time to time but there would be no release of information until after the matters were concluded. I know that didn't satisfy Mr. Williams and I know that, periodically, along the way, I had discussions with him up until the point where, ultimately, he told me that unless I cooperated with him I wouldn't like what ended up in the book about me in particular.[4]

"He wanted me to introduce him to the families, the French and Mahaffy families in particular. I couldn't, in good conscience, do that.[5]

"I seem to recall that I did have conversations with the families, telling them of Mr. Williams' interest in them but certainly they had no desire in meeting with him and speaking to him and, ultimately, he sent them letters saying that unless they cooperated with him, they

4. I never made any such statement. After I came into possession of a copy of then Inspector Bevan's will-state, I no longer needed or wanted to talk to him about anything. Because tricks and lies are acceptable investigative tactics for the police, when talking to police persons it has been my experience that the closest one is going to get to the truth from any individual officer's perspective or point of view is contained in their sworn will-states which even so, are all too often filled with convenient errors and omissions.

5. This is also incorrect. I did not ask Inspector Bevan to introduce me to the families. The one letter I sent to the Mahaffy and French families (the one in which I misspelled Kristen's name) distinctly stated that I did not need or want to talk to them unless, of course, they wanted to talk to me.

wouldn't like what he wrote about their children in the book. And I think it's fair to say that they don't like what he wrote about their children in the book.[6]

"But Mr. Williams was a regular in court, although some days his absence was quite noticeable. Having met Mr. Williams, you'll know that he is someone that you would pick out of a crowd. When he's not there, it's noticeable.

"For my part, I saw that he had quite a healthy relationship with the defense team during Bernardo's trial and spent a good deal of time with them. There are others who can probably give you information about the nature of that relationship because there are people who have spoken to me about that and understand that maybe he could have got that information first-hand from others.

"It was interesting because right around the time of the verdict, Williams disappeared and we didn't see him again which was somewhat interesting because here he is trying to write a book and he didn't even follow it through to the dangerous offender applications.

"I remember there was some comment about his absence during those applications which was a fairly critical piece in the whole chain of events.[7]

"But, he disappeared from sight and for some time I thought that maybe his book had sort of disappeared because he had been beaten

6. Here, he is correct about only one fact. The families did not like what I wrote about their children in my book because I portrayed them as what they were – normal, teenage girls and not the virgin saints their families and the popular press have so assiduously made them out to be. Otherwise, what Bevan says is utter nonsense. I only sent one letter to each family – in the letter to the Frenches I misspelled Kristen's name which Bevan subsequently used to try and embarrass me in front of the Chief – but I certainly did not make any overt or covert threats. Just as I did not threaten Inspector Bevan, I did not threaten the families of the victims.

7. The dangerous offender applications were a slam dunk and totally irrelevant. If there ever was anyone more obviously guilty than Paul Bernardo and more deserving of a dangerous offender designation, I don't know who it might be. Perhaps Karla Homolka? But Inspector Bevan had made sure that Karla got off with only a dozen years in jail. As I told Inspector Bevan at the time, I had very little interest in Paul Bernardo. He was only one of many avenues through which I intended to get to the truth about Karla Homolka and Vince Bevan's relationship to her.

off the mark by a number of other journalists who produced works on the trial.[8]

"And so, after the verdict and right up until the time that the judicial inquiries into the task force and the Homolka deal were concluded, I used to see Mr. Williams from time to time on television representing himself to be some kind of expert on this whole situation and on serial killers and on the investigation which is something that I would have a good laugh about, but I never had any kind of working relationship with this person and I was never of the view that he was going to be a chronicler and produce any kind of reputable work because he certainly did not impress me as having that kind of ability."

Detective Kollee interjected: "Just dealing with the relationship that he had with the Bernardo defense team, were you aware that he may or may not have had access to the defense team room that was adjacent to the courtroom?"

"I've heard that he did have access to their private office," Bevan replied. "I have heard from one of the witnesses that I understand you have interviewed that he was seen in there alone going through case materials.[9]

"I also seem to recall that, at some point during the trial," Bevan continued, "one of the prosecutors spoke to Mr. Rosen about access to those materials because Williams was in the room alone. I think it was now Judge Leslie Baldwin that actually had that conversation with Mr. Rosen."[10]

---

8. One of Inspector Bevan's more apparent flaws as an investigator, and one which many of his colleagues pointed out to me at the time, is his penchant for jumping to conclusions such as his conclusion about the make of the car in which Kristen French had been abducted, his conclusion about the identity of the young, comatose teenager in the 1:58 videotape, and his conclusion about Karla being the compliant victim of a sexual sadist.

9. Superintendent Bevan is making reference to a tabloid newspaper reporter, Alan Cairns, who, with another reporter, co-authored one of the other books to which Bevan alluded earlier in the interview. A month earlier, Mr. Cairns volunteered for an interview during which he tried to incriminate me.

10. Shortly after the Bernardo trial, assistant prosecutor Leslie Baldwin was appointed to the bench, and is currently a sitting judge in St. Catharines.

"This information, had it come to your attention, that Mr. Williams would have access to the defense room either by himself or when the defense team was there, would that have been a concern to you?" Detective Kollee asked.

"A bit of a flag, yeah. During the trial, there were issues that came up from time to time about the sensitive nature of particularly the banned materials, and I know that the police investigators and certainly the prosecutors had concerns that the material be protected appropriately and there were discussions both before Justice LeSage in chambers and in private between defense and Crown counsel about what was being done to protect it."

"Now with all your dealings at the courthouse during the trial, did you personally ever see Stephen Williams either in or around that defense room?"

"Yes, I did."

"Would it be more than once? I guess I'm referring to right inside the defense room, either when other members of the defense team were present or possibly using it by himself. Do you recall any specific occasions of that nature?"

"I have seen him in the room. There's one instance that I can remember walking past the room where the door was partly open. It was either the door was opening or it was closing, I can't recall right now, but as I walked past the room, I could see Stephen Williams standing in there.

"But, again, during that time period, the relationship that he had with Mr. Rosen was no secret so it didn't surprise me to see him in there. Indeed, I think maybe many of the journalists would have given their eye teeth to be able to go in and talk on that basis with the defense team."

"Okay, do you recall during the trial, there were incidents where material ended up being leaked to the media?" Detective Kollee asked.

"Well, one example in particular was a photograph depicting Karla with the raccoon eyes."

"Are you familiar with how that photograph came to be in the possession of a local newspaper?"

"I know that at that time we did an investigation because there was an allegation that it was one of our people. The journalist who received the information was categorical in his statement to us that it had not come from the suspect officer. So where, indeed, did it come from? I don't have the information. I know that throughout the trial, there were concerns over leaks because, at the end of the day, there would be videotape that came from the search at 57 Bayview Drive. Videotape clips of that material would be on TV. We certainly had not released it. I think that somebody from the prosecution team, and I'm not sure which one it was at this time, raised the issue in court, again because somebody from the defense team had actually passed a copy to one of the TV networks and that material aired that night. So there was some of that going on during the trial."

"Did you or any member of the Green Ribbon Task Force provide any material of any nature to Stephen Williams that he might have used in the preparation and production of his book?"

"Well, I did not and I'm assured, in my discussions with members of the Green Ribbon Task Force, that nobody there had anything to do with Stephen Williams. There were times when, in the hotel, where our office was located, Stephen Williams would quite often frequent the bar downstairs. I know that there were discussions amongst the investigators, some of the investigators and some of the prosecution staff, that he had spoken to Greg Barnett on one occasion. I think that was for a relatively short period of time and I don't have any suspicions of Mr. Barnett. Mr. Barnett did not have access to the videotapes anyway."

"Is there any other information that you might be able to share with us that would help us in this investigation?"

"I can't think of anything at this particular point in time although certainly if I get any information, I'll forward that to you but there's nothing else right now that I can help you with."

"Thank you for your cooperation, Superintendent Bevan."

"No problem."

DEADLY IGNORANCE

About a month before they talked to Superintendent Bevan, the detectives interviewed a man named Alan Cairns. Cairns believed he had damning information about me which he offered to the police on Tuesday, January 20, 1998.

Cairns, a short Scottish derivative with hair sprouting from his shoulders and the back of his neck, said he had recently returned from a scuba-diving trip, so there were several instances during the interview when the tape was stopped or indecipherable while, in the words of the person transcribing, he "horked."

Detective Kollee began: "We're at the offices of the *Toronto Sun* newspaper, 333 King Street East, Toronto, Ontario... It is 10:52. I'd like to start this interview, Mr. Cairns, with a little bit of your background in journalism and your responsibilities with this paper."

"Well, in a nutshell, I have 18 years experience and I've been with the *Toronto Sun*, officially, since September of 1989. I have covered mostly crime cases, some major cases, and one of these cases was the Bernardo case and out of that case, of course, came a book that I co-authored with Scott Burnside, my colleague at the *Sun*."

"And the name of your book was?

"*Deadly Innocence*."

"Okay. There's been an investigation requested into another book author, one Stephen Williams, and he may have breached a publication ban to obtain material for his book. If you can just tell us of any dealings or any experience that you had with Mr. Williams from the time that you started to cover the Bernardo trial until its completion."

"Well, I didn't have a relationship with Williams. I didn't really know him. But, quite frankly, I didn't like him. He is a very abrasive character and I found him to be highly opinionated and certainly, in his mind, a literary snob. He seemed to look down on the daily media. In fact, he went to great lengths at Karla Homolka's trial to put the local media in the light of being amateurish and not part of the literary establishment. 'Ah!' I thought to myself, 'and this coming from a man who had yet to be tested and whose work ethic had yet to be shown.' I found it to be quite insulting. He was thrown out of the court by Judge Kovacs and, to my surprise, returned to the court with a media document from the *Mount Forest Confederate* and his common-law wife, Marsha Boulton, with media documents from a woman's radio station, with whom, obviously, they had no dealings until that point in time.[1]

"I thought this was a gross breach of journalistic ethics. He was ordered out of the court as an author and then he pretended to be a member of the media just so he could get back into court. Now, there is no governing body over the media so in a way, it's our own fault for not policing ourselves but I thought that ethically, it was a gross breach. After that, I really had no time for Stephen Williams. I thought he was a poseur and I didn't like him. As time went on, you know, it became clear to me in an article that was written by Derek Finkle in *Saturday Night Magazine* that Williams had cooperated with Mary Garafalo, the woman from the American tabloid television show *A Current Affair* and, it is well-documented in that article that Williams traveled to New York City and met with Garafalo. I think the quote in the article was for the 'sharing of information.' And this was after Garafalo had broken the publication ban and this was after Williams had entered that court under the jurisdiction

---

1. In fact, it was Ms. Boulton, whose syndicated column "Letters from the Country" was a regular feature in the weekly newspaper, who was given press credentials by the *Mount Forest Confederate*. As noted earlier, I was accredited by CKNX FM-102, an "easy listening" radio station in Southwestern Ontario. Ms. Boulton wrote a feature article for the *Confederate* on the trial.

of Judge Kovacs who had ruled that no direct or indirect breach of the ban could be undertaken. Quite frankly, I was surprised that there was no action taken against Williams for that and I have my own suspicions about how certain information was given to *A Current Affair* and to the *Washington Post* but clearly he met with Garafalo.[2] That's documented. I think that was most unfortunate. We went to great lengths not to discuss this information with any other foreign media. The American media, in particular. In fact, we turned down large sums of money from American tabloids to give them details about the information that was banned."

Mr. Cairns continued: "My disdain for Williams increased after that. When Scott Burnside and I were doing our research, we thought that, you know, someone who described himself as such a prolific author, we would be bumping into him at every corner. In fact, out of something like 50 to 60 people we interviewed in the case, there were only two people who had been interviewed by Williams. As the trial arrived, we were quite aware that Williams had done very little work on his book, very little unique, original research and, not only that, we were very aware that Nick Pron from the *Toronto Star* newspaper had done very little research too. That's a whole other story about Pron; don't get me started on that."

"Just to interrupt you for a second. Are you at liberty to share with us the names of those two people that Williams interviewed?" Detective Kollee asked.

---

2. What Alan Cairns told the police, like a great deal of his reportage, was partially true. He had some facts. The rest he made up. I did have dinner with Mary Garafalo in Toronto in December, 1993. I also was a guest at her wedding at Toronto's Casa Loma in the summer of 1994. Later that year, Ms. Boulton and I had dinner with Mary and her husband when I was in New York to meet with my agent and various publishers. At that time I was planning to incorporate something about the media in *Invisible Darkness* and was trying to pump Ms. Garofalo for information about the machinations of the tabloid juggernaut in New York. I was hardly going to "share" any of my information with her, given that it would have been a breach of my contracts with three publishers, not to mention against the law. In the end, there was nothing about the media or its behavior that impacted on the disposition of these cases and, therefore, nothing to write about with regard to the media's largely provincial and pedestrian coverage

"No, no, I can't because I interviewed them and anything that I do or say with people that I talk with is my business and nobody else's. As I said earlier, I would talk about Stephen Williams with you but if I had discussed something with Williams, even off the record, I wouldn't tell you, but you know, come to think of it, I have never discussed anything with Williams. To my mind, he's not part of the media. To my mind he's an entrepreneur who came into this case and has essentially thumbed his nose at the law. Like it or not, it's the law and I was not going to breach that."

"A refreshing opinion," Detective Kollee's partner observed.

"It's no secret. Christie,[Christie Blatchford, a columnist also assigned by the *Toronto Sun* to cover the Bernardo case] Scott [Scott Burnside, his co-author who has since become a sports reporter] and I, we all thought that the ban was wrong, but it was still the law and we have ways in which the law can be challenged and that's what we did. We challenged it in the courts.[3] We never published anything that broke the ban throughout the trial. We didn't publish anything that could be contempt of court. Arguably some of the stuff may have tainted the jury pool in St. Catharines but that was just the tip of the iceberg.

"However, during the trial Stephen Williams was on TV, professing to be an expert on the case and I guess at that point maybe he was. I mean, all of a sudden, the court case itself had made it an equal playing field and he's certainly as capable of having an opinion based on the evidence as anybody else but he continued to be somebody who – I just wanted to stay away from. I just didn't feel comfortable around him. He's larger than life, he's... he's... he's... he's big, in size and shape, his mouth is big and his head is big and I just find him to be the type of person that I personally find... I just don't like him.

"During the trial, it became apparent that he was very close to the defense team of John Rosen and Tony Bryant. I cannot mention, or

---

3. When Mr. Cairns says "we" he means the large news organization for which he worked. Mr. Cairns undertook no self-financed legal action of any kind with regard to the Bernardo/Homolka cases.

rather, I will not talk about any discussions that Scott and I may have had with Rosen and Bryant just as I won't discuss anything about any other connection that I may have had with this case. We became quite aware that he was very close and in fact, on one occasion that I remember quite clearly, I was in the court and I was wondering where Stephen Williams was?

"Just as an aside – another thing that has struck me as odd was that he really wasn't taking that many notes and for somebody in his position I thought that was pretty odd. And something else that I remember is that when Rosen gave his cross-examination of Karla, Williams actually gave Rosen a thumbs-up from the audience and I thought that was really weird, for someone who professes to an objective book writer. That stunned me."

"You saw him do this?" Detective Kollee's partner exclaimed, incredulously.

"Absolutely! Right on! And I just thought it was weird. We went to great lengths in this case to be almost like a shotgun and to talk to as many people as possible and we succeeded; we talked to lots of people. But I just thought it was weird that somebody who had hardly talked with anybody in the lead-up to the trial had suddenly attached themselves to the defense's coattails. I thought that was really odd.

"Back to my original point: At one point, he wasn't in the court and I, having the investigative mind that I have, I just thought, 'Wow! I think I know where he is!'

"The defense team had a room next to the court in which they had the evidence and it was a locked room and during the break or whenever they would go in there and before court they'd go in there and after court and there were two rooms, you know – but there was a door between them[4] – and I left the courtroom and knocked on the door, just playing a hunch, and after I knocked I just sort of kept walking away and wouldn't you know it, the door opened and there was Stephen Williams coming out of this locked room. And I thought that

---

4. Each room also had a door, a fact which Mr. Cairns apparently failed to observe.

was odd. I thought to myself, 'Why would the defense let somebody be in a room where they have all the evidence?'

"Then I started to wonder 'what evidence is in that room?' I don't think that a reporter or an author, for that matter, should have close relationships like that and I found it odd that a person having a unique, exclusive relationship with the defense team… I just thought it was very odd, in my own mind. I knew that was the only way he was going to get his book done, to be close with the defense and exclusively with the defense."

"Did you see him come out of this particular room, the one with the lock, more than once?" Detective Dowell asked.

"No. That was the only time I saw him in there alone in a locked room, and this was for a number or hours. This is during the trial proceedings. If I had been guarding the evidence that I knew that somebody wanted to see I would have to be, number one, sure that the evidence was not there; number two, that it was locked in a safe; or number three, that the person who was in there, that their reputation, their morals and ethics were absolutely impeccable. And I would have to know them as a friend, like a real, real close friend who wouldn't screw me, no matter what the circumstances. I mean, I just found it really odd because this to me was obviously some kind of friendship of mutual gain."

"Were you aware of what was in that room, Alan?"

"I have no idea."

"When he came out of this room, did you make an observation about the room?"

"No, I mean, when court had recessed and, you know, the door was open I could see that there were books and evidence and all kinds of things. There was a VCR and TV I mean, I chuckled at the time, I just thought it was funny. I mean I was aware that Williams' success was absolutely dependent on the sharing of information from the defense on a large scale because if he had not had it, he would not have written his book, because there were already three. I mean, essentially the main books were ours, *Deadly Innocence* and Pron's *Lethal Marriage* but they were on the shelves, they were already for sale and for him to come out with a book that was essentially the same as *Deadly Innocence* and *Lethal Marriage* a year later would not have worked. He had to come out with something a lot more in-depth and, of course, he came out with his book and I don't know, I can't really guess but, well, maybe I can… It seems to me that everything came from the defense through disclosure, everything in the book. I'm not aware of any other source that he would have had to have obtained pictures and things like that."

"Have you read his book in its entirety?" asked Detective Kollee.

"No. I've read passages of it. It's good. I mean, I would not be critical of his work. I was surprised to the extent that he put in the fringe pornography. I would say that what he has in there, it's not even fringe, it's total pornography. He seemed to forget that these victims were still girls. I think that he went out to just basically do 100 percent on the case including the shock value and I personally think that it could have been handled a lot more generally but I'm certainly not going to get into the debate on whether Karla did this and Paul did that. Some of the words that he uses in the book are offensive to me. When he's talking about the scene in the shower, for example, he says Kristen looks small. Like, how does he know she looks small? And the word 'look' I think is very interesting. You would only use the word 'look' if you'd seen something. That's a word you would not use unless you had seen that tape. In another passage, they're talking about Bernardo handing Leslie a roll of half-used toilet paper. Like, I mean, who could conceive the half roll of toilet paper?"

"Just out of curiosity, in your opinion, that very type of thing you just mentioned about the half-used roll of toilet paper: is it your opinion that that's something he would have to have actual knowledge of, that he actually saw it or could someone such as an author pass that off as, you know, literary license?"

"You could do it. I mean, there's lots of ways in which writers can camouflage where they got information from. In my opinion, it doesn't really mean a hell of a lot. I'm certainly not a trained expert but the word 'look' suggested to me that he either saw the tape or else someone played the tape and told him. It had to be one of the two but with Williams, he's such a big mouth, that if he said he's seen the tapes it could he true but it could also be him talking, being the blowhard that he is. I really can't say, it's just opinion. It doesn't mean anything. He used that word twice. It almost seems to me that he saw them and tried to camouflage it but forgot the camouflage in those two or three instances. You know, there's another part where he talks about the mole on her chin. I forget what it was exactly, but did he get that from the tapes or did he get that from still pictures of Leslie when she was in a bathing suit on the beach in Florida? I mean a lot of things came in disclosure. Williams obviously had access to everything the defense had because he didn't get it anywhere else. What I'm saying is that a lot of what I looked at in the book, stuff that just made my eyes pop, must of come from things that I didn't have access to. I'm not envious or jealous of Williams. I mean, you know, we did our best on this case and we were very successful in terms of what we got and what we did and our book withheld the scrutiny of both the Campbell and the Galligan judicial reports. I mean, you know, they both backed up what we had from first-hand evidence that we have in the book so, I mean, I'm quite happy with my book and I don't really have an axe to grind with Williams. I'm still angry at him for belittling the daily media and blowing his own horn when really there was nothing of distinction that he'd done before. You know, if a Grisham wants to say that then I think we should all sit up and listen but if Stephen Williams says it, it's just a bunch of bullshit. I don't know if that answers your question but my opinion doesn't really mean anything.

"My understanding, Mr. Cairns, is, during the trial, particularly at the times when the tapes were being played, at the end of the day, if members of the media wished access to some of the material that were in those tape summaries, they could go to a room and a court official would come in and bring those tape summaries and read from them."

"Yeah. From the transcripts. Any of the banned tapes which are essentially Ms. Mahaffy, Ms. French, Ms. Homolka, that is, Tammy Homolka and Jane Doe. Anything that involved the teenage victims which we visually did not see but the transcripts were read to us in the anteroom."

"Were you able to tape-record these readings?"

"No. Tape recorders were not allowed in there. It was basically Scott and I did them on our Mac Powerbooks but as far as I remember, there were no audiotape recordings made."

"Were you able to get the transcripts verbatim?"

"Yeah. We had to record it ourselves.

"Excuse me. I'm just back from a scuba-diving trip. We were able to basically transcribe them and ask questions of the court official to repeat the transcript so we did get essentially the transcript but we didn't have access to photographs. We could see them, touch them, but we couldn't take them out and even after the trial that is the rule, unless you get photographs from either the defense or through other sources such as family members. You could not take pictures out of the court."

"So you'd be able to obtain accurate, verbatim transcripts of the banned tapes from what you heard in court and then from what you were able to pick up afterwards?"

"Yeah. From what we were able take down during court and what we were able to get to have read to us afterwards. At one point, I made the point, I think I said this in front of the crowded court, I said to the judge, 'You're gonna have a lot of errors if we are going to have to rely on what we hear during court, if you don't sit down with us and say "this is the transcript from today," there is going to be mistake after mistake in the daily papers.' After I made that point, they came to a conclusion that they had better do it that way."

"Would you be aware if Stephen Williams was sitting in on any of those sessions?"

"Oddly enough, I don't think he was there. I can't remember seeing him in those sessions. I think Williams would sit in on the court and then he would cozy up to Rosen and Bryant afterwards and his whole reason was to schmooze John Rosen and Tony Bryant. Again, I really don't know why. It's because he had no other alternative and after the way he'd shot his mouth off, just for his own ego, he had to come through. We didn't have time to schmooze anybody after the trial. I like to think that we didn't schmooze, that we had struck up relationships but I felt that Williams was – the best word I can think of is a leech. It's almost like a kid in school yard hanging on to the school bully and making sure that he buddied up to the school bully because it was his only protection and at the time, I remember thinking to myself, well, you know, more power to him if he can do that. We really didn't need Rosen and Bryant and you know, whatever we may or may not have done with them then, I mean it's all irrelevant, you know, I'm not going to get into that but more power to him if he could make it work. I guess the thing that pissed me off more about Williams was the relationship he had with Mary Garafalo and also, in his book, I'm not entirely clear on this, but Paul Bernardo's dad was charged with sexual assault on Debbie Bernardo and, in Williams' book, he goes into this whole thing of overkill where he describes the sex assault victim was Debbie Bernardo and how the father had used his finger for this and that, and it seems to me that there was a publication ban on that, and it seems to me there's a standing principle, certainly among the newspapers, that you don't name the victims of a sexual assault. And here is Williams naming Debbie Bernardo in the book and going into graphic detail about what Ken Bernardo did to her. I thought 'Isn't that a breach? Like, why would he do that, you know? What's the point?' So again, I find myself looking at Williams with disdain and he continues to pass himself off as this great literary figure of our times and it just sticks in my throat…"

"Was there any time throughout the period of time that you were there to cover the trial that Stephen Williams made any admissions that he saw the tapes or bragged about seeing the tapes or…?"

"He didn't talk to me at all other than to put down the *Toronto Sun*.[5] The company that he kept – you know, Derek Finkle, the freelance

---

5. I do not recall ever speaking to Alan Cairns whom I did not know or care to know except once, when he interrupted a private conversation I was having with Metropolitan Toronto Police Detective Steve Irwin outside the courthouse during the Bernardo trial. The rudeness of his intrusion and his abrasiveness precluded any discussion about his employer.

writer with the *Saturday Night Magazine* – they were on the fringe. They were fringe people, they were the fringe magazine groupie people that weren't part of the daily media. It's almost like they all band together because they're not in the mainstream. Finkle wrote an article and mentioned Scott Burnside and me and yet he never once even called us. Even in the courtroom, we were sitting three rows away from Derek Finkle and he wrote a three-page article in *Saturday Night* which referred to us on a half-a-dozen occasions and sometimes not in glowing terms and he never once tried to speak with us. I mean, this is the kind of company that Williams kept, that guy and Mary Garafalo. The relationship between Williams, Garafalo and Finkle – they had this threesome going there and this exchange of information and Williams and Finkle were working together.

"Finkle gets him to meet with Garafalo and then after Finkle finds out that Williams has a personal file in his office on him, he writes about it. So you have business dealings going on here between people that should be kept private and suddenly they end up in *Saturday Night*. It's like, wow! There's Garafalo calling Williams this name and the other. On the other hand, she's fully aware of the ban and what it means and she's disclosing that she met with Williams in New York City. I mean, it's like a bunch of jackals just stabbing each other in the back. I mean, like 'go away,' I want nothing to do with these people. There's that old adage: 'You sleep with dogs, you get fleas,' and you know, I don't want anything to do with these people. I wanted nothing to do with them. I don't think Williams particularly wanted anything to do with me either and I'm sure that he has very little affection for me but I couldn't care less. I am disappointed that he never talked to me."

CONFESSIONS OF A
FACELESS BUREAUCRAT

Michael Code paused, fork halfway between plate and mouth, and, with great indignation, declared my theories about Inspector Bevan's role in delivering Karla's future "bullshit."

"No stupid cop," he said, "could ever have that much influence in determining the fate of an accomplice witness." Decisions of that gravity were made in the prosecutor's office, which meant, at the time, his office.

The evening was not going well. It was mid-week in early October, 2001, and I had finally convinced Michael Code to meet me for dinner at Toronto's Bistro 990 at 7:30 p.m.

When I first called him he said he did not have any time to revisit the past. I suggested to him that, in spite of his reputation as an obsessed workaholic, he probably had to eat. He said that he liked to eat and that he probably could discuss Karla's deals in a superficial way over a pleasant dinner – only if I agreed that what was said was not necessarily "on the record."

As he explained to me, he ate a light breakfast, never ate lunch, therefore dinner was an important meal. But he agreed to meet me, not only because he needed sustenance but also because he remained slightly impatient with the lack of public understanding of the deals with Karla – deals for which he was responsible. He had been the man in the Ministry of the Attorney General where the buck stopped.

For my part, we had a mutual acquaintance in the world of journalism, one of a very few for whom Michael Code happened to have a healthy respect, a sentiment that I shared. As it turned out, that friend stood pat for me and said I could be trusted.

Even with our mutual friend's endorsement, Michael Code remained ambivalent. He felt the government's side was misunderstood and no one in a position of authority at the Ministry of the Attorney General had ever spoken publicly about the subject. But he also doubted whether anyone would truly listen.

I convinced him that it was still very controversial and well worth his time. The fact that Karla would soon be out of jail, one way or the other, no later than July, 2005, made the decisions he had made then even more current than they had been at the time he made them, and people would be very interested indeed.

My friend had cautioned me that Michael Code did not suffer fools gladly, and that our dinner might not provide the easiest conversation I ever had or garner the result I wanted. He was right. Like Karla, Michael Code and his motivations were mysterious and complicated.

Just before he joined the Ministry of the Attorney General in 1992, Code had established himself as one of the finest criminal lawyers in the country. He was working in private practice with a boutique law firm established by Clayton Ruby and Marlys Edwardh. Both Ruby and Edwardh are highly regarded criminal defense lawyers in their own right. They are known for their spirited defenses and their abiding belief in the Charter of Rights and Freedoms. At that time, the six lawyers in the firm had led the way in Charter cases. Many of the cases in which Michael Code was lead counsel had been high profile and broke new legal ground. He was well regarded by his peers as a jurist. His industry was legendary. Some called it obsession.

Although many of the lawyers at Ruby Edwardh could be described as left-leaning, liberals or social democrats, in Michael Code's case he was a card-carrying member of the New Democratic Party. In early 1992, he did the unthinkable for an accomplished criminal defense lawyer and went over to the other side.

The vast majority of people in the prosecutor's office take the job out of law school and work their way up. A job in the Ministry of the

Attorney General represents a sinecure with a steady salary and dental benefits, something that the vast number of lawyers in private practice never enjoy. In most cases that come before the courts, the cards are stacked in the prosecution's favor; therefore, they win more often than they lose. The majority of judges are appointed to the bench out of the prosecutor's office.

There is also a certain prosecutorial mindset which is not shared by the mavericks who belly up to the criminal bar. It is not unusual for good criminal lawyers to do a year articling in the prosecutor's office but it is very rare that a seasoned, successful criminal lawyer in mid-career takes a job with the Attorney General.

When the New Democratic Party unexpectedly formed the provincial government in Ontario that year, Michael Code's good friend and colleague, Larry Taman, was appointed Deputy Minister to the Minister of the Attorney General. He convinced Code to join him, not as a prosecutor, which Code would not have done, but as the boss of all prosecutors. Thus he became Assistant Deputy Minister, Criminal. In a way, it was an irresistible proposition. Power is a magnet. In retrospect, the controversy that swirled through the legal community about Code's choice to join the prosecutor's office was based on professional jealousy. It should not have centered around why he took the job, rather who among them would not have taken it?

One of Michael Code's first official acts was the approval of a million dollars to facilitate the formation of Inspector Vince Bevan's nascent Green Ribbon Task Force. In an ironic twist of fate, one of the country's finest criminal defense lawyers became the boss of the highest profile police investigator in the country. The dynamics of such a pairing could have easily formed the basis for a season of *Law and Order*.

Intermittently, between May, 1992, and February, 1993, Inspector Bevan returned to the trough. Code approved numerous subsequent requests for millions upon millions of dollars to support what had become the largest police task force in the province's history. On occasion, Inspector Bevan would meet with Code to rationalize his lack of progress.

Shortly after the Bernardo case concluded in the fall of 1995, the New Democratic Party lost power to the Conservatives and Michael Code resigned his position. He went back into private practice and was soon one of the busiest criminal lawyers in Canada again. By the time he and I met, he was head of the eight person Criminal Law Division at Sack Goldblatt Mitchell and routinely putting in fourteen- to sixteen-hour days, six or seven days a week.

Code was late for our first meeting but on that particular night, it didn't matter. For some inexplicable reason the restaurant was busier than I had ever seen it. Although he showed up at 8 p.m., we were not seated until 9:30. We were given the large round table in the front window beside the bar.

Roughly fifty years old, Michael Code is a tall, dark, square-jawed, no-nonsense, handsome man who, when out to dinner, prefers to sit in the dining room.

"I thought you were going to make reservations," he snapped.

I had, but it was one of those nights. Once someone sat down, they just never left. If we had held out for the dining room we would still be standing in the bar. I tried to explain. He waved me off as though I was making an inferior legal argument.

To make matters worse, conversation had been very difficult above the din and I had, in a gesture of quiet resignation, downed two or three large martinis, which had an effect similar to zombie dust.

Therefore it took a while before I discovered that Michael Code was a rare creature – an egomaniacal Buddhist.

All great criminal lawyers have large egos. The odds in a criminal case are always stacked against the defense. They are the perennial underdog. In many ways, they are also actors. The courtroom is as much a stage as any theater. Except a defense lawyer has to be able to think and seldom has either a sympathetic or large audience. Without an inflated sense of their own importance and a somewhat romantic belief in the good fight, there would be no such thing as defense lawyers, let alone good ones.

I have met many lawyers with egos, but I have never met one who was also a Buddhist. Buddhism teaches a passive acceptance of the world, an almost beatific surrender of both the self and desire, where-as the law, the way Michael Code had chosen to practice it, was adversarial. The world of criminal law was one of atrocities, punishment, contrition, desire, contention, argument and an active defiance of the way things are.

Finally seated and with dinner ordered, I took a sip of the excellent Chablis Mr. Code had agreed to. I then gave him my theory of the importance of Vince Bevan's role in Karla's first deal, to which he bellowed "bullshit."

To begin to try and build my case, I asked him if he was aware of the exact circumstances that drove Karla to George Walker's office? Did he know about the Mickey Mouse watch?

No.

Was he aware that there were two search warrants – one written by the Toronto police and the other one by Inspector Bevan and the Green Ribbon Task Force?

Vaguely, but how was that relevant?

I asked him if he had studied either search warrant?

No.

I asked him if he had reviewed the transcripts of the first Toronto police interview with Karla Homolka – the only interview conducted with Karla in which the police performed as investigators – rather than the facilitators and stenographers they became?

He had not.

"Then you were not aware that she lied to the police on that occasion?" I said.

"What difference would it have made if I was?"

Was he aware that Inspector Bevan sent two of his detectives to George Walker's home at 11:30 p.m. on February 11, 1993?

No.

Then he could not have known that those policemen told Walker, on Inspector Bevan's instruction, that the police and prosecutors would be prepared to do whatever deal might be necessary to get Walker's new client's testimony against her husband.

No.

Was he aware of the circumstances that precipitated Bernardo's arrest?

Vaguely. "It had something to do with the media, right?" Which, of course, would have been exactly the answer Inspector Bevan would have wished for.

Had he ever read Inspector Bevan's will-state, or any other cop's will-state who was involved with the case?

No.

I asked him about the videotape evidence. Did Karla's demeanor and behavior in the 90-minute homemade pornographic videotape she and Paul had made, the one in which she impersonated her recently dead sister, did that not give him pause, at least about her overall state of mind and her demeanor?

He had never seen the videotape.

"What about the others?" I asked, nonplused. "Have you seen any of the other tapes – the ones that show the attacks on Tammy Lyn and Mahaffy and French?"

"No," he replied insouciantly. The only videotape evidence he had seen was the thirteen-minute segment in which Karla and Paul assaulted Jane Doe on June 7, 1991.

How could he have possibly have committed to the second deal with Karla – the one that gave her a pass for Jane Doe – if he had not reviewed all the evidence, all of her statements, all of the relevant police will-states, all of the police interviews with her friends and all of the hundreds of hours of police interviews Karla had given?

How could he possibly have gauged her sincerity or credibility, and made a cogent decision about whether or not Karla was lying when she said she had completely forgotten about drugging and raping Jane Doe – only six months after she had done exactly the same thing to her sister – if he did not review all the evidence available to him?

However, I did not ask these questions – not then. Eventually, over the next few months, I asked them, but in retrospect I did not formulate those specific questions until I reflected on our conversation the following day.

I did ask a question which I believed directly affected the attack on Jane Doe and offered another possible explanation for Karla's behavior.

Karla had enticed the young girl of her own volition, while Paul Bernardo was out of the house, driving around – I imagined – in ever diminishing-circles, like a shark, waiting for some kind of blood signal.

Paul Bernardo did not know Jane Doe from Adam. He had never met her. Karla had never mentioned the girl to him. In the crazed scheme of things, by Karla's own description, Tammy Lyn had been a Christmas present and, only six months after Tammy had perished in that role, Jane Doe was a wedding gift. The great and significant difference between the two, other than the fact that one lived and one died, was that Jane Doe was a complete surprise.

My question was, had Michael Code ever been aware of the anal-sex-loving nurse Alison Worthington? The girl that Paul Bernardo had picked up in Florida just before the attack on Jane Doe?

The anal-sex-loving nurse was very important because she spoke to Karla's state of mind at the time she set up Jane Doe. I suggested that Jane Doe was the Unicorn tied to the tree in the clearing. After Paul had returned from his swinging, bachelor's vacation in Florida in the late spring of that year, he told Karla all about Alison. He even had Karla pose as his sister when Alison called the house to talk to him. Although not particularly well-known, this evidence was on the record.

Paul told Karla that Alison loved anal sex. Karla hated anal sex. Paul told Karla that Alison owned a brand-new Camaro and had a much better job than Karla's. Karla did not drive – she later said that Paul would not let her – and she brought home a meager two hundred dollars a week from the animal clinic. Paul told Karla that he thought he might be in love with Alison and maybe they should postpone their wedding so he could sort out his true feelings.

Michael Code had never heard of Alison Worthington.

Now I was frustrated. I had determined earlier in the evening, during the interminable period we stood in the noisy bar, that Michael lived alone. So I decided to ask him if he had any pets. It was a non sequitur meant to convey my growing sense of incredulity.

If it did, he did not show it. "I do, actually," he said, taking a sip of the Spanish coffee he had just ordered. "I have a Vermont wild cat."

"It must be from Vermont then," I observed.

"I got it a number of years ago while I was on a retreat in Vermont. The cat found me on a mountain. It was wild then."

My eyes glazed over and whatever light there was left in the dimly lit bar imploded through his as though they were piss-ant-sized black holes in an ever-diminishing universe.

Now I was starting to hallucinate. Perhaps it was time to go. Instead, I tried one more question. Had he at least reviewed the transcripts of Carolyn MacDonald's and Ken Murray's examination of Karla Homolka in June, 1994? In direct contravention of the plea resolution that had been finalized in May, 1993, Karla repeatedly lied under oath during the three days MacDonald and Murray cross-examined her.

I may as well have mentioned the Dharma bums. He scoffed. "Of course I never reviewed those transcripts. Ken Murray is an idiot."

Ken Murray was Paul Bernardo's first lawyer who, in amazing arabesques of hubris and stupidity, managed to turn himself into a total pariah and in so doing had long ago become the sacrificial lamb for all of the authorities' sins.

In one of those bizarre sequences of coincidental events that seemed to defy reason and define Karla's life, Ken Murray had secured the videotape evidence Inspector Bevan and his men had missed during their sixty-nine-day search of Paul and Karla's matrimonial home.

That Murray had done this finally came to light when the hapless lawyer resigned under the weight of his unsustainable position, eighteen months after he had pulled the videotapes out of the pot light in the upstairs bathroom. His slow awakening to the untenable legal dilemma that the videotapes created for him finally drove him to the prominent Toronto criminal lawyer, John Rosen. Not that Ken Murray necessarily respected Rosen. Carolyn MacDonald's partner happened to work in Rosen's firm. Ken Murray begged Rosen to take the case. When Rosen agreed, Murray surrendered the videotape evidence. Somewhat reluctantly, because the law that compelled him to do so was vague, John Rosen turned the videotapes over to the authorities in September, 1994.

Shortly after Bernardo was convicted, the Ministry launched a full-scale investigation of Ken Murray's actions which culminated in criminal charges. They were serious charges, including obstructing justice and absurd, vindictive possession-of-child-pornography related offences. His practice already in tatters, if the middle-aged lawyer was found guilty he would spend a decade or two rotting in jail.

Lawyers are generally held in low esteem. Lawyers for monsters who do questionable things in their client's defense are quickly perceived to be lower than the proverbial snake's belly. Ken Murray made an easy target. He was the perfect foil for the bungled police investigations and the real motivations for the Ministry of the Attorney General's complicity in the two deals made with Karla Homolka.

From the moment Murray turned over the videotapes the official position adopted by the prosecutor's office and the police became "If only" Ken Murray had not concealed the videotapes; "If only" he had done the right thing and given them up when he found them on May 6, the deals with Karla Homolka would never have been concluded on May 14, 1993.

The deal with Karla, as are all deals, was done way before anyone put a signature on a dotted line. The deal with Karla was precipitated by Vince Bevan so that he could participate in the arrest of Paul Bernardo and execute his own search warrant on their matrimonial home. It was that simple.

In complicated criminal matters characterized by bizarre sexual deviance which receive a great deal of media and public attention, it is well understood by senior prosecutors and police that perception is reality. The reality – i.e. Inspector Bevan's opportunism, careerism and considerable good luck – many of the details of which are only now being revealed – was too far complicated for easy understanding. Suddenly, the facts meant nothing, and the perception that a smarmy lawyer concealed crucial videotape evidence, thereby facilitating Karla's sweetheart deal, became reality.

All but one of the charges against Ken Murray were ludicrous. A "possession of child pornography" charge, in and of itself tends to ruin the lives and careers of the individual against whom it is brought, guilty or innocent. It, along with seven other charges, was dropped during the two-and-a-half years it took to bring Ken Murray before a judge. In a sensational trial that lasted through the summer of 2000, the wretched lawyer was tried and acquitted on the single charge of obstructing justice.

His prosecution and the attendant publicity were nothing but a subterfuge and it had served its purpose. It did not matter that he was acquitted. In the public's mind, he was still the scumbag lawyer responsible for those terrible deals with that murderous bitch. Ken Murray became the catalyst that transformed all the authorities' leaden missteps into a golden foxtrot. The very mention of Ken Murray's name, or so it seemed to me, allowed Michael Code to spurn reason, ignore the question and its implications, and become quietly, resolutely inscrutable.

"Look" he said, "on second thought I really do not feel like dredging all of this stuff up again. It was one of the worst experiences of my life. It was a torturous process which I have gone over and over again, both in my mind and with others. Read Patrick Galligan's report, it's all there. I had a great deal of input. He listened very carefully to what I said, and the report accurately reflects what my thinking was at the time and the reasons why I did what I did. After you've read that, maybe we'll talk again."

He got up from the table. "Can I give you a lift?"

We did not speak during the five-minute drive to my hotel. I said goodnight and he drove off to feed that wild Vermont cat of his.

I HOLD NO BRIEF
FOR KARLA HOMOLKA

Rereading Justice Patrick Galligan's report, I realized why it had outraged me when it was first tabled in March, 1996. I called it a "total whitewash" on national television at the time and it is. Not because it is dishonest or the judge was mis-intentioned. I am sure that Justice Patrick Galligan is a hard-working, levelheaded, intelligent man. It is a whitewash because it accepts Karla's version of events and ignores crucial evidence that puts her behavior and motivations in a vastly different, brighter light. It harkens back and causes to ring true that old Czechoslovakian saying about the darkest spot being directly under the light. There was a lot of light shone on Karla over the years but none of it seemed to illuminate that dark spot.

In the body of his report, the judge even admits it. He says that he has not "analyzed in detail the evidence of Karla Homolka with respect to the abuse suffered by her at the hands of Paul Bernardo nor have I examined in detail the extent to which she claims she was completely under his control and domination."

Although he could have done, the judge chose not to "test" anything Karla said, or review any evidence that would contradict her version of events. Instead he just accepted it verbatim because the people, whose actions and motives he was supposed to be investigating, accepted it themselves. Where I come from, this sort of tautological ellipticum constitutes whitewash.

The key is the judge's use of language. For instance, the entry for the summer of 1988 in his "Chronology of Certain Relevant Events," (Appendix "B" on Pg. 226 of his report) states "Paul Bernardo begins beating Karla Homolka."

There is absolutely no evidence for this. In fact, there is a great deal of evidence to the contrary, including medical records compiled by numerous doctors Karla saw in 1988 and 1989 as well as numerous statements taken by police from family, friends and co-workers. There are also a considerable number of photographs from that period, including nineteen, explicitly pornographic Polaroids for which Karla posed in the summer of 1988 that reveal a voluptuous, unblemished teenage body in full bloom. The look on her face throughout all of these pictures is one of complicit rapture. There is no fear whatsoever in her eyes, or any marks on her body from abuse.

For the year 1989, Justice Galligan notes "Paul Bernardo becomes increasingly critical of Karla Homolka, insults, yells and screams at her."

Again, the only evidence for this came from Karla, after everything was settled and she understood exactly what the police and prosecutors needed and wanted to hear. As she said more than once, after she said something specific about how she had been made to perform, "I know that's what you want to hear" because that is what they wanted to hear. It was Inspector Bevan and Murray Segal who oversaw the creation of Karla as a battered woman and a compliant victim. They not only "wanted to hear" it, they needed to hear it.

In the late spring and early summer of 1990, Galligan notes "Paul Bernardo tells Karla Homolka that he wants sex slaves brought to him at her parents' home."

The only talk that can be verified about finding sex slaves was Karla's dissertation on the subject during the hour-and-a-half homemade pornographic video that she and Paul filmed shortly after they killed Tammy Lyn, the videotape made on January 6, 1991, the one in which she impersonates her dead sister.

Although Karla said, as she did about everything, that Paul scripted her and made her say everything she said, her dialogue on the video-tape sounds remarkably spontaneous and natural. And she admitted to the police in February, 1995, four months before Bernardo's trial began, that it was extemporaneous, that there was no written script, it was "just, like, I knew what he wanted me to say." Either she was a born actress with remarkable, innovative skills or she was lying.

The Judge continues: "Paul Bernardo asks Karla Homolka to pretend that she is her sister Tammy during sexual relations… Paul Bernardo tells Karla Homolka that he wants to have sex with Tammy Homolka; discussions ensue about obtaining drugs to facilitate that act."

Whatever discussions there were about drugs and their use were initiated by Karla. Paul Bernardo knew nothing about sleeping pills and less about anaesthetics such as Halothane.

On the other hand, Karla knew a great deal about both and studied various entries for many different varieties of each in the *Compendium of Pharmaceuticals and Specialities* that doctors and veterinarians keep in their offices for reference.

She had "borrowed" a copy from the vet clinic where she worked. The police found it beside her bed. The entries for Halothane, Ketamine, Somontol and Halcion were highlighted with an orange marker. There is a great deal of evidence that Karla kept a bag of crushed Valium in her hope chest which she sprinkled on her sister's food and in her drinks throughout the summer of 1990. When that did not work, she turned to the harder stuff. This is all a matter of public record which the judge appears to have completely ignored.

According to the judge's report, on December 28, 1990, less than a week after Paul and Karla killed Tammy Lyn, "Paul Bernardo orders Karla to obtain more Halcion." On March 25, 1991, after they had moved in together at 57 Bayview, "Karla Homolka gets more Halcion pills for Paul Bernardo."

Nowhere in his chronology does the judge mention the fact that the deadly concoction of the anaesthetic Halothane and the sleeping pill Halcion was entirely Karla's idea; that she not only "obtained" more

Halcion pills by stealing them from her employers but also stole more Halothane from the drug cabinet for which she was responsible. And she did all this even after her sister's death conclusively proved the veracity of the contraindications in the *Compendium* against the non-clinical use of Halcion and Halothane.

Nor does Justice Galligan mention that from the time they met until they killed Karla's sister, Paul Bernardo was working full-time in Toronto and the demented lovers only saw each other on weekends.

Although Justice Galligan mentions the important theoreticians and clinicians in the field of battered spousal syndrome including Dr. Angela Browne, Dr. Lenore Walker and Dr. Charles Patrick Ewing, he does not explain that their combined clinical experience states that a woman has to endure at least three clearly defined cycles of abuse over no less than seven years before a diagnosis of battered spousal syndrome can be given.

He does not discuss the fact that battered spousal syndrome which Karla had allegedly developed, never afflicts women who are living at home in the bosom of their family and friends, working full-time and generally living a normal, happy life as all the evidence, including Karla's, confirmed. It was only later, after she understood "what they wanted to hear," that her history began to be systematically rewritten.

Nor does he observe that Paul Bernardo never actually raped anyone until after he and Karla met. Or address the fact that none of his victims ever died until Karla became an active participant.

Paul and Karla were married for approximately eighteen months and had not even known each other for seven years when the marriage "fell apart."

The judge does not discuss the fact that battered women sometimes, although very rarely, strike out and kill their abusers but never, at least in the voluminous literature on the subject, strike out and kill siblings or perfect strangers as a consequence of their abuse.

For me, Galligan's bias was summed up in one paragraph in the 334-page report. He documents that Karla had given hundreds of hours of interviews to the police and the prosecutors.

"Inspector Bevan told me he estimates it as high as 400 hours… and I have spent countless hours reading her many statements to the police, her recorded interviews and her evidence at trial. I am convinced that any suggestion that, at any time from February 14, 1993 onwards, she withheld any vital information about her critical role in those horrible crimes is simply unsustainable. I hold no brief for Karla Homolka."

DECIPHERING CODE

I told Michael Code I had reread the Galligan report and he agreed to meet again for a late supper in February, 2002. This time he was an hour-and-a-half late. I had pretty much thrown in the towel when he suddenly showed up, somewhat apologetic. He was defending one of the Air India bombers. He was flying back and forth to British Columbia to do it.

Over the holidays he had gone up to his cottage on Pender Lake. The cottage was Michael Code's most cherished possession and the one place where he could find haven and commune with Nature. He had built it himself and according to all reports it was an edifice in the Frank Lloyd Wright tradition of integrated architectural integrity. The only cottage on an isolated island, it was hardly noticeable from the water.

The sleeping area was an open loft approximately fifteen feet above the main floor. He had arrived late one night, had a couple of glasses of wine, cooked a steak and gone to bed. He woke up dazed, freezing and badly battered on the main floor in the early morning hours. Apparently, although he had no memory of it, some time in the wee small hours he got out of bed, perhaps to go to the washroom, but obviously not awake and aware of where he was, and walked off the un-railed loft, falling to the floor. He broke a couple of ribs but the only way he could get help was get into the boat, make the half-hour ride across the bay to the mainland and then drive to the nearest hospital.

It was an excruciatingly painful journey. By the time he got to the hospital, he was in very bad shape. Where he had fallen, on his side, his mid-section had swollen up to the size of a large exercise ball. He had been recuperating for weeks and was only just feeling up to snuff.

There had been no problem getting a table this time. Waiting, tapping my fingers on the table, I had read all the papers including the *New York Times*. Once again, I consumed more than the acceptable number of martinis but this time the experience put strength to my arm. Rereading Galligan had so inflamed my sense of righteous indignation that the martinis had the opposite effect and I was wide awake.

Code begged indulgence. He had not yet had a chance to reread the report himself. It was then that I finally came to realize that his heart was simply not in it, either because I was absolutely right about the machinations of the deals or else because he had no faith in my ability to perceive and represent the legal complications within which he had found himself. Either way, he obviously did not see benefit or redemption in either scenario.

I pointed out what I perceived to be the report's inherent flaw. The judge had accepted Karla's mantra – that Paul made her do everything – uncritically, without regard to the mountain of evidence to the contrary.

Code responded by saying that if he recalled the report accurately, the judge had reviewed virtually every word that Karla had spoken, first in her induced and cautioned statements, as well as in her many subsequent interviews with police between 1993, after she had gone to jail, and Paul Bernardo's trial in 1995. The judge had also reviewed her testimony at trial, both in-chief and in cross, with particular regard to the ten days she had spent on the witness stand being cross-examined by one of the finest trial lawyers in the country, John Rosen – had he not?

"Yes," I replied. "That's what he says but that also is only what she had said about what had happened."

"He also reviewed all of the psychological and psychiatric reports?"

Indeed, he had. Galligan said that Karla had "consistently been diagnosed as a battered or abused spouse suffering from post-traumatic stress disorder."

In his report Galligan addresses Drs. Arndt, Long, Malcolm, Hatcher, Hucker, McDonald and Jaffe, all of whom made reference to memory problems. The Judge recorded that Dr. Malcolm, in particular, had noted a history of "some memory loss" which he thought could be attributed to "emotional anaesthesia."

That phrase – "emotional anaesthesia" – had stuck with me. Like many things to do with Karla, it was bursting with an unwitting irony. Emotional anaesthesia is not a diagnostic phrase to be found in the *DSM-IV-R*, or any of the psychiatric literature. It was wholly an elliptical invention of Dr. Malcolm's. He intended it to describe a condition in which Karla's emotions had been rendered unconscious, non-functioning, implying that it was something that had been done against her will, without her conscious knowledge, by a third party – much the way Karla had rendered her sister and Jane Doe unconscious.

Justice Galligan also singled out the prison psychiatrist, Dr. Roy Brown. He noted that Dr. Brown confirmed his colleagues' diagnoses of dysthymia or reactive depression and post-traumatic stress disorder after Karla had gone to prison and been put in the psychiatric care of Dr. Roy Brown by Correctional Services.

The judge went on to quote Dr. Brown at some length about post-traumatic stress disorder: *The Diagnostic and Statistical Manual of Mental Disorders* (DSM) defines this as the development of characteristic symptoms following a psychologically traumatic event that is generally outside the range of usual human experience. Stressors producing this disorder include various natural disasters, accidental man-made disasters or deliberate man-made disasters (bombings, torture, death camps).

"The disorder is apparently more severe and longer lasting when the stressor is of human design." For some reason, this also struck me. What Dr. Brown was saying here was that man's inhumanity toward man apparently caused more severe psychological devastation than tidal waves and twisters. If this is true it means that we have simply learned nothing from history. Or perhaps it is a phenomenon unique to white, middle-class people born in North America since World War II.

"Among the typical symptoms are depression, 'psychic numbing' or a loss of feeling and interest in social activities and impaired memory and difficulty in concentrating."

Justice Galligan recorded Dr. Brown's conclusion. "I am of the opinion that Karla has been consistently truthful in her recollections of the past events of this case. She continues to have no memory of her own involvement with Jane Doe, and this is consistent with her participation having occurred against her will and under the empowered direction of her ex-husband."

That Karla had instigated the attack, enticed Jane Doe on her own, and knocked her out while her husband was out of the house, apparently escaped Dr. Brown's notice. More interesting still, was the fact this false statement escaped the judge's notice, even though he had access to the facts as they had been brought out at Paul Bernardo's trial.

The judge went on to say that Dr. Stephen Hucker and Dr. Chris Hatcher concurred with Drs. Arndt, Long, Malcolm and Brown. Hucker examined Karla for ten hours and reviewed a great deal of the material, including the videotapes.

Dr. Hatcher interviewed Karla for six hours and conducted a number of substantial interviews with people who could provide him with information about her life, and he too had agreed with all the other doctors' diagnoses. Justice Galligan did not leave out Dr. Angus McDonald either.

He pointed out that Dr. McDonald had "allowed that all of his colleagues had agreed with her diagnosis. He noted that there was alcohol abuse and sexual deviation, most likely of the sado-masochistic type and he reviewed the article 'Compliant Victims of the Sexual Sadist.'

"Dr. McDonald wrote in his report with reference to 'Compliant Victims of the Sexual Sadist' that 'the number of parallels with this case is so striking as to be worthy of particular attention.'"

The fact that there are far more dissimilarities than parallels is never countenanced by anyone. For example, the Hookers had a child, the Bernardos did not. The Hookers only kidnapped one woman, the

Bernardos stupefied, and/or kidnapped, raped and/or killed four teenage girls, including Karla's sister.

The Hookers never killed anyone.

The Hooker's one victim, Colleen Slan, was held captive for seven years. After she signed a slave contract, she was allowed to come and go with a certain degree of freedom.

Jane Doe, the only Bernardo victim who survived, was never enslaved or tortured or involved in any sadomasochistic rituals and voluntarily performed fellatio on Paul Bernardo a number of times. She never knew that she had been drugged and raped until the police told her two years after the fact.

Galligan felt the article, "Compliant Victims of the Sexual Sadist" was so important that he included it in its entirety as an Appendix to his report.

He highlighted the fact that Dr. Peter Jaffe consulted the world's leading experts in battered spouse syndrome. "Dr. Jaffe also concluded that the diagnoses of Karla as a battered woman suffering from post-traumatic stress disorder was bona fide.

"Dr. Jaffe said 'that the failure to disclose the assault on Jane Doe was not unusual for a traumatized person.' He said that people who have been traumatized may remember some events in great detail, parts of others and nothing of some."

Justice Galligan noted that "Dr. Jaffe was not surprised that she did not remember the June 7, 1991 assault on Jane Doe. 'He said that in other cases of abuse he had noticed a process of "incremental" disclosure and that he did not find it unusual that Karla Homolka could not recall everything. He said that he would not be surprised if she remembered other things as time went by."

Judge Galligan concluded that "the expert evidence overwhelmingly supports" Karla's contention that she does not remember and therefore she could not have been successfully prosecuted for perjury.

"We accepted the experts' opinions. There were eight or nine, if I recall. They were unanimous," Code said. "But I will grant you that the first deal had a considerable impact on our deliberations about whether or not to charge her with respect to Jane Doe. We were, to a serious extent, constrained by it."

"Surely what is essential here," I said, "is that the first deal, was a powerful impediment to any revision of your relationship with her. I mean, what was Bevan thinking when he arrested Bernardo on February 17? At your direction, prosecutor Murray Segal had just met with Karla's lawyer for the first time the previous Sunday."

Referring to Bevan's arrest of Paul Bernardo on February 17, Code said "that was incredibly stupid, no question. We withdrew those charges almost immediately."

"Right, and how convenient. It just goes to my point that the Toronto-based rape charges were solid enough to keep him in jail – without bail." I said. "Why do you think Bevan thought he could do what he did? What evidence did he have to arrest Bernardo, even before he got into the house to start searching for the evidence that he did not have?"

Code was not hearing me. "How the hell would I know what some cop is thinking?" he replied, as though I was disrupting his train of thought with irrelevant inanities.

Regardless of the reasons the first deal was made, he said, he was very mindful of it when they came to confront the issue about whether or not to charge Karla with the June 7 assault on Jane Doe.

He emphasized that they had *needed* Karla to make Inspector Bevan's case against Bernardo for the murders. And a sharp legal mind like George Walker's could have and would have – according to Walker himself – created a legal quagmire of epic proportions – had they charged her with the assault on Jane Doe.

Walker considered Karla's lapse of memory with regard to Jane Doe as "innocuous" and covered under the terms and spirit of the May, 1993 plea agreement. Walker told Galligan that he would have vigorously fought if Code had decided to bring new charges against her with respect to the attacks on Jane Doe.

Galligan wrote in his report that first Walker "would argue that a prosecution based on the assaults on Jane Doe was an abuse of process because it violated the letter and spirit of the resolution agreement.

"The second line of defense would recognize that the defense of compulsion provided for in Section 17 of the Criminal Code is inapplicable because charges of sexual assault and aggravated sexual assault are specifically exempt from the benefit of that section.

"However, there is substantial evidence that Karla Homolka was a battered spouse to such an extent that she was completely under the control and domination of Paul Bernardo," and Walker said he would have "contended that her acts were not voluntary ones controlled by her own mind."

But George Walker was blowing smoke. As Walker himself had told his client two years earlier, the battered woman defense would never work if she were to be charged and have to defend herself in court. In Walker's opinions, the experts' opinions would not withstand challenge if Karla were tried as a full accomplice and a perpetrator in her own right. All the mitigating facts, such as the ones Galligan leaves out of his report entirely, would complete erode whatever scintilla of credibility such a defense might possibly have. For example, the fact that Karla enticed Jane Doe of her own accord and stupefied her with alcohol, sleeping pills and anaesthetic, while Paul Bernardo was out of the house. Or the fact that the sodomy-favoring nurse, Alison Worthington, presented a clear and present danger to Karla's relationship to Paul Bernardo and her imminent, ridiculously lavish wedding plans.

Not to mention the anti-psychiatry, such as the idea that Karla was a malingering, histrionic hybristophiliac, developed for Bernardo's defense team by Dr. Graham Clancy.

Because the judge at Paul Bernardo's trial refused to allow any expert opinion about Karla's state of mind or alleged condition admitted as evidence, the anti-psychiatry was not given any consideration by Justice Galligan in his report.

However, Galligan recognizes the tenuous nature of George Walker's position when he states that the defense of "moral involuntariness," which is what all Walker's legal mumbo-jumbo was about, is an almost impossible defense to make.

The issue, from Michael Code's point of view, as Justice Galligan recorded, was that Walker's vigorous defense would be time-consuming, seriously disrupting the scheduling for Paul Bernardo's pending trial and in Code's opinion, and Justice Galligan's, that was the far more important proceeding. The situation would become a legal morass with no guaranteed outcome with regard to Karla Homolka's relative guilt. No one was suggesting that she was innocent, it was always a matter of "relative guilt" and how much they could or could not prove.

To further complicate matters, until Ken Murray gave up the video-tapes in September, 1994, the only real evidence they found in the house, beside the 1:58 videotape, was provided by Karla when she pointed out the spot on the upstairs carpet where Kristen French had thrown up. She did that following her induced and cautioned statements, on June 17, 1993, a good month and a half after Inspector Bevan's search warrants expired. The videotapes behind the potlight in the bathroom ceiling were not the only things that Vince Bevan and his team missed during their search.

"What about the 1:58 videotape the cops found on the second day they were in the house?" I asked Code. "Anyone who saw that tape, as you did, could clearly see that Karla was no 'compliant victim' or any-body's battered wife. Galligan passes over this tape in his report. He calls it 'innocuous' but, in my opinion, it was anything but."

"I did not think that tape was 'innocuous,'" Code replied. "I took it very seriously. But you've interrupted me again. I'm trying to explain the situation to you as best I can and you are making it impossibly dif-ficult. Shut up and listen."

It had been years since anyone had actually told me to shut up.

He started to talk about how he had formed what came to be known as the "Management Committee," to oversee the two prosecutions; the one for the two murders in St. Catharines and the one for the rapes in Toronto. It had been his decision, in conjunction with the other mem-bers of this Management Committee to separate the two prosecutions rather than combine them. In his report, Justice Galligan actually taciturnly questions the wisdom of this decision. Code ignored my question about why they did it. Code was the Chair of the four-man committee. The other three members were very experienced, senior Ministry officials – Leo McQuigan, James Trelevan and Jim Wiley – all seasoned prosecutors with a great deal more experience than Code in matters prosecutorial.

In this undertaking to decide whether or not Karla should be charged with any offences for her role in the June 7 attack on Jane Doe, Code reduced Murray Segal's role to that of a consultant – he had no decision-making power but they listened to what he had to say. He also continued to liaison with George Walker.

The way Code tells it, he conferred with McQuigan, Trelevan and Wiley every step of the way over that crucial period between September, 1994 (the date the authorities came into possession of the videotape evidence) and May 18, 1995, when they finally decided to grant Karla immunity from prosecution for Jane Doe. These were not easy deliberations, Code said, they wavered back and forth on a daily basis.

As Code was talking it suddenly hit me. They had only focused on the one attack on Jane Doe, the only one for which they had a videotape record. Strangely, there was no pictorial or videotape record of that entire summer during which Jane Doe kept Paul and Karla company, regularly fellating Paul with Karla's encouragement. Neither was there a videotaped record of the aborted August 10 attack. All the authorities had to verify that second attack was a record of Karla's 911 call. A record of a 911 call seemed like good evidence to me ("similar fact" evidence, as the lawyers call it – Karla did exactly with Jane Doe as she had done with her sister, except Jane Doe started breathing again and Karla cancelled the call), but apparently for the Management Committee, seeing was believing.

Michael Code had already told me that he had not seen any of the other videotape evidence, a revelation that had boggled my mind. He was surprised by my surprise. To him it was simply matter of fact. Why would he review any of the other videotape evidence when there was never any question, at least in his mind, or the Management Committee's collective mind, about revisiting the first deal. And because the prosecutions of Paul Bernardo were divided, technically, Jane Doe (a rape victim who, like all of Paul Bernardo's rape victims, had survived) was the purview of the Metropolitan Toronto Police and the Toronto borough of Scarborough's prosecutor.

In the mind of the prosecutors who were trying Paul Bernardo's case – Ray Houlahan and his assistant, Greg Barnett – charging Karla for an attack on Jane Doe could have a profound negative impact on their ability to successfully prosecute Bernardo, which is why they had formally asked for an adjudication at the Ministry level in the first place. Their opinion was something which the Management Committee also had to consider, given it was their concern that instigated the formation of the Committee.

The majority of the videotape evidence – the sickening attack on Tammy Lyn and the devastating footage documenting the repeated and brutal attacks on Leslie Mahaffy and Kristen French – held no surprises for them.

They did not go back and review everything Karla had told them in such comprehensive, minute detail, and compare and contrast what she said to what they saw on the tapes, or to what others had said, to determine whether or not she was lying under oath at any time during her many, many statements over the previous two years. There was no will to impugn Karla's previous testimony or rescind her plea resolution for the reasons I have already outlined. It would create a legal mess and in their minds might very well collapse the prosecution of Paul Bernardo.

But there were real discrepancies. For instance, in a statement made under oath, Karla told her police interlocutors in May, 1993, that there was nothing special about her taking the Thursday afternoon off, the Thursday afternoon she and Paul kidnaped Kristen French.

This statement was directly contradicted by her boss, Dr. Patti Weir and her co-worker, Sherri Berry, whom Karla had cajoled and systematically coerced over a period of weeks into reluctantly foregoing her

Easter weekend plans so that Karla could participate in what was obviously a well-planned, premeditated abduction. Further, in consideration of the earlier fate of Leslie Mahaffy Karla *knew*, or at the very least surmised, that the teenager she helped pluck off the street would be violently raped and then killed.

On his own, Paul Bernardo could not have accomplished the daylight abduction of Kristen French. Karla had even talked at length about her role as facilitator and co-participant in just such an abduction and rape during the hour-and–half-long homemade pornographic tape she and Paul made in her parents' basement shortly after Tammy Lyn's death.

Also, under oath, Karla had said she held the Halothane-soaked cloth six inches above Tammy Lyn's face at all times during the attack, whereas the videotape shows her literally smothering her sister with it. The segment is short – barely five minutes – the lighting is poor, and the few times Karla can be seen bending over Tammy Lyn, holding the cloth on her face, are only flashes of no more than a few seconds in duration. Without good equipment that would advance the tape slowly frame-by-frame, this fact is virtually unnoticeable. The Ministry certainly had access to the best videotape equipment so that was not an impediment. To further complicate matters, George Walker, on Karla's behalf, had laid Tammy Lyn's demise on the bargaining table even before Inspector Bevan managed to bungle Bernardo's arrest and execute his search warrant. Walker had told Segal all about Tammy Lyn on the previous Sunday.

Given that Tammy Lyn's death had been ruled accidental, and the authorities would not have known about the true cause unless Walker had proffered it, they were pretty much in a hopeless situation with respect to the sister's murder. It was certainly not something that they could redress a year and a half after the fact.

THE MAN WITH WHOM
THE BUCK STOPS

Deep into Michael Code's Committee's deliberations, Murray Segal wrote George Walker a letter. Dated February 8, 1995, it has always puzzled me. The tone was almost chatty. If the tapes were so crucial that no deal would ever have been made with Karla Homolka had they been handed over when Ken Murray found them in early May, 1993, then why was this letter so blasé and casual. But more than just the tone, the letter makes it abundantly clear that the majority of video-tape evidence was not of much interest to the authorities.

"Generally the tapes give rise to three areas of questioning," Segal wrote. "The largest area, by far, relates to *follow up questioning* [italics mine] that arises as a result of the review of the tapes. Previous questioning, quite naturally, focused on what your client saw, heard and participated in. The actual review of the tapes gives rise to many *follow-up questions*. For example, accepting that the tapes do not reflect a continuous record of the confinement of the victims, what is shown suggests areas which the police need to explore in more detail. In addition, the police are also now in a bet-ter position to ask who was behind the camera in which scene and like matters."

In other words, the videotapes did nothing to cause the authorities to reassess their relationship with Karla. They were only being consid-ered as visual aids, useful in elaborating and fleshing out what they already knew with more precision and detail.

Had the Toronto police been fully in charge of the investigation and had they executed their search warrant and controlled the search of the house, the situation would have been dramatically different vis-a-vis Karla. Thanks to Inspector Bevan, that was not how it played out. But this was not something Michael Code or the Ministry of the Attorney General could have fixed either in 1993 or 1995. Because of Inspector Bevan's imperious territorialism and precipitous actions, Code was stuck with the first deal, which, to a large extent, limited what he could do with regard to the attack on Jane Doe.

As his superiors in the Management Committee did, Segal's letter to Walker focused on the thirteen-minute videotape of the attack on Jane Doe.

"Your client has been questioned on a number of occasions, some-times under oath, respecting her recollection of involvement with Jane Doe. My general understanding is that your client appears to be mistaken respecting her own involvement with Jane Doe. You have confirmed that you have now had the opportunity to view a portion of tape, in relation to Jane Doe, and your client's previous responses in connection with her involvement with Jane Doe. In that tape, I understand that your client appears to be committing a sexual assault on Jane Doe and administering what may be a stupefying drug. You reported to the authorities as early as the fall of 1993 that your client was having difficulties in her recollection of involvement with Jane Doe. Now, for the first time, the authorities are aware of the precise nature of your client's conduct.

"I agree with the police that any further questioning of your client, in relation to Jane Doe, should be under caution, respecting the sexually assaultive behavior and the apparent contradiction between her responses under oath and the videotape."

Segal talks about timing and even the sequence in which the police propose to show Karla all of the videotape evidence when they go down to Kingston's Prison for Women for that expressed purpose.

Although the examination of Karla with respect to the Jane Doe segment of the videotape would be conducted "under caution," Segal says the remainder of the interview that concerns all the rest of the videotape will not be "under caution," but under oath. This means that the police and the prosecutors would not be investigating Karla with respect to anything new concerning the attacks on Tammy Lyn Homolka, Leslie Mahaffy and Kristen French but simply refining their understanding and knowledge of those crimes.

Although Murray Segal repeatedly asserted, both at the time and during Ken Murray's trial, that had the authorities had the videotape evidence before Karla's deal was finalized on May 14, 1993, no deal would have been done, his letter to George Walker and the Management Committee deliberations that lead up to it, say otherwise.

After an extensive review of the videotape evidence, between September 1994 and February 1995, a full eight months before Paul Bernardo's trial began, it was abundantly clear to everyone that Karla was no longer a necessary or relevant witness against Paul Bernardo. However, nothing that Inspector Bevan or prosecutor Ray Houlahan saw on those videotapes, which they reviewed over and over again, caused them to rethink their relationship to Karla Homolka, even though certain scenes on the short Tammy Lyn segment and the longer Mahaffy and French tapes demonstrated that Karla had repeatedly lied to the authorities.

Houlahan did not ask Michael Code and the Management Committee for advice about whether or not there was sufficient evidence to rescind Karla's deal, only about whether or not she should be charged for the stupefaction and aggravated sexual assault of Jane Doe.

In his letter, Segal goes on to speculate that this interviewing process using the videotapes as visual aids would take three or four days, and says that these interviews will themselves be videotaped.

"The investigation of your client, respecting Jane Doe, may require other steps to be taken by the police, including obtaining expert opinion regarding the inconsistency between her account to date and what is reflected on the videotape. In the past, the police have relied upon expert opinion to explain other facets of your client's conduct.

"Expert opinion might assist the authorities in understanding her activities with respect to Jane Doe. Expert opinion may also possibly shed light on whether there is any explanation for why she has failed to provide an accurate account to date."

As Justice Galligan had confirmed in his report and as Michael Code told me over our dinners, they had relied very heavily on their host of experts' opinions to rationalize their relationship with Karla. And as Murray Segal said in this February 1995 letter to George Walker, they would continue to do exactly. In fact, as Segal stated, they were going back to the well one last time, to aid in the decision-making process with respect to the question about whether or not Karla should be charged for the crimes against Jane Doe.

Segal closes the letter by saying that "the police may seek legal advice" from the prosecutor's office "to help them determine what action, if any, including criminal charges" may be appropriate.

Between February 20 and February 24, the police made approximately forty hours of videotape showing them screening all the videotape evidence for Karla and then discussing it with her. It was a remarkable visual record that has since, like all of the videotape evidence, been destroyed. In doing so, Karla's "interrogators" eradicated the evidence of their own incompetence. Now, there will never be any "expert opinion" about Karla Homolka's responses or about the techniques, or the lack of technique, employed by her interviewers.

For the police, who often seem to have trouble with recording equipment, the multi-camera set up for these interviews was quite advanced. They had three stationary cameras; one focused on Karla's face, one set for a wide-shot to capture the entire room so that Karla and her two police inquisitors could be seen, and the third to record in real-time all of the videotape evidence Karla was being shown on the monitor they had set up for that purpose.

The result was a series of VHS videotaped records in four quadrants. When these tapes are replayed, Karla is seen close up in the upper left corner of the screen, the wide shot of the two detectives and Karla at a large table in the upper right, and the videotape evidence she is being shown plays in the lower left quadrant. The lower right quadrant is blank.

The attack on Jane Doe was notable for its similarities to the attack on Tammy Lyn Homolka. Jane Doe really was a body-double for Tammy. Except the videotape of this attack is much better lit and longer and the behavior and actions more explicit. Unlike the short Tammy Lyn segment, there is almost no dialogue – an interesting fact, in and of itself.

Most of the dialogue heard on the videotaped attack on Tammy Lyn six months earlier was initiated by Karla; she was constantly urging Paul to "hurry up" or use a condom and he was verbally responding to these instructions and imprecations. With Jane Doe, Karla obviously did not feel any obligation to try and protect the girl from the perils of unprotected sex, or anything else for that matter.

This time Karla is clearly enjoying herself, mugging for the camera, blowing kisses at the lens and generally having a field day with Jane's lifeless body and limbs. Wearing only a sleeveless t-shirt, naked from the waist down, there are no visible signs of the abuse to which she repeatedly told the authorities and the doctors she had already been subjected. Her skin is flawless alabaster. Nor does she seem at all a zombie under the control of some demonic puppet master. For the duration of this video, Karla appears to be the instigator, the director and very much in control.

Bernardo's camera work is still shaky and unprofessional but this time he frequently captures Karla's use of the Halothane-soaked rag, which she periodically refreshes with a bottle of Halothane she has propped up on a pillow to the left side of Jane Doe's head. This video leaves no doubt about Karla's methodology – throughout the thirteen minutes she can be clearly seen repeatedly soaking the rag with Halothane and placing it directly over Jane Doe's mouth and nose.

Given that this tape was made on June 7, 1991, a week after nurse Alison Worthington's last call to Bayview Drive, a week before Paul brought Leslie Mahaffy home and three weeks before Paul and Karla were married in a videotaped extravaganza at historical Niagara-on-the-Lake, it speaks volumes about Karla's state-of-mind, consciousness of guilt and motivation.

If a picture is worth a thousand words, a thirteen-minute sequence of moving pictures must be worth at least a billion – every one of them an indictment of all the experts' rationales and Karla's multitudinous wordy interviews and detailed explanations for why she did what she did.

Although portions of the other videotape evidence were extremely damning to Karla in and of themselves, particularly sections in the short Tammy Lyn segment and the numerous, lengthy segments showing Karla's performance with Kristen French, if any one segment could have been said to be Karla's nemesis, this was it. To truly know Karla, Michael Code did not need to see any other video.

He assigned Inspector Bevan to gather the "expert opinion" which Segal had talked about in his letter to Walker.

I asked Code why he did that? Wasn't that like putting the fox among the chickens? Why Bevan, who not only had a vested interest in the outcome but also had no experience with psychological experts?

"Because," he replied impatiently, "it was Bevan's case and it is the job of the police to gather evidence."

There's the rub alright. It *was* Inspector Bevan's case.

"But," I said, "he turned to Hatcher, Hucker and Jaffe, all experts that were hired under your auspices in 1994, through the Crown Law Office, to reinforce, or possibly rebut, the opinions of Drs. Arndt, Long and Malcolm."

I mentioned assistant prosecutor Greg Barnett's July, 1994 letter to George Walker, talking about the hiring of Drs. Jaffe, Hucker and Hatcher. I noted that it was written very shortly after Karla's examination by Murray and MacDonald.

"What of it?"

"Well, wasn't the fix in? I mean, Jaffe, Hucker and Hatcher had already written voluminous reports unanimously agreeing with Arndt, Long and Malcolm's diagnoses. They were hired in the wake of what must have been a very strange examination by MacDonald and Murray, an examination that had to have made prosecutor Houlahan uncomfortable. It must have been obvious that Karla was lying under oath. It must have been obvious that Murray and MacDonald were in possession of information that the prosecution did not have. Or else what possible reason could there have been to hire three more experts? One of them, Hatcher, was the expert witness who testified in the California case People vs. Hooker that was documented in that article Bevan was always waving around, the "Compliant Victim of the Sexual Sadists." Wasn't it all just a little to coincidental?

"What do you mean?"

"I digress. Never mind why they were hired in the first place. What I'm trying to say is that the three experts to whom Bevan turned, at your instruction, had already unequivocally stated that Karla was a battered woman suffering from post-traumatic stress disorder. Not only did they all agree with Drs. Arndt, Long and Malcolm each one added his own little riffs and elaborations. One or two of these guys had even had the added benefit of being able to review the videotape evidence. What were they going to do when Bevan came back to them about Karla's alleged memory loss – contradict themselves?"

"I told you already that I didn't pay any attention to anything Ken Murray did."

As he often did, Michael Code replied with a non sequitur that was rooted in my own verbosity. I never did get a satisfactory answer.

EXPERT OPINION

Inspector Bevan's letter to Dr. Chris Hatcher, of "People vs. Hooker" fame, is long and detailed. He gives the doctor a precis of the situation regarding the recovery of the videotapes and Jane Doe, with particular emphasis on the videotaped attack on June 7, 1991, and Karla's loss of memory with respect to virtually everything that was criminal in her activities with the young teenager.

He gives the doctor a series of questions which he says he has already discussed with Drs. Jaffe and Hucker. They are quite succinct:

"I have been directed to request from you a discreet report on the issue of Homolka's memory in relation to these incidents. Specifically, I ask that you address the following questions in your report.

"(i) Why does Homolka provide such consistent and detailed accounts on all other aspects of this case but fails to recall anything about the sexual assault(s) upon 'Jane Doe'? In light of all other crimes, for example, Tammy, Mahaffy and French it is not the most traumatic event.

"(ii) As indicated above, Homolka is seen playing to the camera and her facial expressions can be interpreted as a 'demonic' smile. What is your opinion of these actions?

"(iii) Are 'dream-like' recollections consistent with revived memories as per the post-traumatic stress disorder?

"(iv) In your opinion, is there any other rational explanation for Homolka's failure to recall or disclose these events? Could it have something to do with the Tammy incident or could it be the fact that 'Jane Doe' is the only living victim of this type of conduct?

"(v) If 'amnesia' or 'repression' are the explanation, are there other traumatic events known to you which were not remembered by Homolka?

"(vi) Why is Homolka's recollection of these events blocked? She has some recall of the sexual assault which apparently occurred in August 1991, but no memory of the incident in June 1991?

"(vii) Homolka has stated that she was confused by a 'dream' in which the face of 'Jane Doe' appeared in an incident in which the victim French was involved. What significance do you put on this?"

The Inspector then proceeds in seven typed, single-spaced pages to tell Dr. Hatcher exactly what Dr. Jaffe and Dr. Hucker have told him.

Dr. Jaffe said Karla's memory loss is "not unusual. People who have been traumatized may remember some events in great detail, parts of others, nothing of some. It is no surprise that she does not recall."

It has been Dr. Jaffe's experience with other clients with histories of abuse that "there is a process of 'incremental' disclosure."

Inspector Bevan pointed out the similarities between the attack on Tammy Lyn and the attack on Jane Doe and yes, Dr. Jaffe thought the two may well be linked and cause even further confusion in Karla's mind. "It is not unusual that Homolka cannot recall everything because there is so much to recall and that fact itself can cause confusion as to what happened, where, etc."

Concluding the section about Dr. Jaffe's opinions, the Inspector writes, "Dr. Jaffe's opinion remains unchanged. With some of the events, a part of Homolka paid close attention because she never wanted to forget what she and Bernardo were responsible for. Homolka had indicated that she had a 'safe' place, psychologically within herself, to retreat to – a part of her core that Bernardo could not reach. But with some things she just couldn't 'record' the events because she was disassociating herself from what was happening around her."

For his part Dr. Hucker had responded to Inspector Bevan's questions in a "pro" and "con" format. On the "pro" side he found that there was no evidence that Homolka was psychiatrically disturbed or suffering from a personality disorder prior to meeting Bernardo and that analysis had shown that she is pliable and easily influenced by others. There is evidence from others that her personality changed after she met Bernardo and Dr. Hucker claimed there was "ample evidence from others who observed signs of symptoms of physical and psychological abuse."

Following Drs. Arndt and Brown's lead, Dr. Hucker drew an analogy "to studies done on survivors of concentration camps who were forced to endure terrible things at the hands of others. He also referred to experimental evidence derived from Milgram's work (the application of electrical shocks to another) which studied the phenomenon of people who do terrible things to others on a third party's direction."

Dr. Hucker says these studies "may have some similarity to Homolka's experience with Bernardo and thus provide some explanation for her behavior."

On the "con" side, which in Dr. Hucker's parlance is more a dialectical monologue about his various explanations and excuses for her behavior, such as "the 'devilish smile' seen in the 'Jane Doe' segment." This could easily "be interpreted wrongly by some who consider it in isolation," Dr. Hucker explained.

Instead, he says that Karla "was 'conditioned' to perform that way." He explained that "after Tammy, Bernardo allegedly beat her quite severely for not performing as expected. From that experience Homolka learned that she should perform a certain way during these incidents in order to avoid the consequences."

Dr. Hucker also notes that the videotapes indicate that during her captivity Kristen French "was conditioned to smile for the camera," drawing an unsavory analogy that suggests Karla was as much a victim as Kristen French.

Some of Dr. Hucker's "cons" are credible. For instance, he notes that Homolka was "apparently an active participant in the planning stages and sexual assault which resulted in the death of her sister," although he does draw, in the same breath, comparisons to battered women who develop a "learned helplessness" and become paralyzed by the phenomenon." He does not bother to state that it was impossible that Homolka was suffering from battered spouse syndrome when Tammy was killed, given that she was living at home with her sisters and parents and only seeing Bernardo on weekends.

He notes that after leaving Bernardo and moving in with her aunt and uncle in Brampton Karla struck up a sexual relationship with a stranger whom she had met in a bar. Dr. Hucker allows how this could be interpreted as "hedonistic and self-serving" behavior.

While incarcerated at the Kingston Prison for Women Karla wrote a number of letters to friends which subsequently became public. Dr. Hucker told Inspector Bevan that "the substance of these letters may leave one wondering if she was at a resort of some type."

Inserting another "pro" interpretation of a "con" on the "con" side, Dr. Hucker suggests "that this is indicative of Homolka not being in touch with what is really going on in the world around her."

"Dr. Hucker informs me," Inspector Bevan says to Dr. Hatcher, "that 'repression' is itself a very controversial term." [This on Dr. Hucker's "con" side.] "No one disputes that someone who experiences trauma can also experience memory loss... the result is a type of amnesia with no organic basis." Dr. Hucker allows that there is some controversy about this.

However, when all the "pros" and "cons" were weighed, lo and behold Dr. Hucker reaffirmed his opinion that there was clear evidence to support the diagnosis that Karla suffered from post-traumatic stress disorder, and her memory loss was a consistent symptom of that condition.

Dream-like recollections are atypical in persons suffering from post-traumatic stress disorder and Inspector Bevan dutifully records that Dr. Hucker did not leave the subject without complimenting his colleague, Dr. Roy Brown, for the way he handled Karla when she first raised the issue back in 1993.

From San Francisco, Dr. Hatcher wrote back and told Inspector Bevan he wholeheartedly agreed with Dr. Jaffe's and Dr. Hucker's reasoning and concurred with their opinion that Karla's memory loss was a typical symptom of post-traumatic stress disorder.

* * * * * * *

I asked a psychiatrist friend of mine, Dr. Richard Meen, who has been around the block a couple of times himself, how shills such as Drs. Jaffe, Hucker, and Hatcher, could possibly be taken seriously.

"Wow. They're not shills. I don't know Dr. Hatcher, but Dr. Jaffe and Dr. Hucker are well respected. None of their opinions were ever tested in court, were they?"

"No." I told him that at one point during Bernardo's trial, the prosecution tried to get their opinions about Karla admitted as evidence, but the judge would not allow it. The judge said that Karla was not a defendant. She was a witness. It was up to the jury to determine her credibility for themselves, based on her testimony, not based on what a bunch of doctors thought about her.

"Precisely. So their opinions were never challenged," said Dr. Meen.

But how could nine experienced psychologists and psychiatrists come to the same opinion, given the controversial nature of the subject and her behavior?

"Easy. There is a kind of domino effect in these circumstances. One group forms an opinion and gives a diagnosis. Subsequently, another group is called in and asked to give their opinion. First, they are shown what their colleagues have said. All of these guys know what is expected of them. They are all experienced in giving "expert" opinion and testimony. They work within the system. And the system has both spoken and unspoken rules.

"The lawyers that hire them know the doctors by reputation and they know, roughly, what they can expect each one to say. There have been many studies done on the role of psychiatrists in the courtroom and in the judicial process. Most of them are not favorable to the practice. At best, they advise great caution. Psychiatry is more art than it is science. Guesswork and hypothesis are bad foundations on which to build criminal cases.

"There are doctors who most often testify for the prosecution and others who only testify for the defense. It's an adversarial system. There are two sides and they are each expected to have contrarian points of view. Most who play in this arena are not stupid. It is also a job. They get paid for their opinions. It's how the system works. You may not like it, but there it is."

And Dr. Meen was right. Dr. Hatcher, for instance, was paid US$100,000 for his contribution to Karla's post-traumatic stress disorder diagnostic buttress, and his opinions were never entered into evidence or his voluminous report ever made public.

DISCRETE EPISODES

Ordering grilled chicken with a tomato salad for what had become a very late dinner, I pointed out to Michael Code that I thought the way Justice Galligan dealt with Jane Doe in his report was nothing short of bizarre.

Galligan stated that there were three "discrete episodes" of reprehensible conduct by Karla Homolka toward Jane Doe.

This statement was fundamentally wrong, both factually and in the larger perspective of Karla's role in what was a six-month long, concerted attempt on her part to facilitate sex for her husband with her little girlfriend – while everyone was awake. Presumably, it was not as much fun for anyone after Karla had knocked Jane Doe out. Regardless, there was nothing discrete or episodic about those two attacks.

Galligan says that "the first episode was her inviting Jane Doe to 57 Bayview Drive with the knowledge that Paul Bernardo intended to have sexual relations with her."

At the time Karla invited Jane Doe to 57 Bayview Drive, Paul Bernardo did not know Jane Doe existed so how could Karla have known that Paul Bernardo intended to have "sexual relations" with Jane Doe? By Karla's own admission to police and prosecutors, Jane Doe had been "her idea, and her idea alone." Karla had never previously mentioned Jane Doe to Paul. As Karla intended, Jane Doe was a complete surprise.

To Jane, Karla's invitation came out of the blue. Years earlier, the girl hung around the pet store where Karla worked. However, Jane had not seen or spoken to Karla for at least two years.

Jane told the police that she was very pleasantly surprised when Karla called. She thought of Karla as the older sister she did not have. She accepted the invitation without hesitation and went right over to 57 Bayview where she found Karla – alone. Although Jane Doe had never had an alcoholic drink, Karla gave her sweet, mixed drinks to which she added her pre-mix of ground sleeping pills and water from the test tube which Karla had at the ready in the upstairs bathroom.

When Jane Doe passed out, Karla called her betrothed on his cell-phone and told him to come home, she had a wedding present for him. And it worked. He was surprised, particularly when he saw that Jane was a dead ringer for Karla's recently deceased sister. And indeed, there she was – comatose, spread-out on the floor, waiting for his attention.

For some inexplicable reason, Galligan calls this June 7, 1991 attack on Jane Doe the "second episode."

"The second episode was a sexual assault which Paul Bernado and Karla Homolka perpetrated upon Jane Doe the night of June 7-8, 1991. The third episode was a sexual assault which they perpetrated upon Jane Doe in the early morning of August 10, 1991."

As he extrapolates the events, he reinforces his earlier errors. "I digress to say that the police investigation later established that this visit probably occurred overnight on June 7-8, 1991 and on that night Jane Doe was drugged, anaesthetized and sexually assaulted by both Paul Bernardo and Karla Homolka."

Jane Doe was plied with liquor, drugged and anaesthetized by Karla Homolka alone – without any suggestion or pre-planning or encouragement from Paul Bernardo. The judge has only one fact right – Jane was sexually assaulted by both of them.

He is correct when he states that "Jane Doe had no recollection of those acts being performed on her."

"She told police that she became a frequent visitor to 57 Bayview Drive and was a regular companion of Paul Bernardo and Karla

Homolka. She went on at least one trip to Toronto with them. She also told police that Paul Bernardo began making sexual overtures to her to which she finally succumbed. She performed fellatio on him on a number of occasions."

Justice Galligan ignores the fact that the second attack was precipitated by Paul Bernardo's constant complaining to Karla that, in spite of Karla's encouragement, Jane Doe would not go any further than a "blow job." Karla is reported to have said in reply that she would "just have to put the bitch down again."

People are naturally disinclined to believe Paul Bernardo. But in this case, it rings true. And Karla's stories about that summer actually reinforce its veracity. She basically says the same thing in a different way. After all, if Bernardo was being serviced every second day by the girl, why was it necessary to "put her down" again? One explanation would be that Karla wanted to participate, too, and that was definitely not going to happen while Jane Doe was awake. The other possibility was that she wanted to shut Paul Bernardo up. Neither explanation cuts it as a pathological compulsion created by her husband through abuse.

Then the judge makes another factual error. He writes that "the relationship ended in December of 1992 when she (Jane Doe) refused to have sexual intercourse with him."

By Jane Doe's own statements to police, as well as those of her mother, and Karla's subsequent statements about the relationship, it ended at Christmastime, 1991, after Jane Doe had resisted both Karla and Paul's attempts to coerce her into having sexual intercourse with Paul for the past six months.

According to Jane, the three of them fought – Karla being as dismissive and abusive to Jane as Paul – whereupon Jane called her mother who came to pick her up. After that, Jane Doe never went back to the Bernardo household.

Justice Galligan states that it is his view Karla Homolka's "conduct of inviting young women into the presence of a man as dangerous as she knew Paul Bernardo to be was obviously reprehensible. I have serious doubt, however, that it amounted to criminal misconduct constituting an offense pursuant to any provision of the Criminal Code."

That may be so, but administering a stupefying substance is an offense punishable under the Criminal Code with a maximum sentence of life in prison. "Reckless endangerment" is also an offense under the Criminal Code, as is forcible confinement, not to mention "aggravated sexual assault" and a host of other lesser charges that could easily have been brought against Karla as a consequence of her conduct with regard to Jane Doe.

Galligan further rationalizes his portrayal of the "discrete episodes" with Jane by saying, "On May 14, 1993, during her induced statement, Karla Homolka told the police that Paul Bernardo always wanted her to find young girls for him. She said that she did get two young girls who then had voluntary relationships with him."

(This was a false. The second girl, Norma Tellier, did not have "voluntary relationships with him." Unlike Jane Doe, she would not perform fellatio on Paul Bernardo, let alone have sexual intercourse with him. Inexplicably, the girl occasionally stayed overnight at the Bernardo household, and one particular evening toward Christmas, 1992, with Karla's complicity, Paul Bernardo raped her. He was subsequently charged with the offense.)

"She (Karla) specifically named Jane Doe as one of those girls." Galligan continues. "At her trial on July 6, 1993, Murray Segal advised the Court of this conduct on the part of Karla Homolka" [meaning the conduct of soliciting young girls with whom Paul Bernardo might have sex].

Remarkably, Justice Galligan interprets Karla's behavior with Jane Doe only in the context of her solicitation for Paul Bernardo. "If the conduct of Karla Homolka in befriending Jane Doe so that Paul Bernardo could have sexual relations with her could amount to a criminal offence, it is my view that, by the express terms of the resolution agreement, any sentence which she could have possibly received is included in the twelve-year sentence which was imposed.

"The resolution agreement required Karla Homolka to disclose in her induced statement any criminal activity in which she had engaged.

She disclosed that conduct. The Crown and the police were satisfied with her disclosure and proceeded with the agreed charges."

This remarkable rationalization completely ignores the fact that Karla took the initiative entirely of her own volition to invite Jane Doe into her home, drug her and anaesthetize her in exactly the same way she had done her sister only six months earlier; in other words, Karla had full knowledge that her actions were lethal.

The judge describes this bizarre and reckless behavior under the generic term "befriending," declares it "not a criminal activity." And, given that she admitted "befriending" Jane Doe for the purpose of providing another sexual partner for Paul Bernardo during her induced statement, if it were a criminal activity that had to be acknowledged under the terms of her plea resolution, then she had done exactly that and acknowledged it.

"The Crown read in the fact that Karla Homolka had found young girls for Paul Bernardo. In the light of that provision, if Karla Homolka's conduct did constitute a criminal offense, her sentence of twelve years covers that offense. I need not say anything more about this episode because it is clear that the Crown never thought that the conduct of Karla Homolka in obtaining the young women could be the subject of a charge against her."

A PROPENSITY TO LIE

"It was not my view that the plea resolution covered Karla's criminal behavior toward Jane Doe," Michael Code said. "And it didn't matter what George Walker thought." He paused. "At least it's nice that we got into the dining room this time.

"Whether or not she committed perjury was one issue – like Bevan I accepted the experts' opinions about her amnesia being genuine – but that was separate from the question about whether sexual assault charges should be laid, or a charge like administering a stupefying substance. If memory serves, I actually wrote a memo about this."

"I know that Galligan sort of dismisses the 1:58 videotape in his report but I didn't. I took it very seriously and it continued to trouble me."

"But you made the deal anyway," I said.

"We had to," he replied. "I thought you were starting to understand that."

* * * * * * *

With respect to how the police handled the 1:58 videotape, Justice Galligan again misstates the facts: "The subject of the identity of the victim (on the 1:58 videotape) was not pursued further in Karla

Homolka's cautioned interviews nor was she shown any other pictures, or the videotape segment itself. In fact, she was not shown that picture again, or any other picture, or the videotape from which it was made at any time until February, 1995."

In fact, during her induced and cautioned statements Karla was shown two or three still pictures from that videotape.

After she went to prison, during numerous police visits, the record shows that Sergeant Bob Gillies showed Karla the still pictures from the video at least once if not twice again.

Then, on December 6, 1993, Sergeant Gillies and Sergeant Gary Beaulieu showed Karla the entire 1:58 videotape, replaying various segments two and three times, frequently using the pause button.

This interest in Jane Doe and the identity of the comatose girl in the still photographs taken from the 1:58 video and the videotape itself, was rekindled by Karla's October 6, 1993, letter to George Walker in which she only disclosed that she remembered that "Paul raped Jane Doe, a friend of mine."

Typical of all Karla's utterances to do with her role and involvement with the crimes, the letter puts the entire onus on Bernardo, and confuses what the police ultimately determined were two separate attacks on June 7 and August 10, 1991, during which Karla again used her deadly combination of Halcion and Halothane to knock out a young girl.

"I don't remember much of it. I can picture it happening in our living room." Karla's says in her letter. "She was drunk and had passed out. The next thing I remember is her falling off the bed upstairs."

Justice Galligan quotes the letter in its entirety. "What I'm really afraid of is that I was more involved than I can remember. Bob and Ivan..." [Galligan says he could not make out the second name of the police person in his copy of Karla's letter. Therefore, he substitutes the Toronto policewoman, Mary Lee Metcalfe's name for Niagara Regional Sergeant Ivan Madronic.] "Bob and Mary Lee Metcalfe showed me a still photograph taken from that videotape and I couldn't identify it. What if it was me with Jane Doe... I have to tell them but what if they nail me for this too?"

Justice Galligan notes that by the time Walker shared the letter with the authorities, "an agreement had been reached among the authorities that the Metro Police would investigate all sexual assaults allegedly committed by Paul Bernardo, wherever they were committed, with the exception of those assaults which involved Leslie Mahaffy or Kristen French. Under this arrangement, it was the responsibility of the Metro Police to investigate any suspected assault on Jane Doe."

This is exactly what Sergeants Gillies and Beaulieu told Karla after they showed her the 1:58 videotape on December 6, although Justice Galligan does not seem to have been apprised of this "screening." He categorically states that this particular videotape was never shown to Karla.

The Toronto police finally interviewed Karla about Jane Doe on February 2, 1994. Karla told them that she was trying to recall details but to no avail. Her memory was not clear. As he does throughout his report, Justice Galligan accepts as verbatim what Karla told them.

"She said that Paul Bernardo told her to get Jane Doe drunk and then give her sleeping pills. She said that Jane Doe drank quite a bit and then she gave her one Halcion pill… It is apparent from reading the transcript of that long interview that Karla Homolka was not able to recall any more details of the incident herself."

Then Justice Galligan digresses. "The police investigation is outside my mandate…" (The inquiry into the police investigations and their failings was given to another judge, the Honorable Archie Campbell.) "There is probably a valid explanation for the approach taken by the police. They had the videotape segment itself. When Karla Homolka had trouble identifying the person from a photograph of one frame of the videotape, I wonder why she was not shown the whole segment or, at least, more than one photograph of one frame?"

Justice Campbell addresses this issue in his report but it appears that Inspector Bevan, whom he interviewed, either did not tell him that Karla had been shown the 1:58 videotape, or Justice Campbell did not get the facts straight either. He reasons that the police did not show Karla the video clip "because the police at that time did not have the videotapes of Kristen French or Leslie Mahaffy, although Homolka thought they did, and they did not want to show Homolka (who had earlier demonstrated a strong capacity for lying and manipulation) the weakness of their position, or to influence her testimony or to give her a chance to lie, by showing her at that time that they only had a one and a half minute video clip." [This is puzzling. Inspector Bevan had to know that Sergeants Beaulieu and Gillies showed Karla the 1:58 video-tape on December 6, 1993. They would have not have done so without his instruction and authorization. Regardless, there is no mention of any instruction in any officer's will-state. Also, contrary to what Justices Galligan and Campbell state in their reports, Karla was shown at least two stills taken from the videotape during her induced and cautioned statements in May, 1993. She was again shown two or three stills on June 17, 1993, before she drove around with the police looking for the Mickey Mouse watch she told them she had belatedly thrown out the window of Paul Bernardo's car. It was the same day the police video-taped her as she led them on a house tour of 57 Bayview. The tran-scripts make these facts abundantly clear. Between May and December, it is unclear how many more stills she was shown, but the subject def-initely came up again and again and stills were used as visual aids. Karla was also very aware that the police had not found the videotapes. This too is evident in the text of her responses and queries during the four days of induced and cautioned statements.]

Justice Campbell concludes: "In order to keep Homolka as honest as they could, the police had to maintain the upper hand and they had valid reasons for proceeding as they did."

Campbell then states that "the police 'knew' that Karla had a propen-sity to lie." Inspector Bevan and police officers told Justice Campbell that Karla had "demonstrated a strong capacity for lying and manipulation."

And of course that was true. Karla had blatantly and knowingly lied to police on at least two different occasions – on the occasion of her statement the night her sister died, and throughout her first interview with the Toronto police who she thought were investigating the Scarborough rapes.

In spite of the fact that one of the stipulations of her plea resolution bound Karla to absolute truthfulness, by his own statements to Justice Campbell, Inspector Bevan did not sufficiently trust her to tell the truth and therefore, according to Inspector Bevan, they never confronted Karla with the only real piece of evidence they had recovered from the house – the 1:58 videotape. Given the fact that the police did show Karla the 1:58 videotape on December 6, 1993, none of this makes any sense – unless there was another agenda.

It is instructive to note that Inspector Bevan and his cohorts never did anything to test Karla's truthfulness, even after they had all of the videotape evidence and could have identified a dozen areas where Karla had out-and-out lied to the authorities under oath.

The prosecutor in Scarborough, Mary Hall, and Chief Grant Waddell of the Niagara Regional Police wanted Karla charged with respect to Jane Doe. The Chief even wanted her deal assailed. Typical of the topsy-turvy world of modern bureaucracy and policing, the Chief was not in charge.

After he received Drs. Jaffe, Hucker and Hatcher's opinions about Karla's memory loss with respect to the attacks on Jane Doe, Inspector Bevan wrote a letter to the Management Committee in which he said that "after investigating this issue and examining medical reports I conclude that there is insufficient evidence to support" any charges.

Inspector Bevan believed what he heard (from the experts) over what he saw every time he watched the thirteen-minute videotape segment during which Karla viciously and with apparent lascivious, feral joy, attacks Jane Doe and rapes her.

Justice Galligan notes that perjury is defined in Section 131 of the Criminal Code as: "(1) the making of a false statement under oath; (2) the person who made the statement knew that it was false; and (3) the person made the statement with the intention to mislead."

He reiterates that "it is not part of my mandate to review the police investigations and I want to be very careful not to trespass upon the mandate of Mr. Justice Archie Campbell…" Nevertheless, Justice

Galligan goes on to say that he arrived at exactly the same conclusion as Inspector Bevan.

When the police showed the thirteen-minute-long videotape documenting the attack on Jane Doe to Karla at the Kingston Prison for Women on February 20, 1995, Karla said that she simply could not remember the event. If she had she would have disclosed it. She said that she always "thought the videotapes were still in existence." (A statement which confirms that she knew that the police had not found them previously.)

Justice Galligan quotes Karla from that interview: "So why would I not tell the truth? And especially, I mean, I have been honest and forthcoming about everything. Why would I not tell the truth about this? It doesn't make any sense to me."

Because he does he not have all the facts, or have the facts he has straight, Justice Galligan's analysis of the Jane Doe situation becomes hopelessly convoluted.

He engages in a discussion that confuses and separates the two attacks on Jane Doe, the one on June 7 and the second on August 10. The second attack was precipitated by Bernardo's complaints to Karla about his not being able to persuade Jane to have sexual intercourse with him, but Justice Galligan's report of this "discrete episode" does not make this clear.

Justice Galligan then goes on to state the obvious and records that the Scarborough prosecutor Mary Hall wanted to lay charges against Paul Bernardo for Jane Doe and speculates about what role, if any, Karla Homolka might play in that prosecution. [This seems to me to be absolute obfuscation. By this time, Mary Hall had already laid dozens of charges against Bernardo, including numerous counts of aggravated sexual assault, forcible confinement, and sodomy, to name only a few, with respect to the Scarborough rapes. His February 17, 1993 arrest, on numerous charges related to three of those attacks, stuck. He was arraigned the next day, and held without bail for months even though Inspector Bevan's charges on the murder charges had been thrown out. Over the next few months, after Inspector Bevan had regained control and took over the search of the house, Ms. Hall continued to lay charge after charge as more DNA matches to more rape victims were obtained.]

"Of course, if she [Karla] had been jointly charged with Paul Bernardo [n the sexual assault of Jane Doe] as a party to that offense, the Crown would have had no way of proving the offense against him because, as a co-accused, she would not have been a compellable witness to testify against him. Nor would her description of the events to the police be admissible against Paul Bernardo." (Compellable or not, given the fact that the authorities had had the videotape evidence in their possession since September 1994, eight months before Bernardo's trial began, Karla's testimony against Paul Bernardo with regard to any charge that had been laid, or charges that might be laid, was totally irrelevant and unnecessary.)

The judge continues: "The Crown thought the resolution agreement expressly or by necessary implication protected Karla Homolka from prosecution for offences which she disclosed even after her sentencing provided she would co-operate with the Crown by testifying against Paul Bernardo. Paul Bernardo was charged with the August 10, 1991, assault. Karla Homolka was not. That fact confirms my opinion that the Crown thought the resolution agreement protected Karla Homolka from prosecution for it.

"It is unclear why the two assaults, which were very similar, were ultimately considered separately," he continues. Indeed, it was.

Later, Justice Galligan addresses the issue of warring prosecutors: Scarborough rape prosecutor Mary Hall thought that the videotape evidence clearly demonstrated that Karla Homolka participated in a serious assault on Jane Doe and she should be prosecuted for it. Because of the videotapes, Ms. Hall believed that the case was so clear that it would not be at all difficult to prove. Chief Grant Waddell agreed with Ms. Hall. He strongly disagreed with Inspector Bevan's letter to the Management Committee. The Chief wanted Karla Homolka charged and prosecuted.

However, in his jurisdiction, as Justice Galligan records, the prosecutor "Raymond Houlahan and his assistant, Greg Barnett, were of the opinion that charging Karla Homolka with that crime would seriously affect her credibility as the essential witness in the murder cases. For this reason they thought that she should not be charged."

Thus, the ultimate decision about whether or not to charge Karla Homolka fell to Michael Code.

THE FINE ART
OF ADJUDICATION

During our second dinner, I took an entirely different tact in my approach to Michael Code. I became zen-like. I forewent confrontation and argument. What Code had done, it seemed to me, having now read the Galligan report very closely, was implement the Napoleonic war strategy of divide and conquer, leaving both sides weaker while he maintained and wielded the ultimate power. It certainly read, as Justice Galligan parsed it, as an almost endless process of reduction; one large case against two perpetrators in which the perpetrators are considered separately and then the case itself divided in two, and then the two investigations – the one in Toronto and the one in St. Catharines – made separate and distinct.

The survivors, the victims of the sexual assaults and rapes, regardless of where they were from, and regardless of whether or not Karla was involved in the commission of any of the crimes against them, would be handled by the Toronto police and prosecutors. Only the rapes and murders of Leslie Mahaffy and Kristen French, for which Karla had already pled out, would be investigated and prosecuted in St. Catharines.

Ironically, and predictably, Paul Bernardo was ultimately tried in Toronto for the murders committed in St. Catharines. The trial was moved from St. Catharines to Toronto over concerns about tainted jury pools and his ability to get a fair trial in the Niagara region.

When it came to Jane Doe, even the attacks on her were considered separately and analyzed as though they had happened to two different people. If ever there was a recipe for mystification and blame spread so thinly that it could hardly be identified, let alone assigned, it was in the outcome of Michael Code's practice of the fine art of adjudication.

It occurred to me that Mr. Code just might well be an evil genius and this his masterwork. But it had become abundantly clear to me that I was not going to get anywhere being contentious and arguing with him, so perhaps another, more philosophical, relaxed approach would yield better results.

Dabbing his upper lip with his napkin and taking a sip of the Chablis, Code acknowledged that there may well be errors and omissions in Galligan's report but opined that I was not looking at the big picture. They were not about to revisit the first deal with Karla. I had got that much right. By 1995, they were focused on the singular question of whether or not to charge Karla for what she did to Jane Doe on June 7.

"As I said before, I did not think that her plea resolution prohibited the laying of charges with regard to Jane Doe," he said. "That was a horrendous, totally unjustified attack, especially when you consider that she had to have known how dangerous it was, given that she had killed her sister six months earlier in exactly the same way.

"There were six or seven key factors or areas that we focused our discussions on."

"What were they?"

"I don't remember them all. They were things such as public confidence in the administration of justice and whether or not the victim wanted charges laid – if I recall, she didn't – but they are all there in Galligan's report and I know that his discussion of them is a very accurate reflection of exactly what we discussed and the reasons we came to the conclusion we did."

The list in Galligan's report includes "the gravity of the incident"; "the impact on the victim and the view of the victim as to whether charges should be laid;" "public confidence in the administration of justice and the maintenance of public order;" "the degree of culpability of the alleged offender – in relation to another offender;" "the effect of a prosecution on the public order;" "the likely outcome in the event of a finding of guilt with regard to the sentencing options available to the court;" "and the effect the laying of a charge or charges might have upon the successful prosecution of another offender."

Michael Code and his Management Committee were also cognizant of legal concerns that seem esoteric and irrelevant to the untutored in light of the crimes that both Bernardo and Homolka committed but are essential to the rule of law as it is practiced in this democracy.

For instance, as a consequence of her first deal, and regardless of whatever else Karla was or had become, she was an "accomplice witness."

Canadian courts, unlike their British and American counterparts, have consistently held that before an "accomplice witness" can testify against their accomplice any charges against that accomplice witness must have been dealt with and their punishment adjudicated.

And there was another overwhelming concern as Justice Galligan duly records in his report. Huge weight was given to the idea that the murders had to be dealt with before the Scarborough rapes. Although I have no idea exactly why, it was an opinion that Michael Code firmly held and holds to this day.

Even though the authorities had all the videotape evidence, eight months in advance of the beginning of Paul Bernardo's trial – and therefore no longer needed Karla Homolka's testimony to convict him – Karla's "credibility" as a witness was paramount, something that Code also steadfastly maintains.

To me, Karla's "credibility" seemed a huge black hole in that universe into which all common sense disappeared. But arguing about it with Michael Code was futile. Interestingly, Galligan records that the jury was ultimately divided about Karla's credibility, which certainly goes to my point about its irrelevance.

After the trial, one juror said he did not believe the prosecutor's assertions that Karla was a battered woman or that she committed criminal acts in a state of "moral involuntariness." This was the opinion held by the majority of jurors.

The others said they were convinced that she was battered and in a state of moral involuntariness. Two of the jurors even wrote Karla's family letters of support, and Galligan quotes from one of those letters in which the juror says that he "personally believes she was manipulated, controlled and battered."

In spite of this seismic split among the jurors about Karla's status and credibility, it took them less than a day to find Paul Bernardo guilty on all nine counts, including two counts of first degree murder.

Sagely, Code observed that hindsight is always twenty-twenty. There was no way at the time that they were going to take any chances with Bernardo's prosecution.

Galligan reflects Michael Code's opinion that had they charged Karla with offences against Jane Doe her trial would have been "extremely complicated, both legally and factually, and most certainly would have been long, difficult and with an uncertain outcome." He also adds that he is convinced that it would have been impossible to have completed such a proceeding by the time she was required to testify at Paul Bernardo's trial, alluding yet again to the issue of the "accomplice witness" and her credibility.

Michael Code and the Management Committee also accepted the psychiatric and psychological experts' unanimous opinions about Karla's memory loss.

"What else were we supposed to do?" Code asked me, although I still find it ironic that none of this voluminous psychiatric opinion was admitted as evidence during Paul Bernardo's trial. Karla was not on trial, she was a witness. The judge ruled it irrelevant. It was up to the jurors to decide whether she was credible or not.

The judge did allow the prosecution to call Dr. Jaffe and Dr. Hatcher, whom they had flown up from California to wait in the wings just in case the judge ruled in favor of the prosecution's motion to admit the psychiatric evidence. The two doctors were only allowed to testify in general terms about battered spousal syndrome and post-traumatic stress disorder.

Their testimony was short and irrelevant but obviously significant enough that some of the jurors came to share the prosecution's view of Karla.

None of their reports were entered as evidence. And the defense experts that Paul Bernardo's attorneys had retained were never called in rebuttal nor their alternative theories about why Karla did what she did, and who she really was and what she was, were ever entered into evidence or distributed to the jury. As Galligan said in his report, he himself did not really delve very deeply into this topic. The fact that Bernardo's defense team did not bother to attack this generic evidence about battered spouse syndrome and post-traumatic stress disorder suggests that either they were lazy or completely unconcerned about Karla's credibility because in the end, given the finality of the videotape evidence, it was completely irrelevant. Considering the strenuous nature of their defense, the latter seems an obvious conclusion.

Just before Karla took the witness stand, Michael Code and his Committee decided to give her a pass on Jane Doe too. They also granted her the blanket immunity she had sought in the first instance, and not received, thus superceding and voiding Karla's 1993 plea resolution. The succinct but vague reason was that it would not be "in the public interest" to lay additional charges.

In his report, Justice Galligan admits that no one has "been able to define precisely or describe exactly what constitutes the public interest. The public interest" he says "is broad and comprises many diverse aspects which may vary greatly from time to time and from case to case."

There was no explanation for the surprising and seemingly arbitrary gift of "blanket immunity."

Michael Code's opinion was clearly set out in a memo that he distributed to his Committee members. And all of our conversations had only achieved a reaffirmation of his belief in what he recorded in that memo.

The overriding issue for Code was the immediate, successful prosecution of Paul Bernardo on the murder charges. He says that without Karla's assistance, Bernardo "could not have been charged and prosecuted and would likely have gone on to kill and rape other women."

This entirely discounts the very strong DNA evidence that was developed against Bernardo for the Scarborough rapes; the evidence upon which the Toronto police based their search warrant, evidence that was substantial enough to keep Bernardo in jail – without bail – even after Michael Code was forced to stay the murder charges laid by Inspector Bevan on February 17.

Over the course of our discussions, Code was dismissive on this topic. I asked him, on more than one occasion, why it was so imperative that everything be driven by Bevan and the murder prosecution. Why could the authorities have not proceeded slowly and cautiously, based on the Metropolitan Toronto Police search warrant and the DNA evidence?

At one point, during our first, contentious late-night conversation, he told me that the DNA evidence was not strong enough.

"Strong enough for what?" I asked indignantly. "It was strong enough to arrest Bernardo on three counts of sexual assault and rape, sodomy and a dozen other charges that stuck and held him in jail, without bail, until Bevan finally got Karla's signature on a dotted line and Bernardo was sent back to St. Catharines and formally arraigned on the murder charges in May, 1993."

I never got a satisfactory answer.

It is also a fact that, however conveniently, Code believed, and continues to believe, the experts' opinions about Karla's memory loss.

"She has consistently tried her best to disclose the assault on Jane Doe," Code wrote in his memo. "She told her lawyer of her first recollections and he disclosed this letter to the police. She then told her psychiatrist of further recollections and asked him to assist her with hypnosis and sodium pentothal (which he refused to do for therapeutic reasons.) She then gave a partial account to the police. This is all before the videotapes were turned over to the police…"

Contrary to what Murray Segal has steadfastly maintained and what Justice Galligan concluded in his report, Michael Code does not think that the videotapes, had they been found by Inspector Bevan and not by Bernardo's erstwhile lawyer, Ken Murray, would have made much difference.

"But for her genuine amnesia and but for the suppression of the videotapes by Bernardo and his former counsel, the assault on Jane Doe would unquestionably have been made part of the plea agreement with Homolka two years ago.

"It would have had some impact on her sentence, in my opinion, but not a significant impact. Instead of twelve years, the sentence might have been fourteen or fifteen years. The key factors on sentencing would still have been her early guilty pleas, her critical assistance to the prosecution in securing the arrest and prosecution of a more dangerous offender, her subservient role in the offences, the duress exercised on her as a battered wife, the positive psychiatric reports and the lack of any prior record or any reasonable prospect of re-offending. Justice Kovacs might well have imposed the same twelve-year sentence even if the assault on Jane Doe had been part of the plea agreement.

"This series of factors, namely, Homolka's significant assistance… the failure to include this offence in the plea agreement through no fault of her own, her genuine attempts to disclose the offence to the police and the minor impact this offence would have had on her sentence are all factors that weigh in favor of discretion."

Neither his colleagues on the Management Committee nor Justice Galligan, after the fact, could find any flaws in his legal ratiocinations, a noun for thought processes which encompass both the abstract and the logical.

I am here to tell you that today Mr. Code remains steadfast in his defense of the correctness of the decision to not charge Karla with any offences to do with Jane Doe, and grant her blanket immunity as he did, he explained, to bolster her credibility as an "accomplice witness."

What is now abundantly clear is that Michael Code's ultimate decision not to charge Karla with respect to the repeated heinous attacks on Jane Doe, and the subsequent grant of blanket immunity, whereby, theoretically, he reinforced her "credibility" as an "accomplice witness," has done nothing to maintain the public confidence in the administration of Justice – quite the opposite – but that consideration was clearly not the most important on Michael Code's list.

Although there are many facts and arguments to the contrary, which I tried to press on him time and again, he stubbornly asseverated that any prosecution of Karla Homolka would have put the successful prosecution of Paul Bernardo for first-degree murder at great risk. To him, Karla was by far the lesser of two evils, and was not then and is not now a danger to society.

He reasserted, time and again, that the public interest was better served by not laying any charges against her; that they did the right thing by dividing the prosecutions, and that he and his Committee did a good job managing those two prosecutions and their divergent interests; that prosecutor Mary Hall and defense counsel Ken Murray were flakes and that the Ministry was correct to fire Ms. Hall and prosecute Ken Murray. Furthermore, according to Code, he and his Management Committee did the right thing taking as much time as they did to decide the Jane Doe matter and that their careful investigation of Karla's claim of amnesia was thorough and bona fide.

As it turns out, Michael Code and I agree on only one thing. Had Inspector Bevan found all of the videotape evidence during the sixty-nine days he searched the house, it would not have made one iota bit of difference.

Code does not, however, admit that the prosecution of Ken Murray was an elaborate subterfuge. What was it he said in that memo of his? "But for her genuine amnesia and but for the suppression of the videotapes by Bernardo and his former counsel, the assault on Jane Doe would unquestionably have been made part of the plea agreement with Homolka two years ago."

In other words, Murray's "suppression" of the videotape evidence for eighteen months did not really have any meaningful effect on Karla's deal or her relationship with the authorities. Michael Code thinks that it might have had some impact on Karla's sentencing. Maybe, had Ken Murray turned over the videotapes right away, they might have had some effect "but not a significant impact. Instead of twelve years, the sentence *might* (italics mine) have been fourteen or fifteen years… Justice Kovacs *might* well have imposed the same twelve-year sentence even if the assault on Jane Doe had been part of the plea agreement."

When we parted that last evening, we simply agreed to disagree on the reasons why the deal was done in the first place. He said "potato," I said "potatoe." We did, however, agree on two other things. Karla should have been released on her statutory date, that the prison officials far exceeded their mandate and their role when they detained her.

HYBRISTOPHILIA

The day the party pictures were published on the front page of the *Montreal Gazette*, Karla was in her room in Establishment Joliette's House 10 getting ready to go to work. One of the girls had CTV's *Canada AM* morning news program on television and yelled at her to turn it on. Karla became very upset, especially when she saw the pictures of her and Christina Sherry on national television. "Chris," as Karla calls her, was already out on parole and Karla believed that this would destroy whatever life the girl had managed to start rebuilding for herself.

Karla was never happy whenever there was something about her in the media, but this time she felt worse than usual. She actually felt physically ill. She went to work and tried not let herself think about it, but she had a really bad feeling.

Shortly after arriving at work, her parole officer, Ginette Turcotte, called her to the administration office and showed her the front page of the *Montreal Gazette*, and asked her to read the article and look closely at the pictures and tell her who had given them to the *Gazette*. Karla did as she was told.

Karla thought then, as she does now, that it was Mary Smith. She had been in for manslaughter and had a long criminal record. She and her girlfriend were both troublemakers. The other inmates knew it and the prison knew it. Karla did not know it when she moved into House 10 where the two were already residing. As was Karla's wont, she had tried to make friends. She had actually given this woman one of the pictures.

"I know," she confided to a correspondent. "A very stupid move."

It was a long time ago. The pictures were taken in 1998. Today was September 22, 2000. Karla believed some of the photos had been stolen from her room.

Mary Smith was a "horribly bossy, pushy woman" and when she got paroled "everybody was happy."

Karla was no longer happy. She made it through the rest of the day as best she could but she continued to feel really awful. The feeling persisted, like a flu bug. They were supposed to be doing inventory in food services but Karla could not bring herself to count mushrooms and tally cabbages.

"I just felt too awful to do it," she wrote, noting that this was not "normal for me – I can usually put everything aside, but I had a really strong reaction to this."

Karla talked to her co-worker who was also a friend and they decided to just skip inventory that month. They talked to their boss and she was okay with it so that's what they did.

A few days later, Karla was called to the administration office again. When she got there, Ginette Turcotte asked her if it was true that she was refusing another psychiatric evaluation. "Yes, it's true," Karla said.

Having been evaluated and assessed dozens of times, before and after she went to prison, Karla was finally fed up, particularly when right after she applied for those escorted temporary absences (ETAs) and challenged the warden's decision to refuse them, they began sending people to see her who started to write what Karla considered to be ill-informed and negative reports.

After reading what the Montreal psychologist Hubert Van Gijseghem had said in his August 2000 report which he had written without interviewing her, Karla had decided once and for all to exercise her right to refuse any further psychological evaluations. It was blatantly obvious that "the fix was in" so why bother. Anyway, as Karla had patiently explained to Ms. Turcotte, after the fiasco last year over

her ETAs and the court case, she had decided not to contest her detention. They got want they wanted. She would stay in prison for her full
twelve-year term, so what difference did it make now?

About thirty minutes later, Ms. Turcotte called her again. It was a
few minutes before count and Karla was back in her house where she
supposed to be. Twice a day, just like in the movies, all the inmates had
to be in their respective places to be counted. Karla called over the
intercom and told her it was count; Ms. Turcotte said come anyway, so
Karla left her house and walked across the yard.

Everything about that day was indelibly etched in Karla's brain.
About the minutes that followed she wrote: "This is going to sound
absolutely crazy and not true, but I swear it is. On the way there it actually went through my head 'they are calling me to tell me they are going
to transfer me because I am causing them too much trouble.'" And to
Karla's absolute, stunned disbelief that was exactly what Ginette
Turcotte did. She told Karla she was being transferred – to the Regional
Psychiatric Center in Saskatoon – for a complete psychiatric evaluation. Even though the idea had crossed her mind, it was not a serious
thought and Karla had immediately dismissed it, like a bad dream
from which you awake shaken but, within a few minutes, cannot
remember any details. After all, Karla had not really caused any trouble. When her court challenge made the papers, she withdrew it. She
did not know how the media found out about it. Someone tipped them
off, but it wasn't her. Then she decided not to contest their obvious
desire to detain her beyond her statutory release date on July 6, 2001.
She had even apologized.

Karla told the parole officer that they could not transfer her to a
psychiatric facility and prod and probe her against her will, it was
against the law and the prison's own regulations.

Karla thought that Ms. Turcotte felt badly and did not want to be
the one breaking the news to her. But it didn't stop Ms. Turcotte from
telling Karla that not only could they transfer her, that was exactly what
they were going to do, and Karla did not have any choice. "I was so
upset. I cried and yelled. Why Saskatoon, why not Kingston – there is

a Regional Center in Kingston – why not there where at least I can see my family?"

The parole officer said she would inquire about the possibility of Karla going to the Regional Psychiatric Center in Kingston instead. Then she asked Karla if she would go voluntarily. Karla told her that there was no way she would go voluntarily, then immediately wavered and asked if there was any difference, afraid that not going willingly would mean something worse. Ms. Turcotte told her that all it would mean was more paperwork. That was pretty much all that was said. Karla had to wait until the count was over and then she walked back to her house. She was crying uncontrollably. Women from the house next door were sitting at their picnic table. They asked Karla what was wrong but she just shook her head and went inside. Linda, Manon, and Tracy were in the kitchen.

"I walked in, crying like a baby and they all asked me what was wrong. I told them they're transferring me to Saskatchewan. They all stood there with their mouths open." Transfers were very rare, reserved for the hardest cases and always punitive. They had not even transferred that pain-in-the-ass, Mary Smith.

Karla ran upstairs to call her lawyer. Marc Labelle was not in his Montreal office so Karla talked to his associate, Martin Latour. Frantic, Karla explained the situation. Monsieur Latour laughed. He told Karla not to worry, she was not going anywhere. Karla was not convinced. She tried to explain that everything was different for her, she wasn't like other prisoners, but he still said that she was not to worry – an involuntary transfer to a psychiatric facility was against both policy and the law.

When Karla came downstairs the questions started. Karla told the women what her parole officer had told her and started crying again. They all told Karla not to worry. The chairperson of the inmates committee, Karla's friend and housemate, Stivia Clermont, was in the private family unit in the midst of a family visit. It seemed that every time either Stivia or Karla went to the PFV, something bad happened. "All I could think of was that this topped everything that had happened so far." One of the girls wanted to go and tell Stivia. Karla said no.

Karla steeled herself and went back to work for the rest of the day. She did not say anything to anybody because she was completely off balance and not sure what to do. She had gotten so used to keeping everything about her case secret that she just carried on. She was called back to the administration office a couple more times that day. First, Ms. Turcotte gave Karla formal notification of her forthcoming involuntary transfer. It was now obvious that they had been working on it for awhile – it was not something that had just cropped up as a consequence of the pictures in the paper. Like everything the prison did, the form was meticulously typed, repetitive and unnecessarily long. Under the heading "Assessment for Decision" it said "Decision Required: Institutional Transfer (Involuntary) Assessment Purposes."

Reading it, Karla was completely flabbergasted. They were using Hubert Van Gijseghem's ridiculous and unfounded speculations to justify the transfer. "Even I, with only a B.A. in Psychology can see the stupid diagnostic errors he made," Karla scoffed in a letter.

If he had wanted to portray her as a psychopathic monster he could have been a lot more imaginative; like those doctors hired by her ex-husband's lawyers prior to his trial who called her a malingering, histrionic hybristophiliac. Hybristophilia describes the phenomenon of an individual who is sexually aroused by a partner's violent sexual behavior. The term was derived from the Greek, *hybridzein*, meaning "to commit an outrage." Whereas there is a great deal in the psychiatric literature to dissuade anyone from ever diagnosing a woman with anti-social personality disorder, or suggesting that she was a psychopath, as Van Gijseghem had done, there was nothing to say that a woman could not be the driving force in a hybristophilic relationship.

"Histrionic" was good too. The criteria for histrionic personality disorder was a "pervasive pattern of excessive emotionality and attention-seeking, beginning by early childhood and presented in a variety of contexts… People with this disorder constantly seek, or demand, reassurance, approval, or praise from others and are uncomfortable in situations where they are not the center of attention…" and so on and so forth.

Drs. Graham Glancy and Nathan Pollack had not interviewed Karla either, but that had not put a crimp in their style. All this had long been a matter of public record. It was published in that horrible book called *Invisible Darkness*. The book was very mean to Karla and said that she was the one most responsible for everything. And maybe she had been. Karla was filled with self-loathing and self-hatred. She knew she was a horrible person who had done horrible things. But she was not solely responsible. And she had been tried and sentenced. Her deals had been reviewed by a judicial inquiry and they were found to be just and correct in law. How much more did anyone want? She *should* pay for her crimes and she was paying for them, as sentenced by the court. Her lawyer, George Walker, in consultation with the prosecutor Murray Segal, had told her when she first went to prison what twelve years meant: If she *was* good, it meant four years in jail, and eight years on parole. If she *was* bad, it meant eight years – with four years on parole. She remembered it as though it were yesterday. He had said if she was "the worst prisoner ever" she would only do eight years. She had been the best prisoner ever. And look what they were doing to her now!

Karla's case management team, in preparing the "Institutional Transfer, Involuntary" forms were relying on the conclusions in Dr. Van Gijseghem's report where he says "a serious investigation of Ms. Teale" is required "to test the following hypotheses:

"Is an Antisocial Personality Disorder present that has not been detected by the clinical and actuarial tools used up to now?

"Is Narcissistic Personality Disorder present? (Her unconditional infatuation for a 'perfect narcissist' like Paul Bernardo would lend weight to this hypothesis.)

"Is either of these two Disorders not complicated by one or more genuine types of paraphilia?"

How many more "actuarial tools" could be applied to her? She had been given every psychological test known to man and then some, many twice or three times over. And, no, Karla did not meet any of the criteria for antisocial personality disorder, at least not according to the *Diagnostic and Statistical Manual of Mental Disorders IV*, to which Van

Gijesghem repeatedly referred throughout his report, as though it were the Bible.

According to the *DSM-IV* the essential feature of antisocial personality disorder (ASPD) "is a pattern of irresponsible and antisocial behavior beginning in childhood or early adolescence and continuing into adulthood. For this diagnosis to be given, the person must be at least 18 years of age and have a history of Conduct Disorder before the age of 15. *By definition, the Conduct Disorder symptoms begin before the age of 15.* The first symptoms of Conduct Disorder in females who develop Antisocial Personality Disorder usually appear at puberty, whereas in males the Conduct Disorder is generally obvious in early childhood."

That let Karla out. Throughout her childhood, until Karla met the "asshole" when she was seventeen and a half, Karla had been a wonderful, happy child. Her childhood had not been characterized by "lying, stealing, truancy, vandalism, initiating fights, running away from home, and physical cruelty…" In fact, just the opposite was true. The only time she had ever "run away from home" was when she went to Kansas to see her high school sweetheart, Doug Liddell, but she was already seventeen. And she did not "run away," she simply disobeyed her parents and went on a two-week vacation. She even called them when she arrived to tell them when she would be home. That was hardly "running away."

All the weird stuff came later, after she hooked up with Paul Bernardo.

Karla was twenty years old when she killed her sister. There was nothing in Karla's childhood, or her behavior up until that remarkable act to even hint at antisocial personality disorder.

ASPD was modern psychiatry's concession to the idea of psychopathy, a word that had not been officially recognized by the profession since 1963. Van Gijesghem's hypothesis about ASPD may well have been his way of suggesting that Karla was that rarest of all creatures, a female psychopath. But if she was, would that not have been discovered by Dr. Sharon Williams when she administered the *Psychopathy Checklist – Revised (PCL-R) to* Karla in 1996?

Van Gijseghem said he reviewed both of Dr. Williams's "Psychological Assessments." Karla had scored 5. To be classified a psychopath she would have had to score at least between 20 and 30. Obviously, Van Gijseghem was making it up as he went along, doing the bidding of Jacques Bigras, the senior psychologist seconded to CSC headquarters in Quebec – the man who had ordered Van Gijseghem's report and who in turn, was doing someone else's bidding, someone higher up.

The *DSM-IV* criteria made the possibility of a narcissistic personality disorder diagnosis a little more plausible: "The essential feature of this disorder is a pervasive pattern of grandiosity (in fantasy or behavior), hypersensitivity to the evaluation of others, and lack of empathy, that begins by early adulthood and is present in a variety of contexts.

"People with this disorder have a grandiose sense of self-importance. They tend to exaggerate their accomplishments and talents, and expect to be noticed as 'special' even without appropriate achievement.

"These people are preoccupied with fantasies of unlimited success, power, brilliance, beauty, or ideal love, and with chronic feelings of envy for those whom they perceive as being more successful than they are."

There is a bit of a problem with narcissistic personality disorder since it is arguable that our society is built around it and generally rewards those who display its symptoms. So how does one really tell if someone "suffers" from it? And if one can make such a diagnosis, if it were as simple as that, would that not in turn mean that dangerousness can be predicted and criminal behavior curtailed? Having said that, narcissistic personality disorder does not necessarily lead to criminal behavior anyway.

If Karla were ever suffering from narcissistic personality disorder, seven years of prison and prison therapy had pretty well eradicated it. She was no longer preoccupied with "fantasies of unlimited success, power, brilliance, beauty" and certainly not "ideal love," but it was true, sometimes she was still envious of others who had not been bad and stupid like her and led decent, productive lives.

Drs. Arndt, Long and Malcolm specifically said that she did not suffer from any personality disorder. And Drs. Jaffe, Hatcher, Hucker and McDonald had concurred. And why, if she had developed this narcissistic disorder after she had spent a few years in prison had not someone else such as Dr. Brown or Dr. Williams picked it up and treated her for it – five, six, seven years ago?

Dr. Van Gijesghem refers to "her unconditional infatuation for a 'perfect narcissist' like Paul Bernardo…" Actually, if Van Gijseghem had really done his homework he would have known that Paul Bernardo had been found to be a sexual sadist by one of the world's leading clinical forensic psychiatrists, Dr. John Bradford, who examined and tested him over a ten-day period prior to his trial. Nowhere in Dr. Bradford's report did he use the term "perfect narcissist." There was no such thing as a "perfect narcissist" in the psychiatric literature. Dr. Van Gijseghem had culled that term from an article written by an layperson newspaper reporter; an article filled with psychobabble that had been published in *Saturday Night Magazine* during Paul Bernardo's trial in the summer of 1995.

But the rhetorical *pièce de résistance* in Dr. Van Gijseghem's report was his last interrogative: "Is either of these two Disorders not complicated by one or more genuine types of paraphilia?"

Given the fact that Karla was not diagnosed by fourteen other experts with "either of these two Disorders" and in fact, did not suffer from them, how could they be complicated by "one or more genuine types of paraphilia?"

Again, according to the *DSM-IV*, as well as the test results obtained by Dr. Racine-Rouleau through her administration of the *Abel Screen Test*, and the opinions of prison psychiatrists and psychologist Drs. Brown, Williams and Arbut, Karla did not suffer from any sexual dysfunction or paraphilias.

"The Paraphilias are characterized by arousal in response to sexual objects or situations that are not part of normative arousal activity patterns and that in varying degrees may interfere with the capacity for reciprocal, affectionate sexual activity. They include 'Exhibitionism,'

'Fetishism,''Frotteurism; (a term defined as "recurrent, intense, sexual urges and sexual arousing fantasies, of at least six months duration, involving touching and rubbing against non-consenting person"), 'Pedophilia; ("recurrent, intense, sexual urges and sexually arousing fantasies, of at least six months in duration, involving sexual activity with prepubescent children"), 'Sexual Masochism,' 'Sexual Sadism,' 'Transvestic Fetishism,' and 'Voyeurism.'

"Except for Sexual Masochism, in which the sex ratio is estimated to be 20 males for each female, the other Paraphilias are practically never diagnosed in females…"

Karla was not a "sexual masochist." As Dr. Glancy had said in his report to her ex-husband's lawyers, "a female hybristophiliac is not a masochist. The idea that she herself might become a victim is not in the cards. So long as the two partners remained in sync then the victim would always be someone else. If one partner became unstable, as did Paul Bernardo, and threatened the other partner, as he did Karla, then the partner would dissolve the partnership, as Karla did."

Neither were Karla or her husband pedophiles; their victims were not prepubescent, they were teenagers.

Then Van Gijseghem's last statement: "If one of the above hypotheses is confirmed, is there a possibility or probability that she will reoffend?"

Who could really say? The people who the police and the prosecutors said could say, such as Drs. Arndt, Long, Malcolm, Jaffe, Hatcher, Hucker, McDonald, Brown and Williams, all said she was not a danger to society nor likely to reoffend. The judge at her trial accepted Drs. Arndt, Long and Malcolm's conclusions.

Afterwards, the judicial inquiry thoroughly reviewed the question and Justice Patrick Galligan conclusively stated that he was satisfied that Karla was no longer a danger to society and would not reoffend.

Karla knew that she was not going to reoffend, but that did not matter because who would believe her? Surely the question was, was she less or more likely to reoffend if released (a) on parole on her statutory date, with its attendant strict conditions, so that she could gradually get used to life on the outside again, or (b) suddenly, after she served her last day on July 6, 2005, having been betrayed by the system and locked down for the balance of her sentence in Cellblock A at Sainte-Anne-des-Plaine?

It was all terrible. It was all made up. No one cared. And even if they did, as Karla sincerely believed some of the people who worked in Joliette did, they could not do a damn thing about it. She could not remember exactly who it was who told her but she wrote that it was someone working at Joliette who let it slip that "the Warden had received a phone call in the middle of the night telling him to get me out of that prison, that they didn't want it to become an election issue. They were just following orders."

The "Institutional Transfer, Involuntary" form documented Karla's family name as "Teale" even though Van Gijseghem suggested that her continued use of the name in prison somehow represented a lack of remorse and was indicative of some kind of unspecified perversity.

It recorded her prison number, 283308 D; given names, Karla Leanne; date of birth, May 4, 1970, and described her as a divorced Canadian citizen who could not be deported. It also listed important dates to do with her "Sentence Management":

July 6, 1993 – the day she went to prison; July 6, 1995, the day Karla was first eligible to apply for full parole, June 1, 1997; the day she was transferred to Joliette, July 6, 1997; her statutory release date, July 6, 2001, the date to which this "Assessment for Decision" was addressed, and, of course, the last day Karla would spend in prison, July 5, 2005.

It went on to explain the reasons for the involuntary transfer.

The purpose of this transfer of Ms. Teale is to allow the CSC to conduct a thorough psychiatric assessment for a potential detention referral. Over the past few months, we have begun gathering pertinent information in order to carry out an exhaustive analysis according to the criteria required for a detention referral. Although Ms. Teale has stated that she will not contest her continued detention beyond the period of Statutory Release, we must nevertheless carry out a complete review within the prescribed legal time frames.

As it now stands, we have reached an impasse because the assessments available to us were insufficient. In our opinion, a thorough psychiatric assessment is essential in order to clearly determine the true risk the subject may represent. Furthermore, in light of the assessment recently submitted by the psychologist, Mr. Hubert Van Gijseghem, we believe that the hypotheses he suggests merit further exploration. This would allow us to obtain more precise understanding of Ms. Teale's personality traits and also help us to complete a thorough risk assessment.

It is because of the requirement to obtain all pertinent information, that is accurate, up-to-date and complete as possible, that we consider it essential Ms. Teale be assessed in a setting specializing in the field of psychiatry.

They first discussed Karla's transfer to Saskatoon with the facility there on September 27, 2000, and blah, blah…

With regards to preventive security, we consider it important to note that Karla Teale was the subject of threats on numerous occasions. It is therefore paramount that her security be properly assured during any transfer.

These threats had been reported in the media but no one in Joliette or at RPC in Saskatoon was ever able to confirm them or identify a source. What this little paragraph did though, as Karla knew it would when she read it, was ensure that she would be held in maximum-security solitary confinement at RPC – for her own protection.

Ironically, following on that, the report notes that her overall security classification had always been "medium" and that there would be no "modifications" to that status.

As we previously mentioned, we are presently reviewing all of Karla Teale's file in order to conduct a thorough detention review. We therefore require all information related to the dynamics of her personality. Since her first contacts with the justice system, Karla Teale has been the subject of numerous psychological and psychiatric assessments, none of which have offered a clear prognosis or orientation with regards to her dangerousness.

This statement is patently false. All the assessment reports, including those of Drs. Arndt, Long, Malcolm, Hatcher, Hucker, Jaffe, and CSC's own Dr. Brown, stated unequivocally that Karla was not a danger to society.

Inspector Bevan repeatedly told reporters, while Karla was wandering around free on bail awaiting her trial in 1993, that she was not a danger to society and, indeed, CSC's own Dr. Sharon Williams said the same thing to justify Karla's transfer to Joliette. Nobody in the system with whom Karla had come into contact thought Karla was a danger to society or else she would not have been designated and maintained at a medium-security classification all these years.

The judge who presided over Karla's trial, Francis Kovacs, stated in his sentencing remarks that Karla was not a danger to society although he did qualify that opinion by saying "unless she met another Paul Bernardo." This caveat was not sufficient for the judge to reject the terms of Karla's plea bargain and sentence her to life in prison which he would have been well within his authority to do.

All of the voluminous experts' reports in Karla's file also stated that her prognosis and her prospects for recovery were good.

The "Institutional Transfer, Involuntary" report went on, oblivious:

We therefore believe that a thorough assessment of the internal dynamics of the subject must be carried out, especially in view of the fact that we are now in possession of all factual information related to her offences. It is important to keep in mind that at the time her sentence was handed down, the videotapes of the circumstances leading up to the crimes were not yet available. These (the videotapes) must be taken into consideration in order to fully appreciate the offender's participation in the perpetration of the criminal acts which resulted in the loss of life.

Neither was this true. A number of Karla's assessors and evaluators such as Drs. Hatcher, Hucker, McDonald and even CSC's Dr. Brown, had seen the videotape evidence. Also, a consultant to the prosecutors and the families of her victims, Dr. Catharine MacKinnon, reviewed them extensively and advised the prosecutors and the families about their relevance and how they should be used as evidence during Paul Bernardo's trial. MacKinnon had written in her report that it was obvious that Karla was also a victim of a sexual sadist.

Dozens of senior police officers and individuals in the judicial system, who had unquestioningly accepted the decision that Karla would get two concurrent twelve-year prison terms for her crimes in return for guilty pleas and testimony against her former husband, had seen the videotapes and had every opportunity to strenuously object and attempt to revise her sentence.

The videotapes had come into the authorities' hands in the third week of September, 1994, eight months before Paul Bernardo's trial started. In spite of this fact, and the extensive review of the videotape evidence conducted by the police and Bernardo's prosecutors, just before Karla took the witness stand in July, 1995, Michael Code and the Management Committee gave her a pass for her role in the stupefaction and rape of Jane Doe. They also bestowed on her the blanket immunity her lawyer had sought in the first plea resolution in 1993 but had not received.

The courts had already decided Karla's fate and the conditions of her deal dictated that she be released on parole at least by her statutory date. It is not supposed to be the role of the Correctional Service to re-evaluate the sentence imposed by the Court. The language in her file was unequivocal on this point and it was certainly the understanding of all involved that she would be released at the earliest possible date, contingent on her "good behavior."

Reading the transfer form, Karla knew once and for all that it was never going to happen.

Therefore, although at this time, Ms. Teale states that she is unwilling to participate in the assessment process, it is our duty to insure that all possible analyses are carried out in order that the CSC's detention review is as thorough as possible. It is with this duty in mind that a transfer to a specialized psychiatric center, even if it is involuntary, must be brought into effect. The chosen site of such a transfer is the Regional Psychiatric Center in the Prairies.

This center is presently the only federal institution which both car-
ries out assessments and treatment of women offenders. Our choice
was also based on the fact that our obligation to respect the legal
time frame for detention review can be better controlled if she is
incarcerated at a federal institution.

The report goes to remark about a fact that was irrelevant to the
Correctional Service's role:

Ms. Teale has always aroused much controversy in the public
arena. Many individuals have clearly and publicly expressed their
discontent with the plea bargain which was reached between Ms.
Teale and the justice system; although we remain constantly aware
of the public's scrutiny, we have tried to keep in mind that our role
is to manage the sentence which was handed down. This being said,
we are also aware that Karla Teale remains an enigma; it is a case
which challenges us with regards to analysis, assessment and iden-
tification of the personality traits as well as the level of dangerous-
ness. Although several psychological and psychiatric reports are
presently on file, a precise portrait of Karla Teale which takes into
account the many facets of her personality, continues to escape us.
There exist so many contradictions or unclear statements in her file.
These need to be properly explored in order to allow us to carry out
a thorough and professional detention review. We therefore believe
that it is essential that the offender not only be thoroughly assessed,
but that this assessment take into consideration the multiple
hypotheses put forth (by Dr. Van Gijseghem) so far, as well as the
impact, if any, that her participation in institutional programming
has had.

The document is signed by Karla's parole officer, Ginette Turcotte,
and team leader Julie Cobb.

Here was the scenario: None of the psychiatrists, psychologists,
primary workers or parole officers including those whose signatures
were affixed to this document, under whose supervision and in
whose care Karla had been for the past three-and-half years, were
capable of discovering the dynamics of Karla's personality — dynam-

ics that were long a matter of public record and contained within her prison file. Somehow, those dynamics were ignored or overlooked or misunderstood by all the various individuals involved in construing Karla's punishment and prison term. However, not to fear: the authors of the rational for Karla's involuntary institutional transfer were supremely confident that those elusive dynamics would be suddenly and miraculously discovered by psychologists and psychiatrists in the employ of Correctional Services at the Regional Psychiatric Center in Saskatoon.

It gave Karla vertigo. It was a blizzard of bureaucratic mumbo jumbo and factually incorrect statements and assumptions. Through the haze of a kind of psychic brown out, Karla could hear Ms. Turcotte's voice.

No, Karla could not go to the Regional Psychiatric Center in Kingston because they did not take women. Pinel, the psych hospital in Montreal with whom Joliette had a transfer and treatment arrangement, could not take her because it was a provincial institution and the federal prison authorities did not feel that they could "control the time frame for the evaluations," whatever that meant.

Patting Karla's arm, Ms. Turcotte also told her that this was all happening because of the photographs in the newspaper, "plain and simple."

The warden had received a phone call from Ottawa in the middle of the night telling him to get Karla out of Joliette, that they did not want her to become an election issue. A Federal election had just been called. The ruling Liberal party was, at the time, very concerned about an imagined threat to their mandate from the neo-conservative, right-wing Alliance party. This was before then Alliance leader Stockwell Day's name was changed to "Doris" by a satiric public referendum. The Liberals were re-elected in a landslide.

The fact that the staff at Joliette were just following orders did not make the situation any less devastating. But it did teach Karla that none of these people, no one, not even prison staff she had previously trusted implicitly, were really in charge nor could they be trusted.

News travels fast in the joint. Stivia heard and left the PFV unit a few hours later. They began a vigil. Karla did not know what else to call it. As Karla later characterized it: "It was like someone had died in that house. Everyone stopped eating. Everything came to a standstill."

Karla stopped working. Stivia stopped working. They just sat there together, being together.

Karla tried to keep on working but could not. Every time she tried to go into work, she ended up getting called somewhere else, so what was the point?

"I gradually told people what was going on," Karla recalled. "Everyone was in shock. Nobody was happy. People were crying and coming up to me telling me to fight, coming up and hugging me. I cried all the time."

Karla tried to fight. Her lawyers filed suit in Federal Court to try and stop the transfer. She called the Correctional Investigator.

Correctional Services has a special investigative unit known as the Correctional Investigator Office meant to oversee the Service's activities and prevent, or correct, breeches of protocol and policy.

The investigator told Karla in no uncertain terms not to worry, that she would never be transferred because it was illegal and contrary to policy.

Everyone was trying to reassure her but somehow Karla knew not to believe them. She had learned over the years that nothing, absolutely nothing, was the same for her. Although it was only a period of sixteen days between the time the pictures appeared in the newspaper and her transfer, the world Karla had diligently and carefully built for herself over the past seven and a half years collapsed.

Karla does not remember very much very clearly about those days. The time seemed to run together. She started having panic attacks and taking Ativan and sleeping pills again. When she didn't, she couldn't sleep and sat up all night, rocking back and forth.

To Karla's way of thinking it was another complete betrayal. "This may sound like an extreme reaction," Karla wrote "but you have to look at my past. I was in a wonderfully loving family, and then condemned to hell on earth with Paul. Then I was sent to a prison in which I was locked away in a small unit with very few other people for four years. For that time, I was verbally abused, threatened and escorted everywhere. The only time I spent alone was in the PFV. Then I went to Joliette where I was almost free. I really hated it at first, but grew to love it. You visited my house in Joliette so you have a glimpse of what it was like. We really try to make it a home and we live as a family for the most part. There are five of us who had been together for years. We are very close. We cook together, eat together, have fun together, etc. It really was like a family. I was accepted in that prison. For the first time in my whole sentence, I had real friends, a real life. I was able to work on my problems and issues just like everyone else. I had a job I liked. I worked hard for what I had and I deserved it. And here it was all about to be taken away from me for no good reason except that I was bringing heat on the prison through no fault of my own. If I sold those photos, if I caused trouble, I would understand. But I didn't. And everyone around me telling me that they were against what was happening made me feel even more helpless because a) I couldn't appeal to them to change their minds because they weren't the ones making the decisions, and b) I couldn't get mad at them for the same reason. Talk about frustration."

Karla was a model prisoner. And most of the many reports written by prison staff reflected that.

It was crazy. In Van Gijseghem's report he listed all the reports he had allegedly consulted. For instance, he sited reports by Dianel Lariviere, Gilbert Richer and Joanne Fenessey.

Dianel Lariviere was Karla's second Primary Worker in Joliette. She started off with Linda Clermont and then they switched her to Dianel. She was a very compassionate woman who did her best to help Karla – she always told her what was what; for instance, she told Karla that it didn't matter what Karla did things were already decided. But her reports were not negative. She wrote her papers in a helpful way.

Gilbert Richer did a program called "*Pouvoir D'agir sur Soi*," loosely translated, meaning "self-empowerment." It was a program that he created himself and was now doing in prisons in France.

Karla had asked to take the program but he denied her first application because it was designed for people who came from dysfunctional families, and the prison was well aware that Karla's family background was not dysfunctional. She convinced him to let her take it because her relationship with her ex-husband was so dysfunctional and she was so young when that had started. Gilbert Richer agreed, but probably just because she was going to do it in English. There were not many English-speaking women participating, so Karla did not take up anyone else's space.

M. Richer's report, to which Van Gijseghem refers, was excellent and said, among other things, that he never saw Karla deny or minimize her responsibility for her crimes.

Joanne Fenessey gave the program called "Survivors of Abuse and Trauma." It was supposed to be in two parts but the women who took it with Karla asked for a third session which they ended up doing on Saturdays. Ms. Fenessey's report about Karla was very positive. If Van Gijseghem actually read any of these reports, he had completely ignored the substance of what they said.

The fact that she had never caused any trouble and was a model prisoner was recorded in her voluminous prison files – there were so many: Admission and Discharge; Visits and Correspondence; Education and Training; Case Management; Preventive Security; Sentence Management; Psychology; Discipline and Disassociation; Health Care and Parole – files that, when stacked one upon the other, were taller than she was.

Everyone around Karla, both other inmates, her friends, the prison staff, the CSC's own institutional investigators, and her lawyers, told her they were against what was happening. There was absolutely no one within Karla's purview with whom she could get angry and vent her growing embitterment and malignant frustration.

* * * * * * *

The Elizabeth Fry Society has an office in the Administration area of Joliette. Karla sat there with three of the women from her house and one of her caseworkers, waiting for her lawyer to call. When the telephone rang, Karla was too upset to take it. She knew it was hopeless. When the caseworker told them the news, everyone started crying. Ginette Turcotte walked in and was also told. Ms. Turcotte had no idea. She went into her office, made a few calls, came back and said, "I'm sorry, Karla, but you're leaving in an hour." Karla freaked out. It was 4:00 p.m. She and Stivia and Linda ran to the personal effects station to get a cart to put Karla's things in. André, the guy in charge, could not believe that Karla was leaving. Nobody could really believe it. It was a tempest in a teapot. The stories and pictures in the newspaper had not caused any trouble for Joliette. Although that's what it said in the media followups, it was not true.

André told Karla and her friends to go back home, that he would bring a cart over to the house. Karla went back to her house to say goodbye. Everyone was crying. Karla was crying. André arrived with the cart. Karla and the girls went into her room and started throwing stuff into some bags. She had already put some clothes out on the bed, knowing that she would lose in court. Karla quickly called her mother. It was freezing outside. One of the girls gave Karla her winter coat. They walked to the door near the canteen and the keeper would not let anyone go the rest of the way with her, except for the caseworker. They all hugged goodbye and cried some more. Karla's worker and the keeper walked with Karla to Personal Effects where her stuff was packed up for the journey. Karla was searched and then met with the RCMP officer who would escort her to Saskatoon; coincidentally he was the same guy who had brought her to Joliette from Kingston four years earlier. He and Karla's parole officer told her that they were not going to handcuff or shackle her because they knew that she would not do anything. On the way out they stopped at the clinic where they gave Karla a bunch of Ativan because they were afraid that she was going to have another panic attack. Then they walked out and got into the truck.

"We were turning around to pull out of the parking lot. I looked out and what must have been the whole population was standing at the fence watching. I started crying again and put my hands up to the window as if to hold all their hands. Of course, no one could see because it was dark by then and there was no light inside the truck."

They drove to Montreal and got on the plane. From there on, things are a little vague. Karla was so stressed out she had popped a couple of Ativan. For months, in fact until she got to the Regional Center at Sainte-Anne, she did not realize that there was another officer from the Regional Reception Center with them on the transfer. She was there all the way from Joliette to Saskatoon. She was the one who searched Karla. She remembers the RCMP guy handing her a Coke, a bottle of water and a KitKat and putting them in her pocket. She does not remember landing in Thunder Bay and going inside the restaurant at the airport there. She does remember landing in Saskatoon and getting handcuffed and being put in a car. She remembers arriving at the prison, insisting on calling her lawyer, but calling her mother instead. It was 3 a.m. and Karla was a complete emotional wreck.

* * * * * * *

Opened in 1978, the Regional Psychiatric Center in Saskatoon is a diamond-shaped building with an inner, open-air courtyard that sits on the city's eastern river bank. It is described on the CSC Web site as "a forensic mental health hospital operating in a multi-level security setting, providing a therapeutic environment to meet both the health and correctional needs of patients."

When Karla arrived that Saturday morning, October 7, 2000, there were 194 men and 12 women in residence.

Karla was placed in a 3.5 by 2 metre windowless, cinder block "transition" cell with a sink, toilet, desk and dresser. The steel cot which was firmly fixed to the wall was covered by a mattress. The solid-steel cell door opened onto a small corridor where Karla would allegedly meet with the assessment team as well as have controlled access to a little kitchenette.

Kept in isolation, not allowed to interact with the other women who were all classified as maximum-security and considered dangerous, if not deranged, Karla immediately felt an enormous psychic dissonance and sensory deprivation that would ultimately have as debilitating an effect on effective assessment as the panoply of psychiatric medications she had been on between 1993 and 1995.

For doing as she was told and being a model prisoner for seven and a half years all Karla's privileges were revoked and she was put back in isolation. For seven and a half years Karla saw her parents and her sister regularly on holidays, particularly Thanksgiving and Christmas. Now Karla was barely able to talk to her mother on the telephone. For all her discipline and hard work, Karla was far worse off than she had been when she first went to prison.

The next day Karla woke up horrified. It was so dry. Already her skin was parched. Karla had dry skin to begin with and she was quickly dehydrated. She had nothing – no toiletries, no clothes. They gave her a sweatshirt to wear but no underwear or bra or anything – it was Thanksgiving, a long weekend and Personal Effects at RPC was closed and her belongings were unavailable to her. Karla begged one of the nurses to go and get her a bra and panties. She did but Karla had to wash them every day because she did not get her own clothes for a week.

"The nurses were super with me," Karla later explained. "They brought me the unit TV to watch during the day. I had nothing. The first letters I wrote from there were total desperation. They put me in segregation because of threats against my life and I was locked up in this little room with a cell, a shower and a tiny kitchenette which was really a counter-top, bar fridge and cupboards. It was terrible."

After four years, Karla was suddenly totally alone with no one to talk to. The nurses tried to come back and see her but Karla was "super suspicious" and they really were too busy anyway. They had twelve other women to deal with.

Dr. William Shrubsole, the associate clinical director at the Center, told the *Saskatoon Star Phoenix* that Karla's evaluation would be done by a diagnostic team consisting of a psychiatrist, a psychiatric nurse, a psychologist and a social worker. This team would try to interview Karla and gather information about her mental state, forensic history, background and her "psycho-social situation."

"They will also observe her to see how see copes," he disclosed, "what her interpersonal skills are like."

The duty psychiatrist came to see her. He did not give Karla his name and she never found out what it was. Karla refused to answer anything except the most basic questions, and she refused to sign the acceptance of treatment papers or the agreement to abide by the unit rules.

Later, after it had been explained to her that if she did not cooperate they would change her security classification from medium to maximum, Karla sat down and read the papers they wanted her to sign. "I laughed... when I looked at the treatment papers. It said that if you refuse to follow treatment you will be thrown out of RPC. Ha! That never happened to me, unfortunately."

On December 4, 2000, a month and a half after Karla had been transferred to RPC and refused to sign the admission papers, Correctional Investigator Ronald L. Stewart sent a letter, delivered by hand, to the Commissioner of the prison service, Lucie McClung.

Referring to S.177 of the Corrections and Conditional Release Act (CCRA), he said he was writing to inform the Commissioner that based on his extensive review he found "that the decision to transfer Ms. Teale from Joliette Institution to RPC was unreasonable, contrary to law and contrary to an established policy. This is because she was admitted to RPC... for a psychiatric assessment contrary to her expressed wishes. No procedures under relevant provincial legislation were implemented to permit her placement or treatment (including assessment) in these circumstance."

He goes on to cite the provisions Karla's transfer contravened: Ss 88(1) which provides that "treatment shall not be given to an inmate, or continued once started, unless the inmate voluntarily gives an informed consent thereto; and… an inmate has the right to refuse treatment or withdraw from treatment any time."

Paragraph 2 of the Commissioner's Directive 803, which provides "The consent of the offender must be obtained for a: all medical procedures b: all psychiatric and psychological assessment and treatment c: involvement or participation in any form of research, and d: the sharing of heath care information…" He cites a number of other Commissioner's Directives, including 840 and 850.

He notes that the response to his letters of September 28, and October 5, 2000, argued that Karla's transfer "occurred within the Service's purview under s. 28 of CCRA, as a 'service' rather than a treatment."

The Commissioner's response reiterated what Karla's parole officer had written in the "Decision for Involuntary Transfer" form and underlined "the necessity of such assessment for release review purposes" and distinguished "between 'assessment' and 'treatment.'"

Mr. Stewart found the Commissioner's response to be empty rhetoric and gobbledygook. "First," his letter continues, "I find that these responses ignore the pith and substance of the transfer, which was patently for treatment. Irrespective of the Service's obligation in case review prior to release decisions, its obligations to obtain informed consent are paramount and a condition precedent to providing treatment by means of admission to the RPC.

"Second, to attempt to distinguish from 'treatment' a procedure as detailed and personally invasive as is contemplated here is at odds with the plain meaning of the term, not to mention the Service's own policy of specifically enumerating assessment and treatment as requiring informed consent.

"The responses simply do not address our own clearly expressed inquiries which related to the issue of informed consent…"

In conclusion, he recommends that the Commissioner immediately "rescind the decision and permit Ms. Teale to return to Joliette Institution or to another institution which meets her security classification requirements as well as the other criteria for placement and transfer," and secondly "that you apologize for the transfer," and lastly "that you take measures to ensure that compliance with the law on informed consent to treatment is the condition precedent to taking any decision (including, but not limited to transfers to medical/psychiatric facilities) whose purpose is to provide treatment (including assessment)."

BIBLIOTHERAPY

Dr. Lucinda (Cindy) Presse, the senior clinical psychologist at the Regional Psychiatric Center in Saskatoon, was, like her friend, Dr. Sharon Williams, an adjunct professor at Queen's University. Cindy (as Karla called her) graduated with a B.A. from McMaster University in Hamilton and then went on to do her graduate work, an M.A., Diploma in Clinical Psychology and Ph.D. at Queen's. She received her doctorate in 1984. Like Dr. Williams, Dr. Presse was also a student of William Marshall, the guru of sex offender programs for the Correctional Service. She had always had a strong interest in psychopathy and sex offenders and gave her first paper on the subject in 1982. It became her dissertation. It was entitled "Paradoxes in Treating Penitentiary Psychopaths."

On her curriculum vitae, Dr. Presse's clinical interests are listed as "creating choices for female offenders" and "rational approaches to therapy, for instance, RET, DBT, and bibliotherapy," so it should not surprise anyone that she lent Karla her dissertation on psychopathy to read.

Dr. Presse's research interests include women offenders, correctional treatment approaches, cognitive factors in psychopathy, cognitions and belief systems within populations, and childhood precursors of psychopathy.

She delivered a paper entitled "Correlates of female psychopathy in a remand population" to the Canadian Psychology Association meeting in St. Foy, Quebec, in 2001.

It was co–authored with Leslie Spencer from the University of Saskatchewan and stated out of the gate something well-known in therapeutic circles, that there were few studies of criminal psychopathy in females.

In the paper, Dr. Presse documents that they had access to archival files on all women remanded to a local forensic ward (likely the one in the Regional Psychiatric Center) since it opened in 1994. Scores on the *Psychopathy Checklist-Revised* (*PCL-R*, Hare, 1991), available on 45 participants, were examined on nine demographic variables, psychiatric diagnoses, two MMPI-II scores, six criminal history variables, and six social history variables.

She and her colleague noted significant differences between high and low *PCL-R* groups were found on two demographic variables – self-reported histories of childhood abuse, substance abuse, and psychiatric diagnoses if personality disorder traits were included.

PCL-R scores were correlated with MMPI-II Pd scores, age at admission, age at first adult conviction, and number of previous adult convictions. Psychometric properties of the PCL-R scores revealed an alpha correlation of .9 and a pattern of item-total correlations similar to Hare's (1991). The paper then compared the results Drs. Presse and Stewart got with the female PCL-R results attained in a early study authored by Salekin, Rogers and Sewell (1997).

Other papers Dr. Presse had given over the years included "Moral Reasoning and Criminal Psychopathy," "Violence, Sexual Assault and Psychopathy-related Personality Traits in College Students' Dating Relationships" and "Managing and Treating the Psychopathic Offender." The point is, Dr. Presse, like Dr. Williams, could easily be considered expert on psychopathy, psychopaths in prison and sex offenders.

After receiving her doctorate, Dr. Presse became a professor of forensic psychology at the University of Saskatchewan. Her colleague there, Dr. Stephen Wong, one of Dr. Robert Hare's most ardent acolytes, was also the Research Director of the Correctional Service Regional Psychiatric Center. Dr. Presse joined the Center shortly thereafter as a clinical psychologist and, in September, 2000, just before Karla arrived, received her pin for thirty-years of distinguished service.

She was assigned to administer Karla's evaluation and give her yet another full battery of psychological tests, including the ubiquitous MMPI-2 (Karla had been given that test so often over the past eight years that she had virtually memorized all 500 questions) as well as the Weschler Intelligence Scale and a host of others. As the ranking, senior Correctional Service's psychologist, she was also the team leader.

Karla liked Cindy. She found that she had a "real nice attitude." Like her friend and colleague Sharon Williams, Dr. Presse believed in good bedside manners; that the therapist and evaluator were likely to be far more effective in a collaborative rather than a confrontational relationship with their "patient." She was very kind to Karla and treated her nicely, an approach which tended to make Karla open up even more. Cindy also took time to help Karla with her situation, its suddenness and unfamiliar isolation.

She introduced Karla to two of her graduate students and they came to see Karla often over the duration of the time she was there, even after the evaluations were completed.

Although obviously fully qualified to do so, Dr. Presse did not even think about administering Dr. Hare's *Psychopathy Checklist-Revised*. Dr. Williams had already administered the test in 1996. With regard to psychopathy, nothing would have changed over the past few years. People did not suddenly become psychopaths. According to Dr. Williams' test results, Karla was not a psychopath and that was certainly good enough for Dr. Presse.

As a proponent of bibliotherapy, Dr. Presse was pleased to see that Karla was a voracious reader. Besides her Ph.D. thesis, Cindy also brought in all kinds of books from her own library for Karla. The one Karla liked the most was *The Man in the Gray Flannel Suit* by Sloan Wilson, a popular American novelist from the 1950s who also wrote *A Summer Place*.

It said on the jacket flap that *The Man in the Gray Flannel* Suit was the most insightful and influential post-War novel about Madison

Avenue, advertising and suburban life. The title was familiar to Karla. She wondered if they had ever made a movie from the book. She had certainly not seen it in a theater. Maybe it was old and she had seen it on television.

Earlier that year, Dr. Presse's colleague and the RPC's Research Director, Dr. Stephen Wong, had delivered a paper entitled "Outcome of an Institutional Sex Offender Treatment Program: A Comparison Between Treated and Untreated Offenders." It was latterly published in *Sexual Abuse: A Journal of Research and Treatment.* He was also one of the developers of a controversial assessment tool called the *Violent Risk Scale* or VRS, which they did administer to Karla. During the past decade, assessing "dangerousness" and "risk" had become big (and controversial) business in Correctional Service circles all over the world. Both Dr. Wong and Dr. Presse had done a great deal of research about sex offender programs and administered and overseen a number themselves. It was one of the major programs offered at the Regional Center.

After collating all the results of Karla's tests and scoring them, Dr. Presse found Karla not to be dangerous to either herself or society, and her report recommended Karla's immediate release from prison on parole. She did not recommend that Karla be enrolled in any sex offender program.

Karla wondered why, after transferring her over 4,000 miles to one of two specialized Correctional Service's facilities devoted to the assessment and treatment of offenders with psychological and psychiatric problems – both of which specialized in the treatment of sex offenders – CSC hired two outside psychiatrists, Dr. Gene Marcoux and Dr. Robin Menzies, as consultants to participate with Dr. Presse in Karla's assessment and evaluation.

Surely in major cities such as Montreal or Kingston or Toronto, there were hundreds of forensic psychiatrists and psychologists as well qualified, many undoubtedly better qualified, than were these two practitioners who had set up shop in the middle of nowhere.

Dr. Marcoux was a nice enough guy, but all he really did, after talking with Karla a couple of times, was write another review of her file. At least it was fair and balanced and reflected the file's content. Karla got the sense that Dr. Marcoux was a genuinely caring individual. He was also nice enough to come back and see Karla after the examinations were over, to inquire after her well-being and see how she was.

Robin Menzies was another story altogether. He described himself as a clinical professor, consultant psychiatrist in private practice, focusing on adult and forensic psychiatry but never said with which university he was affiliated. Karla disliked him immediately.

She asked one of her friends to try and find out about him and his affiliation on the Internet but they drew a blank. What they did find out, however, was that Menzies had testified on behalf of Robert Latimer, the Saskatchewan farmer who had killed his severely disabled daughter.

Menzies testified under oath that Latimer's sole motivation for ending his daughter's life was to stop her suffering. Apparently what Dr. Menzies thought was of no consequence. The jury found Latimer guilty of murder and sent him to jail for a minimum of ten years.

Menzies had also examined Colin Thatcher prior to a hearing being held to determine if Thatcher, another prairie boy, who had been convicted of murdering his wife decades earlier and sentenced to life in prison, was entitled to a reduction in his 25-year sentence. Thatcher, a former Saskatchewan cabinet minister, told Menzies that his dead wife was not "one of his favorite persons" so he did not feel particularly bad when she passed. The hearing decided that Thatcher was not entitled to a sentence reduction.

Menzies had also testified as an expert on behalf of a plaintiff known as D.W. in a lawsuit against the administrator of a student residence, one William Starr, and the Attorney General of Canada.

D.W. had been sexually assaulted by Starr while he was a student at the Gordon Student Residence. The Attorney General of Canada operated the residence and employed Starr as its administrator. Apparently, Starr played with D.W.'s penis and stuck his finger up his anus and made him fellate him on two different occasions.

According to Menzies, who saw and evaluated D.W., he was suffering from post-traumatic stress disorder accompanied by depressive disorder as Karla had been when she first entered the prison system.

As defined by Dr. Menzies for the court, PTSD is a mental disorder precipitated by exposure to traumatic experience such as sexual abuse. PTSD is a little more complicated than that, but the court took Dr. Menzies' word for it.

Dr. Menzies also noted that the prognosis for PTSD is guarded; even with treatment. He testified that D.W. was likely to suffer reoccurring episodes of flash backs to the assaults, as Karla claimed she still did.

He also told the court that PTSD occurs in only one to ten percent of the population and D.W.'s background may have made him susceptible to the disorder.

In his ruling, the judge took Dr. Menzie's point. In a section where he calls himself a "tortfeasor" the judge wrote "a tortfeasor must take his victim as he finds him, even if the victim's losses are more dramatic than they would have been for the average person."

It was clear to Karla from the beginning that Dr. Menzies was not on the up and up, that he was another Correctional Service's "beard" like Dr. Van Giseghem. She *knew* from the moment they first met that he was only there to write a negative report. On the last day of her sessions with him, Karla felt as though she was back on the witness stand being cross-examined by John Rosen. Menzies conducted a totally aggressive interrogation and it was not nice at all.

Karla seemed to exist in a constant state of suspended irony. Both Dr. Sharon Williams, who was, after all, the Corporate Advisor to the Commissioner on Sex Offender Programs in Correctional Services' facilities across the country, and her friend, forensic psychologist, Cindy Presse, had written extensively on evaluator's methodology, and the role of the psychologist and psychiatrist in the penitentiary. They maintained that the physician or psychologist could get a much better, more accurate result by doing assessments and examinations in exactly the opposite manner to the approach taken by Robin Menzies,

Aggressive, pushy, in-your-face, confrontational tactics, the doctors repeatedly said – both in papers they had presented and in workshops they had conducted – make the patient/inmate nervous, less responsive and, therefore, less accessible, making the task at hand even more difficult and the results even less reliable than they might otherwise be. Assessing "dangerousness" was already a tenuous exercise, fraught with empirical danger as the Correctional Service's dismal track record aptly demonstrated. The doctor's bedside manner should not make it worse.

Nevertheless, Robin Menzies, contrary to Drs. Presse, Marcoux, Williams and the fourteen other psychologists and psychiatrists by whom Karla had seen and assessed since 1993, not only wrote a negative report, but said Karla was a psychopath who continued to be a danger to society, and would most probably reoffend if released on parole. In the end, Dr. Robin Menzie's report trumped all others. Apparently it was the only report taken into consideration by the Correctional Service and the National Parole Board.

* * * * * * *

Karla remained in RPC until early January when she was finally transferred to the place her parole officer at Joliette, Ms. Turcotte, had explained she could not go – Institut Phillipe Pinel in Montreal, the psychiatric hospital with which Joliette had a treatment and assessment agreement.

MACABRE CYNICISM

In spite of the fact that Karla had waived her right to statutory release and refused to appear in front of the Parole Board on March 6, 2001, the Parole Board convened in Montreal and formally denied Karla's statutory right to be released on parole on the forthcoming sixth of July.

In their written decision, which was immediately made public, the three-panel board said that Karla was likely to repeat her "monstrous and depraved" crimes.

Parole decisions address the prisoner directly: "The board is satisfied that, if released, you are likely to commit an offence causing the death or a serious harm to another person before the expiration of the sentence you are now serving, according to law."

In a rhetorical flourish, it opined that Karla's crimes were too atrocious, her psyche too deranged, and her conscience too unaffected to merit release at this time.

These statements all fly in the face of the diagnoses and conclusions of nearly a dozen psychiatrists and psychologists, and ignore the decision and written opinions of Justice Francis Kovacs. They also disregard the determinations reached by Justice Patrick Galligan when he was tasked to make formal inquiry into the merits of the plea resolutions that made Karla an issue for the prison and the Parole Board in the first place.

The Board's decision also failed to confront the fact that the prison had, for the past seven years, aggressively treated Mrs. Teale (as they addressed her) as she had been diagnosed by Drs. Arndt, Long, Malcolm, Hatcher, Hucker, Jaffe, Macdonald, Brown, Heney, and Williams.

Written in French, the decision instead refers to psychiatric reports which assert that Karla is a continued threat. The decision does not name the authors of these reports nor discuss their content in any meaningful way. Nor does it qualify this conclusion by stating that there is only one report that asserts that Karla is a continued threat, authored by Saskatoon forensic psychiatric consultant, Dr. Robin Menzies.

"Recently, the diagnostic experts have seen a personality disorder, for example an antisocial personality or psychopathy."

This should read "recently *a diagnostic expert* has seen a personality disorder, for example an antisocial personality or psychopathy."

For the sake of argument, let us assume, as the Parole Board and the Correctional Service did, that, contrary to all the the opinions and diagnoses of Drs. Arndt, Long, Malcolm, Jaffe, Hatcher, Hucker, McDonald, the prison's own Drs. Brown, Heney, Williams, and Presse, that Dr. Menzies is right, that Karla has a "deranged psyche" and is a dangerous, unrepentant psychopath. Further, that this condition has only "recently" been discovered. This means two things: that Karla morphed into a psychopath while imprisoned, and that Dr. Menzies' has incredible diagnostic powers that none of his esteemed colleagues who evaluated Karla over the past decade share.

If Karla has recently become afflicted by antisocial personality disorder, then the effect of incarceration and all those programs the prison compelled Karla to take transformed her from a battered woman suffering from post-traumatic stress disorder into a psychopath. Ergo, the prison and its programs do not rehabilitate as their proselytizers vociferously proclaim, rather they systematically take their charges and transform them into monsters before releasing them back into society.

The Parole Board's decision is not a particularly coherent document. On the surface, it seems lucid and logical but its observations and remarks are repetitive and pleonastic, as though they were uncomfortable with their subject matter, their decision and the basis on which it was made.

Although it has already stated that "diagnostic experts have seen a personality disorder, for example an Antisocial Personality or psychopathy," elsewhere the decision elaborates: "Two out of three psychiatric evaluations done at the Regional Psychiatric Center in Saskatoon recommended your continued detention," a statement which only partially reflects reality.

As the reader will recall, Karla was seen and evaluated by three individuals while she was resident in the Regional Psychiatric Center in Saskatoon – the facility's senior clinical psychologist, Dr. Cindy Presse, and two outside consultants, Dr. Neil Marcoux and Dr. Robin Menzies.

Dr. Marcoux had the singular task to once again review Karla's file and write a report about its contents as per Dr. Van Gijseghem, except he had the benefit, thanks to the coercion used to convince Karla, of her "cooperation."

His report does not actually make a recommendation one way or the other, but it does go out of its way to highlight the negative or ambiguous language and the more heady speculations contained in some of the more discursive reports and documents contained in her file.

The Parole Board's decision states in a brief moment of lucidity that "the most recent psychiatrists and psychologists, having seen you in group therapy… recommend generally, although not unanimously, that you remain incarcerated."

In her report, Dr. Presse holds for Karla's immediate release, which is substantively different that recommending "generally, although not unanimously," that she remain incarcerated.

The report goes on to say: "Your entire *modus operandi* demonstrates a high level of indifference when it comes to the consequences of your acts on others… Numerous specialists emphasized your superficiality and great indifference toward the victims."

Of the seven psychologists and psychiatrists who wrote reports prior to Karla's incarceration, only one, Dr. Angus McDonald's, makes reference to Karla's apparent "moral vacuity," a turn of phrase that could be interpreted to suggest that she was superficial and indifferent. But one can also read Dr. McDonald's report the way Justice Galligan did, as an endorsement of Inspector Bevan's Karla, the "compliant victim of a sexual sadist."

"Despite the numerous programs you followed, you have shown yourself resistant, evasive and disinclined to really open yourself up and fully grasp your role as an aggressor."

This does not jive with literally dozens of reports and daily observations contained in Karla's voluminous file made by a phalanx of her handlers over the previous seven years.

"You continue to paint yourself as a victim, which indicates that your problems are still very present."

For the first two years Karla was in prison, the police, prosecutors, psychologists and psychiatrists not only "painted" Karla as a victim, in the process of readying her for her role as key witness at her ex-husband's trial, they created her as victim and left her with the indelible, ever-expanding vocabulary of victimhood.

When Karla returned from testifying at Paul Bernardo's trial in the fall of 1995, the prison continued to treat her as a victim, redoubling those professionals' efforts by forcing her to enrol in programs such as "Survivors of Abuse" and allowing her to enrol in others such as Gilbert Richer's self-empowerment course "Pouvoir D'agir sur Soi."

"Your *modus operandi* and the meticulous care that you devoted to getting rid of traces of your crimes also shows considerable indifference."

The police, prosecutors and the Court were fully cognizant of Karla's "*modus operandi*" and her "indifference." Nevertheless, Karla was sentenced by Justice Francis Kovacs on July 6, 1993, with no parole recommendations, which meant that even a very early parole would not be opposed by the authorities, who, the record shows, anticipated that Karla would be released on parole the moment she was eligible in 1997.

The Parole Board's decision also states in a sort of "by-the-way" fashion that Correctional Service told the Board that it knows of no program that would adequately protect the public if Ms. Homolka was released early. If Karla is dangerous, what program will "protect the public" when she is released at the end of her sentence on July 6, 2005?

Echoing Dr. Van Gijseghem, the Board's decision continues: "The new name you deliberately chose, 'Teale,' is, according to you, that of a serial killer in a movie. Under the circumstances, this can be qualified as both cynical and macabre."

Again, this was a fact well-known and understood by the authorities and the court when Karla was tried and sentenced. Neither the Parole Board nor the Correctional Service are supposed to adjudicate. Their only mandate is the management of the offender's sentence.

The Board's decision states that it is concerned that Karla intends to go about her business "as if nothing happened" when she is released. What else might she do? And will she go about her business "as if nothing happened" with less or more impunity, when released, free as a bird, on July 6, 2005?

The decision notes that Karla was more concerned about her safety than about her risk of reoffending which, given the source of this information (reports by two news organizations well known for their penchant for tabloid hyperbole) is a meaningless and unfounded statement.

Her crimes were "monstrous and depraved… All these crimes are extremely grave… the fact that you continued your crimes after the death of your sister, which occurred during your sexual abuse of her, demonstrates clearly your difficulty in controlling your violent sexual impulses to the point of putting in danger the safety of others… All your *modus operandi* demonstrate a high degree of indifference to the consequences of your acts against everyone."

Elaborating, the decision states that Paul Bernardo had said that Karla's little sister would be a "really beautiful Christmas present…" and that Karla enticed Jane Doe "knowing she would be drugged and violated by you and your accomplice."

In relation to the French and Mahaffy murders, "hours after killing the girls you went off and had sex with him [Paul Bernardo] without any concerns" and then the decision accuses Karla of showing "macabre cynicism."

No kidding. We can all rest easier now knowing that it was "macabre cynicism" that allowed Karla to commit her bizarre and horrific transgressions. That said, her "macabre cynicism" was known and understood by the police, prosecutors and the court when they all sanctioned the plea bargain and sentenced Karla to two concurrent twelve-year terms in return for her guilty pleas to two counts of manslaughter.

The decision concedes that according to her psychological reports, again, not saying which ones, Karla is described as "an intelligent person, polite, courteous, but superficial... with a tendency to control" and then, contradicting itself, states that Karla has no identifiable "mental or physical sickness."

In the next breath, the decision reiterates the point that recent expert analysis has declared Karla "an antisocial personality or... a psychopath."

If an antisocial personality disorder or psychopathy which manifests itself in violent, sexual impulses that ultimately prove fatal to its victims are not "mental or physical sickness" then what are they? And when did superficiality and a tendency to control become indicative of dangerousness and criminal behavior? If that were the case, we would be compelled to lock up most of the mothers and middle-class housewives in America, not to mention corporate managers and Chief Executive Officers.

Of the treatment Karla received in prison over the past seven and a half years, the Parole Board pronounces that "it has had little impact," opining that Karla failed "to truly open up and take responsibility for (her) crimes..." and that she continued to choose "to portray herself as a victim which suggests your problems are still very much present."

Not according to Gilbert Richer's reports about Karla's performance in his "*Pouvoir D'agir sur Soi*" or "Self-Empowerment" program. And not according to all the many reports of a half dozen other program leaders and primary workers who had sustained congress with Karla. Richer noted that Karla accepted full responsibility for her crimes.

Buried in the copy, in another small flurry of contradiction, the decision states that there is "no evidence that you are planning any serious crimes…" but adds the non sequitur that Karla seems to take delight in "controlling" and "scheming."

The decision concludes with the statement that the panel is convinced that if Karla were released before the completion of her full sentence, she would "commit an infraction causing death, or a serious injury to a person," and in consideration of this "fact" orders her continued detention.

The Director of Communications for the National Parole Board, John Vandoremalen, had the last word. Toward the end of the dozens of newspaper reports about the Parole Board's decision that seeped across the country in March, 2001, Mr. Vandoremalen was quoted stating the obvious: "No matter what, after 12 years, the sentence ends. Once the sentence is over, she's a free citizen."

With that fact in mind, there are a few, very important questions that the Parole Board, and the Correctional Service, in their wisdom, apparently did not consider.

After her court challenge became public in 1999, Karla withdrew it and waived her right to release on her statutory date. She said she was content to stay where she was and do her time.

Why then was it necessary to take the excessively aggressive, punitive, expensive and public action of flying Karla halfway across the country to a maximum-security psychiatric unit where she was kept locked down in isolation for four months, only to be returned to the local psychiatric hospital, Phillipe Pinel, where the Correctional Service said she could not go in the first instance?

This action and the subsequent Parole Board's decision was an blatant betrayal of the prison authorities' custodial mandate with respect to Prisoner 283308D, and also a betrayal of everything Karla had been assured would happen by the judicial and law enforcement personnel with whom she had fully cooperated between the years 1993 and 1995.

For seven years the Correctional Service treated Karla one way and then suddenly reversed itself. What will the cumulative effect of such institutional hypocrisy be on Karla's newly discovered "deranged psyche" and "unaffected" conscience?

Assuming that Karla's psych is deranged and that she is dangerous, how does punishing her for good behavior and locking her down in a maximum-security prison for men make her any less a risk when she is released at the end of her sentence?

How does promising her that if she cooperates with the doctors in the Regional Psychiatric Center in Saskatoon she will be returned to Joliette to serve the remainder of her sentence and then reneging and placing her in the maximum-security Regional Reception Center in Sainte-Anne-des-Plaines move Karla toward her inevitable release in a productive and rehabilitative way?

If the first seven years of incarceration and intensive therapy provided by Correctional Service in relatively humane conditions transformed Karla from a battered woman suffering from depression and post-traumatic stress disorder into a conscienceless, rabid psychopath, what will the next few years do for her, locked up in maximum security with five other violent, unrepentant women?

If she was a benign monster before, a duplicitous accomplice to unspeakable crimes, does this kind of erratic, politically-motivated institutional intransigence not guarantee that she will be released a malignant monster, even more dangerous and a greater "risk to reoffend" than she was when she entered the prison system?

If they could not resolve her personality and her dangerousness in the first seven years with a panoply of programs and therapy, how will they resolve these notional wills-o-the-wisp over the few years remaining in her sentence with none?

If Vince Bevan and Michael Code were wrong to do what they did when they gave Karla the deals that saw her "walk away" with only a twelve-year prison sentence, which they themselves knew would likely amount to only four but no more than eight years in jail, how would this third, highly public, institutional sophistry on the part of Correctional Service and the National Parole Board make that original wrong right?

BACK TO THE FUTURE

"Hi there. I was very happy to receive your letter the day before yester-day," Karla wrote on November 24, 2001. "I had agonized for so long whether or not I should ever write back to you, but when I finally did and sent the letter I couldn't wait for your response."

Against her better judgement, Karla had responded to her corre-spondent back in April to offer thanks for Dr. Arndt's obituary and tentatively provide a bit of innocuous information about some of the psychiatrists and psychologists she had seen and a few details about her life in prison, particularly between the time she was sent to Joliette and her present housing.

Karla had sent three or four short, handwritten letters between April and June, 2001. Then she had second thoughts about whether or not it was a good idea. Karla felt very unsure of herself. "I have such a hard time knowing what I should do about anything. It is very hard when every little decision you make can have such a large impact on every aspect of your life. I don't think anyone can really understand how my life is. I am afraid to make any decision as I am afraid of the impact it may have."

Had she not done everything that was expected of her? She had been well-behaved, a positive force in the prison population. She had taken all their courses. She had done the peer group thing and consis-tently done peer support. She had educated herself, even got a univer-sity degree. She had no demerit marks on her voluminous record. And what had the prison done? There was no point going over and over that. What were the possible consequences of corresponding with this person? There was a caveat in her first deal about talking about her crimes but this correspondent was not interested in her crimes only her experience in prison. Besides, she had been given blanket immunity before she took the witness stand in 1995. Theoretically, that superceded whatever caveats had been written into the first plea resolution.

Still, she was hesitant. And doing time does something to one's sense of time. You pass through it as though it is a vast mucilaginous bubble, emerging three months later none the wiser, feeling as though only three or four days have gone by. The way Karla explained it, being in jail was a form of suspended animation. Between June and October she received four or five letters and sent none. It was a letter dated Sunday, September 9, 2001, that jarred her out of her lethargy and indecision. It began "I have just realized that you really do not want to get out of jail. Not because you have some phobia, like a cloistered nun, fearful of the outside world or that you fear for your life on the mean streets of Montreal. You do not want to get out of jail – at least, not on parole – because, were you to make parole – appear before the board on the anniversary of your statutory release date, somehow make your case and prevail – it is for certain that the parole conditions would prohibit you from associating with anyone who had a criminal record. And that would seriously threaten Linda Véronneau's access to you and yours to her.

"The way things are, at least you can talk to her on the telephone every night, see her every Thursday for three and a half hours (and every second Saturday for a couple more,) and, as I have just discovered, soon, on every sixth weekend, you may even be permitted conjugal visits."

Karla was flabbergasted. Somehow, the letter writer had found out that her friend Linda was visiting her at Sainte-Anne. The person must have someone on the inside, or else how could they have possibly known? It would have to be someone very senior, like a warden or someone who worked in Visitors and Correspondence (V&C). But how was that possible? The person was from out-of-province and spoke only English.

The letter went on: "Let me say at the outset so you do not misconstrue and think me either perverse or prurient, I don't care about your sexual preferences or whether you and she plan to live happily ever after. I suspect, in this relationship, Ms. Véronneau is the love-sick aggressor but that's neither here nor there. All is fair in love and war, n'est-ce pas?"

This was followed by a detailed biography. Linda Véronneau had been born on December 11, 1961, the second child of Monique and Alfred Véronneau, and had three siblings all of whom were now living in or around the Montreal area, including older brother Mario, younger sister, Marie Josée, and younger brother, Claude.

Since her father died, Linda's mother has gone by her maiden name and lives in Saint Luc, a sprawling Montreal suburb on the shore of the St. Lawrence River. Her father had been a jeweler and boxing promoter. As it is everywhere else, boxing in Montreal, particularly in the sixties and the seventies, was inextricably bonded with organized crime. Being a jeweler and a boxing promoter would suggest that Monsieur Véronneau was mobbed up, but there is no definitive record to confirm it. He died in a light plane crash on Valentine's Day, 1981. Not yet twenty when her father was killed, Linda had already been raising hell for years.

Karla did not know any of this background stuff. She and Linda had met when Karla went to Joliette in June, 1997. Linda arrived a few months later. She was soon elected Chairperson of the Inmates Committee.

"Today, Linda's rap sheet is the unfortunate registry of a petty, career criminal that stretches back thirty convictions to 1980. Besides being busted for drugging and drinking, she appears to have specialized in Break and Enter.

"Botched B&Es, that is. Linda recently completed back-to-back sentences – a four-year and a two-year stint in Joliette for drug-fuelled robbery sprees committed between 1995 and 1997. Recidivism is relatively low among women who have done federal time. Therefore, among female offenders in Canada, Linda belongs to a very small, exclusive club. She is a career criminal. (I'm not judging, I'm just telling it like it is.) Who knows, your love may have rehabilitated her...

"In December, she will be forty. Her long criminal history cannot be explained away by socio-economic factors or an abusive childhood, as so many criminal behaviors are today. At least, not that I have been able to determine through any of her records. She has a $24,000 per annum annuity, thanks to her father's success and foresight. Not bad; only a few thousand less per year than your ex-husband was making when you married him. As no one knows better than you, there is no money quite like steady money."

The letter went on to say that Linda's position as Chair of the Inmates Committee reinforced all the things in her files that describe her as an outspoken, head-strong character, a domineering individual who bends people and circumstances to her will even when confined in a commune of like-minded characters. It also documented the dissolution of Linda's relationship with her former girlfriend and partner-in-crime, a cocaine-addicted stripper named Lyn Vallee who had been conveniently incarcerated with her.

Lyn Vallee was granted early parole on April 28, 1998. The Parole Board rationalized Ms. Vallee's early release as just reparation for what they perceived to be a healthy, pro-active move on her part, i.e. breaking up with Linda.

"Six months later, on November 5, 1998, Linda herself was paroled. On November 18, her parole was revoked – at her own insistence.

"Apparently, she could not stand to be separated from you and proclaimed that she would not adhere to any of the conditions of her parole so they might just as well lock her back up and save everyone the trouble. They did.

"However, a mere three months later, on January 28, 1999, she was paroled again "

Karla's correspondent commented on the inexorable irony in all this. Here was Karla, a model prisoner, detained on her statutory date, and there was her friend Linda. It was like George Walker had told Karla years ago. A twelve-year sentence meant four years unless she was the worst prisoner ever, then she would do eight. Twelve years never meant twelve years, except when your name is Karla, Karla thought ruefully.

Linda Véronneau was actually an excellent example of the veracity of George Walker's maxim. Despite constant and consistent bad behavior, including fifteen drug busts while incarcerated at Joliette, despite the violent component to her crimes and her best contrarian efforts, Linda Véronneau could not seem to stay in jail.

The letter went on to describe how on the second occasion of her release on parole, Linda voluntarily "copped to an unsolved B&E, committed on February 3, 1997. She did this by picking up the pay phone in House 10 and calling a cop in Varennes named Gilles Vallemaire. As far as I can determine, Linda grew up in the Montreal suburb of Varennes and liked to return there to do dastardly deeds. (I do not know whether or not you know all this, but trust me, I'm not making any of it up.)"

None of it really surprised Karla. A lot of cons try to figure out a way to get back in after they get out.

"Linda apparently told the cop that she was doing what she was doing so that she could remain in Joliette with you until your statutory release date. According to Detective Sergeant Vallemaire, she said that she was in love with you and could not stand to be separated from you.

"The fact that Linda's statutory date on her new two-year sentence (a term which she had specifically requested), would coincide almost exactly with your July 6, 2001 statutory release date is simply too coincidental to be coincidence. For a while I was sceptical but now that I have pieced this together, I see a compelling – if somewhat dark – love story.

"Back to the future: as a result of Linda's allegedly Eros-driven confession, on February 15, 1999, her statutory release on the four-year term she was already serving was formally revoked and on March 5, she was sentenced to the extra two years she sought for the unsolved crime to which she confessed.

"Apparently, right around that time, March/April, 1999, various individual members of your Case Management Team started to report concern about your relationship with another, dominant inmate who seemed to have undue influence over you, and staff, such as parole officer Ginette Turcotte and primary worker Daniel Cournoyer began to write negative reports about your attitude and your unwillingness to open up and take responsibility for your crimes."

To Karla, this was outrageous not only because it was not true, but also because of all the letters she had received from this correspondent, this was the first that contained blatantly incorrect information. For instance, none of her handlers in Joliette, or anywhere else for that matter, had ever written a negative report about any of her relationships with other inmates; her relationships with the other inmates were, by and large, very good, positive relationships. Karla knew that the bare bones of all this had already been published in a tabloid newspaper in Toronto – not the part about Linda visiting her at Sainte-Anne-des-Plaines or Karla's reasons for wanting to stay in jail for her full term but rather the idea that she and Linda were lesbian lovers.

The reporters for the newspaper had apparently highjacked Linda's brother Mario in Varennes and then he became cooperative and put them onto his sister Marie-Josée where Linda was staying at the time. Linda spoke briefly to one of the reporters and denied everything but facts and denials never stopped the media. Then came Karla's faithful correspondent's *pièce de résistance.*

"With Linda's help and guidance, you decided to go around your team and apply directly to the Elizabeth Fry Society for sanctuary if and when you were granted ETAs. Then, with their agreement to house you in hand, you again circumvented your team and applied directly to the warden for those ETAs which, predictably, were refused… It is too much *déjà vu*, this idea that love and a lover hold sway with you, and take precedence over everything else, including common sense.

"Infuriated by the Warden's recalcitrance, and again with Ms. Véronneau's help, you turned to Sylvie Bordelais, the Elizabeth Fry Society's lawyer in Montreal. It took her and Pascal Lescarbeau a month and a half or two months to prepare and file a court action to have the warden's decision to refuse your application for escorted temporary absences overturned.

"Between September and November, 1999, when the story about your court challenge hit the newspapers, you must have felt strong, defiant even, pleased with yourself, self-reliant, a woman standing up for her rights – this is implicit in your affidavit – only you were none of these things. Once again, you were deluded. Instead, you were once again someone else's puppet, and/or your legendary negative response to rejection was bolstered and buttressed into untenable actions by the one you loved.

"For the longest time, I was having trouble understanding your bold lawsuit-launching salvo followed by your tail-between-the-legs retreat as soon as the shit hit the fan."

The letter went on to say that no one other than a career criminal like Linda Véronneau would have been familiar with the gaggle of lawyers from Montreal by whom Karla was variously represented, including Pascal Lescarbeau, Marc Labelle and Sylvie Bordelais, and asserted that no lawyer "not even a stupid one and, god knows, there are lots of those around" would advise an inmate to do what Karla did. The letter stated that the inmate would have to instigate the court challenge and then insist on it, both on the challenge to the warden's decision and latterly, her capitulation.

"Then I realized there was a "hidden" dimension to your retreat. If you were released on your statutory release date the conditions of your parole would automatically dictate that you could not associate with anyone who has a criminal record, i.e. Linda Véronneau. You would be out, sure, but you would be without your own true love and after all, have you not done everything you have ever done for love?"

The letter then went on to document how Linda had come into hundreds of thousands of dollars. In the fall of 1999, her maternal grandmother, Marie-Paule Bessette, died. She named Linda and her older brother Mario co-executors of her will.

"Considering all of the estate issues, and the other siblings, my research suggests that Linda may cull as much as $800,000 when all is said and done. Not bad for doing nothing. Certainly a much bigger score than she ever netted from any of her myriad, ill-conceived heists.

"Time goes by and once again Linda Véronneau is finding it impossible to stay in jail. On February 11, 2000, she is again released on parole – to a halfway house. This time, thanks to her grandmother's demise and largesse, she has a good deal of money in her jeans – something to tide her over until the will is probated. Money being a great equalizer, Linda is reunited with her estranged siblings. She buys herself a nice convertible and gets a cell phone. Not forgetting her annual annuity of $24,000, Linda is, as they say, in funds. Understandably, this pecuniary redemption would ameliorate behavior and provide relief from stress and deliver some good old-fashioned middle-class stability. At least this, according to the records, is how the Parole Board regarded Linda's windfall."

Continuing to provide information, some that Karla knew and some she didn't, the letter went on to describe how various Parole Board decisions about Linda talked about her crimes being fuelled by her habitual drug and alcohol abuse.

"In spite of the 15 reports of her using drugs while incarcerated, Joliette did not oppose her February parole. They, too, were influenced by the fact that Linda was now an heiress and perhaps by the idea that you and Linda should be separated as well. They even went so far as to state that Linda's completion of a substance abuse program as well as psychological and aptitude programs had reduced the risk that she would fall back into drug and alcohol abuse in the future.

"The most recent Parole Board decision with regard to Linda talks about her predisposition to criminal behavior being linked with a dysfunctional milieu evolving, in part, from major emotional dependence. This is psychobabble to describe an obsessive woman with a big hole in her heart who is possessive to the point of madness.

"With the additional, new two-year term, Linda's statutory release date became September, 2000. She was paroled six months in advance of that date and this time, she made it through an entire six months – from March to September – the longest she had made it on the outside for years. But alas, she just could not seem to make it on the outside without you. Her parole was revoked for drunk driving and like a boomerang she was back, just in time to wave you goodbye as you boarded that seven-seater Pilatus to Saskatoon.

"Four years is four years, and two years is two years, and the two terms although probably not concurrent, certainly had some overlap and now, just before you were housed in Sainte-Anne, the door swung open and Ms. Véronneau stepped out, a free woman. Her debt to society paid, she is no longer hamstrung by parole conditions, which explains why she can associate with you. And, indeed, now she can drink, smoke, snort and shoot up to her heart's content, as long as she does not run afoul of the law and get caught. I'm guessing now, but right around the middle of June, 2001, a few weeks before you wrote me that last letter dated June 24, Linda, often accompanied by her sister, started visiting you on Thursday afternoons. A little brisk drive out into the country in her new convertible, off to see her true love in prison, man, you could write a very contemporary country song about it."

That did it.

Karla decided to break her self-imposed months of silence. "It is true that I have taken the position of silence from the beginning," Karla wrote back, grinding her teeth. "Obviously that position has not served me very well... For your information, your characterization of my relationship with Linda is absurd."

First of all, Karla had never met Linda's sister or brother or any of the other family members and had no desire to do so. Neither was Karla the only person from Joliette that Linda was visiting. Nor did Karla have any plans to live with Linda when she got out of jail. "She is not or has not helped me or guided me in any of the decisions that I made or continue to make."

The suggestion that Linda Véronneau had anything to do with either Karla's application for ETAs or the subsequent court challenge was not only wrong, it was ridiculous.

"I was put in contact with Pascal Lescarbeau by a carceral lawyer who frequently comes to Joliette. She had explained the process to me and said that when Joliette denied my ETAs (as we believed they would) we would apply to the court and they would likely grant them as I met all of the criteria. She told me Pascal had lots of experience in federal court. What she didn't tell me was that he is also her husband. Some referral. Pascal told me that in federal court we have the option of keeping everything confidential. The lawyer just has to ask. 'It's as simple as that,' he said. You know the old saying 'If it seems to good to be true it probably is?' Well, I should have been thinking of that. When the file was copied to the media I freaked. Understandably, as I was told it would be confidential. One of the lawyers came to see me (I don't remember which one as there were three of them involved) and explained that the confidentiality request had not been done. Now the media was in court asking for permission to print my personal file. I was told the only way I could prevent that was to withdraw my request for my ETAs. So that is exactly what I did. I fired Pascal and hired Marc Labelle… I was then informed that the Federal Court never had jurisdiction to grant my ETAs. The only thing they could have done was invalidate the CSC's decision and order another CSC employee to make a new decision. Great. Had I known that from the beginning I would never have gone through with anything… Oh, to correct two more of your inaccuracies: Daniel Cournoyer is not a primary worker, and I met Sylvie Bordelais at Joliette as she used to come there every Wednesday to meet with the women. Nobody introduced her to me – she introduced herself."

All this information turned out to be true.

Although Karla decided she had to set part of the record straight, she had no great expectations. She understood that no matter what she did, or said, her actions and words were only going to be seen one-dimensionally and portrayed as indicative of unbridled egotism and lack of remorse. The reality was something quite different but Karla, as long as she remained Karla, was condemned to occupy the world as she was perceived. She could say a thousand "sorry's" a day and it would be interpreted as false and self-serving or insincere and self-serving.

Karla had never underestimated how vile a shadow she cast. And there was nothing anyone could have done about the bad timing or the political expediency that determined such swift and punitive action as had recently been meted out by the prison authorities. Karla knew she was an easy target.

She went on to say that when she wrote her application for ETAs "*that* was when the reports written by my case management team became so negative. I have two reports, one written the day after the other in which my attitude is discussed. One report is for the purpose of Private Family Visits and describes me as open, respectful of other inmates and staff, and working on every aspect of my correctional plan." Karla's correctional plan was designed to try and address her role as both a victim and an accomplice/aggressor. To a large extent, her correctional plan was shaped by the anomalies described in "Compliant Victim of the Sexual Sadist" which Inspector Bevan and Murray Segal had made sure was included in Karla's prison file.

The other "Progress Report," the one written a day later, (normally "Progress Reports" are written once every six months) was tabled to justify the denial of Karla's ETAs. It describes her as "demanding and defiant and working on only one aspect" of her correctional plan.

Karla continued: "There is nothing written anywhere that says that another inmate had undue influence over me. I'm sure Stivia [Stivia Clermont, the current Chairperson of the Inmates Committee at Joliette] will concur that *nobody* influences me. I am hypersensitive to people trying to dominate and control me now."

This also checked out.

However, Karla's correspondent had been right about some things: Maybe her biggest mistake was backing down once she had committed herself to the court challenge. Maybe she should have gone through with it. At least then, some of the truth about the double-dealing which characterized the way the prison handled her over the past few years might have come out.

She agreed that this would not necessarily have changed the outcome, the prison would have invariably recommended her detention, and the Parole Board in all likelihood rubber-stamped it, as they almost always did.

The letter writer had said, quite correctly, that Karla's fear of the media and her almost pathological adherence to ideas about protecting her privacy were unnecessary impediments. No one's life in all its horrific, perverted detail had ever been made more public than hers. Obsession with the detritus of the lives of the famous and infamous was an indelible mark of our culture. It was one of the contradictions of Karla's "being," these obsessions with the media and privacy.

Even though the prison was "dedicated" to maintaining her privacy, as long as she was in prison, Karla would have no real privacy. Being in prison was the fundamental antithesis to privacy. There was nothing that Karla had done, whether it was apply for ETAs, gain weight, challenge the Warden's denial of the ETAs, participate in a birthday celebration, receive letters from her sister, have her picture taken, develop friendships with various inmates, paint her nails, imagine a future, absolutely nothing that some one had somewhere made public. In prison, she was a proverbial sitting duck.

There was something else that made a lot of sense: her correspondent said that there was nothing more anyone could say about her that had not already been said a thousand times. Given that she had been called every name in the book – killer slut from Niagara Falls, the Barbie of murder and mayhem, murderous psychopathic bitch, to name only a few, what difference would more of the same make?

That was a very good point but one, like her obsession with the media and privacy, that never really took hold. An inability to comprehend complex ideas when she was at the center of the metaphor was one of Karla's profound deficits. She would say that she understood something, that indeed this or that statement was correct but then she would stubbornly adhere to her own, old ideas even though she had intellectually discounted them.

Karla was not nearly as smart or street-wise as she appeared during the year leading up to her incarceration. Under the media's distorted microscope, it appeared as though she were navigating the treacherous waters of her tenuous legal position with savvy and aplomb. In reality, she was merely a cork bobbing in an already safe harbor. Many of Hitler's henchmen were well-educated and cultivated men. Because one gets good school grades and reads books does not mean they are capable of holding two opposing thoughts in mind simultaneously. It simply means they are not completely dim.

Karla pointed out that it was Van Gijseghem who wrote in his report that she associated "with the strongest people among her peers." He did not say where he got that information or how it was germane to any diagnostic assessment. Karla had never met Dr. Van Gijseghem. Nor had he met any of her peers. Although none of the voluminous reports in her file alluded to such a thing, Karla felt compelled to point out in her letter that "the strongest characters in prison are also the most sociable."

Dr. Van Gijseghem's remark was undoubtedly a thinly veiled allusion to Judge Kovacs' observation that Karla was not a danger to society unless she happened to fall into the thrall of another domineering character like Paul Bernardo. Perhaps Van Gijseghem was trying to plant the seed that some of Karla's prison "associates," such as Linda Véronneau, might be just such a person. After all, the prison officials knew Karla's file and had read Justice Kovac's sentencing remarks many times. They also read the newspapers. They had people in the communications division in Ottawa who clipped everything to do with prisons and prisoners. Van Gijseghem obviously read newspapers and magazines. A few of his remarks even appeared to have been plucked directly from a few old magazine articles and newspaper reports about Karla and what she might or might not be.

It was true that had Karla been released on parole on her statutory date, she would not have been able to see Linda Véronneau. One of the pro-forma conditions of parole was that of association. Parolees are not allowed to associate with anyone who has a criminal record. On the other hand, visiting in prison was relatively free of restriction. Since Linda Véronneau had served her time and been released, she was no longer a parolee herself. She had paid her debt to society and was a citizen again. She could associate with anyone she chose, whether they were in prison or not.

"The idea that I want to do my full time so that I can get out of prison and have a relationship with Linda is ridiculous. That is the last thing I want. I have said many times that I don't care what conditions I would receive upon my release. I would spend three hours a day standing on my head should that be required. Whether you want to believe me or not, the reasons I want to do my whole time are complex... If I were released on statutory release I would be subject to the condition of meeting regularly with a parole officer. To do that would place my *reintegration* at risk... If I have to meet with a PO, it makes it easy for someone to find my whereabouts, and therefore impossible to "disappear." As well, and you may think this to be nothing but a self-serving statement, I have enough feelings of guilt and self-hatred that perhaps, maybe if I do my entire sentence rather than just two-thirds of it, I will feel a little less guilty. If you choose not to believe that, so be it."

It was certainly believable that Karla had convinced herself that this is what she believed. However, by not applying for ETAs and parole when she was first eligible in 1997, and every year thereafter, as was her right, by not appearing in front of the parole board to appeal her detention beyond her statutory date in March 2001, and then subsequently waiving her right to appear on the anniversary of the Parole Board's decision in March 2002, Karla taciturnly became complicit in her own reconstitution.

If she did not have the courage of her own convictions or those of the legion of experts and legal authorities who said she was a battered woman suffering from post-traumatic stress disorder, brainwashed and abused to such an extent that she committed unspeakable crimes out of an instinctive need for self-preservation, why would anyone facing the prospect of doing the politically incorrect thing and releasing her on parole hesitate to redefine her as an antisocial personality and a psychopath? Karla's lack of foresight, her inability to see the consequences of her actions, or inaction, as the case may be, pointed to another fundamental flaw in her character, not one that necessarily made her dangerous and a murderer but rather one that made her a pawn.

The relationship with Linda was not sexual anyway. "We are friends. She was in love with me (and I don't know why – I'm probably the worst person to be in a relationship with), but that's as far as it goes. Perhaps there was something there at one time, but, if so, it is long over."

And her correspondent's provocative statement about conjugal visits in the private family unit were simply wrong. Karla did have access to the unit both by herself and for visits with her immediate family. To go there alone, she had to do an initial application and then see a psychologist for a suicide evaluation. Usually they make the inmate do an evaluation every time but the psychologist said it was not necessary in her case. They were sure Karla was not going to commit suicide.

Regardless, the nature of the bureaucracy in prison means that the inmate has to apply every time they want to go into the unit. In Joliette and at Sainte-Anne-des-Plaines, the two houses reserved for private family visits on the prison grounds are relatively new, fully equipped, pleasant two-bedroom bungalows. In Sainte-Anne, Karla was allowed to use the unit once a month, allowing for availability. Family visits have priority over solitary visits. Each application passes in front of a prison committee that meets once a month and is accepted or rejected. Then the V&C officer goes to the inmate and books whichever date the inmate wants. The inmate fills out an order form for their food which is purchased from a local grocery store. "You can order anything you want, except seafood and alcohol," Karla advised. "But it is very expensive." When Karla goes, she eats mostly chicken, fruits and salads and her order usually costs her between fifty and eighty dollars.

"There is a very strict list of people who are allowed to come to these visits. It usually has to be family – parents, siblings, grandparents, nieces and nephews, grandchildren, spouses. Sometimes they allow girlfriends and boyfriends, but it really depends on the situation and the prison. Legally, they do not have to. Everyone who does come has to have a community assessment with a parole officer prior to being accepted, as well as a security check."

Even if Karla wanted to have a conjugal visit with Linda Véronneau, and she most certainly did not, Linda would likely not pass the community assessment.

In the context of the mad speculations about Karla's reasons for wanting to stay in jail and her relationship with Linda Véronneau, her correspondent had also made reference to the lawyer for her victims' families, an oleaginous man named Tim Danson.

"As I am sure you are aware, Danson has you firmly in his sights. One of the things he is investigating is the notion of having you charged with perjury since you swore under oath in 1995 that you were not a lesbian. If you want, I can send you the clippings in which he floats this balloon. Of course, such an idea is patently absurd. Prisons change people. Whether you are or are not a lesbian is irrelevant. To me. But not to him. I think he and his poppycock grandstanding – which is all about raising more money to finance his poppycock grandstanding – are quite absurd and dangerous on a larger scale. But I am probably as alone in that view as I am about the fact that you should have made your statutory release date.

"Mr. Danson holds sway with a large, powerful lobby that would like to see you locked up forever and is looking for any way, absurd or otherwise, to achieve that goal."

The letter goes on to document that Tim Danson attacked the Elizabeth Fry Society for supporting Karla's bid for ETA's and suggested that they "reevaluate themselves as an organization."

All the while he was spouting off in the press, he was lobbying the federal government to review the Society's funding because they were publicly supporting Karla. The Society receives approximately

$450,000 a year from the government, a paltry sum considering the vast scope of the work they try to do and the billions upon billions of dollars the government devotes to prisons and incarceration.

"Tim Danson has earned five to six times that amount lobbying on behalf of the victims' families, all of it from donations to the families' 'Integrity Fund.' No one really understands what Tim Danson and the families are on about, or what they really want, but they send money anyway and to date, that money has amounted to millions of dollars…

"Danson is like a heat-seeking missile. Whenever the war chest is skimp, he searches out another *cause célèbre*. Anything to do with you and your ex-husband and videotapes and evil-in-general and in particular, your imminent release – suddenly the donations start to pour in. Right now, the coffers are somewhat depleted and Mr. Danson is very alert for new headline-grabbing circumstances upon which to pounce.

"From a February, 2000, *Toronto Sun* report about what they effusively described as an intense lesbian relationship between you and Linda (which Linda denied, to no avail), Mr. Danson has already reconnoitered a potentially explosive situation.

"He played some of his cards when he submitted opinions from the victims' families to Joliette during your 'assessment' and spoke bombastically to the press. He cited the rumor of your relationship with Linda (both publicly and behind closed doors in the corridors of power) as a prime indication that you have not rehabilitated yourself and now and in the future represent a "clear danger to public safety."

"He was quoted as saying that you invariably 'seek out people who like to dominate…' and that you are the kind of 'person who likes to be dominated.' Certainly, this *idée fixe*, that Linda is a dominatrix who led the passive and pliable Lynn Vallee into a string of robberies, is a matter of public record and fuel for the Danson jet.

"At some point, Danson will point to the assessment of the late Judge, Francis 'Doc' Kovacs, who noted in his sentencing remarks at your trial that 'absent the influence and association of someone whose behavior bears the characteristics of what truly may be one of this province's and the country's most feared individuals, she is unlikely to reoffend.' Meaning, that provided you do not fall 'under the spell' of another dominate and criminal person like your ex-husband, you will not be a danger to society. Antithesis: If you do, you will.

"The idea that you might be released into the loving arms of a career criminal/lesbian with a history of violent crimes and a history of female-to-female domination that has led others to violent acts in the past is definitely not going to sit well with the extremely well-financed Mr. Danson and his large, well-financed, highly politicized lobby."

Of course this reasoning was absurd. Karla was not a lesbian and even if she was, or had become one in prison, or was perhaps bisexual, which might be closer to the truth, Danson's ludicrous statement about perjury was not worth the ink and paper it had been printed on. Neither was her relationship with Linda in any way similar to her relationship with her murderous ex-husband, and Karla could prove it. Even if it were true that they had once been lovers, Linda Véronneau had never committed any sexual assaults or murdered anyone or forced her partners to commit horrendous acts of sexual deviance and murder. It was all too absurd. Clearly, it made headlines and on its surface was sensational and could indeed fuel Tim Danson's depleted "war chest" and, therefore, like many others he was likely to remain undaunted by facts, reason or common sense.

Karla knew all about Tim Danson. He had served her with a lawsuit while she was still in Kingston's Prison for Women. She often got clippings about things that he said in the newspapers. However, a recent clipping talked about the fact that Danson proposed to do an "examination for discovery" on her while she was incarcerated in Sainte-Anne-des-Plaines.

"What a jerk," she wrote, hoping the news report was not true. "I have nothing to say to him or anyone else about those crimes."

Also, Karla was virtually penniless. So what was the point. She had never contested her responsibility or tried to negate her role so she did not understand what he could possibly be planning to question her about. Besides, she had survived many interrogators more voracious and adept than Tim Danson, such as John Rosen and Robin Menzies. Compared to those two, Danson would be a walk in the park. She put him out of her mind.

AMENDE HONORABLE

Karla had been resident in the Regional Reception Center at Sainte-Anne-des-Plaines for a year. She was now into her tenth year in jail. As much as things on the outside had changed, some things remained exactly the same. For instance, the media still got most everything wrong. It was not just a question of wrong facts. Some facts were wrong but it was more about selective facts from selective sources and imbalance.

For instance, what had been remarkable about the breathless reporting about her and Linda Véronneau was the underlying assumption that it was somehow unusual or shocking that there were lesbians and lesbian relationships in prison and that there was something inherently wrong or scandalous in that. What did people think that young women locked up together for years do?

When Karla was denied early release for the second time, there had been a flurry of reports on the news wire and in the tabloid papers.

"Karla will remain behind bars: Board" the headline in the *Toronto Sun* proclaimed. Was that news? Karla had signed away her right to appeal the National Parole Board's decision to keep her in jail seven months earlier.

And to the point about the media's sources. These news reports repeated only the most superficial and sensational details, provided by the National Parole Board itself.

These media reports did not refer to any of the documents upon which the Board had allegedly relied in making their decisions and slavishly regurgitated whatever the Board gave them.

"Believing Homolka has not made any significant progress in the last year, the Board rejected her release in a federally mandated annual review of her case" one of the stories read.

"Last year, in her first mandatory parole review, the Board ruled that Homolka was likely to kill again because of the seriousness of her crimes and an apparent antisocial personality or psychopathy."

The unquestioning acceptance of such statements was galling. What exactly did that mean, "likely to kill again because of the seriousness of her crimes?" Were her crimes not always serious? Were they not just as serious when the police and the prosecution made the deals with her? Were they less serious when the original nine experts said that she did not have an "antisocial personality disorder" and was not a danger to society?

And what did "the seriousness of her crimes" have to do with the idea of recidivism? Was there some kind of proven link between serious crimes and the repetition of those crimes? *Qu'est-ce que c'est?*

What was to prevent her from killing again when she was released from prison free and clear? Following the logic of the Correctional Service and the Parole Board, the repetition of her offences was only a question of time. Why would she be less of a danger to kill again in three years time when she was released after serving her full sentence? None of it made any sense and for some reason it was really starting to irritate Karla. Perhaps her correspondent was right. She had remained silent far too long. After all, if she did not speak up, who would speak up for her? If she did not argue her side, no one else would and the only side available to the media would be the federal prison officials' and the Parole Board's. Maybe she was making a mistake. Maybe next year, on the anniversary of the Board's decision, she needed to appear, if for no other reason other than to force the world to pay some attention to the bureaucratic hypocrisy that was at work. They say two wrongs don't make a right. Let's give her critics their due and say that all the prosecutors', police and psychiatrists' opinions and decisions were wrong as were Justice Galligan's retrospective conclusions. Let's say no deals should ever have been made with her.

Instead, she should have punished like Damiens, the French regicide who was on March 2, 1757, "condemned to make *amende honorable*" as Michel Foucault described in his book, *Discipline and Punish*. Like Damiens, the flesh should have been torn from her "breasts, arms, thighs and calves with red-hot pincers," and her hand, the one which held had the Halothane-soaked cloths and Kristen French's long, black hair, "burnt with sulfur and, on those places where the flesh will be torn away, poured molten lead, boiling oil, burning resin, wax and sulfur melted together" and then her body "drawn and quartered by four horses" and her "limbs and body consumed by fire, reduced to ashes..." just as they did to Damiens. Like him she should have remained alive, for almost twelve hours, until finally only a torso with a head, she was tossed into a huge fire that took four hours to reduce her to ashes.

But that is not the way society chose to deal with Karla. Nor was she given a life sentence without any possibility for parole. And if society should have dealt with her that way, if it was wrong that she had not been tortured, drawn and quartered, the time to redress that wrong was long past. Her deals stood. And part of her deals were, if well behaved, she would be paroled. How did betraying her after she had upheld her end of the bargain make the first wrong right?

One psychiatrist, of the legion she had seen since 1993 – the hired consultant in Saskatoon, Dr. Robin Menzies – suggested that Karla was suffering from an antisocial personality disorder and could be a psychopath. The fact that Saskatoon was not the Vienna of modern twenty-first-century psychiatry seemed to have escaped notice.

Perhaps it should be made public that Dr. Sharon Williams, the Special Advisor to the Correctional Services Commissioner on Sex Offenders and Sex Offender Programs, did not think Karla was a psychopath or a risk to reoffend. Nor did her colleague, Dr. Cindy Presse, the Senior Psychologist from Saskatoon, with whom Karla had spent the most therapeutic time while she was incarcerated in the Regional Center out there.

Dr. Presse knew that Karla was not suffering from antisocial personality disorder – she had administered all the tests and tabulated the data. Karla did not meet any of the criteria for ASPD.

Dr. Presse also knew it was ludicrous to even suggest that Karla was a psychopath. Her colleague, Dr. Williams, had administered the only recognized test for psychopathy, Dr. Robert Hare's PCL-R, and her test results definitively showed that Karla was not what Dr. Menzies said she was.

Dr. Presse's report had recommended that Karla be released on parole immediately. Karla did not see any reflection of this reality in any of the Parole Board's perfunctory pronouncements or in the written decisions they so readily shared with the press. Nor did she see it reported in the media. If Karla continued to hold her tongue, as she had done for the past nine years, none of this would ever be known.

It was interesting how it worked inside. Even though she had waived her right to appear in front of the Parole Board, her parole officer, whom she seldom saw, composed her SPC (*Suivi du Plan Correctionnel*) and the "*Évaluation en Vue d'une Décision*," largely based on the Parole Board's previous decision. She also included observations and reports that her prison guard had made about Karla from the day she arrived at the Reception Center in April 2001, through September, 2001. And those six months had been, understandably, Karla's worst since she went to prison.

Even so, what did the two reports actually say? Karla retrieved her copies from her desk drawer.

They overlapped and were repetitive and phrased slightly differently. Both were dated November 16, 2001. "Mrs. Teale has not participated in any specific programs while in the Regional Reception Center (RRC) even though she had successfully completed many programs in Joliette."

That was true for the six months between April and September. But there were no programs (at least ones that she had not already taken two or three times) for women at the men's Reception Center at Sainte-Anne.

"Mrs. Teale is dedicated to her job; her first job at RRC was that of cleaner; she is now a clerical person who prepares the files for the new arrivals at RRC."

Was it not a good thing to be dedicated to your job, no matter how menial? There was no mention that the preparation of "the files for new arrivals at RRC" took Karla about three hours a week to complete.

"She maintains the same quality of good standards at her job as she employs in the various activities offered to all women in the women's unit in RRC, including her work in the art studio, and the animal therapy clinic in which she participates once a week."

Animal therapy clinic – *L'atelier de zoothérapie* in French: A guy who took his dog to visit lifers in Archambault on the other side of the complex came over to Cellblock A one afternoon a week and yes, Karla did enjoy that, the dog was wonderful. Was it not also a good thing that she maintained the "same quality of good standards" at work and at play?

"She also benefits from the Private Family Visits Program, both alone and with her family. *Et elle reçoit hebdomadairement la visite de sa copine…* And she benefits from regular visits from her friend."

The latter was a reference to her regular visits with Linda Véronneau. On this particular point, the Toronto media and Tim Danson would certainly differ with her parole officer's assessment, Karla thought to herself. Even this was no longer entirely true. For some reason, Linda had not been back to see Karla since Christmas but these reports had been finalized and submitted a month before Christmas.

"Since her arrival at the institution, Mrs. Teale has not had any new psychological and psychiatric evaluations. In September, 2001, she requested psychological therapy to help her adjust to her arrival at RRC, which was started but quickly terminated because she could not establish a bond of trust with the provider."

That was true. Given the circumstances, and how clearly Karla had come to understand that the prison manipulated psychologists and psychiatrists to arbitrarily say whatever the Correctional Service wanted them to say, was it any wonder that she could no longer "establish a bond of trust" with any psychologist or psychiatrist in the prison's employ?

"There has been no identifiable change in Mrs. Teale's attitude. She maintains an adequate attitude but is nevertheless somewhat standoffish to prison personnel."

"Standoffish?" That had been true – for the first little while. It had not been true since September, something that was very subtly reflected later on in the report. True or not, it did beg that question – why would she be anything else other than "standoffish?" Being open and friendly had landed her in maximum security in the Regional Psychiatric Center in Saskatoon and now here at Sainte-Anne-des-Plaines, probably for the rest of her sentence.

It had also taken Karla some time to adjust to living in a tiny, all-woman island in a sea of men. As she wrote: "I have been so isolated from the world for so long that when I first came to this prison and had interaction with the men I didn't know how to act. When I saw one walking down the hall I immediately looked at the ground. I'm sure they all thought I was the biggest snob in the place, but it was pure shyness and insecurity."

The report went on to specify that Karla "is polite and does not require any special attention or vigilance."

In a place reserved exclusively for the hardcore female prisoner – women beset with such acerbated mental health and behavioral problems that no other prison in the country could handle them – would the fact that Karla was polite, quiet and independent not be a major plus? Add to these fact the fact that "she has not had any disciplinary infractions since she arrived at the Regional Reception Center." In fact, Karla did not have any disciplinary infractions on her prison record, period, but it was painfully obvious now that her exemplary good behavior was totally irrelevant.

"Her file was reviewed on October 10, 2001, and there was no new information. She is constantly requesting a transfer back to Joliette and demands a regular review of her security status. She does not understand why she was transferred to maximum security at RRC and still does not accept it."

That was certainly true during the limited time period that these reports addressed. Were she not demanding of a review and questioning her involuntary transfers then she truly would have been a mental health case and belonged right where she was.

She was promised by staff at the Regional Psychiatric Center in Saskatoon that she would go back to Joliette if she cooperated with the assessment which they could not ultimately do without her cooperation. She cooperated, but when she looked out her window she did not see rue Marsolais.

Karla had stopped making those requests and demands by Christmastime. She came to accept her situation and even told her IPO, in a gesture of openness and *esprit d'corps* that she was "fine with it now." Karla had decided that there were even some good things that happened to her as a consequence of her being transferred there. As she wrote: "Everything happens for a reason and some good things have happened to me since I came here, things that never would have happened elsewhere."

The prison reports continued: "She is showing difficulty adapting to the other female prisoners and has a different way of life than others in her unit."

No shit, Sherlock. "Yes, my way of life was different than everyone else's," Karla wrote. "I do not smash up my cell or bang my head against the wall or scream at the 'screws' when things do not go my way. Most of the women here are like that, but are seriously attempting to change (most of them anyway)."

In reality, Karla had a calming effect on the five other female prisoners in her unit, an effect that her unit manager, IPO and parole officer privately acknowledged but never recorded in any of their reports.

"Over all," Karla continued, "I would have to say that all of us have changed as a result of my being here. They are all more calm than they were before but I am less calm. I have definitely become 'harder,' for the lack of a better word."

This change in Karla was not reported. In a section entitled "Attitudinal Change" it says "There has been no noticeable change in Mrs. Teale's attitude."

The SPC goes on to parrot both the text in the Parole Board's first decision to detain her as well as Dr. Van Gijseghem's off-hand statement about Karla being largely "conformist."

"She demonstrates a particularly conformist's attitude" was how her parole officer put it in the evaluation.

Since she had seen it in Van Gijseghem's "expert report" in August 2000, Karla had wondered just what that meant? Even with her degree in psychology she was none the wiser. Did it mean that she conformed to rules and regulations? She had been told that was what she was supposed to do. She was told if she did that, she would be paroled.

Perhaps "conformist attitude" was code for "pretending" to conform. Maybe it was institutional lingo to suggest that she was playing possum or "malingering," as it would have been categorized in the *Diagnostic and Statistical Manual of Mental Disorder – IV*.

Nevertheless, was having a "conformist attitude," no infractions on your prison record, being polite but "utilitarian" in your dealings with prison staff akin to other institutional infractions such as trafficking in drugs, or stabbing another inmate, or attacking a guard?

Was benefiting from the use of Private Family Unit and regular visits from "your friend" and family, not requiring vigilance or any special attention, were those sufficient justifications to continue detention? In Karla's unique case, the answer was a resounding "Yes."

The most acerbic part of the reports dealt with Karla's alleged attitude toward the sex offender program that the prison had only recently started telling her she needed to take. It described how Karla had been willing to participate in the program provided it was given in Joliette.

In the section "Motivation – Moderate" the report stated that Karla "shows very superficial interest in programs in general, except she has requested the sexual offender program in Joliette and again, she is only requesting it to get back to Joliette. She is adverse to any therapy that would try to get at the root of her aggression – she does not want to go back and discuss the reasons for her actions or her crimes."

It was so frustrating for Karla to read this, given that she had enthusiastically taken every program the prison had proffered over the past eight years, and was reported to be, up until she applied for escorted temporary absences, making excellent progress with both aspects of her Correctional Plan – that part of the plan that addressed her role as an aggressor as well as her documented role as the compliant victim of a sexual sadist. Without going into the hundreds upon hundreds of therapeutic hours that had already gone into discussions about "the reasons for her actions and her crimes," this statement did not reflect what Karla told her parole officer.

Prior to Christmas, Karla had never discussed a sex offender program with her parole officer. What she said was said to the "screw" – slang that Karla would never have used before she was transferred to Sainte-Anne-des-Plaines – and they were words to the effect that she knew enrolment in a sex offender program would be a good reason to send her back to Joliette because she knew there was a sex offender program beginning there soon, and that would be a good pretext to send her back. She said this during one of those periods when she was trying to open up and be less "standoffish" with prison personnel.

"I never said I would *only* do it if it were given to me there," Karla explained.

She had tried to get the parole officer to correct this misstatement in the report for months but to no avail. Ms. Dufor, Karla's parole officer at Saint-Anne-des-Plaines, ignored her attempts to clarify her position and the report was filed the way it was written.

In the meantime, Karla had changed her mind. She had now decided that she would not do a sex offender program under any circumstances, no matter where it was offered or what they might try and do to her to make her take it. All the promises they had made to her had been empty.

Over the year she had been in the Regional Reception Center, she started to fully realize the absurdity of their position. Right up until they moved to detain her in 1999 she was treated as a battered woman.

Suddenly, she had been mysteriously transmogrified into a danger-ous sex offender. It wasn't something that Karla, or anyone else, could see happening. Her head did not start to swivel the way Linda Blair's head did in *The Exorcist*, nor did she get Sissy Spacek eyes, the way they grew large and pooled and shot blinding shafts of laser light that exploded the walls of Ewen High School in the movie *Carrie*. There was an old English saying for being in jail: held at Her Majesty's Pleasure. Karla morphed at Her Majesty's Pleasure.

The more Karla thought about it, the more she realized this sudden institutional preoccupation with sex offender programs was another set up. Karla had not been convicted of any sexual offences. Her lawyer had gone to a good deal of trouble to make sure that did not happen and there must have been a reason. If the police and the prosecutors and the courts did not find her to be a sexual offender, nor the prison for the past seven years, why in God's name should she become one now?

Karla made a note to herself in her computer to make sure that she asked her parole officer (and anyone else with whom she might have a conversation for that matter) why exactly she should enter a sex offender program when she had not been convicted of any sex offences and the system had never defined or treated her that way before?

The computer was a very useful tool. Karla had bought hers and a printer from Purchasing after she arrived at Sainte-Anne. She did not know much about computers but it suited her needs. It ran Windows 98 and Karla had recently bought a program called PrintShop that let her design her own greeting cards and stationery.

Now that she thought about it, it was apparent that they had been setting up to do this since the time they called in Dr. Racine-Rouleau to give her the Abel Screen Test and put a report called "Sexology" in her file. Karla did not think there was such a word but there it was, and it would obviously trigger an adverse response in anyone who even glanced at her file.

Everyone – the carceral lawyers, the other inmates, her lawyers, many of the prison staff at Joliette, the Correctional Service Investigator – they all said that Karla could not be transferred against her will to Saskatoon for a psychiatric assessment and what happened? She was transferred to Saskatoon – and kept there for four months – for a psychiatric assessment.

In Saskatoon, they told her if she cooperated she would be sent back to Joliette. She cooperated and she was sent to Sainte-Anne-des-Plaines. Why was her natural desire to return to Joliette – a return she had been promised – a negative akin to an institutional infraction in the parole officer's report?

When she had last talked to her parole officer, Ms. Dufor told Karla that she thought Karla should do her last year "in the community" but she would have to take the sex offender program first.

When Karla told her guard that she had decided not to do a sex offender program, the guard looked at Karla as though she had a screw loose and told her that if she did not do it, she would never get out on parole and would spend the rest of her time in jail. Big deal. Karla fully expected to remain in jail until the last day of her sentence – July 6, 2005. Getting out early was no longer an incentive. The prison had already seen to that.

As Correctional Services had demonstrated over the past two years, there was always more behind their decisions with respect to Karla than Karla's well-being or even the general well-being of the community-at-large. After thirty years, there was still controversy about the real effectiveness of sex offender programs, even in the male population for whom it was designed. Further, there really were no sex offender programs for women – the programs that were offered were experimental. That had been part of Dr. Williams's mandate since 1995 – to begin a series of test programs toward establishing a bona fide treatment for women.

Karla was by far the highest profile female prisoner in the country. They wanted her as a guinea pig. What was in it for Karla? Absolutely nothing. Whether she "passed" or "failed" the Correctional Service would have what they wanted – a document that labeled her a sex offender. They would have accomplished what the police, the prosecution and the courts eschewed.

It was interesting. After their discussion about Karla doing her last year in the community but having to take a sex offender program first, which happened in January or February, 2002, the parole officer confided that she had a great deal of difficulty in writing Karla's reports because there really was nothing to say.

Rereading the documents Karla realized how true Ms. Dufor statement had been. They were filled with non sequiturs and ridiculous things such as the idea that Karla's "requests" were "too scattered," a reference to the fact that Karla asked more than one guard questions instead of just interacting with her own IPO. What is the point of putting that on the record? First she was marked for being "standoffish," now she was cited for being too garrulous.

In the section entitled "Potential for Social Reintegration" Ms. Dufor's writing most reflected the difficulty she was having trying to invent something to say. "Mrs. Teale has all the right assets to live in society but we believe that were she released into society that she would again do harm." And then the *pièce de resistance*:

"The reason for her transfer from Joliette to RRC was to protect her personal security. In our opinion, the risks are still real, the media attention is still high profile. Recently a Quebec paper did an article about the great killers of Canada and Mrs. Teale was prominently featured. This kind of media attention brings rage and disgust from the general public."

This statement made Karla laugh. "Yes, the official reason I am in max is for my protection. It is a joke. The parking lot here faces our yard. If someone wanted to shoot me they could do it just as easily here as they could at Joliette."

Ms. Dufor also repeated the new line about Karla's risk to society still being very high and very real. "The different psychological and psychiatric evaluations state that her [Karla's] unique criminal behavior remains unaddressed and untreated."

The last statement was simply a lie. Karla's many psychological and psychiatric evaluations state that her "unique criminal behavior" was a consequence of her twisted relationship with Paul Bernardo and that she was the "compliant victim" of a "sexual sadist." That was, in a nutshell, what nineteen out of twenty psychological and psychiatric reports concluded.

Frankly, during her first seven years in prison, Karla would have taken any program the prison offered – she did, in fact – and would have willingly submitted to any kind of therapy including an experimental sex offender program. Back then, she had trusted them.

It had now become apparent to Karla that she would be out of her mind if she agreed to enrol in a sex offender program. She had recently become aware of something called Section 810.2 in the Criminal Code. It was relatively new, having been enacted in 1996. Here was the hidden agenda in the prison's recent imprecations for her further cooperation. If she did enrol in a sex offender program, she could easily be subject to Section 810.2 and its onerous implications. Up until now, the application of Section 810.2 had been relatively rare, always involving men – mostly pedophiles. But things were moving very fast in the world after the bombing of the World Trade Center on 9/11 and Karla knew that it was a very different, more strident, more conservative, more anti-crime place outside the prison walls than it had ever been before. She could easily imagine that with Section 810.2, they would try and make yet another exception for her.

The way it was written Section 810.2 allowed for any person (including any representative of Corrections Canada) who feared "on reasonable grounds that another person will commit a serious personal injury offence, with the consent of the Attorney General, to lay an information before a provincial court judge, whether or not the person or persons in respect of whom it is feared that the offence will be committed are named." Karla did not quite know exactly what that meant, but it sounded menacing and all-inclusive.

Section 810.2 had, over the past few years, been used by the Correctional Service and the police to shadow sex offenders and alert communities into which they try to relocate after they had served their time and been released from jail.

In the last couple of years, it had been made impossible for certain individuals, even though they had done their full sentence, to get out and try to start over.

Karla had recently read some articles from American newspapers about satellite surveillance and sex offenders and how some offenders were not being released even after they had served their full terms. To her the stories pointed to a trend in what had become a culture of extreme vigilance, not only in the court of public opinion, but in the courts and in Parliament, where the laws got made.

Under Section 810.2, "a judge may order a person who is perceived to be a high-risk offender under a peace bond for a duration of one year or less if the court is satisfied that the released offender poses a significant risk. The court may place specific conditions on the offender that must be met or the defendant will face further sanctions."

On the surface, this high-risk, peace bond measure might seem reasonable (to many people it seemed imminently reasonable), but when a number of conditions are imposed, particularly when they are not realistic, the individual may not, regardless of their best intentions, be able to abide by them. Consequently, released offenders subject to a peace bond have had an inordinately difficult time not ending up back in jail, even after they had served their full sentence.

There was a case in Alberta that Karla had read about. A person identified only by the initials L.J. was a convicted sex offender. He repeatedly denied sexually assaulting a fourteen-year-old girl. Regardless, he was convicted and sent to federal prison. Like Karla, he had been detained and forced to serve his full sentence. Upon his release, a peace bond was ordered according to Section 810.2 and L.J. was compelled to abide by several conditions.

First, he was required to inform police about any change in residence, providing at least 24-hours notice. Second, L.J. had to report weekly to a designated detective who just happened to be in a city about 60 miles away. This was particularly problematic because L.J. did not have a vehicle. Third, he was not to come within a hundred meters of a public area where children under the age of fourteen might be present nor was he to enter a residence where children under the age of fourteen years were living.

After his identity and sexual offender status was made public, L.J. was summarily evicted from the hotel where he had rented a room. When evicted, he was immediately in breach of the peace bond for failing to notify the police twenty-four hours in advance of a change in residence. Ergo, he was arrested and returned to prison.

* * * * * * *

The "*Évaluation en Vue d'une Décision*" was like a covering memo to the Parole Board. It asked and answered the question about whether or not Karla's detention should be maintained. It repeated everything that was in the SPC. It also mimicked or copied a great deal from the Van Gijseghem report, which was the least authoritative of all the pscyh reports in Karla's file.

Karla was being kept locked down by a redundant rhetorical tyranny which she could now see was going to prevail until she had served her full sentence. Her parole officer was simply giving back to the Parole Board in these two reports what the Parole Board had originally written the previous year when it upheld the prison's referral for her detention.

"At thirty-one-years of age, Karla Leanne Teale is eight years into her federal sentence of twelve years for two involuntary homicides or manslaughters. Her case was last called for review in March, 2001, through Sections 192 2(a) & (I) of the laws that govern statutory release.

"In September, 2001, Mrs. Teale refused to appear in front of the Parole Board to appeal CSC's recommendation that she be detained past her statutory release date..."

Under a section headed "Analysis of the reasons for detaining the prisoner" the report went on to summarize the Board's original reasons for revoking Karla's statutory release.

It contained all of the non sequiturs and phrases: "a threat to society," "considering the seriousness of the crimes," "the cynical and macabre name change," "indifference to the victims," "needs to be protected from society and society should be protected from her."

"In summary, the lack of change is significant in the last year, the motives to maintain her incarceration are still very real and we believe that Karla Teale is capable of committing crimes that could cause death or serious bodily harm to an individual before the end of her legal incarceration date. It is for this reason that we will recommend that her detention be continued."

Considering all this, Karla decided to dig in her heels. They had recently told her they had a sex offender program ready for her to take. That was simply not going to happen.

Did they actually think that she was going to take their advice now and trust their judgement? Forget it. These reports clearly demonstrated the hopelessness of her situation. They were rhetorical exercises.

Van Gijseghem suggested she might be an antisocial personality, and via Menzies she became one. Van Gijseghem suggested that her choice of name was cynical and macabre, and it became so.

What the Parole Board stated in the decision to detain her was now fed back to them by a parole officer to justify her continued detention even though she remained a medium-security prisoner with no institutional infractions whose behavior was exemplary.

As well as not taking any more prison courses or "therapy" programs, including any sex offender program, Karla resolved to appear in front of the Parole Board on her next anniversary and began to make notes:

Consider this: According to seven experts, when I came into prison I was a clinically depressed, battered woman suffering from post-traumatic stress disorder.

After seven years in custodial care, in a system that is now, according to its own public relations, all about healing and rehabilitation, I have become a dangerous, unredeemable psychopath. How is that possible? What does that say about the supposedly new prison system for women and its effectiveness?

I entered the Kingston Prison for Women in July, 1993, with seven reports from reputable physicians which stated that I was a battered woman, suffering from PTSD in "urgent need" of "comprehensive therapeutic intervention." The Correctional Service psychiatrist for P4W, Dr. Roy Brown, concurred.

The idea that I was the "compliant victim of a sexual sadist" and a heavily depressed, battered woman suffering from PSTD and had "learned helplessness" through numerous "cycles of abuse" was not my idea. It was the opinion of Drs. Arndt, Long, Malcolm, Hatcher, Hucker, Jaffe, and McDonald. These reports are all contained in my prison files.

When I first saw Dr. Arndt in March of 1993, I did not know there was such a thing as clinical depression. I had never been to a psychologist or a psychiatrist. I had never heard of Lenore Walker and "battered spousal syndrome" or "post-traumatic stress disorder."

I did not reinvent myself as a battered woman to save myself. In fact, my lawyer told me that the battered woman's defense would not work in my case.

Nevertheless, I was diagnosed by the doctors as a woman suffering from BSS and PSTD. Nine experts (including two in the employ of the Correctional Service) who examined me between 1993 and 1995 concurred and the police, prosecutors and the courts believed them.

Is it my place not to believe what they said? Should I have stood up and said "No, no, wait a minute, I'm not a battered woman?" Other than the fact that such behavior would be against human nature, I believed them. I felt battered. I looked battered. What I now want to know is who or what empowers the Correctional Service to overturn those diagnoses and ignore the tenets of the plea resolutions that were based on them?

The prison service accepted those diagnoses and proceeded to treat me as diagnosed for seven years!

In those first months at Kingston's Prison for Women, I made a request to be transferred to a psychiatric facility, which would ostensibly have been better equipped to assess me and provide appropriate therapy and manage my rehabilitation.

Correctional Service refused that request and I was assured that I would get the comprehensive therapy I needed in their prisons.

CSC psychotherapist Jan Heney and psychiatrist Dr. Roy Brown were immediately made available to me for therapy three to four times a week. According to Dr. Brown's reports, which are included in my files, over the next two years, I made excellent progress.

If CSC were ambivalent about who and what I was, why did they insist on keeping me in the prison facility and treating me exclusively as a depressed woman suffering from battered spousal syndrome and post-traumatic stress disorder? There were myriad options. They could have treated me as a sex offender and a psychopath. They could have granted my request and transferred me to a psychiatric facility. As you can see in my file, prosecutor Murray Segal and the Ministry of the Attorney General for Ontario, in whose jurisdiction I committed my crimes, had no objection to such a transfer.

If the Correctional Service did not accept me as I was diagnosed when I entered the prison system, why did they not start to treat me as a sex offender and a psychopathic monster right away?

I suppose, today, in retrospect, they could argue that such an approach would have been in conflict with the police and the prosecutors with whom they were compelled to cooperate in order to get me ready to testify as the key witness in my ex-husband's murder trial.

But what about after the trial in the fall of 1995? I have letters from police officers congratulating me on my performance and telling me to just ignore all the nay sayers and critics who called me a murderous psychopath and a monster.

If it was a question of my role as a witness for the prosecution and the constant presence of police officers and prosecutors from Ontario that prevented the prison authority from treating me contrary to the way I had been diagnosed, why was I not immediately treated as a sex offender and a person suffering from antisocial personality disorder after I testified?

After Paul Bernardo's trial, the police and prosecutors were through with me and never came back. What was to prevent the prison from treating me as what they now say I am then?

Instead, after I held up my part of my plea resolution, testified and returned to jail, the prison continued to treat me as I had been originally diagnosed.

The prison officials insisted that I enrol in many programs directed toward battered and abused women and their attendant psychological problems. I did, and as the various reports show, I did well in all these courses and completed them to everyone's satisfaction.

All through this process, both before and after my ex-husband's trial, the prison officials and psychologists and psychiatrists consistently wrote reports which said I was making good progress and getting better. Before Dr. Brown retired in 1996, he considered me healed.

In 1996, the special advisor to the Commissioner of Correctional Service on sex offender programs and adjunct professor of psychology and psychiatry at Queen's University, Dr. Sharon Williams, examined me and administered a battery of tests which included the Psychopathy Check List – Revised (PCL-R)– and found me not to be a psychopath. Dr. Williams did not find me to be a threat to myself, other prisoners or the community. Her report was used by the Correctional Service to support my transfer to general population at Joliette.

The Correctional Service Sex Offender Program (which had been built and financed by CSC in conjunction with Queen's University over the past thirty years) was developed by a Kingston-based psychologist Dr. William Marshall. (I took Dr. Marshall's Introduction to Deviant Psychology undergraduate course by correspondence.)

Dr. Williams is a student and disciple of Dr. Marshall's. Part of Dr. Williams' mandate as Special Advisor to the Commissioner was and is to set up sex offender programs for women and she has personally overseen a number of cases and delivered numerous papers on the subject. I am told that some of her work is available through the CSC Website. One of the premiere sex offender programs in the world was right there in my own backyard, as it were, while I was incarcerated in P4W. No one ever suggested that I participate in it.

Although officially, there are no programs for female sex offenders, over the past eight years Correctional Services has treated over two dozen women as sex offenders. This information can easily be found and verified on the Correctional Service's Web site.

Dr. Williams did a second "Psychological Assessment" in 1999, shortly after I applied for the Escorted Temporary Absences, which, although it was my right to do so, precipitated a series of events that placed me here in front of you today. Again, she did not find me to be a psychopath or suffering from any personality disorders or a candidate for the sex offender program.

My recent Correctional Plan and other reports from my Parole Officer to the Parole Board say that I have not shown any interest in new programs or therapies since I was transferred to the Regional Reception Center at Sainte-Anne-des-Plaines in April, 2001.

What more do psychologists and psychiatrists in the employ of Correctional Services really have to contribute?

What more can be said that has not already been said?

Given the dramatic differences of opinion between the majority of the psychologists and psychiatrists who have examined me over the years and those of Drs. Van Gijseghem and Menzies and the weight those two reports have been given by Correctional Service and the National Parole Board why would I subject myself to any further programs or assessments at the behest of the Correctional Service?

Is there something new that can be learned? If it is the dim opinions of my state of mind and personality expressed by Van Gijseghem and Menzies that currently has vogue, there are much more inventive and credible opinions on the public record than the ridiculous idea that I am suffering from an antisocial personality disorder or psychopathy. It is clear to anyone with even a cursory familiarity with psychology and the *Diagnostic and Statistical Manual of Mental Disorders – IV-TR* that I am not.

Not to suggest that any of the doctors at the Regional Psychiatric Center in Saskatoon found anything Dr. Van Gijseghem said credible. In fact, they all tore his report apart, saying that it was irresponsible and baseless.

For an interesting alternative to the majority of expert opinions that say I am a battered woman suffering from post-traumatic stress disorder and clinical depression, the opinions of the doctors retained by my ex-husband's lawyers have apparently never been countenanced by Correctional Services or anyone in their employ. This anti-psychiatry is liberally quoted in the book *Invisible Darkness* by Stephen Williams. Although I personally have not read the book, I am told that it is by far the most accurate book about my case, and the most damning to me.

It was published in the fall of 1996. It talks about the opinions of Dr. Graham Glancy, Dr. Nathan Pollack and Dr. John Money from Johns Hopkins.

Those doctors called into serious question the opinions of the nine doctors who diagnosed me as a woman suffering from BSS and PSTD.

The fact that the diagnoses of Drs. Arndt, Long, Malcolm, Hatcher, Hucker, and Jaffe were controversial and contained some inherent contradictions was available to everyone when the opinions of Drs. Glancy and Pollack became a matter of the public record.

These doctors opined that I was a malingering histrionic hybristophiliac, a far more plausible diagnosis, according to the axis in DSM-IV than antisocial personality disorder or narcissistic personality disorder or psychopathy.(There is no listing for "psychopathy" in DSM-IV. Neither is there for "hybristophiliac" for that matter.)

On the more prosaic side, there were various experts consulted by women who wrote voluminous articles about me in *Saturday Night Magazine*, and, more recently, in *Elm Street*.

Like Van Gijseghem and Menzies, these experts suggested psychopathy and/or narcissistic personality disorder but they did it with considerably more flare. Dr. Van Gijseghem culled some of his ideas from the *Saturday Night* article which was written by a newspaper person with no training in psychiatry or psychology.

I have been called every name in the book and then some. However, the opinions that were accepted by the police, the prosecutors and the courts are what they are and I am what I am.

I would underline the fact for the Parole Board that Correctional Service once again called on Dr. Sharon Williams in 1999 to administer tests and reassess me shortly after I applied for escorted temporary absences. She did not find that I was suffering from antisocial personality disorder or psychopathy at that time either and her conclusions did not support a transfer to a psychiatric facility nor did she recommend that I be reclassified as a maximum security prisoner or be enrolled in a sex offender program. Shortly after her report was reviewed, it was obviously not satisfactory to the Correctional Service because my file was referred to Dr. Van Gijseghem, a some-time outside psychological consultant to the Correctional Service.

I do not know how many people who sat on the jury at my ex-husband's trial agreed with the prosecutors and the court that I was a battered woman suffering from post-traumatic stress disorder. After all, I was a witness. I was not on trial and no psychiatric evidence about my condition was allowed into evidence. Nevertheless, at least two jurors felt strongly enough that I was what the prosecutors and police and psychologists and psychiatrists said I was to have written letters of support to my family and me. These letters are also in my file.

I was given intensive therapy both in and out of prison, but most particularly, for almost seven years – while in prison. I was taught, and learned to have that which I had lost – self-esteem.

Just as I had done before I met Paul Bernardo, I was able once again to assert myself and stand up for my rights. I was encouraged to do this by the prison authorities every step of the way and that is abundantly clear to anyone who reviews my file. I was shown the way to self-reliance. I am relying on what I learned in prison and falling back on it in order to make this presentation to the Board.

My current parole officer worries about the media and public opinion and holds, as does the Parole Board, that I am in danger from an enraged public. This is utter nonsense. There is no such thing as vigilante justice. It is a purely fictional concept created by the tabloid press.

I was very worried, prior to my ex-husband's trial, about all the leaks about my trial and my crimes. Contrary to the publication ban levied by the judge at my trial, all the details were published in the United States and England, in both respectable newspapers such as *The Washington Post* and *The New York Times* as well as in the tabloid press and on tabloid television shows such as *A Current Affair*.

The publication ban that Justice Kovacs had ordered was repeatedly broken here in Canada as well as in North America and England.

Dr. Jan Heney and Sergeant Robert Gillies told me not to worry about it, that even the breaking of the publication ban in the media would not have any significant impact. They were right. It didn't.

The *Toronto Sun* and a few others actively campaigned for years to have my deals rescinded. Hundreds of thousands of people from Southwestern Ontario have allegedly signed petitions to have those plea resolutions quashed. Tim Danson, the lawyer for the families, has repeatedly publicly denounced me and the plea resolutions that gave me a twelve-year sentence in return for my assistance to the authorities and my guilty pleas. It is relevant, at least to me, that Mr. Danson and the families of my victims approved my plea resolution. If they had not, the deals for my testimony would never have been made.

Today, the plea resolutions and my sentence stand. As a result of public opinion, there was a judicial inquiry conducted by Justice Patrick Galligan. After exhaustive study, the Honorable Justice Patrick Galligan found that the deals were just and correct.

(*Note to self: request complete copy of my prison files and thoroughly review Judicial Inquiry by Galligan before next Parole Board hearing.*)

The issue about whether or not I should be charged with sex offences was thoroughly discussed during the plea negotiations prior to my trial as well as between the time I was sent to jail and my ex-husband's trial.

The police and the Ministry of the Attorney General for Ontario had the opportunity to charge me with sex offences. They did not. I was not convicted of any sex offences.

Is it the role of Correctional Service and the Parole Board to rescind the court's decision and the decision of the provincial authorities and now find that I am a sex offender and force me to take a sex offender's program?

If the two psych reports – the one from Dr. Robin Menzies from Saskatoon, and the one from Dr. Hubert Van Gijseghem from Montreal – that suggest I am a psychopath suffering from an antisocial personality disorder are right then all the other reports by all the other psychiatrists and psychologists who have attended me and provided therapy and counseling both prior to my incarceration and after, including Drs. Arndt, Long, Malcolm, Hucker, Hatcher, Jaffe and Macdonald, and CSC psychiatrists and psychologists Drs. Brown, Heney, Williams, et al. must be wrong.

The question I want to ask the Board is why do the opinions of one psychologist (who never examined me) and one psychiatrist from Saskatoon who obviously came into the assessment process with a bias, hold sway over the opinions of a dozen, equally well-qualified experts?

The Correctional Service's and the Parole Board's reliance on these two reports does not seem to me to be appropriate, rational or fair.

For the sake of argument, let's say that these two reports are right and all the others are wrong – that would then suggest that my prolonged incarceration has made me into a different person than I was up until my eighth year of incarceration – the year I was supposed to be automatically released.

Prior to December, 2000, I was a battered spouse suffering from post-traumatic stress disorder who had made real progress and whose prognosis was good.

I had made many proactive, positive steps to better myself and rehabilitate myself up until I made a request for escorted temporary absences and my file was sent to Dr. Van Gijseghem.

It would appear that if Dr. Van Gijseghem's speculations and Dr. Menzies' report hold sway, rather than help and rehabilitate me, as my Correctional Plan was supposed to do, long-term incarceration in the federal facilities for women has had the opposite effect and transformed me into a some kind of monster.

(I am not saying that I'm a monster. Correctional Services is. It is worth pointing out that the Senior Psychologist from the Regional Psychiatric Center in Saskatoon, Dr. Cindy Presse, does not agree with Dr. Menzies and says in her report, a report that the Board has completely ignored, that I am definitely not suffering from antisocial personality disorder nor am I a psychopath nor a risk to reoffend nor a danger to society and should have been released on parole immediately upon my return to Quebec.)

Nevertheless, assuming that the Board's decision was the right one, and Drs. Van Gijseghem and Menzies are right, it would follow then, that incarceration is having the opposite of its desired effect and I should be paroled immediately and enrolled in an aggressive therapy program such as the treatment I received from Dr. Arndt from March 1993 through June, 1993 and also received from Drs. Brown and Heney immediately after my incarceration in P4W.

Otherwise, I will soon turn into a full-blown monster, being held as I am now in maximum security (my classification mysteriously remains "medium" and always has been) in the men's Regional Reception Center at Sainte-Anne-des-Plaines.

If the logic that found in favor of the Correctional Services Referral for Detention is sound it suggests then, that right around the time I have to be released, on July 6, 2005, a free woman having paid my debt to society in full, I will have become the equivalent of a female Hannibal Lector, an intelligent, macabre, cynical, malingering killer, ironically, one created my the prison system itself

How much more sensible would it have been to allow me to begin becoming reintegrated into society with guidance and support from the system and a parole officer, with conditions and disciplines set by Correctional Services and the National Parole Board that would have to be strictly observed over the next few years until my sentence expires.

I do not fear for my life. That was lawyer and media hype. Nobody is going to try and find me, except maybe for a few reporters from a newspaper.

On parole, I also have the option of not talking to reporters. If they are harassing me, I can call on the authorities' help.

It is obvious that Correctional Services does not want me out on parole but the question is why?

The reasoning, as they have presented it to you in their Referral for Detention, as I think I have demonstrated, is very flimsy.

I think it would be far more honest of them to say that from their point of view, it would be far too much work for too little gain.

They would take a great deal of public heat – it would be embarrassing and not "politically correct" to release me on parole and I would require a great deal of attention from the Board and the authorities and that would be costly. There is simply no upside, from the prison system's point of view.

But the question the Parole Board must consider is what really is in the public interest and not what Correctional Services and the politicians consider in their best interest.

In a few very short years, I am going to be released from prison (regardless of who likes it and who doesn't) and I will have to try and reintegrate into a society and a world that is very different from the one I left. Would it not be far more desirable that I have some help and guidance for a few years, rather than simply be put out on the street two years from now?

It came out in a flood and Karla was exhausted. There was more and any presentation she might make to the Parole Board should be much more succinct and controlled. Karla resolved to try and get it all together before her next mandatory parole review. She did not have hope. She did not think for a second that she would prevail and they would change their mind and release her on parole. But at least for the first time in ten years, the world would hear her own voice.

* * * * * * *

Alas it was not to be. Between the early summer of 2002 and September/October, 2002, when Karla was compelled to advise the Parole Board whether or not she intended to appear at the mandatory hearing that would convene in March, 2003, Karla's resolve dissolved.

"I just can't bear the idea of going there to a media-filled room with the Frenches and Mahaffys in attendance and being verbally beaten," she explained. "I agree that a gradual release is better, but I can forget about that in my case."

Karla's third denial of parole made public by the Parole Board in January, 2003, caused a two-day boost in circulation for Canadian tabloid newspapers which ran pages of color pictures taken of Karla when she was still in Joliette. In these pictures, Karla appears to be an attractive, healthy young woman in good spirits.

The photographs were sold to the *Toronto Sun* newspaper by Linda Véronneau, who portrayed herself to crime reporter Alan Cairns as a scorned lover.

Linda claimed to not only have had a sexual relationship with Karla, but one that was characterized by masochistic demands. Karla liked to tied up and spanked, Linda exclaimed in broken English peppered with obscenities. According to Ms. Véronneau, this would happen all the time in the house she and Karla occupied at Joliette with six other women – just before lights out at eleven o'clock.

For women in prison degrees of separation seldom span six. Spurned by Homolka for over a year, Véronneau has now taken a new lover, former Cellblock A resident and another Karla confidant,

Chantal Meunier. A slatternly blonde, Chantal breathlessly claimed Karla had taken a male inmate who worked in the library as a lover. Chantal said she watched as Karla masturbated him through a fence and slipped him her soiled underwear. Given that there is not an inch of fence line that is not watched twenty-four hours a day by the tower guards at the maximum-security Reception Center, this seems highly unlikely but it makes for good copy.

Without descriptives, the Parole Board's denial once again cited Karla's refusal to acknowledge her role as a "sexual aggressor" and added to her list of trespasses the secret undertaking of an "emotional relationship" with a male inmate which the Board declared had become "sexual."

Whatever, the newspaper reported that the male prisoner who had caught more than Karla's eye had been transferred and Linda Véronneau was going to marry Chantal.

Jean Paul, the inmate trustee who worked in the prison library, was a tall, handsome, sandy blond with just a few years left on the sentence he received for murdering his father. Years earlier, he had been extradited from a Mexican prison and told me that he very much enjoyed working in the prison library in Saint-Anne-des-Plaines. If any of this were true, Karla would no longer have anyone with whom to speak the Spanish she had been studying.

Although it was highly unlikely that any of this took place, it would be abnormal if Karla was not interested in having a sexual relationship with either a man or a woman. Something, anything to kill the monotony and pass the time. How was the fact that she formed an "emotional relationship" with another prisoner reflective of a "deranged psych" or indicative of her dangerousness or in any way predictive of the possibility that she might reoffend when released from prison?

Once again, if any of this were true, the Parole Board and the Correctional Service only had themselves to blame. After all, it was those bastions of discipline and punishment that decided it was best for all concerned that Karla be detained for the balance of her sentence and resolved that she should do that time in an all-male prison.

BEGIN AT THE END

Karla was reading *Torso Murder: The Untold Story of Evelyn Dick*. Evelyn Dick was easily as notorious in her day as Karla was now. Even so, according to the book, Evelyn vaporized after she walked out of Kingston's Prison for Women in 1958, having served almost twelve years of a life sentence for manslaughter. To this day no one knows whether she is alive or dead.

Like most true crime books, *Torso Murder* had pictures. People in pictures from the forties usually looked ugly to Karla unless they were movie stars. But Evelyn Dick was an exception. Evelyn Dick was a truly vivacious, stunningly beautiful woman who turned heads whereever she went. Karla did not think of herself as vivacious or beautiful. She was alright but she really had a pretty common look. If a woman with Hollywood-starlet good looks managed to drop off the edge of the earth, it should be a cinch for Karla.

Evelyn was exactly the same age as Karla – twenty-four – when she was tried for her crimes. And they shared geography; Evelyn was a Peninsula girl too, born in Beamsville, a small town right up the road from St. Catharines, where Inspector Bevan had his Green Ribbon Task Force headquartered.

Evelyn Dick's reputation and the attention paid to her criminal trial were mostly a regional phenomenon. At the height of her trial in the late forties, the story was picked up across country but it was predominately a sensation in Southwestern Ontario. Karla's experience in Quebec had taught her that this was true in her case as well.

The way Evelyn's story goes, police found the remains of her seven-month-old illegitimate son, John Patrick White, encased in a block of cement. Explaining his disappearance to her family, Evelyn had lied and told them that she had put the child up for adoption. This was in 1948. No one bothered to ask any questions.

The cement block containing the child's remains was stuffed in a large suitcase and stored in the attic of Evelyn's house. It was discovered while the police were searching for evidence with regard to Evelyn's estranged husband's murder and dismemberment.

John Dick's torso had been found at the base of Hamilton Mountain in 1946. Eventually, the authorities found his limbs but they never found the head.

They did find teeth and pieces of his bones buried in the ashes in Evelyn's furnace. They found other incriminating evidence including a revolver, cartridges, saws, and bloodstained shoes that belonged to the dead man in Evelyn's father's basement. The Packard Evelyn had been driving the day her husband disappeared belonged to one of her father's friends. It was bloodstained inside and out. There was no DNA analysis in those days but forensic testing showed the blood to be the same type as John Dick's. And then there was the infant in the suitcase in the attic.

As in Karla's case, Evelyn's demeanor and responses were deemed inappropriate by the media and the public-at-large. Cavalier, she gave four different accounts of John Dick's demise. She even suggested that the taciturn Mennonite streetcar driver had been mobbed up and his death a professional hit. She bragged about how many important men she had bedded and handed over her little black book. It turned out that she had even had sex with the son of the judge who presided at her first trial. It was an amazing story, and so close to home.

At the time, psychiatrists found Evelyn on the borderline between dull/normal and moronic intelligence. They concluded that, at the age of twenty-four, she had the mental capacity of a thirteen-year-old.

That seemed very convenient and certainly did not jive with the rest of her life and what other people thought about her. Psychiatric testimony was allowed at her trial but it had no impact. Evelyn was convicted of her husband's murder and sentenced to death. The sentence was overturned on appeal.

A second lawyer, famed Toronto defense attorney, J.J. Robinette, won a new trial for Evelyn on a technicality. This time Evelyn was acquitted. However, not even J.J. Robinette could beat the manslaughter rap having to do the dead, cement-encased child in the attic.

Unlike the childless Karla, by the time Evelyn Dick was tried and convicted she had borne three children. A stillborn boy, the murdered enfant in the suitcase and a daughter, Heather Maria, who was born in 1942. Heather Maria disappeared from public view a few years after her mother went to prison.

What about Evelyn? Some say that she died at eighty where she had been born, in Beamsville. If that were the case, in a weird six-degrees-from-separation scenario, Evelyn would have still been resident in Beamsville right around the time Karla and Paul had kidnaped and killed Kristen French. But no one knows for sure.

There had been books about the case, movies, a play, even a song – by someone called Mickey DeSadest. There was a new movie made for television called *Torso* which was based on research by Brian Vallee, the author of the book Karla was reading. *Torso* was supposed to have been shown on CTV but the terrorist attack on the World Trade Center on September 11, 2001, pre-empted it. Karla made a note to watch out for it when it was rescheduled.

Karla read some place that the cast and crew of the movie celebrated what would have been Evelyn Dick's eighty-first birthday on October 30, 2000. It would seem that celebrations of famous female criminals' birthdays are common occurrences both in and out of prison.

Although Evelyn Dick had a lot of help from the Parole Board when she was released – a prominent member, Alan Edmison, appeared to have been enthralled by Evelyn and arranged a new identity and a job for her in another part of the country – Evelyn was never ratted out or recognized. Karla found this very interesting. According to those in the know, in particular a retired Parole Board member who knew Evelyn and knows who and what she became, Evelyn went on to live a happy, successful and prosperous life.

* * * * * * *

From where Karla was sitting, *Torso Murder* was not only a hell of a good story, ranking right up there with some of the best true crime she had read, it was also a parable. And Evelyn's story mirrored the story of other women who had committed atrocious crimes that Karla had read about. Women such as the "Trunk Murderess" Winnie Ruth Judd, and "Heavenly Creatures" Juliet Hulme and Pauline Parker. Their stories were not only fascinating but instructive too.

Winnie Ruth Judd arrived in Phoenix, Arizona, in 1929, with her physician husband. She suffered from tuberculosis and, like thousands of others, the Judds moved to Phoenix for the dry, desert climate.

Dr. Judd was twenty-two years Winnie's senior and had a few problems of his own, not the least of which was an addiction to heroin. Phoenix was a small town and it had a veneer of respectability. Such flaws, particularly among professionals, were not tolerated. Had he been a drunk, it would have been a different story. When Dr. Judd could not find work in Phoenix, he simply left twenty-two-year-old Winnie behind and went to work for a mining operation in Mexico. Later, he moved to Los Angeles.

Left alone in Arizona, Winnie Ruth got a job as a receptionist at a medical clinic. There she met and befriended a thirty-two-year-old nurse and x-ray technician named Anne LeRoi.

Anne was a twice-divorced, attractive, fastidious farm girl from Oregon. She lived with a waifish, beautiful, twenty-four-year-old woman named Hedvig "Sammy" Samuelson. Sammy had tuberculosis, too.

Winnie Ruth moved in with Anne and Sammy and the three formed a kind of smoldering *ménage à trois*, tainted by titillating rumors of lesbianism, which, in turn, attracted a bevy of male sybarites, including a socially prominent and wealthy lumberyard owner named Jack Halloran.

Although the three women were promiscuous and accepted money and gifts in return for sexual favors, Winnie Ruth decided that she was in love with Jack. On the other hand, "Smiling" Jack, as he was known, was a married philanderer who had many female admirers, including Anne and Sammy.

Around 9 p.m. on Friday, October 16, 1931, during the course of an argument over Smiling Jack, Winnie Ruth shot and killed her roommates.

With help from someone, (assumed, but never proven to be Jack Halloran), Winnie packed the two corpses in steamer trunks. One trunk was large enough to accommodate Anne LeRoi's body but Sammy had to be dismembered so that she would fit in the second. That exercise was accomplished with such precision that it was assumed, although again, never conclusively proven, that Halloran had enlisted the help of fellow voluptuary and drunk, Dr. Charles W. Brown.

Talking about Halloran's participation in front of a grand jury many years later, Winnie Ruth said, "He told me that he had operated on Sammy... He said Sammy had been operated on and that she was dead. Every time he gets drunk he starts saying he is Dr. Buckley from Buckeye. He was always wanting me to introduce him to nurses."[1]

Even though Winnie Ruth had inadvertently shot herself in the hand while shooting Anne and Sammy, she returned to work the following day. After work, she repacked the second trunk, putting some of Sammy's body parts in a valise to reduce the trunk's weight. With Sammy's head in her hatbox, Winnie Ruth then asked her landlord to

1. Boomersbach, Jana, *The Trunk Murderess: Winnie Ruth Judd, The Truth About an American Crime Legend Revealed at Last* (New York, 1992) Simon & Schuster

take the trunks to the train station, explaining that they contained books her husband needed in Los Angeles.

She made the 400-mile trip to Los Angeles on the Union Pacific with the trunks in the baggage car. The valise containing some of Sammy's body parts and the hatbox sat beside her on the seat.

By the time she arrived in Los Angeles, one of the fetid trunks was dripping blood, and the station master refused to release the luggage until it was opened and inspected. Winnie fled. After three or four days, she gave herself up.

A caravan of heavily armed lawmen escorted the diminutive woman back to Phoenix where 20,000 people lined the streets to catch a glimpse of the woman who Randolph Hearst's Los Angeles newspapers had dubbed "Trunk Murderess." The owner of the duplex where the murders occurred sold ten-cent tickets for tours of the site. Press from all over the world descended on the town.

Winnie Ruth Judd claimed self-defense. She admitted that she and her girlfriends had quarreled violently over Jack Halloran.

She described how she had introduced old "Doctor Buckley" to a nurse who Sammy and Anne knew to have a venereal disease. They were appalled that Winnie Ruth would do such a thing and they fully intended to tell Jack. Then Sammy and Anne threatened to tell Winnie's husband about her infidelities with Jack Halloran. In turn, Winnie Ruth threatened to reveal to the world that the two girls were "perverts." In thirties' Phoenician parlance the word "pervert" was understood to refer to homosexuals and lesbians. Such a revelation would have most assuredly cost Anne her job. Winnie Ruth said that was when Sammy and Anne attacked her.

In a sensational trial that lasted five months and had media attention comparable to the O.J. Simpson trial three decades later, Mrs. Judd was convicted of first-degree murder and sentenced to hang. She was sent to the State Prison in Florence to await execution.

Seventy-two hours before she was scheduled to die, Winnie Ruth was declared insane by the authorities and sent to the Arizona State Hospital – with one absurd caveat. As long as she remained insane, her life would be spared. If Winnie Ruth ever became sane, she would be returned to prison and executed.

Not surprisingly, Mrs. Judd became the perfect patient – albeit one with a penchant for wandering away from the asylum, which only seemed to reinforce her status as a mentally challenged person.

In 1939, she escaped for six days. Six weeks later, she was missing again. Using an alias, this time she managed to stay out for twelve days. In 1947, she escaped for twelve hours and in 1951 went AWOL for thirteen hours. In 1952, she left again and returned when the hospital administrator promised that she would be allowed to appear before a grand jury to plead her case.

The administrator fulfilled his promise in 1954. Winnie Ruth's testimony about Jack Halloran's involvement in her crimes was so convincing that her death sentence was commuted to life.

Winnie Ruth escaped from the hospital again in 1962 and this time disappeared completely.

There it was again, Karla thought when she read this. The most notorious, photographed, female criminal in the history of the United States and she was able to disappear completely without a trace. And what was her big secret? She changed her name. Not even officially, as Karla had done when she changed her married name to Teale. Winnie Ruth Judd simply started calling herself Marian Kane.

Over twenty years and seven escapes, media and public attention about Winnie Ruth's escapades went from ranting hysteria and fear to mirth and laughter to complete indifference.

One day, there was an infamous woman called the "Trunk Murderess," a woman whose persona and deeds had become a media fetish and the stuff of legend, a woman who was despised and deposited for life in an insane asylum. Suddenly, that woman disappeared completely and a matronly, fifty-seven-year-old, soft-spoken woman named Marian Kane arrived in Oakland, California and rented a modest apartment.

The following day Ms. Kane walked into an employment agency, and one of those things that just happen happened. That very morning the wealthy Nichols family had asked the agency to find them a maid and companion for the family matriarch. Marian Kane was exactly what they were looking for. She was sent to the Nichols' home in Piedmont, California, a twenty-three-room mansion overlooking the San Francisco Bay and given the job on the spot.

Piedmont was and is a privileged section of the Bay area. In a neighborhood of millionaires, the Nichols lived at Crocker and Lincoln, Piedmont's finest corner.

Mrs. Kane got on famously with her employer whom she soon took to addressing as "Mother Nichols." If Marian admired a scarf or a vase or a piece of jewelry, Mother Nichols would buy it for her. When Mrs. Nichols ordered monogrammed handkerchiefs for herself, she ordered them for Marian as well. One Christmas, the woman gave Marian a sapphire ring in which she had inscribed "E.N. to M.K., Love."

Marian would spend the morning hours sitting with her mistress, braiding her hair. In the evenings they would discuss current events, campus unrest and social upheaval, the Doors, Janis Joplin and Vietnam. The Age of Aquarius was dawning a few miles away at the corners of Haight and Ashbury in the heart of downtown San Francisco. A period of transformation and social upheaval, for Marian Kane it was also a period of redemption. Without abandoning the real details of her past – born to a minister and his wife in the Midwest, married to an older doctor who had since passed away – Winnie Ruth completely reinvented herself as Marian Kane.

Mother Nichols died in 1967. When the big house in Piedmont was sold Marian moved into a small cottage on Mrs. Nichols' daughter's farm north of San Francisco. The farm was a magnificent piece of property in the shadow of Mount Diablo.

On June 27, 1969, as Marian Kane was in the midst of giving a small house-warming tea social to a select group of elderly women, the police drove up. Whatever enchantment had facilitated the total subjugation of Winnie Ruth Judd to Marian Kane was about to be dispelled by pure serendipity.

Although Marian did not drive, in gratitude she bought a car and gave it to her nephew. Her brother and his son had always been close and had helped Winnie Ruth get to Oakland after she escaped from the asylum in Arizona. The car was a gift but it had remained registered in the name Marian Kane. It was an oversight that no one had noticed. One day her nephew left the car parked in a San Francisco neighborhood where a woman had been killed. The police, checking all the license plates of cars parked in that vicinity, discovered that the car was registered to Marian Kane.

A veteran police officer, only days from retirement, happened to remember that when the infamous "Trunk Murderess" Winnie Ruth Judd had previously escaped and gone to Yuma, Arizona in 1939, she had used the alias Marian Kane. He dutifully followed up. When they fingerprinted Marian, Winnie Ruth Judd magically reappeared. At the age of sixty-six, Winnie Ruth was once again America's most notorious female criminal.

The Nichols's extended family descended from all over the world to stand behind the woman they had come to know and love as Marian Kane. They hired famed San Francisco lawyer, Melvin Belli, to fight Winnie Ruth Judd's extradition to Arizona. Belli was, at the time, busily working for the Rolling Stones organizing their free concert at Altamont. Although Belli lost infrequently, he failed to win this time and Winnie Ruth was returned to the State Hospital in Phoenix. A petition from Belli for release was proffered and a pardon granted a year later on the condition that Winnie Ruth not return to Arizona during her lifetime.

In 1971, Marian Kane returned to work for the Nichols' family and their heirs in northern California. She retired comfortably in 1982 and lived quietly in a pleasant apartment in Stockton, California, for the rest of her life.

Before she died in 1999, at the age of ninety-six, Marian Kane told a reporter that she remained amazed that her new identity was never compromised during those six and a half years. Given her immense notoriety, the level of the media coverage her case had received and the fact that she was constantly in compromising situations whereby she found herself in the company of men and women she had known on a first name basis through her husband before she went to jail, it was truly miraculous that no one ever recognized her and revealed her true identity.

For Karla, the story of Winnie Ruth Judd was like a redemptive fairy tale, even more poignant because it was true.

But of all the stories about women who had overcome a fate Karla perceived to be similar to hers, her favorite was the story about Juliet Hulme and Pauline Parker.

* * * * * * *

In a diabolical twist too perverse for one of her own rather prim novels, renowned British mystery writer, Anne Perry, turned out to be an identity layered over New Zealand teenage murderess, Juliet Hulme. In spite of the fact that Ms. Perry was known to readers all over the world, she managed to keep her true identity secret for over thirty-eight years.

The film, *Heavenly Creatures* (1994), starring Kate Winslet as Juliet, rekindled interest in the strange New Zealand murder case and motivated a few local reporters to try and find out what had become of the girls who committed the crime.

After their release from prison, Pauline Parker and Juliet Hulme had somehow vanished into thin air. Anyone familiar with the case, as millions of people throughout the British Commonwealth were circa 1954, would have categorically denied that such a feat was possible.

The story was bizarre. In the middle of the afternoon on Tuesday, June 22nd, 1954, Pauline and Juliet ran up to the manager of a tea kiosk in a small park on the outskirts of Christchurch, New Zealand. They blurted out a garbled account of an accident which had apparently befallen Pauline's mother. Following the girls back to the park, the police discovered a woman's body so badly battered about the head and face that it was unrecognizable.

Both girls were covered in blood. A broken brick in a blood stained stocking was found near the body. The autopsy report revealed that Mrs. Parker had been struck by the brick in the stocking more than forty-five times.

When Pauline Parker and Juliet Hulme were interviewed later that evening, Pauline, then sixteen years old, admitted she had bludgeoned her forty-four-year-old mother to death.

Juliet followed suit with an admission that she conspired with Pauline and that they had taken turns bashing in the woman's skull.

When the Parker's house was searched, two of Pauline's diaries were discovered. From her voluminous writings it was clear that the murder had been premeditated.

The entry for June 19th, 1954 read: "Our main idea for the day was to moider Mother... it's a definite plan we intend to carry out. We have worked it out carefully and are thrilled by the idea. Naturally, we feel a trifle nervous but the pleasure of anticipation is great."

It turned out that both teenagers were prolific writers and note-keepers. During their trial, psychiatrist Reginald Medlicott testified that the violence in the two girls' writing increased to a "fantastic crescendo" during the immediate period leading up to the murder.[2]

Their fictional world with its multi-variant saints and sinners was broad, medieval, violent, and surfeit with sex and death. By the time they murdered Pauline's mother, Pauline and Juliet had between them written six books, as well as various plays, poetry and an opera.

The psychiatrist and other expert witnesses for their defense testified that the girls were suffering from "paranoia of the exalted type" or *folie à deux* and therefore insane at the time of the killing.

Folie à deux or "communicated insanity" has been frequently described in psychiatric literature and, unlike psychopathy, remains in the current edition of the *Diagnostic and Statistical Manual of Mental Disorders (DSM – IV)* as "Shared Psychotic Disorder."

"In the majority of instances," Dr. Medlicott wrote in his report, "it is induced by a stronger character, the inducer, upon the weaker, the inducee (*folie impossée*), but delusions may occur simultaneously in predisposed associated individuals (*folie simultanée*). There is no

2. R.W. Medlicott, "Paranoia of the Exalted Type in a Setting of Folie à Deux: A Study of Two Adolescent Homicides." *British Journal of Medical Psychology*, 28 (1955), 205-223.

evidence of either of these girls imposing their ideas on the other, and there seems no doubt that they developed their psychoses simultaneously."

Lawyers for Juliet and Pauline vigorously argued that the girls were clinically delusional and paranoid. The psychiatrists for the defense also suggested that these paranoia and delusions were symptoms of the girls' homosexuality. The gist of the argument was a "communicated insanity," which made them insane but only in each other's presence.

On the other hand, as the diaries made clear, as did the girls' confessions, Pauline and Juliet knew exactly what they were doing. Both were highly intelligent. Prior to entering secondary school, Juliet Hulme was given intelligence tests and her quotient was in the region of 170.

As fifteen-year-old Juliet said shortly after her arrest, "I would have to be an absolute moron not to know murder was against the law." Neither did she ever express any qualms of conscience. "Conscience," she said, "was bred in people so that they punished themselves; it was senseless."

The police officer who had arrested them committed suicide. His daughter said that what really upset him was that they were not only the same age as she was but they also appeared to be "two normal girls."

Experts for the prosecution testified that drawing a link between homosexuality and insanity was nonsense. Sexual encounters, both heterosexual and homosexual, were normal adolescent phases.

The newspaper headlines proclaimed "A Nation Divided by Matricide!" Were the teenagers lesbians, "precocious and dirty-minded," as the prosecution painted them, or were they insane, as the defense argued? Possibly the most disturbing scenario of all was the idea that allegedly drove the troubled arresting officer to take his own life – that they were just two, normal, teenage girls.

As it most often is, the psychiatry for the defense was wholly discounted and considered irrelevant. Both girls were convicted of first-degree murder and sentenced to indefinite incarceration.

Pauline served most of her time behind bars near Wellington, at the Arohata Women's Reformatory, a far more lenient, minimum-security facility compared to Mt. Eden, where Juliet was sent. Juliet was punished differently because she came to be seen by the media, and hence the public, as the motivating force in the partnership. Over the course of the trial and the intense media scrutiny, Pauline Parker was perceived to be the victim of Juliet Hulme's magical powers of persuasion and the murder "understood" as a "thrill killing" committed at Juliet's instigation. It became politically expedient for the authorities to appear to be tougher on Juliet. Held in separate institutions, they were forbidden to communicate. Prison records show that Pauline was extremely distraught by this inevitability during the first few years of their imprisonment.

During this time, Pauline converted to Roman Catholicism. She also enrolled in courses in English, French, Latin, Mathematics, Drawing, Design and Maori. She completed university entrance requirements and made considerable progress toward her Bachelor of Arts degree, which she completed after she was released from jail.

In late 1959, after only five years in prison, both women were released on parole. Pauline was furnished with a new identity. Juliet simply chose her stepfather's surname, Perry, and took her mother's middle name, Anne.

During their parole, Pauline and Juliet were subject to stringent conditions. Department of Justice officials noted their concern over Pauline's association with lesbians during her probation period which lasted until 1965.

According to the press, the public was outraged by the light sentences and what was perceived to be Pauline and Juliet's privileged treatment. The media went into a frenzied hunt for both of them. It was so obsessive for a time that one commentator called it "horrible" and remarked that it was not as though "these girls are Nazi war criminals."

As usual, the media's fixation was of the moment and current affairs quickly replaced what is, at the best of times, a short attention span.

Public outrage dissipated, as it is bound to do, and Pauline Parker and Juliet Hulme vanished – for thirty-seven years.

Although Ms. Hulme was revealed to be the crime fiction writer Anne Perry in the wake of *Heavenly Creatures*, it would be another three years before Pauline's cover was blown – by her sister.

In an article for the *New Zealand Women's Weekly*, Pauline Parker was revealed "to the world" to be living under the name Hilary Nathan and running a children's riding school in a quiet rural village in the southeast of England. No one in the village of Hoo, near the historic town of Rochester, knew of Ms. Nathan's ignominious past. The journalist who wrote the article was surprised. After all, doesn't everyone in a small town know everyone else's business? Another *ad hominem* without substance.

The story recounted how, in 1965, Anne Perry, a.k.a. Juliet Hulme, and Hilary Nathan, a.k.a Pauline Parker, left New Zealand and went to England. As Anne Perry, Juliet went to live for many years with her mother and stepfather. She took a job as an airline stewardess on domestic UK flights. She lived and worked in Newcastle, in the northeast corner of England.

In 1967, Ms. Perry was granted a visa to live and work in the United States, demonstrating that convicted felons can and indeed do get into the United States, one way or the other.

She immigrated to San Francisco from Newcastle just about the time the "Trunk Murderess," Winnie Ruth Judd, was inadvertently discovered living as maid Marian in the Bay area. When famed criminal lawyer Melvin Belli took on both Winnie Ruth Judd and the Rolling Stones, Anne Perry was thirty-one and working for an insurance company three blocks away from Belli's office.

Ms. Perry returned to England in 1972. Her first novel, *The Cater Street Hangman*, was published in 1979. Between then and now Anne Perry has published over thirty mystery novels. She also became a devout Mormon and has written a history of the Church of Jesus Christ of the Latter Day Saints in England.

Still living only a mile from her mother, Anne Perry occupies a huge, renovated, stone barn overlooking the sea on the eastern coast of

Scotland. She has three dogs, two cats and a neighbor who raises pigs. Her community is small and close-knit. She regularly travels all over the world. Her books are international best sellers.

When first in London, Ms. Nathan (Pauline Parker) worked for a library but eventually quit and retired to the country. Her sister said "she leads a very unusual existence. She hasn't got a radio or a TV, so she would never have heard what Anne Perry had to say and wouldn't care. She doesn't have any contact with the outside world – she's a reclusive, really. She's a devout Roman Catholic and spends most of her time in prayer."

Even though the two best friends, who once swore they would rather die than be separated, have lived in close proximity for decades, as far as anyone knows, they have never seen or spoken to one another again.

Still, there remain the many things in common. They are both deeply religious. Neither woman has ever married. They have both lived in the British Isles for decades. Both women are doing exactly what they dreamt of doing and they have prospered doing it. They also share a voracious love of reading and, as far as anyone knows, neither woman has ever killed again.

These true stories suggested limitless possibilities to Karla. After all, when Karla was released, she would be released free and clear, not encumbered by the stringent conditions of parole as had Evelyn Dick, Pauline Parker and Juliet Hulme.

Contrary to how Karla used to think, she now knew that no one ever recognizes anyone from pictures in the newspapers. To be recognizable on the street you had to be a famous actress or television personality, always up front somewhere, larger than life. Also, the truly famous – or infamous – were always somehow, even if reluctantly, complicit in their own recognition.

Hilary Nathan, a.k.a. Pauline Parker was betrayed by her sister. After a while, Anne Perry did not really care very much and did not do anything extraordinary to try to keep her true identity a secret. In the wake of the movie, the world found out what had become of Pauline Parker and Juliet Hulme. If anything, the revelation was a boon to Anne Perry's career. Otherwise, in the aftermath of this flurry of attention, their lives were unaffected.

Years after her release, after she had firmly established a new life for herself, Evelyn Dick decided to see her daughter, Heather Maria, and meet the granddaughter she had never seen. After a pleasant weekend in Ottawa, Mrs. Dick refused to disclose her new identity to her distraught daughter. They never saw each other again.

If all these notorious women who had committed heinous, infamous crimes could disappear completely, once and for all, even given notoriety that has persisted to this day, Karla knew for certain that she could.

* * * * * * *

If the future contains both the present and the past, as the Bible and T.S. Eliot suggest, then the history of women who have committed heinous, sensational murders that for a time made them infamous and reviled, suggests a future for Karla defined by new identity, prosperity, and even happiness.

The American journalist and raconteur, H.L. Mencken, defined mediocrity as "the ready acceptance of received opinion." With regard to Karla there has been a good deal of "ready acceptance of received opinion." However received opinion and reality are most often mutually exclusive. Contrary to received opinion which suggests that Karla will become a victim of vigilante justice, exposed by the somehow magical machinations of the World Wide Web ["Death Pool Worries Karla" (*Calgary Sun*, Feb. 7, 2001) and "Homolka a Hot Topic on Web Death Pools," (*Kitchener-Waterloo Record*, Feb. 7, 2001)], the wired world will be Karla's oyster.

Another book that Karla found instructive was *How to Mutate and Take Over the World* by R.U. Sirius and the female hacker who called herself St. Jude.

How to Mutate and Take Over the World is an ideal primer for the uninitiated. It takes the reader into the digitally fueled, anarchistic world of the cybergeek and rapidly accelerated Karla's transformation into one of the electronically enlightened.

Styled as a collection of e-mail correspondence, the book is crammed with hacker anecdotes and revelatory moments. Hints and how-to's, existential rants and vicious debates vividly recreate the evolution of the subversive duo who wrote the book. It is a document about the transmogrification from geek to guerrilla.

Women in prison are taught computer skills.

"Yes, I know about the Internet," Karla wrote in response to a question. "It is true that we do not have access, but not that we are not taught Internet access skills. That's a part of a basic training (introductory) computer class taught in Joliette. I know about the Internet and Web sites because I read everything I can get my hands on (except newspapers). I've always been like that. Also, good people like you send me stories off the Internet."

Free, with unfettered access, Karla will become a highly sophisticated Web mistress and very possibly, given her disposition and the way she has now been betrayed by the authorities, cynically minacious.

Along with *How to Mutate and Take Over the World*, somewhere along the way, Karla also encountered *How To Disappear Completely and Never Be Found*.

One of the all-time classic texts of subversive literature from the infamous publisher of *The Anarchist's Handbook*, *How to Disappear Completely and Never Be Found*, first published in 1986, teaches methods that have withstood the test of time.

Begin at the end, author Doug Richmond advises. Make a new start by studying others' demise – scan the obituaries, visit cemeteries, closely check the headstones.

Mapping out the basics, from faking one's death (better to simply disappear, which is surprisingly easy) to landing a job (must find new skills is core advice, as Karla had done), the author is a stickler for pre-planning. Unlike her life in Joliette, in Sainte-Anne-des-Plaines, Karla has nothing but time for pre-planning.

How to Disappear and Never Be Found has been reinforced and updated by two new books, *Advanced Fugitive: Running, Hiding, Surviving and Thriving Forever* and *International Fugitive* both by Ken Abaygo.

There are many other manuals available, including *The Modern Identity Changer: How to Create a New Identity for Personal Privacy and Personal Freedom* by Sheldon Charrett, which can only supplement and update the fundamentals elucidated in *How to Disappear Completely and Never Be Found.*

For anyone wanting a new identity, the Internet is a bonanza of sources as well as facilitation.

"There are many reasons that a person could want or need an extra ID," says Cat Darrington, a purveyor of the identity shuffle and the proprietor of "The Identity Guy" – a Web site source for social security cards, FBI and police Id's, birth certificates, award certificates, degrees and driving licenses. ("The Identity Guy" has since been shut down, but the Cat is lurking out there somewhere in cyberspace.)

"Just because a person obtains an ID in another name doesn't mean that person is up to no good. They could be tired of everyone prying into the little bit of privacy allowed them by big government. Maybe they want to impress someone, or perhaps even deceive them. They could be wanting to drop out of a dead-end life and start all over again."

Among Darrington offerings: A "camouflage (a.k.a fake) passport," birth and baptismal certificates at $15[3] a piece.

With a new identity Karla can easily enhance her hard-won university degree in psychology and buy whatever graduate degree she fancies. Internet University diplomas can be had for $15, plus $5 for shipping and handling.

Shape-shifting has long been a hallmark of evil forces. Karla might remake herself as an instrument of God rather than Satan.

---

3. All prices are in US dollars.

"Ministerial Ordinations" are $25. An extra $20 will get her a copy of "Minister's Guide for Performing Weddings." A doctorate in "biblical counseling" (no course attendance required) costs $75. A Ph.D. in Theology can be had for $150 US.

If Karla preferred, she could become a certified "tarot advisor," "palmist," or "dream analyst."

* * * * * * *

What kind of person can behave monstrously to another human being? A sadist, a psychopath, a sexual deviant – someone with an authoritarian upbringing who was mercilessly abused by their parents? A disturbed personality afflicted in some way by errant genes?

On the contrary: the Nazis who tortured and killed millions during World War II "weren't sadists or killers by nature," Hannah Arendt reported in her book *Eichmann in Jerusalem*.

Many studies of Nazi behavior have concluded that monstrous acts, despite their horrors, were often simply a matter of faithful bureaucrats slavishly following orders, just as Karla said she did.

In a 1976 study, University of Florida psychologist Molly Harrower asked 15 Rorschach experts to examine ink blot test results from Adolph Eichmann, Rudolf Hess, Hermann Goering and five other Nazi war criminals just before their trials at Nuremberg.

In the same bundle, she included the test results from a cross-section of Americans, some with well adjusted personalities and others who were severely disturbed. The anthology of test results was sent to the experts blind. Although they were given the names of those who had been tested, the results were not correlated to the individual names.

The experts were unable to distinguish the Nazis from the Americans and judged an equal number of both to be well adjusted.

The true horror lies in the fact that extreme evildoers are not freaks, they are disarmingly ordinary people. The realization that this is true can be devastating, as it was for the policeman who investigated the murder of Honore Parker by her daughter Pauline and her teenage friend Juliet Hulme.

Just as the concentration camp carpenter in Primo Levi's short story *Lilith*, knew the real name of the woman whom they glimpsed as they took shelter from a storm in a sewer pipe, I too know the woman's real name.

According to Levi's carpenter, there are two different stories about Creation involving two radically different women.

In the second story, the one in Genesis, the one everyone knows, God fashions Eve from Adam's rib. God decided to do this because Adam was lonely. Eve's conception was that of subservient companion.

Although Eve naively, perhaps mischievously, took the Serpent's advice and got Adam to bite the apple, the dynamics of Adam and Eve's relationship remained the same, even after the two were expelled from Paradise.

The other story is substantially different. The woman that the carpenter sees in the concentration camp that afternoon he recognizes as the woman from the other Creation story.

In this version from Jewish folklore, God created a golem, a two-backed creature, a form without form, from a block of clay. Then he split it, creating equal parts, male and female, Adam and Lilith.

Adam's first impulse was to rejoin his severed half and he insisted that Lilith lay down on her back so he could accomplish the task. Lilith was anything but subservient. She flatly refused, saying she would only comply if she could be on top.

God, being male, sided with Adam.

Lilith rebelled. Cursing God's name, she petulantly left the Garden and went to live at the bottom of the sea, a place, I imagine, not unlike St. Catharines, Ontario.

Now, rising nightly from the depths, Lilith flies around looking for unsuspecting children to asphyxiate.

The ancient cabalists elaborated on the story.

They said that in the beginning God was so lonely that He took a companion: He chose the *Skekhina*, that is, His own presence in the Creation.

When the Temple in Jerusalem was desecrated by the Romans and the Jews were dispersed and enslaved, the *Skekhina*, enraged by God's failure to intervene, promptly left him and went into exile with the Jews.

In the aftermath, God could not stand being alone so he took Lilith as his mistress.

An unimaginable scandal, more like a quarrel than a love affair, the alliance between God and Lilith nevertheless intensified.

According to this story, as long as the relationship between God and Lilith lasts, there will be blood and chaos on Earth.

Given the current state of world affairs, it would seem that their relationship is steadfast.

Lilith has adapted and evolved and she is anything but faithful to her God. She now has some remarkable capabilities. For instance, she can enter men's bodies at will, and whomever she enters becomes possessed.

The way the carpenter in Levi's story tells it, Lilith is always "greedy for man's seed, and she is always lying in wait wherever it may get spilled... All the seed that doesn't end in the only appropriate place – that is, inside the wife's womb – is hers," the carpenter says.

"All the seed that every man has wasted in his lifetime, in dreams, or vice, or adultery. So you see she gets a lot of it and so she's always pregnant and giving birth all the time."

The only way Lilith can be prevented from asphyxiating children during her nightly rampages is to know by the rustling at the window that she is about to enter a house and capture her under an overturned bowl.

For anyone who has tried to catch anything under a bowl, this is no easy task.

Of course, whenever the bowl is set right, Lilith flies off to the next atrocity.

One day, and I remember that day quite clearly, I heard Karla rustling at the window. For a split second, I caught her under my bowl. The bowl was made of description and explanation. But I was mistaken. Her capture was an illusion. She had possessed me as she had legions before, including Dr. Arndt, Inspector Bevan and prosecutor Code. When I peeked under the bowl, she was gone.

Although flushed and hesitant, the gatekeepers are now busy about the business of setting the bowl under which they have her captive, right side up. It will not be long now. Karla will soon be free again, without any restriction, a vital young woman of thirty-five. Perhaps she will have learned the key to her capture and simply avoid windows.

Over the past decade, many of the atrocities in the seemingly endless Liberian civil war have been tied to the natives' belief in juju spirits. According to many reports, the insurgents and warlords in Sierra Leone often take a young woman with them to the battlefront. Once there, she strips off her clothes and walks backwards into enemy territory, using a mirror to guide her way. According to juju lore, her nakedness and the fact that she is walking backwards makes her invisible. Thus, she crosses enemy lines with impunity, infiltrates the opposing army's position and buries charms that curse their enterprise.

The world into which Karla Teale will walk after she is released from prison is a very different world than the one she left, and, to her, very much enemy territory. In a sense, Karla's strange, taciturn, schoolgirl demeanor and murderous ways were a harbinger of things to come. I think of Karla as that backward-walking, looking-glass navigating, naked woman. Released from prison, she will move imperceptibly among us, invisible, burying charms that I imagine will increase the dark forces' power. With Karla back in the world, there will simply be a few more possibilities that we may never see coming. As Leonard Cohen sang in his song *The Future*, he has seen the future and "it is murder."

My evocation of Primo Levi's Lilith in the previous section may have been a bit arch but I am by no means the first to reference the Holocaust and concentration camps in an attempt to describe Karla.

At least four psychiatrists, including Dr. Hans Arndt and Dr. Roy Brown, compared Karla to a concentration camp survivor. Her comparison to a nocturnal rampaging succubus rings far truer than the psychiatrists' turgid analogies to a death camp survivor. It is also an accurate adjuration of how Karla has possessed me for over a decade.

Talking about Karla in the context of Lilith and concentration camps also echoes an idea first observed by Hannah Arendt in *Eichmann in Jerusalem*. Ms. Arendt argued that the Nazi purveyors of the death camps and the Holocaust were ordinary men and women who were merely "following orders" in what is now historically understood to have been a massive bureaucracy of genocide. "Following orders" does not exonerate. The fact that Adolf Eichmann and hundreds upon hundreds of lesser-known war criminals hunted down by Simon Wiezenthal and other Nazi hunters were simply "following orders" did not save them. All but one of the defendants at the Nuremberg trials were put to death. Karla is more like an obscure war criminal who has escaped justice than any survivor of the death camps.

Dr. Graham Glancy came closest to explaining what Karla was in psycho-pathological terms when he called her a malingering, histrionic hybristophiliac. But inherent in its accuracy is its irrelevance.

As Ron Rosenbaum concludes in *Explaining Hitler*, his riveting, ten-year study of Hitler explainers and their theories about the wellspring of evil, explanations exculpate their object. To explain Hitler's actions as a consequence of some neuroses or psychoses, which in turn are excused as the culmination of a dysfunctional upbringing or a lack of sexual prowess and genital deformity, is to ultimately excuse and humanize him.

For example, there are among Hitler explainers those who believe that Hitler had only one testicle. In turn, that physical deformity, which the eminent historian Alan Bullock called "the one-ball business," has been seriously invoked to explain why Hitler hated Jews and ultimately decided to exterminate them. Go figure.

Ours is a culture that values explanation over consequence. There can be no excuse for what Hitler did. It does not matter why he did it.

How and why he was allowed to get away with it is another story. There is great scholarship on that topic but there is little will to confront its ugly conclusions: The Holocaust was not only a manifestation of Hitler's diseased mind but also the consequence of the deliberate ignorance or even the collusion of other nations, the German people themselves, and global corporations including the Catholic Church. However the pie is cut, psychobabble about psychopathology is a subterfuge for the truth about culpability.

There is no excuse for Karla. It doesn't matter why Karla committed her barbarous acts. Unacknowledged by Dr. Hubert Van Gijseghem, Dr. Graham Glancy had long ago answered the question about Karla's "underlying personality structure" and how it may have compelled her to act out as she did. But that explanation has not solved the enigma that is Karla or altered her exculpation.

Karla was the creation of men in power who clearly understood the cultural dynamics of explanation and excuse. Moving to immunize her against any and all dissent for their own idiosyncratic reasons, they sacrificed the truth about the extent of her culpability.

There are a number of things that can be known for certain about Karla. She is equally, if not more, responsible for the crimes she and her partner committed. No one died until Paul Bernardo moved in with Karla Homolka. She could have chosen not to do what she did to her sister. She did what she did with the full knowledge that her actions put her sister's life at risk. She had many opportunities to save her sister, Leslie Mahaffy and Kristen French. Lastly, Karla has nothing in common with women such as Winnie Ruth Judd, Evelyn Dick, Pauline Parker and Juliet Hulme.

None of these women went to prison with an expectation of a future. Winnie Ruth and Evelyn Dick were both initially sentenced to death. Pauline and Juliet were sentenced to indefinite terms.

None of them committed serial sexual homicides. None of them murdered their sisters for the singularly utilitarian purpose of pleasing a lover. None of them procured young girls for the sexual gratification of their fiancés or husbands. None of them participated in sexual games with teenagers they had rendered comatose with drugs, alcohol and anaesthetic. The only thing that is relevant about the stories of Winnie Ruth, Evelyn Dick and the Heavenly Creatures is exactly what Karla took from them. In spite of media circuses and worldwide attention, it is possible for notorious female criminals to completely disappear.

* * * * * * *

Karla's former boss at the Number One Pet Store, Kristy Mann, had been the unwitting catalyst for Karla's first meeting with Paul Bernardo in 1987. In the few years prior to Paul Bernardo's trial, Ms. Mann carried on a voluminous correspondence with Karla, perhaps fuelled by her sublimated guilt over her inadvertent role as matchmaker or her need to try and understand how someone she liked, someone she thought she knew, could have participated in such perverse and grotesque crimes against humanity.

In one of her letters, Kristy mentioned a book to Karla about England's infamous Moors murders, a book that Karla said she would love to read.

The book recounted how Myra Hindley, in tandem with her partner Ian Brady, committed the Moors murders. It was the first known case in British history in which a woman was involved in serial sex killings. Predating the Manson family murders by a few years, the direct involvement of a young woman made the horrific crimes she and her partner committed seem even more evil and unforgivable.

On their first date Ian took Myra to see Spencer Tracy in *The Nuremberg Trials*. He also gave her his copy of Hitler's *Mein Kampf* and compelled her to read it. Myra's greatest desire, her entire aim in life, after that first date, after reading *Mein Kampf*, was to please Ian. She changed the way she dressed to a kind of Nazi-jackboot-mini-skirts-bleached-blonde thing. She encouraged Ian to take pornographic pictures of her similar to those Paul and Karla took in the heady summer of 1988. Brady's ideas became increasingly paranoid and outrageous, but nothing fazed Myra. When Ian told her there was no God, God-fearing Myra stopped going to church. When he told her that murder was the "supreme pleasure," she agreed. Their personalities fused. Myra became what she beheld: a secretive, surly, overbearing and aggressive Ian Brady. The pair quickly became greater than the sum of their parts. Ultimately, Hindley and Brady were held responsible for the rape and murder of nine children.

A luggage ticket, found folded in a prayer book Myra always carried with her, led police to a locker at Manchester Central Station. Inside were two suitcases filled with pornographic and sadistic paraphernalia. There were nine photographs of one of their victims, 10-year-old Leslie Anne Downey. They showed the girl naked, bound and gagged in a variety of poses. The pictures had been taken in Myra's bedroom. There was also a cassette tape. On the tape, Lesley Anne could be heard screaming, crying and begging for her life. Punctuating the child's imprecations, Myra and Ian cajoled and threatened her. The fact that they took Polaroid pictures, a new way of privately making instant images, as well as made tapes of their victims' tormented screams, seized the collective imagination with exacerbated horror.

Hindley and Brady escaped the death penalty by a hair's breadth. Four weeks before they were arrested, "The Murder Act" of 1965 abolishing the death penalty in England took effect. Ian Brady was sentenced to three lifetimes in prison. In a nod to the gentler sex, for her part Myra got two.

A model prisoner, Ms. Hindley maintained her innocence until 1987. Although she finally admitted her involvement in at least five of the murders, until her death on November 15, 2002, from a combination of pneumonia and hypertension, she insisted that she was under Ian Brady's spell and did not actually commit any of the murders, in the sense that she stopped anyone's breath.

* * * * * * *

The crimes of Fred and Rosemary West make the exploits of the Moors murderers and Paul and Karla look like warm-up exercises.

On December 27, 1973, when Karla was a three-and-a-half year-old toddler, the Wests pulled up to a local bus stop in Gloucester, England and offered Lucy Parkington a ride.

An attractive, twenty-one-year-old, Lucy was studying medieval history and English at the University of Exeter. It was a cold afternoon and the bus was late. Lucy thought nothing about getting in a car in broad daylight with a young, married couple and their four-month-old baby.

Lucy was kept alive in the West's basement for a week. Eventually, after repeatedly raping and torturing her, the Wests killed the girl and dismembered her body. They separated some of her remains for their trophy case and buried the rest in the basement.

Like the sudden disappearance of Kristen French an ocean away and decades later, Lucy's abduction was extremely well publicized. It was made even more newsworthy because she was the niece of famous English novelist Kingsley Amis. Regardless, it would be twenty-two years before Lucy Parkington's fate was known.

Because they were a nondescript part of the social fabric of Gloucester, like Paul and Karla in St. Catharines, the Wests were invisible. Unlike Paul and Karla, the Wests remained centered and happy in their deviance. Neither unraveled and turned on the other. As a consequence, their spree lasted for twenty-five years.

Fred was a good provider and Rose took in lodgers to help make ends meet. They had children – his, hers, theirs, other people's – so many, in fact, that none of the neighbors could keep track. When a couple of the children went missing over the years, no one noticed.

Whereas Karla's family was disarmingly normal, to describe Rose West's family as dysfunctional would be a gross understatement. Rose bedded her father, her father bedded her, Fred bedded Rose, Rose bedded her two brothers. Rose even occasionally bedded her father and Fred at the same time.

Unlike Rose, Karla was not promiscuous. More a throwback to the conventional housewife of the 50s, Karla said she dreamed about staying home and having children. About the only thing Karla had in common with Rose West was the unrestricted fulfillment of her husband's every wish.

Holes and tools got Fred West hard so Rose talked incessantly about filling great, big, gaping holes and always made sure there were plenty of hammers, pliers and power tools strewn around the house.

Dirty talk about teenage virgins and lurid rapes got Paul hot, so Karla talked the talk and encouraged him to make his fantasies real. From the time they met until the time they were caught, Karla "inspired" Paul Bernardo to rape at least nineteen different women, all strangers whom he followed and attacked in heavily populated suburban areas. All of the women Paul Bernardo raped of his own accord survived their attack. No one died until he and Karla started living together.

Paul Bernardo would not abide Karla looking at another man, let alone sleeping with one. Fred West, on the other hand, was forever bringing home big black men from the foundry where he worked so he could watch Rose seduce them. Half of Roses' children were sired by her black "lovers." Still, the West's neighbors thought nothing odd.

About things sexual, Paul Bernardo was clumsy and prosaic. Fred West, on the other hand, had an insatiable curiosity and an unfettered, deviant imagination. He enthusiastically set up scenarios and procured for Rose.

Karla was the procurer in the Bernardo household.

Rose never wore panties unless she was collecting "samples" for Fred. Afterward, the semen-stained knickers were partially cremated, labeled and put in jars. They were memorabilia, something for the Wests' dotty years. Fred and Rose kept all sorts of trophies – reams of videotape, Polaroids, love notes, even seventy-two bones, including Lucy Parkington's left knee cap.

When police searched Paul and Karla's house in Port Dalhousie, they found panties in paper bags, newspaper clippings galore about Paul and Karla's rapes and murders, all manner of insipid love notes, a videotape showing Karla having sex with a comatose teenage girl and a hooker from Atlantic City, burned bones they never did identify, and a lock of Tammy Lyn's hair.

Heather West, Fred and Rose's first-born, the four-month-old baby who had been in the car when the Wests picked up Lucy Parkington, was strangled and chopped up in the summer of 1987, a few months before Paul and Karla met.

Fred had been raping Heather all of her life, asserting it was his fatherly right. At 16, Heather rebelled. She told her father she was going to blow the whistle. Fred buried her in the backyard. Seven years later, Fred's "family joke," that Heather was "under the patio" somehow got back to the police and finally provoked an investigation.

Lucy Parkington's remains were the second set of eight found in the Wests' basement. Heather and a few others were in the backyard, another few were unearthed in surrounding fields. No one is sure how many victims Fred and Rose West raped, tortured and murdered over the quarter century they were active. Some informed observers speculated there may be have been as many as a hundred victims.

Myra Hindley was jailed before Karla was born. Rose and Fred West were apprehended just after the authorities came into possession of the videotape evidence of Paul Bernardo and Karla Homolka's spree in September, 1994.

Fred West's suicide while in custody awaiting trial in 1995 was barely noticed in North America. Rose's trial was coincident to Bernardo's in the summer of 1995. Both were eclipsed by the O.J. Simpson fiasco. The story of Fred and Rose West remains obscure in North America.

Like Myra Hindley before her, Rose West tried the "he-made-me-do-it" defense and claimed that she was the compliant victim of a sadistic, dominant partner. As George Walker had explained to Karla, that defense would never work were Karla compelled to go to trial and defend herself against the evidence. It certainly did not work for Myra, or Rose. Rose West was found guilty on all counts and given a life sentence with no possibility of parole.

* * * * * * *

In the summer of 2002, Karla once again changed her mind and decided that she did not want to continue her correspondence. She cut it off with a short note. Her disappointed correspondent replied:

"Over the past few months I have done a good deal of thinking and I have come a conclusion which I believe the prison authorities have long understood and one that has guided their actions. I have come to the conclusion that you do not have the courage of your own convictions. Let me explain:

"Inspector Bevan and his legion of police officers explained that you were the 'compliant victim' of a 'sexual sadist.'

"The psychiatrists and psychologists explained that you were a battered wife suffering from clinical depression and post-traumatic stress disorder. Even though it was never offered or admitted as evidence, at least two jurors at Bernardo's trial believed these explanations strongly enough to write letters on your behalf. Some people in the media even believed it. But you didn't. Not really. You gave it lip service. Had you really believed it, you would have applied for ETAs and parole the first moment you were eligible – back in 1995-96. Nobody in their right mind would stay in jail a second longer than absolutely necessary. Anybody with the courage of their own convictions (backed by a legion of cops, prosecutors and health professionals), would have done everything in their power to get out of jail at the earliest possible moment.

"When the applications were denied, as they invariably would have been, a woman with the courage of her convictions would have appeared in front of the Parole Board and boldly made a cogent argument such as the one we discussed you should be making when you next are entitled to appear in March. These actions would have told the prison, the National Parole Board, the press and the public that you had the courage of your own convictions; that you really believed that you were what the police and the psychiatrists said you were.

"By not applying, by burying your head in the sand, by not going in front of the Parole Board consistently, every time, whenever you were eligible, until the last second of your sentence, by allowing your lawyers to say that you feared for your life, by telling me that you actually felt too guilty to be released (you did not feel that way for one second before the press got hold of your prison file in the wake of your application to the Federal Court to have the warden's decision about ETAs rescinded), by your actions you have told me, the federal prison authorities and everyone else that you do not believe in the persona that was so painstakingly constructed for you.

"(That's another thing that continues to perplex me. You continue to worry about your privacy and now, steadfastly, re-impose your self-imposed silence but you must understand that the cat is already out of the bag. The major media organizations all have copies of your complete prison file and literally dozens of people in those organizations have combed through them. If you think for one minute that just because there is a court order against your file's publication that any point of interest will not come to public attention then you are far more naive than I think you are.)

"The fact is your actions have always spoken much louder than your words. In spite of your diffident and articulate rhetoric, and your subscription to all those courses and your dedication to 'good behavior' and your degree in psychology, in your heart of hearts, you do not actually believe that you are a victim of a sexual sadist, or a battered wife or clinically depressed or post-traumatically stressed out. You do not really think any of that about yourself and you never did. That is why the prison authorities have been able to manipulate you as easily as they have.

"In your heart-of-hearts, you know who and what you are. And so do I. Obviously what you have also failed to understand is that none of this changes my opinion that you should have been released on your statutory date; or that your detention and the manner in which it was accomplished will probably cause irreparable harm to you and society-at-large. Nor does it change my opinion that you will be able to disappear and adopt a new identity after your release if you get good advice and use your head. For a while I saw some glimmer of possibility that you were able to look at the big picture and take advice and think things through. But now I am more skeptical than ever. For what it's worth. After all, if you don't hear it from me, who are you going to hear it from?"

Thus my source for information about Karla's life in prison dried up.

* * * * * * *

When I was in New York negotiating the contract for my first book, an editor expressed the opinion that she hoped the book was not going to be another tedious story about police bungling and prosecutorial malfeasance because nobody wanted to read books about that stuff.

Since then there have been a lot of stories about police bungling, bungling that has had far worse consequences than Karla's light sentence and pending future. Perhaps if there had been more books about the breadth and depth of that bungling, more than just the torture and murder of a couple of teenage schoolgirls could have been prevented.

For instance, in 1990, the New York police and the FBI were in a position, not only to prevent the destruction of the World Trade Center on September 11, 2001, but also to preclude a forthcoming series of atrocities. These included the bombing of the World Trade Center in 1993, the attacks on the United States housing complex at Khobar Towers in Saudi Arabia, the bombing of the two American embassies in Africa in 1998 and the Navy destroyer Cole in Yemen in 2000. Right up to the last few weeks before September 11, the FBI leadership in Washington ignored compelling evidence that al-Qaeda fighters were planning to turn passenger jets into airborne firebombs.

It starts with the assassination of Rabbi Meir Kahane. On November 5, 1990, El Sayyid Nosair assassinated the Jewish right-wing extremist Kahane in a New York banquet room. Nosair was wounded during the attack and quickly apprehended. When the New York police raided Nosair's apartment, they found compelling evidence that he was at the heart of a terrorist conspiracy firmly rooted in North America and extending to Egypt, Saudi Arabia, Pakistan, and Western Europe.

The New York City police were already aware of the radical mosque in Brooklyn where Nosair hung out, and his connection to the infamous blind Egyptian cleric, Sheik Omar Abdel Rahman, who openly preached jihad in America.

In Nosair's apartment they discovered a Lego set for jihad: instruction manuals from the U.S. Army Special Warfare School at Fort Bragg, bomb-making materials and maps highlighting New York City landmarks. One of Nosair's papers urged like-minded individuals to knock down the "tall buildings of which Americans are so proud."

The NYPD brass turned a deaf ear to their detectives' imprecations about this evidence. There was an institutional disinclination to transform what was a solved murder case into an unsolved conspiracy. The NYPD Chief of Detectives reportedly told his senior detectives that the FBI "do conspiracies," the New York City police solve murders.

Ultimately, Kahane's assassination was described to the press by the NYPD as the act of a "lone, deranged gunman." A few days later the FBI confiscated all the evidence from Nosair's apartment. None of it saw the light of day until after the World Trade Center bombing in 1993.

The trail of indifference, intractable territorialism and bureaucratic bungling from the revelations and evidence found in Nosair's apartment to that fateful day in September, 2001, became a sixteen-lane interstate highway.

One of the very few top FBI officials to take al-Qaeda seriously, John O'Neill, was forced out of the Bureau in July 2001. He was killed on 9/11 during his second day at work as the new director of security for the World Trade Center.

A recent book documenting this massive systemic failure of modern policing called 'The Cell': Cops and Plotters, by John Miller and Michael Stone, contains an epilogue listing nine pages of missed opportunities. It is printed single-spaced in mice-type.

I do not fear a free Karla. I fear the people who created Karla and gave her that freedom. It is the policemen like Vince Bevan and the prosecutors